Ungifted

UNGIFTED

Intelligence Redefined

~

Scott Barry Kaufman

Illustrated by
George Doutsiopoulos

BASIC BOOKS
A Member of the Perseus Books Group
New York

Books published by Basic Books are available at special discounts for bulk purchases in the United
States by corporations, institutions, and other organizations. For more information, please contact
the Special Markets Department at the Perseus Books Group, 2300 Chestnut Street, Suite 200,
Philadelphia, PA 19103, or call (800) 810-4145, ext. 5000, or e-mail
special.markets@perseusbooks.com.

A CIP catalog record for this book is available from the Library of Congress.

ISBN: 978-0-465-02554-1 (hbk.)
ISBN: 978-0-465-03789-6 (eb)
10 9 8 7 6 5 4 3 2 1

This book is dedicated to everyone who feels trapped by a label. May this book inspire you to believe in yourself and set yourself free.

Here's to the kids who are different,
The kids who don't always get A's
The kids who have ears twice the size of their peers,
And noses that go on for days . . .
Here's to the kids who are different,
The kids they call crazy or dumb,
The kids who don't fit, with the guts and the grit,
Who dance to a different drum . . .
Here's to the kids who are different,
The kids with the mischievous streak,
For when they have grown, as history's shown,
It's their difference that makes them unique.

—DIGBY WOLFE, "KIDS WHO ARE DIFFERENT"

CONTENTS

ABILITY

ACKNOWLEDGMENTS

I would like to express my deepest gratitude to the many people who have supported me over the years in my pursuit of the truth about human intelligence. You will meet many of them throughout this book, but a few deserve singling out before we begin the journey.

I owe a deep debt of gratitude to my agent, Giles Anderson, for believing in the concept of this book and helping to make it a reality. I am also very grateful for my editor at Basic Books, TJ Kelleher, who gave me this chance, Tisse Takagi for her astute editorial assistance, and my production editor, Melody Negron, and my copyeditor, Wendy Nelson, for their thoroughness and patience. I am also very thankful I found the perfect illustrator for this book: George Doutsiopoulos. I appreciate his keen artistic skills as well as his immense patience!

Warm appreciation goes to the following mentors during high school for believing in me: Joyce Acton, Paul Spencer Adkins, Mary Brown, Tom Elliot, Regina Gordon, Debra Hobbs, Joyce Jeuell, and Mr. O. I am also incredibly appreciative of my mentors in college: Anne Fay, Herbert Simon, and Randy Pausch. Thanks to Fay for taking my dream seriously and helping me get there, Simon for teaching me how to take science seriously, and Pausch for teaching me the importance of not always taking life so seriously. I am also very appreciative to Nicholas J. Mackintosh, Jeremy R. Gray, Jerome L. Singer, and Robert J. Sternberg for their mentorship and collaboration in graduate school.

Thanks to the many other collaborators over the years I've had the great pleasure of working with and learning from, including Balazs Aczel, Joshua Aronson, Melanie Beaussart, Ronald Beghetto, Sheila Bennett, Jamie Brown, Sarah Burgess, Elise Christopher, Colin DeYoung, Kendall Eskine, Gregory J. Feist, Marie Forgeard, Liane Gabora, Justin Garcia, Glenn Geher, Luis Jiménez, Alan S. Kaufman, James C. Kaufman (my brother-in-spirit), Deidre Kolarick, Aaron Kozbelt, Kevin McGrew, Geoffrey Miller, David Moore,

Kate Plaisted, Jonathan A. Plucker, Jean Pretz, John Protzko, Matthew R. Reynolds, and Krishna Savani.

Thanks to the good folks at *Psychology Today*, including Hara Estroff Marano, Kaja Perina, Matthew Hutson, Lybi Ma, Carlin Flora, Jay Dixit, Andi Bartz, and Jane Nussbaum, for their support of my blog *Beautiful Minds* (now at *Scientific American Mind*), a platform that allowed me to test out many of the ideas in this book. Indeed, some of the content of my blog posts at *Psychology Today*, *Scientific American*, *Harvard Business Review*, the *Huffington Post*, and The Creativity Post made its way to these pages. Special thanks to Hutson for offering me the blog in the first place, and Marano for being such a strong supporter of this book and commissioning my article "Confessions of a Late Bloomer." You may notice that the opening vignette in Chapter 8 is a modified version of the opening to my "Confessions" piece. I should also note that some of the material in Chapter 13 on new approaches to learning appeared in the special "Radical Openness" issue of *Design Mind Magazine*, published by frog in partnership with TED. I am very appreciative of my editor on those pieces, Reena Jana, for her excellent editing skills and valuable additions to the piece.

Warm gratitude goes out to the following colleagues who were kind enough to read drafts of sections of this book and offered helpful feedback: Daniel Bor, Christopher Chabris, Jason R. Cooperrider, Colin DeYoung, K. Anders Ericsson, David Henry Feldman, Dawn Flanagan, Jack Fletcher, Margaret Gayle, Rachael Grazioplene, Mary Helen Immordino-Yang, Wendy Johnson, Rogier Kievit, David Lohman, Nicholas J. Mackintosh, Kevin Mc-Grew, Rebecca McMillan, Nancy L. Segal, Dean Keith Simonton, Jonathan Smallwood, and Darold Treffert. From this list, I must single out Rebecca McMillan for going beyond the call of duty in her support, guidance, generosity, and input from the earliest days of my writing this book. She has not only seen me through many moments of despair and frustration, but also greatly helped me *get past* those moments. I must also thank Tamara Day for making my vignettes more fully express the moment. Of course, I take the blame for any deficiencies in this book.

My acknowledgments wouldn't be complete without thanking my other friends and colleagues who have supported me over the years, including (but certainly not limited to) Diederik Aerts and the rest of the Center Leo Apostel for Interdisciplinary Studies, where I did a postdoctoral fellowship, Amy Alkon, Catharine Alvarez, Alice Andrews, Piers Anthony, Kanya Balakrishna and the rest of The Future Project team, John Bargh, Deborah Bial and the rest of The Posse Foundation team, Paul Bloom, Marc Brackett, Louisa Egan Brad, Becky Burch, Lynn Butler, Susan Cain, Shelley Carson, Mark Changizi, Saalim Chowdhury, Marvin Chun, Barry Cohen (my dentist), Barry Cohen (the psychologist), Jordan M. Cohen, Kathy Colwell, Matt Conant, Andrew Conway, Erin Coulter, Alia Joy Crum, Orin Davis, Jennifer DiMase, Carol Dweck, Brian Earp, Mo El-Sherif, Seymour Epstein, Jane Erickson, Barbara Esham, Alvaro Fernandez, Kurt Fischer, Milena Z. Fisher, Diana Fleischman, Eugene Ford, Howard Gardner, Syreeta Gates, Sandeep Gautam, Mark Gerban, Kristin Gilmore, Adam E. Green, Sarah Green and the rest of the *Harvard Business Review* team, Jennifer Odessa Grimes, Corin Barsily Goodwin and the rest of the Gifted Homeschoolers Forum staff, Abby Gross, Heidi Grant Halvorson, Maria Konnikova Hamilton, Joy Hanson, Nicole Hendrix, Erin Joy Henry, Whitney Hess, Adam Horowitz, Sallomé Hralima, Laura Jonkman, Melanie Kahl, Daniel Kahneman, Michael Kane, Yoona Kang, Nadeen L. Kaufman, Barbara Kerr, Justin Khoo, John Kounios, Kristof Kovacs, Andrea Kuszewski, Markus Labude, Matt Lanken, Valerie Kaefer LeCureux, Marina Livis, Bret Logan, Max Lugavere, Andrew Mangino, Gary Marcus, Art Markman, Dan McIntosh, Sam McNerney, Rose Swan Meacham, Martha J. Morelock, Paul O'Keefe, Lauretta Olivi, John-Michael Parker, Annie Murphy Paul, Esther Perry, Steven Pfeiffer, Patricia Phillips, Zorana Ivcevic Pringle, Kristen Pring-Mill, Sasha Raskin, Arthur Reber, Ruth Richards, Cat Rogerson, Blanche Rubin, Gabrielle Santa-Donato, Lori Schomp, Rebecca Searles and the rest of the *Huffington Post* team, Emma Seppala, Timbo Shriver, Steve Silberman, Jason Silva, Paul Silvia, Allan Snyder, Lynne Soraya, Lori Stone, Ian Temple, Nienke Venderbosch, Jill Vialet, Jonathan Wai, Joshua Waitzkin, Pascal Wallisch, Jim Westgate, Michael Anthony Woodley, Darya Zabelina, and Bora Zivkovic and the rest of the *Scientific American* team. I'd like to also thank my new friends at Milkboy Coffee in Ardmore, Pennsylvania (particularly Daniel Keller and Hugh Morretta) for their constant encouragement and for providing me with copious amounts of much-needed dopamine. In recent years, I've also been fortunate enough to form a friendship with Trina Paulus, author of *Hope for the Flowers*, a book which inspired me tremendously when I was very young. I appreciate Paulus's constant support, and thank her for kindly granting me permission to reprint the illustration at the end of this section, which originally appeared on page 77 of *Hope for the Flowers*. I am particularly grateful to my two closest friends—Elliot Samuel Paul and Ben Irvine—for their ongoing friendship, support, and stimulating conversations. Their philosophical and compassionate minds have enriched my life greatly.

Finally, I must acknowledge my family for encouraging all of my zany pursuits. I will never forget my grandfather's warm touch on the cello and intense practice routines, nor my grandmother's dogged persistence and determination to succeed no matter what got in her way. My greatest appreciation goes to my parents, Barbara and Michael. Without their encouragement, love, and guidance at every stage of my life, this book would have remained a mere pipe dream.

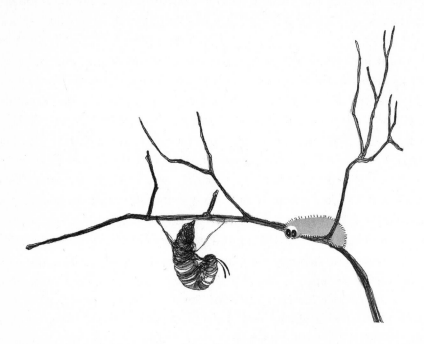

PROLOGUE

PROLOGUE

I am sitting alone in a dimly lit classroom, peering out a slightly cracked door. Across the hall is another classroom. It is full of my peers, who seem alien to me. The door is open just enough for me to see a small section of the classroom. I think it's a biology class, because the students are dissecting something that looks like a frog. I can hear the teacher's voice getting louder and closer to me. I strain to hear what he is saying but can't make out the words. Sounds technical. Maybe something relating to frog organs. Suddenly, the teacher appears at the door.

The teacher looks at me. I look at the teacher. He has a cautious expression on his face. Which, I suppose, is warranted, considering he is holding a live frog. He slowly holds the frog out to me at eye level. *Ribbit!* the frog calls out. I stare into its glossy eyes and it's like he is talking to me. I reach out my hands and take him from the teacher. I clutch the frog as I walk up to the door of the biology classroom. The aliens turn to look at me skeptically. I shout out one of the technical terms I just heard the teacher use—*Tympanum!*—to demonstrate that I am worthy of learning how to dissect frogs, just like them. The frog smiles. I think the frog is impressed. The teacher does not smile and does not seem impressed. In a snap, the teacher slams the door and I am jolted awake.

When I was very young, I was diagnosed with a learning disability. By the age of 3, I'd already had twenty-one ear infections. Even though I had an operation to remove the fluid in my ears, I developed central auditory processing disorder (CAPD), which made it very difficult for me to process words in real time. Blind people who have successful operations aren't able to see right away. It takes time to adapt to their new world.

Similarly, after my ear operation I had to re-learn how to process auditory input. Speech entered my ears, but it took an extra step before I could process its meaning. Unsurprisingly, my auditory processing problems caused me to lag behind my peers in school. When I performed poorly on an IQ test, I had to repeat third grade. I remember thinking to myself: *Gosh, I must be really behind if they don't think I'm ready to handle fourth grade.*

My early life experiences ignited within me a fascination with how and why people differ from each other. Playing in the park with my friends as a very young child, I noticed that some were generally more athletic than others. They just seemed to move with a natural precision and grace. I remember scrutinizing my friend Lee effortlessly swing himself across the jungle gym, as I repeatedly tripped. Why, I thought? What kind of bug juice was he drinking? More importantly, *where could I get some*?

Likewise at school, I noticed that some students seemed to understand the material effortlessly, whereas I required more time to process things. Even so, I wondered whether that actually made me learning *disabled*. It seemed that no matter where I went, or what I did, I couldn't escape that label. I was placed in special education and entered an environment where the teachers had very low expectations for my future success. But deep down I knew that I was capable of more. I was eager to challenge and express myself. All I wanted was a chance.

As I got older, my desire to understand intelligence became stronger. In high school I read voraciously on the subject, took every type of IQ test I could find, and meticulously analyzed why some questions were more difficult than others. Once I reached college, I embarked on a more formal, scientific journey to understand human intelligence. As I learned everything I could about how psychologists measure human intelligence and unexpectedly won awards for my research, I kept my own past a secret out of fear it would shatter my colleagues' perceptions of my objectivity. That it would somehow invalidate everything I worked so hard to achieve.

I set out on my journey convinced that it was simply not possible to accurately measure a person's intelligence. But what I found surprised me. I became so engrossed in the complex debates and methodologies used to investigate intelligence that I found myself, at times, forgetting my own past. Then I would come across studies that clearly contradicted—even invalidated—my own personal experiences and I had to reconcile the research with my own sense of self.

I often wondered: Which is *the* truth? Can there be multiple, contradicting truths? Which truth should I trust—the cold, impersonal generalizations based on large groups of people, or my deeply personal, subjective experience? Subjectivity or objectivity? Both sides within me have been incredibly suspicious of the other.

To give you a flavor of my internal struggles, consider the following typical statement from my colleagues:

> **COLLEAGUE:** The IQ test is just a brief assessment of one trait. It doesn't say anything about a person's past or future potential. It's only used to match a person to an intervention. Each person has numerous opportunities to demonstrate their intellectual prowess. A single test score certainly has no impact on a person's chances of success in life.

In response to which the following internal battle would ensue in me:

> **SUBJECTIVE SCOTT:** I wish this were true, but it isn't. First of all, we don't *really* view learning disabilities as being easily overcome. We stamp people with the label "learning disabled" really early on and treat those kids as if they are actually *disabled*. We clearly see them as being opposite from those *other* kids who do really well in school and who are really good at taking IQ tests—the kids we label *gifted*. Speaking of which, the IQ test isn't the only measure that determines people's fate. In fact, many tests may *appear* on the surface to be measuring a diverse set of skills, but they are really just disguised IQ tests. They may be *called* something different—academic achievement, SAT, ACT, GRE, LSAT, whatever. But don't let them fool you—they are all measuring the same thing. But what is this *thing*, anyway? And why do psychologists call it *intelligence*? Who gave them the right to define and then own that term? Surely many of *them* do well on these standardized tests. But just because *they* do well, does that mean that we must all accept that the thing they are measuring—which they are really good at—is *the* pinnacle of human intelligence? Why do we listen to them? Why do we take everything they say as fact? Just because they are doing science, there's no subjectivity involved? None? *Really*?! What if these careful, objective scientists had completely different experiences as children? What if they grew up being denied opportunities because of a low score on one of their very own tests? Would they be so quick to label their tests as intelligence tests? Would they fight their subjectivity and still come up with the same label, because they still believe that what they are capturing is the essence of human intelligence? Or would they see their tests a bit differently? Maybe they would hold different views about

the development and nurturance of intelligence, and focus more research on how IQ interacts with the many other important life traits that are on offer, many of which aren't neatly captured by a single brief test administered one slice in time? [panting, out of breath]

OBJECTIVE SCOTT: Calm down, kiddo. You are letting your subjectivity get in the way of the truth. That long rant, full of many annoying italics, was unnecessary and unprovoked. I'll be much calmer in tone, more efficient in my word choice, more organized in my thoughts, and I will include only one italicized word. My argument is thus: First, those who study learning disabilities are well aware of their developmental nature. You can't blame the researchers for the fact that many educators don't know the latest scientific research and can't apply it in their schools. Second, you aren't being fair to the incredibly thoughtful and careful intelligence researchers who have worked very hard to try and discover the true nature of human intelligence. They would be the first to admit that they are only talking about averages, or odds if you will. They are fully aware outliers exist. You certainly aren't being fair to the applied intelligence researchers, who have done a fine job constructing tests that are reliable and valid and that statistically correlate with lots of real-world outcomes. We owe a huge debt to them for creating some of the most predictive tests in the history of psychology. Sure, most of them probably do score very highly on their own tests and therefore don't know what it's like to go through life being labeled unintelligent. It's also true that IQ tests have unfortunately been abused many times throughout their history, and they have caused a lot of harm to many people—including my subjective self. But when properly administered, and the scores properly interpreted, the tests can be incredibly useful in helping children reach their maximum potential. Although I must objectively note that I have absolutely no idea what in the world the word *potential* actually means.

Subjective Scott is eager to respond, but I really must get on with the book.

~

Right from the start, I had a million questions about human intelligence. Just how general is IQ? Is there more to life than IQ? What if you don't do well on IQ tests—should you just write your life off, check yourself into a mental institution and enjoy the free food and care? Can you compensate for a low IQ? How much can you compensate? Does the compensation necessarily differ depending on the environment? If I want to be an announcer on *American Idol* alongside Ryan Seacrest, what's the minimum level of IQ required? Is that number different if I want to be a physicist?

I had just as many questions about talent. What is talent, really? Everyone throws the term around like they know what it means. We know that no one is born with fully formed traits; no one is born with the ability to read Shakespeare. So talent isn't inborn. But we also see clear differences in how fast people learn things. Is that—whatever that is—talent?

Then I wondered whether all paths to success *require* talent. Take Mary, who writes a best-selling novel after 15,000 hours of hard labor, and John, who writes a best-selling novel in 5,000 hours. Clearly there were differences in how long it took each of them to complete their novel. Is either more deserving of the label "gifted" than the other?

Also, isn't talent highly specialized? Some fields, such as mathematics, may demand more inclination toward numerical reasoning whereas other fields, such as dart throwing, may be more dependent on rote repetition of motor functions. Even within a domain, there might be multiple paths to achievement. Maybe Frank achieves worldwide musical acclaim by crooning whereas Sarah achieves it by belting out the high notes. Different talents, but both achieve success in the musical domain.

Practice left me equally perplexed. How do you get to Carnegie Hall? The typical answer is "practice, practice, practice." But no one ever asks: Who are those people who *ask* how to get to Carnegie Hall? It may turn out that they are a special population of folks, with already high intelligence, musical ability, or drive. If this is so, then we have a problem of restricted range: those without the necessary skills have already weeded themselves out of the competition. If we study those folks—and only those folks—and find that ability doesn't differentiate the great from the not-so-great, can we really conclude that ability plays no role whatsoever in the development of musical greatness?

So maybe it's all in the genes—including the will to practice! But there are many different genes, and all of those genes are constantly interacting with environment. No two people have the exact same genes or the exact same experiences. So then, how are we ever to figure out *the* role of genes in determining achievement?

Then came the torrent of questions about imagination and creativity. Do all domains require imagination and creativity? Does achievement always involve being original? What separates the good from the truly great? Where's the dividing line?

By the way, don't unique life experiences matter? You see the world through a very unique lens. Doesn't that count at all? Or what about your very unique talents? You know—that rare ability you have to yodel while break-dancing. Let's say you score really low on the SATs, but you can do a mean head spin while yodeling to the tune of "I Want It That Way" by the Backstreet Boys. Does that count at all? Must you do well on standardized tests to achieve in life?

Where do roadblocks fit in? How do harsh life experiences—such as growing up with a disability—contribute to achievement? Being labeled "learning disabled" in a school setting can be an incredibly painful experience, but can't that experience be just the fuel that is necessary to drive someone to make a change in the world?

I wish I could say I solved all of these mysteries. But the truth is, I ended up with even more questions.

~

There are so many moving parts to the puzzle of human intelligence. And no easy answers. Nevertheless, there are some things I do know. Everyone has unique needs and is worthy of encouragement. In the real world, people clearly differ in their inclinations, passions, dreams, and goals. But environments also differ, so people in theory (but unfortunately not always in practice) have the opportunity to seek out or create their own unique niches.

Not so in school. In this peculiar microcosm of reality, you aren't supposed to be different. We have general education, where we group children together by such arbitrary criteria as age, ability, grade, and subject matter. Information is presented in discrete units, with little information given about how it is all connected or how any of it can be applied in the world at large. If you deviate from the norm, you may be lucky enough to be eligible for special education.

In this artificial world of school we created, labeling is important. Individual differences collide with limited resources, creating a situation where parents are scrambling for special services for their children. With the future of so many lives at stakes, it's crucial that we scrutinize exactly how we identify those who don't fit the norm, since the methods we use affect our interventions as well as our expectations of just how high we allow them to soar.

I firmly believe we can recognize and value every kind of mind without diminishing the value of others. I don't see intelligence as a zero-sum game: just because someone is talented (whatever that means) by the standards set by society doesn't mean that the person who isn't doesn't have dynamic potential for intellectual functioning. There are so many different paths to success.

All of us—no matter what labels we have been given—have areas of strength and weakness. What is viewed as a great asset in one culture may be overlooked in another culture. Some people get lucky and are born into environments that support and highly value their particular strengths. Others have to alter their environments to *display* the value of their strengths.

Is this book personal? Absolutely. I *want* readers to see the world through my eyes. This includes the early pain and confusion I felt at being labeled *ungifted* as well as the tremendous sense of victory and success I felt later when I defied everyone's expectations of what was possible. Through engaging in fascinating research on the subject of human intelligence, I was able to overcome my own obstacles and began to question the system that told me I shouldn't have succeeded. I began to question our entire understanding of human intelligence and possibility, and wondered how many other people were being stifled by an unfair and often arbitrary label. Even though scientists can reveal real, observable behaviors, the concept of intelligence has no fixed meaning. Scientists, indeed all of us, interpret behaviors according to our own beliefs and experiences. Therefore, it is worth taking a very close look at the meaning we give the word "intelligence," for it has an immense impact on millions of lives.

Throughout this book I do my best to make it obvious when subjective Scott is creeping into the pages, and I hope I make it equally as clear when I am presenting the research findings as objectively as possible. A major aim of this book is to lift the curtain off of the many labels that scientists have put on the phenomena they have discovered, and show the underlying mechanisms for what they are rather than what the scientists have decided to call them.

Our journey takes us through various stages. In the first section, *Origins*, I lay the foundation for the rest of the book. I want to arm you with the truth about how traits actually develop, and the history and current measurement of IQ, before we get into all the nitty-gritty debates.

With that knowledge as our base, we enter the world of *Labels*, where children are stamped according to their early abilities. Debates about who qualifies for what label—whether it's learning disabilities or giftedness—rage on in this standards-based educational climate.

Leaving the labels behind, I then lay out the rules of *Engagement*. In recent years psychologists have discovered many crucial factors that either promote engagement and perseverance or cause students to zone out and avoid challenges. As we'll see, motivation, mindset, and self-regulation are *intimately* linked, and are incredibly malleable and heavily influenced by context.

With knowledge of these key drivers of success, we leave the world of school and consider how *Ability* develops on the stage of life. There are numerous studies showing that expertise and deliberate practice are important causes of success. But does deliberate practice explain everything? In this section we look at other abilities (deliberate practice is an ability, after all), including "general intelligence," "talent," and "creativity." In each case we will get our hands dirty as we try to understand what's really going on beneath the labels.

Finally, in the last chapter, with all of the fascinating strands of human intelligence exposed, I will present you with my reconceptualization of human intelligence. I believe the new definition best describes how people live and learn in the real world, and provides people with the understanding they need to realize their dreams. After laying out the theory, I will discuss the broad implications for education and society, and present some examples of programs in line with my new definition.

As we take this journey together, I encourage you to question everything, just as I have questioned everything. My criticisms notwithstanding, it must be acknowledged that I wouldn't have been able to take this journey without the hard work and dedication of large numbers of scientists and educators who have thoroughly inspired me over the years. I have an immense appreciation for their hard work and dedication in their attempts to solve the many puzzles surrounding human intelligence.

I also owe a huge debt of gratitude to the recent flurry of journalists and authors who have written books for a general audience, in highly digestible form, about the determinants of talent, practice, and high achievement.[1] Journalists, authors, scientists, and educators have all provided glimpses of how the world works and have increased our awareness of the social problems that currently exist. That is immensely important. After all, knowing how the world works is the only way we can initiate the change required to create a *better* world.

So come join me in my ongoing journey to understand the vastness of human possibility. Let's take a complete tour of the human mind and its many manifestations. Not all of the research will make us feel good. Some pieces of the puzzle may even seem to contradict one another. But stick with me. I hope to convince you that the overall picture of human intelligence is far more beautiful, exciting, and hopeful than any of the one-sided alternatives.

ORIGINS

Chapter 1

DEVELOPMENT

1988

Face down on the bathroom floor, I wait for the bullying to end. "Hey loser, you failed again," says the chubby kid with long blond hair. Another kick, followed by nervous laughter from his cronies. He pulls me up by my collar and looks me in the eyes. I stare back.

His name suddenly pops into my head: *Rob. That's why he looks familiar; he's also in the resource room.* I smile. He tilts his head and looks at me confused. "You're gonna be in third grade forever!" he says with broken bravado. I'm not sure if the words are meant to scare me or if he is just voicing his own fears. He pushes me down again and turns around. Just like that, he leaves, his followers shuffling closely behind. On to torment the next special education student, I imagine.

As I straighten my shirt and feel my bruised rib, I replay his words in my mind. *He's right.* This is my second time in third grade. The school psychologist said I needed some catching up, but what does that mean? Familiar worries surface inside me. *I really don't want to be in third grade forever. Am I doomed to always be one step behind?* An overwhelming urge suddenly comes over me to run home and hide.

This was just one incident of many that characterized my childhood, but the feelings and questions that it evoked within me persisted. I *was* different. I knew it, the teachers knew it, even the bullies seemed to know it. While the other kids sat calmly in a circle listening to the teacher read a story, I was running around the circle with a superman cape. Instead of playing cops and robbers with the kids in my neighborhood, I acted out entire soap operas alone in my room. Instead of doing my math homework, I wrote short stories about time travel. In every way, and at every turn, I seemed out of sync with my peers. I was living in my own head, and consequently people treated me like I was disabled. But no one knew my inner world.

Later That Week . . .

I'm enraptured. There, right in front of me, is one of the world's greatest symphony orchestras—the Philadelphia Orchestra, known around the world for its lush, deep, "Philadelphia Sound." One of the principal cellists winks at me from the stage. He is a friend of my grandfather, Harry Gorodetzer, who himself was a cellist before retiring from the orchestra a few years back. There is no one I look up to more than my grandfather. He embodies everything I want to be: charismatic, charming, friendly, and successful. He is friends with everyone, including many of the big-time conductors and musicians of my generation, including Simon Rattle, Ricardo Muti, and Yo-Yo Ma.

I beam with pride and wave at the cello section. They wave back with their bows as the concert mistress comes on stage. Applause reverberates throughout the Academy of Music. I feel special just being in their company. I feel as though I've been allowed *entrance into a world of greatness.*

I can't wait until the concert is over and I can go backstage. Every time I get to meet one of the great musicians, I feel on top of the world. Being with them allows me to forget the mess at school. They don't know any of the labels I've been given or that I've been placed in special education. All they know is that I am Harry's grandson, and that makes me special in another way. They ask me all sorts of questions about my dreams and desires like I'm just a normal kid capable of anything I set my mind to. I tell them I want to be a cellist or doctor. Their comments are encouraging, and they genuinely seem to believe my ambitions are attainable.

In contrast, the situation in school is only getting worse. I've been taken out of the normal classroom and placed in special education, with untimed tests and a lighter course load. Even though the new environment allows for more freedom, most of the time I just feel bored. I feel like I'm capable of more, but because others don't believe in me, it's hard to believe in myself. I assume the teachers must be right.

Every time the intercom makes an announcement for the gifted students to report for their activities, I wonder: *Who are those kids who hang out in the gifted room? What do they have that I don't? And why can't they remember their room number?* I assume they have more potential:

plain and simple. They were born with the mind to excel. I wonder what I'm capable of. More importantly, I wonder if I'll ever get a chance to find out.

But tonight I don't have to think about any of that. I can get lost in the music and the rush of excitement backstage. I can dream about a world where other possibilities exist, possibilities beyond school and tests and the scrutiny of my teachers. Moments like this allow me to imagine a world in which I might be able not just to get by but to flourish.

~

What are the origins of greatness? Throughout history there has been no shortage of speculation.[1] In ancient times, genius was considered supernatural or divine. The Greek Muses—mythological goddesses—were thought to be the source of inspiration for literature and the arts. Philosopher Immanuel Kant believed the ability to produce something that is both original and exemplary was inborn and could not be taught.[2] Taking the opposite extreme, Sir Joshua Reynolds, an influential eighteenth-century British painter, proclaimed to his students at the Royal Academy, "Nothing is denied to well directed labour; nothing is to be obtained without it."[3]

While there were a plethora of opinions on the subject, the topic received its first scientific treatment in 1869 when Francis Galton published *Hereditary Genius*.[4] Galton, who was Charles Darwin's half cousin, was so enthralled with Darwin's ideas of genetic variation as the seed of natural selection, that he became convinced that a similar idea could be used to explain why people differ from one another in genius.

His evidence came not from genetics—modern genetic analyses were not available back then—but rather by investigating family lineage. Galton collected data on distinguished European men by scouring the obituaries in the *London Times* and showed that eminence (at least among men) appeared to run through bloodlines. He found that this held across a wide range of occupations, including statesman, military commander, scientist, poet, painter, and musician.

Eventually Galton grew dissatisfied with anecdotal evidence and decided to set about measuring human intelligence. At the International Health Exhibition in London in 1883, he set up his "Anthropometric Laboratory." For a mere threepence, people could have a wide range of their abilities measured, including "Keenness of Sight and of Hearing; Colour Sense, Judgement of Eye; Breathing Power; Reaction Time; Strength of Pull and of Squeeze; Force of Blow; Span of Arms; Height, both standing and sitting; and Weight."[5]

Although Galton focused on the nature of eminence, he did acknowledge the importance of passion, zeal, and persistence. Still, he argued that regardless of the environment, exemplary and natural abilities inevitably rose to the top.[6] This idea didn't go uncontested. In 1873 the French-Swiss botanist Alphonse de Candolle showed that the environment mattered a great deal in cultivating genetic expression, showing that eminent scientists from Western civilization tended to do their best work under particular political, economic, social, cultural, and religious conditions.[7]

Still, the question of individual differences remained. Although de Candolle's results helped explain why scientists growing up in very different environments differed from one another, his findings weren't able to explain why people differ from one another within the *same* cultural environment. Could the environment be the sole explanation? Or do genetic differences play any role at all?

The jury was out for over a century, with fierce arguments favoring one position or another. What was severely lacking was a systematic investigation of the issue.

∾

In 1990 the behavioral geneticist Thomas J. Bouchard Jr. and his colleagues at the University of Minnesota published a striking finding: about 70 percent of the differences in IQ found among twins and triplets living apart were associated with genetic variation.[8] What's more, the identical twins (whose genes were assumed to be 100 percent identical*) were remarkably similar to identical twins reared together on various measures of personality, occupational and leisure-time interests, and social attitudes, despite spending most of their lives apart.

This study, and the hundreds of twin and adoption studies that have been conducted since then, have painted a consistent picture: genetic variation matters.[9] The studies say nothing about *how* they matter, or *which* genes matter, but they show quite convincingly that biological variation does matter. Genes vary within any group of people (even among the inhabitants of middle-class Western society), and this variation contributes to variations

---

*Although there is a growing consensus that this assumption is not true. See E. Charney, "Behavior Genetics and Post Genomics," *Behavioral and Brain Sciences* 35 (2012): 331–358.

in these people's behaviors. The twin findings shouldn't be understated; it counters many a prevailing belief that we are born into this world as blank slates, completely at the mercy of external forces.[10]

The most important lesson researchers have learned from over twenty-five years' worth of twin studies is that virtually every single psychological trait you can measure—including IQ, personality, artistic ability, mathematical ability, musical ability, writing, humor styles, creative dancing, sports, happiness, persistence, marital status, television viewing, female orgasm rates, aggression, empathy, altruism, leadership, risk taking, novelty seeking, political preferences, television viewing, and even rates of Australian teens talking on their cell phones—has a heritable basis.* Because our psychological characteristics reflect the physical structures of our brains and because our genes contribute to those physical structures, it is unlikely that there are any psychological characteristics that are completely unaffected by our DNA.[11]

Unfortunately there is frequent confusion about the meaning of heritability. The most frequent misunderstanding is the purpose of twin studies. Heritability estimates are about understanding sources of similarities and differences in traits between members of a particular population. The results apply only to that population. The purpose is not to determine how much any particular individual's traits are due to his or her genes or his or her environment. Behavioral geneticists are well aware that all of our traits develop through a combination of both nature and nurture. Heritability estimates are about explaining differences among people, not explaining individual development. The question on the table for them is this: *In a particular population of individuals, what factors make those individuals the same as each other, and which factors make them different?*

Therefore, twin studies aren't designed to investigate human development. In recent years developmental psychologists, including L. Todd Rose, Kurt Fischer, Peter Molenaar, and Cynthia Campbell, have been developing exciting new techniques to study *intraindividual variation*.[12] Intraindividual variation focuses on a single person and looks at how an integrated dynamic system of behavioral, emotional, cognitive, and other psychological processes change across time and situations. New intraindividual techniques allow researchers to focus on a single twin pair and see how nature

---

*Although a few traits, such as love styles and materialism, don't appear to have a heritable basis.

and nurture interact in nonlinear ways to explain both their similarities and their differences.[13] Both levels of analysis—twin studies and developmental analysis—are informative, but the results from the one do not apply to the other.[14]

Many people also confuse heritability with immutability. They hear the word "heritable" and immediately think of "genes," which then conjures up pictures of a fixed trait that can't be altered by external forces. In contrast, many people hear the word "environment" and breathe a sigh of relief, thinking the trait is easily modifiable. This requires quite a strong faith in social engineering!

Just because a trait is heritable (and virtually all of our psychological traits are heritable) doesn't necessarily mean that the trait is fixed or can't be developed. Virtually all of our traits are substantially genetically influenced *and* are influenced by environmental conditions. Even though television viewing has a heritable basis,[15] most people don't think of the activity as being outside our personal control. Indeed, parents frequently control (or try to control) the length of time their children spend sitting in front of the tube.

Another source of confusion is the role of parenting in the development of traits. A common finding in twin studies is that the environments experienced by twins (or any two siblings) do little to create differences in intelligence and personality as adults. In other words, the heritability of traits tends to *increase* as one ages and escapes the influence of parents.[16] Judith Rich Harris showed that peers exert a greater influence in creating differences in personality among adolescents than parents.[17] But do these findings mean that parents cannot effectively help their child develop their unique traits? Absolutely not. That's like saying that water has no influence on a fish's development because all fish live in water. A nurturing family environment is a *necessity* to help the child flourish, just as a fish needs water to swim and survive.

Just because a variable doesn't vary doesn't mean it has no causal impact on a particular outcome. Genes could "account for" 100 percent of the variability in a trait in a particular twin study, but this does not mean that environmental factors, including parental quality, are therefore unimportant in the development of the trait. Instead it turns out that parenting matters in a way that is different from what was originally assumed: Parents matter to the extent that they affect the expression of genes. Parents can exert important influence in the child's development by nurturing productive interests and helping the child channel destructive inclinations into more productive outlets.

The importance of parenting becomes more salient when we look at a wider range of environments. Only a few of the twins in Bouchard's original study were reared in real poverty or were raised by illiterate parents, and none were mentally disabled. This matters. Consider a recent study by Eric Turkheimer and colleagues. They looked at 750 pairs of American twins who were given a test of mental ability when they were 10 months old and again when they were 2 years.[18] When looking at the group of kids aged just 10 months, the home environment appeared to be the key variable across different levels of socioeconomic status. The story changed considerably as the children got a bit older and differences in education became more pronounced. For the 2-year-olds living in poorer households, the home environment mattered the most, accounting for about 80 percent of the variation in mental ability. For these kids, genetics played little role in explaining differences in cognitive ability. In wealthy households, on the other hand, genetics explained more of the differences in performance, accounting for nearly 50 percent of all the variation in mental ability.

Prominent behavioral geneticists, including Bouchard, eventually realized that it was time to move on from simply calculating heritability estimates. In a 2009 paper entitled "Beyond Heritability," researchers Wendy Johnson, Eric Turkheimer, Irving I. Gottesman, and Bouchard concluded that "given that genetic influences are routinely involved in behavior," "little can be gleaned from any particular heritability estimate and there is little need for further twin studies investigating the presence and magnitude of genetic influences on behavior."[19]

Twins studies had their day, then modern genomics arrived, full of promise. At last—we could look at differences in DNA and see exactly how people or groups genetically differ from one another! In 2000 the renowned behavioral geneticists Robert Plomin and John Crabbe optimistically predicted, "In a few years, many areas of psychology will be awash in specific genes responsible for the widespread influence of genetics on behavior."[20]

Their prediction came true. We received an embarrassment of DNA riches. The most recent technology, genome-wide association studies (GWAS), enabled us to easily and cheaply search through the entire human genome in search of genetic markers (more technically referred to as single nucleotide polymorphisms, or SNPs) associated with different traits. Just put hundreds, even thousands, of people's DNA on chips, read them out, and look at the bits that differentiate different levels of schizophrenia, personality, intelligence, or what have you. Seemed straightforward.

It wasn't. Consider height. It seemed a pretty sure bet that we'd find the genes that contribute to differences in height. Height tends to have extremely high heritability (.90, averaged over many different populations).[21] So the genes pretty much have to be there. And sure enough, lots of genes have been found. The problem is, only a vanishingly small proportion of that number have actually been replicated.[22] When you go fishing for a million fish, you're bound to find an awful lot of seaweed.

We find the same story when it comes to complex psychological traits. Consider a recent study led by Ian Deary in Scotland.[23] They conducted a genome-wide analysis of 3,511 adults in search of the genes that underlie IQ, collecting information on over 500,000 genetic markers for these participants. Taking all of these genes into account explained about 40 to 50 percent of the differences among IQ test scores. No single gene, however, explained more than a tiny fraction of the differences in IQ. Another recent study led by psychologist Christopher Chabris sought to replicate the association between twelve specific genetic variants and IQ.[24] Across three independent samples and almost 10,000 individuals, only a single test was marginally significant.

These findings confirm what we already knew from behavioral genetics research: nearly every human trait is polygenic (that is, involves many interacting genes).[25] As developmental psychologist Eric Turkheimer puts it, "GWAS is always bound to produce a few 'results' because everything is heritable, and heritability is instantiated in the genome, in the same not very useful sense that cognition is instantiated in the brain."[26]

The causes of human behavior are complex. For every single action we take, there are a huge number of causes, each one small in its effects but large when taken together. You don't have access to how all of the various genetic and environmental factors interacted throughout the course of your development. This poses a problem for scientists in search of *the* causes of development, because there is no single cause. The long and winding road that leads from genotype (DNA) to a phenotype (outward behavior) differs considerably from person to person.

What really matters is not whether genes influence behavior or not, but how we take what we've got and steer the course of our lives. For that, we need a developmental perspective.

∼

Michael Jordan didn't pop out dunking a basketball from the free-throw line. Full-blown abilities and traits aren't prepackaged at birth. That's because our genes don't code for traits; they code for the production of proteins. Although it's true that proteins are the building blocks of everything we do— they contribute to the formation of cells and the transport of elements from one location to another, and are the foundation for chemical reactions—they are far removed from anything we would recognize as psychological traits.[27]

One of the most important discoveries in recent years is that the environment triggers gene expression.[28] Findings from genetics, neuroscience, cognitive psychology, and developmental psychology demonstrate that the nature versus nurture question is highly misleading. We are neither born nor made. The environment is inseparable from our genes. Every trait develops through the interplay of genes and the environment. Nature and nurture are complementary, not at odds.

But where is the environment? You may think of the environment as existing *out there*, far and away from what's going on inside you. Truth is, the environment can be internal or external. The external environment includes things such as light, noise, heat, and food. Internal factors include hormones, nerve impulses, and other genes.[29] Both internal and external factors contribute to the activation and deactivation of genetic expression.

Every single step we take in life is registered by cells within us and alters the configuration of all the other cells in our body. As science writer Matt Ridley notes, "[Genes] are devices for extracting information from the environment. Every minute, every second, the pattern of genes being expressed in your brain changes, often in direct or indirect response to events outside the body. Genes are the mechanisms of experience."[30]

The human genome has plasticity built right in by giving us considerable redundancy. Many of our genes serve more than a single function and can produce more than one protein, depending on genetic and environmental factors. Many different genes can even contribute to the production of the same protein. In the language of science, the development of traits is "canalized."[31] As developmental cognitive neuroscientist Gary Marcus notes, "Nature is not a dictator hell-bent on erecting the same building regardless of the environment, but a flexible Cub Scout prepared with contingency plans for many occasions."[32]

All of us are born with a range of possible expressions of a trait (what scientists call "norms of reaction").[33] Because your genotype (your genetic makeup) continually interacts with the environment, we don't know at any point in time how your genotype would respond if plucked up and put in a completely different environment. Some genetic expression lies dormant in all of us, waiting for the perfect environmental circumstances to trigger it. This phenomenon is called "cryptic genetic variation" and has received quite a bit of research attention in recent years.[34]

Genes are like players in the Philadelphia Orchestra. There are many different sections responsible for contributing to the development of different traits. For the symphony to sound beautiful, lots of syncing is required. All of the players within each section have to be in sync, and all the different sections have to coordinate as well. Just as the percussion section might have difficulty getting its rhythm together, the genes that underlie a particular trait might be activated later than the genes for other traits that contribute to an ability. So one trait, like extraversion, can develop early, while another trait, like speech production, may lag—which may be awkward until the two come into harmony. Not only that, but if the orchestra plays in a totally unresponsive environment—for example, an audience of techno fans—the players will be discouraged from reaching higher and higher levels of achievement.

What's the role of the conductor in the gene symphony orchestra? The conductor is analogous to all of the environmental influences that can guide the various sections and help them sync up and sound beautiful.

～

So is there any hope of understanding how traits develop? One key is to recognize that tiny genetic and environmental advantages multiply over the years—in what is called the "multiplier effect."[35] This idea can be traced back to sociology's notion of "Matthew effects," named for the biblical aphorism "For to him who has shall be given and he shall have abundance; but from him who does not have, even that which he has shall be taken away" (Matthew 25:29).[36]

The environment can take even a tiny genetic or environmental advantage and "multiply" it again and again as such interactions are reiterated through the course of one's development. The other side of the coin is also possible, of course. A slight genetic or environmental disadvantage can lead a youngster to avoid situations where that difficulty would be revealed. Yet those are precisely the situations that would enable the child to practice the task and make up for the disadvantage. Instead, the child misses the boat while peers sail off ahead.

Multiplier effects have been studied from a number of different perspectives—including Urie Bronfenbrenner and Stephen Ceci's bioecological model of abilities and chaos models, in which "tiny differences in input could quickly become overwhelming differences in output."[37] This idea is encapsulated in the "butterfly effect," in which a small change at one point in a nonlinear system can result in large differences at a later state.

The dynamic, nonlinear, and probabilistic nature of human development has received large support in recent years. Some of the very same genes that have been associated with our lowest lows (such as depression, anxiety, and the inability to concentrate on an important task) have been shown under nurturing conditions to lead to our highest *highs*—such as positive emotions, intellectual curiosity, and an enhanced ability to regulate our emotions.[38]

Adopting a Swedish idiomatic expression, W. Thomas Boyce and Bruce Ellis refer to *dandelion children* as those who survive and thrive in whatever environments they encounter, just like dandelions prosper regardless of soil, sun, drought, or rain.[39] In contrast, they describe *orchid children* as individuals whose survival and flourishing is heavily dependent on the environment. As they poetically note, "In conditions of neglect, the orchid promptly declines, while in conditions of support and nurture, it is a flower of unusual delicacy and beauty."

In recent years there have been a number of studies that support the "Orchid Hypothesis" (as journalist David Dobbs puts it).[40] To be sure, each genetic mutation only explains a small fraction of behavior, and it remains to be seen how many of the genes actually replicate. Also, it's surely a gross simplification to split the world up into two groups—orchids and dandelions. Nevertheless, these results highlight the importance of taking into account gene–gene interactions as well as gene–environment interactions in understanding human development. Our latest understanding is that many of our genes don't code *for* positive or negative outcomes. They are related to heightened sensitivity to the environment—for better *and* worse.[41]

This is why it's crucial to intervene as early as possible and set the trajectory of the child's genes for the *better*. By the time children enter their first year of school, they already come to the table with substantial differences in environmental support and the amount of time and money invested in them.[42] This matters. According to psychologist Keith Stanovich, the child who starts off reading well, or has been put in a position early to accumulate a large vocabulary, will read more, learn more, choose friends who are also good at reading, ask for more books, receive more books, and ultimately read better as a result. The child with a lower vocabulary will read more slowly, gain less enjoyment from reading, and not construct such a reading-enriched environment. The result is that the intellectual gap between the two children will become greater and greater.[43]

The environments of low-SES (low socioeconomic status) homes and high-SES homes differ markedly in a number of factors relevant to the development of intellectual functioning. In one study, the researchers estimated that children raised by professional parents heard approximately 30 million words by the age of 3, and their vocabulary was much richer.[44] In comparison, they estimated that children growing up with working-class parents heard 20 million words, while children of unemployed African American mothers were estimated to have heard only 10 million words by the age of 3. There were also important differences in parental treatment, with children of professional parents receiving considerably more encouragement relative to the number of scoldings.

There are other important differences between high-SES and low-SES environments. The HOME Inventory (Home Observation for Measurement of the Environment) measures the quality and quantity of intellectual stimulation and support available to children at home. Some indicators include (a) how much the parents talk to the child, (b) access to books, magazines, newspapers, and computers, (c) how frequently the parents read to the child, (d) how many trips are taken with the children to places outside the home (such as museums), and (e) degree of warmth and friendliness in the family. Various studies using this inventory have found significant differences between the social classes on these various dimensions, and these differences are associated with as much as a 9 IQ-point difference.[45]

Critics have argued that perhaps the children are inheriting both the genes for lower IQ *and* the lower-SES environment from the parents. Although this is a fair criticism, this can't be the whole story. Children adopted from lower-SES backgrounds and living with genetically unrelated but higher-SES parents show a 12- to 18-point increase in IQ, on average, compared to their siblings who are left behind.[46]

These differing experiences add up. Bennett Shaywitz and his colleagues found that "a child with a mean IQ for Grades 1–5 of 80 would be expected to show a decrement of −1.1 per year, while a child with a 140 IQ would tend to show an increase of about 4.5 points a year."[47] Likewise, Herbert Walberg and Shiow-Ling Tsai found that general science achievement among young adults depends on three factors: prior educational background, current educational activity, and motivation. Critically, they found that these three factors are cumulative: it was the prior educational experiences that predicted current educational activity and motivation.[48]

Of course, we aren't completely passive recipients of our environment. All of us actively make choices on a moment-to-moment basis that influence our development, and genes influence these choices. The possibility that our genes help direct our experiences was proposed by Sandra Scarr and Kathleen McCartney in 1983.[49] More recently this premise has been incorporated into Experience Producing Drive (EPD) Theory.[50] According to the EPD theory, natural selection sculpted our genes so that we would be active agents of our environments, constantly seeking out situations that maximize our chances of survival and reproduction. In other words, we evolved to find the best environmental fit for our genomes. In Darwinian terms, that just may be the meaning of life.

Under this view, genes exert their influence on the development of our traits by controlling our motivations and preferences. Eventually people will surround themselves with environmental influences that reinforce their genetic drives. In Wendy Johnson's formulation of the theory, this pull and sensitivity to certain aspects of the environment applies to all areas of individual differences, including motivations, interests, attentional foci, personality, attitudes, values, and quirky traits unique to each individual.[51] Genes influence the development of traits indirectly, by controlling our tendencies to engage in the world.

Think of the kid who is immediately attracted to the violin and spends hours and hours practicing without anyone telling him to do so. Or the young girl who finds numbers beautiful and spends many hours playing with numbers in her head. These children find these activities inherently rewarding. And their skills in their respective areas build up because they seek out opportunities to do the things that they find rewarding, gaining lots of practice along the way.

Genes indirectly pull us in certain directions, and take us away from other directions. We all have our own unique set of things that capture our attention, and this is partly rooted in our genes. Genes influence our traits and abilities by motivating us to seek experiences that in turn develop the neural brain structures and physiology that support even higher levels of achievement.

~

Things get even more complicated when we try to understand the developmental path to greatness—achievement that is both original and exemplary.[52] Most human traits—including IQ and personality—have a "normal," or bell-curve, distribution in the general population. This means the distribution is symmetrical, with equal numbers of people on both sides of the bell curve. In terms of most contemporary IQ tests, about 68 percent of the general population can be expected to score between 85 and 115, with virtually everyone scoring between 40 and 160 (see Chapter 2).

Not so with greatness. When you look at the distribution of greatness in the general population, you see something very different. *Greatness doesn't conform to a normal distribution.* Instead, it's highly "skewed," with the right side of the tail reaching all the way out. To see what this looks like, consider a computer simulation conducted by Dean Keith Simonton on two different distributions: IQ and greatness.[53] In the simulation he assumed a population of 10,000 people, and he assumed that both distributions have an average score of 100 with a standard deviation of 16. Figure 1.1 shows what Simonton found. As you can see, the distributions couldn't have been more different. The simulated normal distribution conformed quite well to the distribution of IQ. The distribution is symmetrical, with the number of people with IQ scores above average equal to the number of people with IQ scores below average. The lowest IQ score was 37, the highest was 155, and the range was 118 points. Now look at the other distribution, which is typical of greatness. As you can see, it's not at all symmetrical. Although the average score was still 100, the range was 254 points! The lowest score, 87, was much closer to the average than the highest score, 341. In fact, out of 10,000 people, there was only a single person with a greatness quotient (GQ) of 341.

Contrast that with some of the highest IQ test scores in our generation and they pale by comparison with some of the highest GQ scores.[54] And that's only with a population of 10,000 people. You can expect GQ scores to be much higher among larger populations. Clearly, there are many people whose actual levels of greatness far exceed their prediction based on their IQ test scores alone, or any other single trait for that matter. What's going on?

The answer to this puzzle is that greatness is the result of many factors operating *in combination*—including the development of many personal characteristics, accumulation of life experiences, opportunities, and chance.[55]

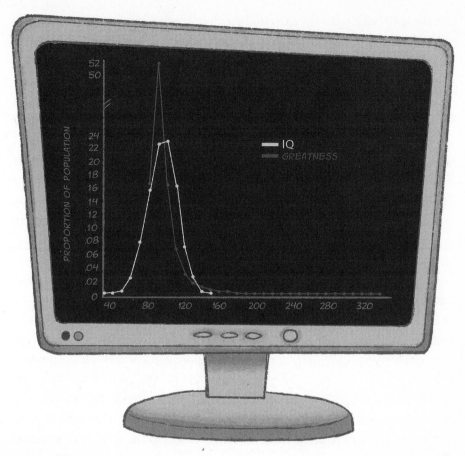

FIGURE 1.1.
Source: D. K. Simonton, *Scientific Genius: A Psychology of Science* (New York: Cambridge University Press, 1988). Adapted with permission.

Once we understand that the skills that underlie IQ test performance are only some of the many factors contributing to greatness, we can see how a less than stellar IQ score can be offset by other factors. The higher the level of other factors—such as opportunity, perseverance, or motivation—the higher the total product. This also means that people can arrive at the same GQ score through a very different combination of factors.

These ideas form the core of Dean Simonton's model of talent.[56] According to Simonton, additive models—in which a bunch of different traits are simply added on to each other to determine a person's level of talent—are too simplistic. Instead, Simonton argues that talent must be viewed as a multidimensional and multiplicative developmental process. Talent is multidimensional in that many different traits combine to make up a talent, and multiplicative in that the genes that underlie each trait aren't independent of each other in their effects, but are constantly interacting with each other and the environment.

Think of it this way. Every single sphere of socially valued achievement—from opera to acting to visual arts to break-dancing to banjo playing to physics to psychology to being president of the United States—draws on a different constellation of traits. Let's call this constellation the "X-factor." Consider the music "X-factor." As Gary Marcus points out in his book *Guitar Zero: The New Musician and the Science of Learning*, musical talent is influenced by many different genes.[57] There are genes that affect memory, curiosity, and sensitivity to absolute pitch. There are genes that relate to tests of musical composition and improvisation (but these same genes also seem to play a role in social interaction in humans and other species). Marcus argues that "music is a skill that builds on a multiplicity of brain circuits" and "a skill that draws on many different genes—each of which may contribute in some way or another to any individual's talents for music."[58]

Of course, the importance of a person's constellation of personal characteristics depends on the domain. The "X-factor" for the TV singing competition *American Idol* may consist of a combination of style, vocal quality, pitch, rhythm, charisma, and persistence.* Is this the same X-factor as the scientific discovery X-factor? Heck no! Scientific discovery often involves a different constellation of traits, some of which may sometimes be at odds with the pop music X-factor (such as detail-oriented thought, restraint, and introversion).

But even X-factors in a single domain can be individualized. Muggsy Bogues made it to the NBA through his speed and agility, whereas Wilt Chamberlain relied more on his height and strength. Sure, psychologists could go in and find a strong correlation between height at age 10 and success in the NBA, but this would only isolate a single trait—height—and ignore the most interesting aspect of achievement: *the combination and capitalization among traits.*

Of course, capitalization isn't always easy. For instance, a person without vocal chords will not become a great national anthem singer, no matter how high they score on other traits that contribute to national anthem singing ability (such as emotional expressiveness). Simple math shows that in the multiplicative talent equation, a value of 0 on any single trait (such as the absence

---

*Fun fact: I was rejected from *American Idol* twice! See http://www.psychologytoday.com/articles/200912/how-win-american-idol.

of vocal chords) times any number of other values (such as an extremely high level of emotional expressiveness) will always end up being 0. But while this is theoretically true, trait values are rarely zero in the real world. Even a raspy singer like Bob Dylan would probably still be appreciated as a national anthem singer—he has such a distinctive combination of traits.

In sum, there are many different traits on offer, and each trait is on a continuum. Where each of us lies on that continuum at any moment in time is influenced by a lifetime of developmental experiences dancing with nature. The key to understanding the development of greatness lies in understanding how initially small genetic and environmental advantages lead a person to self-select environments that are the best match for them and how the environment then reinforces or squelches those advantages. Greatness is not born, but takes time to develop, and there are many paths to greatness.

Keep this big picture in mind as we take a journey through each of the pieces of the intelligence puzzle—beginning with the most traditional metric of intelligence, IQ.

Chapter 2

IQ

1990

"Will it hurt?" I ask my Mom as we drive up the winding road to the school psychologist's office. "No Scotty, painless," she reassures me. I tick that question off my list. "OK, well what if he discovers that I'm really stupid and I have to go to a really special school?" Mom sighs and does her best to alleviate my fears, but they are still there. I know what's at stake.

The result of this test will determine my school placement for next year. It's the end of fourth grade, and my public school is discontinuing the resource room. They are throwing the kids with learning disabilities back into mainstream classes with minimal additional support. This greatly concerns my parents, so they have decided to take me to see a licensed school psychologist. I am terrified to take his test, especially considering my poor showing a few years back when my IQ was tested. I really want to go to Haverford Boys Prep—the prestigious local private school. Every time I pass by Haverford on my way to school, I look at the neatly uniformed kids with envy. There is no doubt in my mind; today is judgment day.

"Hi," I say shyly as I enter the testing room. "Hi Scott," the psychologist says with a smile. "No pressure today. We're just going to do some puzzles." This makes me feel even more nervous. He puts some blocks on the table and asks me to put them together in a way that matches a picture. I try my best to concentrate but can feel myself beginning to sweat. I've never been good at spatial tasks. I often get lost on the way to the bus stop at the bottom of our street. And my Mom drives me to the bus stop!

I mix the blocks around, trying different combinations, but feel like I'm getting nowhere. "You had it," the psychologist says reassuringly. "Believe in yourself!" He writes something down on his notepad. I continue to sweat.

Question after question, I second-guess myself. With each new test, I see multiple possible answers, and repeatedly ask myself: *Why do I have to pick one of the answers provided? What if I can justify why more than one answer is correct? Would they mind if I modified this question a bit?*

The test ends and I leave the room feeling discouraged. "So he found out I am really dumb after all?" I ask my parents later that week over dinner. "No," says my Dad sighing deeply. "But he did note your test anxiety. In fact, he also noted that you were one of the most creative test takers he's ever seen but said it's a shame there's no way to score creativity on the test."

My worst fear comes to pass. Instead of being sent to the prestigious Haverford Academy, as I dreamed, I am pulled out of my current public school and shipped off to a school for children with learning disabilities—my fate sealed by a single test.

~

The inventor of the modern IQ test—Alfred Binet—was a loner. An indifferent student, Binet declared after a brief stint in law, "That is the career of men who have not yet chosen a vocation."[1] He later spent a short stint volunteering in Jean-Martin Charcot's neurological laboratory at Salpêtrière Hospital in Paris, and at age 37 received his doctorate in the natural sciences with a dissertation on "the sub-intestinal nervous system of insects." But none of this is what really consumed him.

Starting around the age of 22, Binet spent most of his days in the French National Library burning through books on human behavior from the major thinkers of the time. Soon he was publishing on psychology. His first published article, at age 23, and his first book, just six years later, took a broad approach to understanding various mental processes, including attention and perception.

Though he was denied all three professor positions for which he applied, he eventually landed a post as director of the Laboratory of Physiological Psychology at the Sorbonne (a position he would keep until his death). Don't be fooled by the fancy-sounding title: this was an unpaid position, divorced from mainstream academia in France. The only thing economically sustaining his psychological research was his family wealth.

This makes Binet's tremendous output—both in quality and quantity—all the more remarkable. From 1890 to his death, Binet published over 200 books, articles, and reviews, spanning virtually all of psychology. Binet's research was strikingly original for its time. He lived in an era where everyone seemed to be obsessed with abnormal behavior. Instead, Binet probed the depths of the human psyche in all its varied forms. Fascinated by individual differences, he investigated every corner of the human mind, including consciousness, will, attention, sensation, perception, aesthetics, creativity, suggestibility, hypnotism, cognitive styles, love and erotic fetishes,* pain thresholds, mental fatigue, language development, memory development, and conceptual development.

Not content with just studying clinical populations, he sought out an incredibly diverse range of populations, including children, adults, those with mental disabilities and other clinical disorders, chess experts, human mental calculators, and professional actors, directors, authors, and artists. As developmental psychologist Robert Siegler, notes, "It is ironic that Binet's contribution should be so strongly associated with reducing intelligence to a single number, the IQ score, when the recurring theme of his research was the remarkable diversity of intelligence."[2]

Binet was light-years ahead of his time. His work on prose memory, eye-witness testimony, group pressure toward conformity, intrinsic motivation, and expertise in chess and mental calculation all foreshadowed modern-day research on these topics. Even his work on cognitive development preceded Piaget's groundbreaking research.[†] As Robert Cairns notes, "It has taken experimental child psychology 70 years to catch up with some of Binet's insights on cognition and the organization of memory."[3]

Most remarkably, Binet was entirely *self-taught*. As Binet wrote in a letter to a friend in 1901, "I educated myself all alone, without any teachers; I have arrived at my present scientific situation by the sole force of my fists; no one, you understand, no one, has ever helped me."[‡,4]

This was due, in part, to his personality. Interviews with Binet's family, friends, and colleagues paint a picture of a shy, reclusive man with very high energy devoted to his work. This description of Binet, written after his death by his daughter Madeleine, seems to capture much of his character: "My father was above all a lively man, smiling, often very ironical, gentle in manner, wise in his judgments, a little skeptical of course. . . . Without affectation,

---

*Binet coined the terms "erotic fetish" and "sexual fetish."

†Curiously, Piaget rarely acknowledged Binet's work. It's hard to imagine how Piaget could have been unfamiliar with Binet's thinking and findings. I won't dare speculate on Piaget's motives for his glaring omissions of Binet's pathbreaking work.

‡In her biography Theta Wolf suggests that Binet may have overstated his case, as some scholars, such as Theodule Ribot, did lend him some patronage.

straightforward, very good-natured, he was scornful of mediocrity in all its forms. Amiable and cordial to people of science, pitiless toward bothersome people who wasted his time and interrupted his work. . . . He always seemed to be deep in thought."[5]

A great tragedy is that much of Binet's brilliant research was ignored in his time. This was no doubt due in large part to a combination of his personality and his estrangement from mainstream academia. He never left France, he did not present his work at academic conferences, and because he didn't have an official post, he didn't have a large number of students to carry on his legacy. As Siegler notes, "Binet's product was strong, but his marketing was weak."[6]

～

The year 1894 was monumental for Binet. He received his doctorate in the natural sciences, founded the journal *L'Année Psychologique* (which is still in existence today), published a book on the psychology of human calendar calculators, and with his collaborator Victor Henri and other scientists in the laboratory at the Sorbonne, published a book and many articles on suggestibility, memory, character, and educational psychology.

But it was Binet's collaboration with Henri from 1894 to 1898 that was particularly important for the development of the first IQ test. Together, Binet and Henri sought out new methods that would allow for the "precise observations of individuals considered in all the complexity and variety of their aptitudes."[7] In 1895 they announced their intention to develop an intelligence test, outlining an ambitious project consisting of the measurement of ten separate abilities: memory, imagery, imagination, attention, comprehension, suggestibility, aesthetic sentiment, moral sentiment, muscular strength/willpower, and motor ability/hand-eye coordination.

Even though lower-level sensory processes were included in their outline, they made it quite clear that—in opposition to the work of Galton, James McKeen Cattell, and other intelligence researchers of their day—more complex reasoning measures provided a better test of intelligence. Foreshadowing later findings (see Chapter 10), they argued that "if one wishes to study the differences existing between two individuals, it is necessary to begin with the most intellectual and complex processes, and it is only secondarily necessary to consider the simple and elementary processes."[8]

As a first pass, Binet began observing and even testing his two young daughters, Madeleine and Alice, on a variety of cognitive and personality tests. Many of the psychological tests he gave his daughters are still in use today, including the ability to generate words, make associations between words, complete sentences, describe objects and pictures, and recall a variety of information, including pictures and foreign-language sentences that were unknown to his children.

Interestingly, Binet's initial analyses of his children were *qualitative*. Binet believed in the importance of qualitative analysis, looking closely at errors, cognitive styles, and patterns of strengths. Binet scored the thought processes of his children along the dimensions of linearity, conventionality, and originality. In his earliest published papers on the fruits of his observations, he went into great detail on the many differences between his children, noting that Madeleine displayed more "stability," being able to voluntarily focus her attention at will. He also noted she was more practical and had a poor imagination. In contrast, Alice showed greater "variability," having difficulty learning material that didn't interest her, but displayed a much richer imagination.[9] A particular distinction that seemed to preoccupy Binet was that between reflection and impulsivity. His culminating observations were presented in his 1903 book *The Experimental Study of Intelligence*, when his children were already in adolescence.[10]

After presenting his findings, he noted in a footnote that it was time to move on. He noticed substantial changes in the character of his daughters, and he remarked that the latest descriptions of them were less applicable than they were just a few years earlier. Binet believed in recognizing mental development progression from childhood through adulthood: "In case one should succeed in measuring intelligence—that is to say, reasoning, judgment, memory, the ability to make abstraction—which appears not absolutely impossible to me, the figure that would represent the average intellectual development of an adult would present an entirely different relation to that of the figure representing the intellectual development of a child."[11]

As fate would have it, around 1892 Binet was contacted by Theodore Simon—a young intern physician with access to a clinical population. Simon sought Binet's advice about how the "abnormal" people in his psychiatric internship should be educated. Even without a formal academic position, Binet agreed to supervise Simon's doctoral dissertation, leading to one of the most important collaborations in the history of psychology.

~

As the nineteenth century came to an end, business and civic leaders across a number of Western European and North American countries united to promote compulsory universal public education. But this posed a serious problem: How should a diverse population of children be educated? Advocacy groups, teacher organizations, and educational psychologists lobbied for special schools to meet the needs of children with mental disabilities.

The opportunity of a lifetime came in October 1904, when Joseph Chaumie, the minister of public instruction, established a commission to create a way to identify students in need of alternative education. Binet, an active member of the French group, saw an opportunity to complete his tests and put them to practical use. Binet and Simon immediately went to work. The closest they came to a working definition of intelligence is the following: "It seems to us that in intelligence there is a fundamental faculty, the alteration or the lack of which, is of the utmost importance for practical life. This faculty is judgment, otherwise called good sense, practical sense, initiative, the faculty of adapting one's self to circumstances. To judge well, to comprehend well, to reason well, these are the essential activities of intelligence."[12]

Binet argued that there were three distinct aspects of judgment: direction, adaptation, and criticism. Direction involved the ability to concentrate on the task and figure out what needs to be done to solve a problem. Adaptation involved selecting appropriate strategies and monitoring the usefulness of the strategy. Finally, criticism referred to the ability to criticize one's own thoughts and behaviors, and to make changes based on this criticism that increase task performance.

Binet and Simon's assessments were described as having "the air of a game" for children, and they stressed the need to encourage the test taker. Using the many items Binet had developed over the prior years, the first edition of their test was finished in record time—just one year later—culminating in the publication of the Binet-Simon Intelligence Scale.[13] True to their conceptualization of intelligence, the original items measured everyday practical skills, including the ability to name various parts of the human body, to name objects seen in a picture, to give definitions, to repeat a series of digits or a complete sentence, to copy a diamond, to say the difference between paper and cardboard, or a fly and a butterfly, and to find as many rhymes as possible in a minute.

Binet and Simon made clear the purpose of their test:

> Our purpose is to be able to measure the intellectual capacity of a child
> who is brought to us in order to know whether he is normal or retarded.
> We should, therefore, study his condition at the time and that only. We
> have nothing to do either with his past history or with his future; conse-
> quently we shall neglect his etiology, and we shall make no attempt to
> distinguish between acquired and congenital idiocy . . . we do not attempt
> to establish or prepare a prognosis and we leave unanswered the question
> of whether this retardation is curable, or even improbable. We shall limit
> ourselves to ascertaining the truth about his present mental state.[14]

Their twenty-minute test consisted of 30 items presented in order of
increasing difficulty. Each task was thought to be representative of a typical
child's ability at various ages. They initially gave their test to 50 children aged
3 to 11. Individuals considered "idiots" generally could not move beyond the
sixth of the 30 tasks, while "imbeciles" rarely went beyond the fifteenth task.[15]
In their first edition, they came up with a five-part classification scheme:
blind, deaf, medically abnormal, intellectually backward, and emotionally
unstable.

Along with their test, they also published a number of caveats. First, they
made clear that their test does not measure a person's absolute level of intelligence. They warned that their test couldn't possibly offer precise measurement like inches as measured by a ruler. Instead, a score on their test was
simply a classification entirely relative to that of other children of the same
age. Binet was undoubtedly influenced during his library reading days by
the nineteenth-century English philosopher John Stuart Mill, who wrote that
"the science of human nature . . . falls far short of the standard of exactness
now realized in Astronomy."[16]

Binet and Simon also acknowledged that many factors other than intellectual ability could influence performance on their tests, such as the un-
naturalness of the testing situation and the potential for the test to intimidate
children.[17] They also mentioned longer-term influences, such as background,
upbringing, health, and effort. Due to these other potential influences, they
stressed the need to compare any person's test results only with those of
comparable backgrounds.[18] Finally, they noted the importance of constant
retesting, pointing out that individuals' intellectual development progresses

at variable rates, due to different rates of maturation as well as differences in intellectual experiences.

Binet and Simon soon revised their test, in 1908 and again in 1911. Their revised scale had 56 tests presented in order of level of difficulty based on the percentage of children at each age who passed their test (they tested about 200 children between the ages of 3 and 15). Most importantly, they introduced the notion of *mental age*. For example, if a child passed the 10-year-old level tasks but failed the ones at the 11-year-old level, then that child was thought to have the intelligence of a typical 10-year-old, regardless of that person's actual age. By the 1911 edition, the scale was extended from age 3 through adulthood, with eleven levels and five items at each level.[19]

It's noteworthy that the Binet-Simon scale never yielded an intelligence quotient (IQ). In fact, long after Binet's death, Simon indicated that the use of a summary IQ score was a betrayal of the purpose of their test.[20] While Binet and Simon's purpose was noble, let's be absolutely clear: most people in France just wanted to weed out the intellectually disabled so that the "normal" students would not be slowed down.[21] There were no actual provisions in place to educate those with "alternative" educational needs. Their primary focus was identification, not remediation. This concerned Binet and Simon: "To be a member of a special class can never be a mark of distinction, and such as do not merit it, must be spared the record."[22]

Alas, Binet's efforts, caveats, and cautions were almost completely ignored by the French establishment. Once again Binet found himself on the periphery. The French legislature on April 15, 1909, stated that decisions about eligibility for special education should be made by a group consisting of a physician, a school inspector, and a director or teacher. The legislature made absolutely no mention of any role for psychologists or intelligence tests for assessing students.[23] Binet and Simon's intense efforts were wasted in their native France. Binet personally felt as though he was a failure.

Soon his test would spread like wildfire across the globe—particularly in America—and to his horror, his test was used for purposes he never intended. Toward the very end of his life, in response to statements that children with lower test scores would *never* achieve certain things, he wrote in exasperation: "'Never!' What a strong word! A few modern philosophers seem to lend their moral support to these deplorable verdicts when they assert that an individual's intelligence is a fixed quantity, a quantity which cannot be increased. We must protest and react against this brutal pessimism. We shall attempt to prove that it is without foundation. . . . With practice, training, and above all method, we manage to increase our attention, our memory, our judgment and literally to become more intelligent than we were before."[24]

Binet even developed various "mental orthopedics"—intellectual exercises— to show the potential for remediation. But it was too late. On October 28, 1911, Binet suffered a stroke and passed away at the young age of 54. The mass testing movement in America had just begun, with the testing proponents carrying with them a completely different conceptualization of human intelligence.

~

Henry Goddard, director of the Vineland Training School in New Jersey, came across Binet and Simon's scales twice—first during a visit to Brussels in the spring of 1908 and then again a year later. Both times he shrugged them off, without recognizing the relevance for the "feebleminded" individuals with whom he worked.* As Goddard would later note, "Probably no critic of the scale had reacted against it more positively than I did at that first reading. It seemed impossible to grade intelligence in that way. It was too easy, too simple."[25] But the seed was already planted.

Goddard gave the test a try and was immediately impressed. "Our use of the scale was a surprise and a gratification. It met our needs. A classification of our children based on the Scale agreed with the Institution experience," he noted. It apparently didn't take him much convincing! Goddard immediately translated Binet and Simon's 1908 test into English and became the test's chief evangelist in the United States. At academic conferences he presented his results showing that the tests reliably classified various degrees of "feeble-mindedness," and in his 1914 book *Feeble-Mindedness: Its Causes and Consequences*, he adopted Galton's flawed methodology to show that feeblemindedness ran in families and was by consequence hereditary.

No matter that Goddard couldn't actually go back in time and administer Binet's test to the ancestors of the children at the Vineland Training School. Goddard was on a clear mission, informed by his own personal definition of intelligence as "a unitary mental process . . . conditioned by a nervous mechanism which is inborn . . . that is but little affected by any later influences except such serious accident as may destroy part of the mechanism."

---

*Historical note: The term "feeblemindedness" was eventually replaced by a series of other terms: "mental deficiency," then "mental retardation," then "intellectual disability."

Goddard must have been quite convincing, because he persuaded the superintendent of a local school district in New Jersey to let him test ordinary schoolchildren. Goddard published his findings in a 1911 paper titled "Two Thousand Normal Children Measured by the Binet Measuring Scale of Intelligence." Even educators were enthusiastic. In 1914 a few dozen school districts were administering Binet and Simon's tests. By 1916, 22,000 copies of Binet and Simon's 1908 published paper (which Goddard translated) had been distributed, along with 88,000 test blanks.[26]

But Goddard didn't stop there. In 1892 Ellis Island in New York Harbor opened its doors to immigrants eager and excited to settle and work in the great "land of opportunity"—the United States. Immigration reached its peak in 1907, with more than a million hopeful immigrants arriving on Ellis Island. To prove their "worth" as citizens, they had to demonstrate mental and physical fitness. Goddard came over to Ellis Island in 1917 with a revised version of the Binet-Simon scale. As a result, the number of immigrants who were deported increased greatly.

Let's put all this IQ testing in historical context for a moment. Long before Goddard ever set his sights on Binet's test, there had already been enormous public pressure to come up with eugenic methods, not just for the feebleminded but for a wide range of "undesirables," including the mentally insane, epileptics, habitual drunkards, criminals, prostitutes, tramps, and paupers. By the time Goddard brought Binet's tests to the attention of teachers working with the feebleminded, six states already had sterilization laws on their books and many others states had laws that forbade marriage between undesirables.[27]

So the IQ testing movement can't be blamed as the sole cause of sterilization in the United States. Nonetheless, Goddard wasn't entirely innocent either. He did bring wider public attention to the "problem" of the feebleminded, and IQ tests were certainly used to justify sterilization. By 1964, about 60,000 human beings up to that point were subjected to compulsory sterilization in the United States, with many more in Germany. Mental disability was the justification for almost half of these victims, and IQ tests certainly informed the diagnoses.

∾

Goddard wasn't the only American exalted by Binet's scales. Lewis Terman, a professor of psychology at Stanford University, was equally smitten. Unlike Goddard, Terman never hesitated. He immediately saw many uses for Binet's test. Like Goddard, he believed that the tests should be used to identify the "feebleminded" so that they could be put "under the surveillance and protection of society." Terman believed this would "ultimately result in curtailing the reproduction of feeble-mindedness, and in the elimination of an enormous amount of crime, pauperism, and industrial inefficiency."[28] Terman advocated institutionalization, but others argued sterilization was a better method.

But Terman saw another use. He was interested in the *upper ends* of the distribution. As he noted, "The fact is that previous to the publication of Binet's 1908 scale the significance of age differences in intelligence was very little understood. Psychologists were not aware of the extraordinary and detailed similarity that may exist between a dull child of twelve years and a normal average child of eight. No one recognized the significance, for future mental development, of a given degree of retardation or accelera-tion. . . . The value of the Binet method in the identification of the intellec-tually gifted became immediately evident to the writer when . . . he made trial of the 1908 scale. It was obvious that children who showed marked ac-celeration in mental age were, by any reasonable criterion, brighter than children who tested at or below their chronological age."[29]

Eager to start putting Binet's scales to use, Terman revised the 1911 Binet-Simon scale, producing the Stanford-Binet test in 1916.[30] In essence Terman developed an entirely new test. He added 40 new items, allowing for 6 items for each age, spanning ages 3 through 14 (the Binet-Simon scale had 5 items for each age). The test for 9-year-olds had the following kinds of items:

1. Dates: What day of the week is it today? What year?
2. Arrange five weights from heaviest to lightest.
3. Mental arithmetic.
4. Backward digit span of four.
5. Generate a sentence containing three particular words.
6. Find rhymes.

While Binet and Simon originally gave their test to approximately 50 children rated by their teachers as having "normal intelligence," Terman tested about 1,000 children aged 4 to 14. He took children from each age group from schools comprising students of average social status. This larger standardization sam-ple allowed him to obtain much more accurate information than Binet on the difficulty level of the different items. Based on this information, he found it necessary to rearrange the majority of Binet's items into different age levels.

Another major advance was Terman's scoring procedure. He maintained Binet's notion of mental age but borrowed German psychologist William Stern's idea of the intelligence quotient—mental age divided by chronological age.[31] This formula was useful because it distinguished between people who all have the same mental age but differ in their actual age. Terman didn't like decimals, so he decided to multiply Stern's formula by 100. Therefore, the formula for IQ became:

$$IQ = MA/CA \times 100$$

To see how this works, let's look at three people with the same "mental age." As you can see in the following table, three different people can all score the same on the test (that is, have the same "mental age"), but their IQ score will depend on their chronological (actual) age. This was surely an advance from Binet's scales, but its weaknesses immediately became apparent. What does an IQ score mean for adults? Let's say your actual age is 60 but you've got the mental age of a 50-year-old. Your IQ would be 83. But let's say your actual age is 50 and your mental age is 60. Your IQ would be a whopping 120! Can we really assume that the difference between a mental age of 20 and 10 is the same as that between 60 and 50? I hope you see the problem.

Mental Age (MA)	Chronological Age (CA)	Quotient (MA/CA)	IQ ($\times$ 100)
10	5	2	200
10	10	1	100
10	15	.67	67

Terman's workaround was to put a chronological age of 16 in the denominator when testing adults. In his revision, he changed this number to 15, finding that the average IQ score stopped increasing around that age.[32] Of course, this was all just guesswork, because he never actually tested anyone older than 18. His defense was simply: "A mental age of fifteen years represents the norm for all subjects who are sixteen years of age or older" (31). Modern-day aging research has not confirmed this, but to be fair, Terman was in the dark on this research.

Terman recognized another pesky "problem" with IQ—variability. Not every age group showed the same amount of intellectual growth. The average

IQ fluctuation was 16 points—but ranged from 12 to 20 points depending on the age group. At first Terman just chalked up these fluctuations to chance, but it was hard to ignore variability as large as 20, which is what he found for the 12-year-old age group. Eventually, he attributed this to the "onset of pubescence," although he acknowledged it hadn't been demonstrated that pubescence is related to the rate of cognitive development.

It became inevitable: Terman had to get rid of IQ. Standard scores—which indicated how far a test score deviated from the average—were much more appropriate, because they took into account age-to-age fluctuations. But dropping IQ wasn't so easy. IQ had already become entrenched in the American public education system's psyche, and standard scores were messier and not as easy for school psychologists to interpret. So in their 1937 revision, Terman and Merrill kept IQ scores, but included a conversion table that allowed school psychologists to convert IQ scores to standard scores.

What about classification? Terman had to come up with labels for different bands of IQ scores so school psychologists could interpret the scores. With the first edition of the Stanford-Binet, Terman introduced the world's first-ever classification system for IQ.

IQ	Classification
Above 140	Near genius or genius
120–140	Very superior intelligence
110–120	Superior intelligence
90–110	Normal, or average, intelligence
80–90	Dullness, rarely classifiable as feeble-mindedness
70–80	Border-line deficiency, sometimes classifiable as dullness, often as feeble-mindedness
Below 70	Definite feeble-mindedness

He didn't stop there:

> Of the feeble-minded, those between 50 and 70 IQ include most of the morons (high, middle, low), those between 20 and 25 and 50 are ordinarily to be classified as imbeciles, and those below 20 or 25 as idiots.[33]

Terman's true biases can be found if you read further on the same page. He didn't see much use for distinguishing between different levels of "feeble-mindedness," claiming that "in the literal sense every individual below the average is more or less mentally weak or feeble." Let's be clear: the first classification scheme for IQ was entirely based on one man's personal views of what his tests were measuring. Like Goddard, Terman fully believed that "feeble-mindedness," as assessed by his tests, was fixed, enduring, and hereditary.

One thing is for sure, Terman's *decisions* proved to be enduring. Not only did his test become the gold standard to which later IQ tests would be compared, his labels influenced a whole new generation of IQ classification schemes. Interestingly, Terman's impact surprised even Terman himself! As he noted about 15 years after the first edition of his test was published, "I knew that my revision of Binet's tests was superior to others then available, but I did not foresee the vogue it was to have and imagined that it would probably be displaced by something much better within a few years."[34]

Well, it wasn't.

The Stanford-Binet remained America's IQ test of choice for a half century. While everyone else in America seemed to be caught up in the IQ mass-testing craze, David Wechsler—chief psychologist at Bellevue Hospital in New York City—viewed intelligence a bit differently. Wechsler's practical sensibility was a return to the IQ test's founding principles. Like Binet, Wechsler viewed intelligence as a person's ability to understand and cope with his or her environment. Also like Binet, he saw IQ tests as clinical instruments that could reveal important information about a person's personality.

What Wechsler produced in 1939—the Wechsler-Bellevue Intelligence Scale—was an important achievement in the history of IQ testing.[35] Many of the decisions he made have affected IQ test construction ever since. Some of his advances were technical. He introduced the notion of deviation IQs and distinguished them from the older ratio IQs (MA/CA). This term didn't stick: the notion of IQ was so firmly ingrained in the public's psyche, everyone still referred to his deviation scores as IQ scores. Nonetheless, the notion of deviation IQ scores was an important advance.

In coming up with deviation IQs, Wechsler had to make some arbitrary decisions. First, he chose 100 as the average person's IQ. He picked this number because the number 100 had become quite common in the old formula. He also had to pick a standard deviation. So he picked 15, because it was an easily divisible number close to 16—the number Terman and Merrill had used.[36] These were arbitrary decisions, but they were fairly sensible because they allowed a range of scores that the public had become quite familiar with since Terman first published his test.[37] Deviation IQ scores allowed the

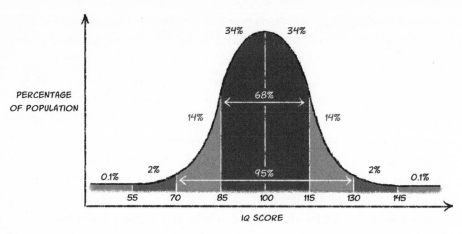

FIGURE 2.1. IQ SCORE DISTRIBUTION

examiner to place scores on a bell curve. (See Figure 2.1.) If the average IQ score is 100, and a person's IQ is 115, that means that person is 1 standard deviation above the average score. Conversely, an IQ of 85 is 1 standard deviation below the average score. About 68 percent of the human population will score between 85 and 115, and 95 percent will score between 70 and 130. This leaves 5 percent at the extreme ends of the curve—2.5 percent at the lower tail and 2.5 percent at the upper tail.

For those who prefer dealing with numbers rather than graphs, the following table is a list of percentile ranks corresponding to various standard scores ("IQs"). IQ scores (in the sense of CA divided by MA) haven't been in use since the 1930s, yet the term is still very much a part of the public's consciousness. Today a person's IQ score is strictly a percentile rank: it tells you how many people of the same age scored lower than you on the same test you took at that one slice in time. For example, if you score 110 on the Wechsler test, this means that you scored better than 75 percent of representative individuals in your age group who were given the exact same test.

IQ	Percentile Rank	IQ	Percentile Rank
160	99.997	125	95
155	99.99	120	91
150	99.91	115	84
145	99.87	110	75
140	99.62	105	63
135	99	100	50
130	98	95	37

IQ	Percentile Rank	IQ	Percentile Rank
90	25	60	0.38
85	16	55	0.13
80	9	50	0.04
75	5	45	0.01
70	2	40	0.003
65	1		

Technically, that's all an IQ score means. As Binet first noted all the way back in 1898, your mental test score is not an absolute measure of your intelligence; it's only a relative score. There is no absolute zero for IQ, like there is for height or weight. You can't brag that just because your IQ of 160 is twice your friend's IQ score of 80 that you are twice as intelligent. It's also not clear that the 20-point difference between two IQ scores (such as 140 versus 160) has the same psychological meaning as the 20-point difference between two other IQ scores (say, 90 versus 110).

But Wechsler's most important innovation was not the content of the tests—he took many of his items right from earlier tests. Nor was it replacing the MA/CA formula with deviation scores—although this was certainly important. No, the major advance of his test was its purpose: that it should be used as a *clinical instrument*. He grouped items together into a Verbal Scale and a Performance Scale, so practitioners in an individually administered setting could observe the *quality* of the student's pattern of responses.

The test publishers were skeptical. Why take so much time to measure a person's intelligence? This was antithetical to America's obsession with a fast, cheap, and efficient way to categorize the totality of a person. So Wechsler published the test himself. He took the initiative and tested 2,000 children, adolescents, and adults in Coney Island, Brooklyn, and New York City. Importantly, he realized the importance of finding a representative sample. For instance, if you want to know how well Americans aged 7 to 70 do on an IQ test, then test people at each age who are representative of the U.S. population at large on a number of demographics, including sex, age, social class, region of country, and so on.* After carefully norming his test on other important demographics, The Psychological Corporation suddenly became interested in publishing it.

Wechsler's tests weren't an instant hit, due to long-standing loyalty to the Stanford-Binet. But in the 1960s, the balance began to tilt toward Wechsler's

---

*Of course, since Wechsler's initial studies were conducted in New York, he did not have a representative sample by region.

scale. People saw the need to go beyond a single IQ score. Educators saw the benefit of being able to assess a child's pattern of scores. Wechsler's original test included ten subtests and included a separate Verbal IQ and Performance IQ. Until its fourth revision,[38] the Stanford-Binet only offered a single IQ, and was verbally oriented.

One of Wechsler's collaborators on the revision, Alan Kaufman (no relation), expanded on Wechsler's emphasis on IQ tests as clinical instruments. In 1979 he introduced the notion of *intelligent testing*. This approach elevated the clinician above the test and enabled the test administrator to treat each child as an individual: "The focus is on the child, with . . . communication of the test results in the context of the child's particular background, behaviors, and approach to the test items as the main goals. Global scores are deemphasized, flexibility and insight on the part of the examiner are demanded, and the test is perceived as a dynamic helping agent rather than an instrument for placement, labeling, or other types of academic oppression. In short, intelligent testing is the key."[39]

Many modern IQ tests have the intelligent testing approach built into the test. The fourth edition of the Wechsler Intelligence Scale for Children (WISC-IV) and the Wechsler Adult Intelligence Scale (WAIS-IV) include "process scores" (based on Edith Kaplan's Boston process approach), which allow the clinician to gain insight into the processes that may lead a child to get a problem wrong. The latest edition of the WISC also includes a companion that allows the clinician to qualitatively better understand why the child is responding in a particular way to the test items. Other modern IQ tests, such as the Kaufman Assessment Battery for Children, Second Edition, also include qualitative indicators (QIs) built in, which guide the examiner's observations of the child during the testing session. As Alan Kaufman notes in *IQ Testing 101*, "The important lessons here are that IQ tests are built based on clinical observations, they offer far more to the skilled examiner than a bunch of test scores, and a psychologist's experience with a test is an invaluable commodity that cannot be overlooked."[40]

The Stanford-Binet is now in its fifth edition and is a much more sophisticated test, but Wechsler's test, now in its fourth edition, remains the test of choice for most practitioners in the United States.[41]

～

For most of the twentieth century, there was a stark divide between intelligence theory and practice. Scientists, with very little interest in the practical utility of cognitive tests, were off on one end of the planet debating the existence of a general factor of intelligence (see Chapter 10), and IQ test constructors were in another corner doing minor refinements to test items created in the 1920s and 1930s. There was very little cross talk, almost to the point that it seemed like they were all living on separate planets!

In the 1960s, the field of neuropsychology was also getting off the ground. A particularly influential team of neuropsychologists was Nobel Prize laureate Roger Sperry and his graduate student Michael Gazzaniga, who conducted research on epileptics in whom the corpus callosum—a bundle of fibers connecting the two hemispheres of the brain—had been severed. These "split-brain" patients who had undergone surgery did show fewer symptoms of epilepsy. But unexpectedly they also appeared to have two completely separate minds.

Around the same time the split-brain research was in full swing, Alan Kaufman came across neuropsychological research and was curious why IQ test makers weren't incorporating the latest findings into the creation of their tests. As fate would have it, he and his wife, Nadeen, soon received a call from Dr. Gary Robertson, director of test development at American Guidance Service (AGS).*,42 Robertson asked if they would be interested in developing a new test of intelligence. They eagerly accepted the invitation.

Their test was a radical departure from other IQ tests at the time. A major advance was the use of "teaching items" where the examiner goes over a few sample items and explains the reasoning behind the answers to make sure the test taker understands the test. Also, examiners were required to communicate with the child in a variety of ways, if necessary, using different words, gestures, language, even American Sign Language. These advances allowed for individualized test instruction and increased communication between the test examiner and the test taker. This increased the chances that they were measuring something significant, and not just an inability to understand directions.

Although it soon became clear that their test was primarily measuring short-term memory and visual processing, their test was important in that it was the first theory-based individually administered clinical IQ test.†,43 By the late 1980s, a number of other neuropsychological and cognitive tests had proliferated, tapping into a range of cognitive functions. It was time for all the different tests to speak the same language.

---

*Now called Pearson Assessments.
†In 2004, Alan and Nadeen revised their Kaufman Assessment Battery for Children (KABC-II) to include additional tests of planning and learning.

At a historic 1986 meeting in Dallas, a number of influential theorists, IQ test constructors, and one test publisher made an important realization: the different cognitive abilities measured by contemporary IQ tests could be mapped onto the language the theorists had been using for the entire century. Kevin McGrew recounts that "a collective 'Ah Ha!' engulfed the room" and the meeting "was the flash point that resulted in *all* subsequent theory-to-practice bridging events."

The deal was sealed in 1999. At a meeting in Chapel Hill, North Carolina, organized by Riverside, an important IQ test publisher, a number of influential people got together to discuss ways of bridging the gap between theory and practice. In attendance were the authors of the third edition of the Woodcock-Johnson IQ test as well as the authors of the latest edition of the Stanford-Binet. Also in attendance were the influential intelligence theorists John Horn and John Carroll (see Chapter 10) and members of the Riverside publishing staff.

According to McGrew, the goal was "to seek a common, more meaning-ful, umbrella term that would recognize the strong structural similarities of their respective theoretical models, yet also recognize their difference."[44] Shortly after the meeting, through the coordination of Richard Woodcock, author of the Woodcock-Johnson Test, the two intelligence theorists at the meeting (John Horn and John Carroll) agreed to merge their theories into a single coherent framework. The Cattell-Horn-Carroll (CHC) theory of cognitive abilities—the single most influential framework of cognitive abilities in existence today—was born.[45]

Finally practitioners had a common language they could use, regardless of which specific IQ test they used. School psychologists could also pick and choose which tests they wanted to administer to assess a student's areas of cognitive strengths and weaknesses. They could then use that information to develop a specific plan of action to help the student compensate for areas of difficulty. This technique—called the *cross-battery approach*—was initially proposed by Woodcock, then Dawn Flanagan and McGrew developed the principles and methods, and more recently Flanagan and her colleagues have extended the approach even further.[46]

The CHC framework consists of a hierarchy of cognitive abilities. At the bottom of the hierarchy are seventy or more "narrow" abilities that make up nine "broad" abilities at the next level up in the hierarchy. At the very top of the hierarchy lies a single "general" cognitive ability (see Chapter 10), although that level of analysis is deemphasized in the CHC framework because it has the least practical utility for devising interventions. Figure 2.2 shows the nine broad cognitive abilities that are part of the CHC framework (see the Appendix for the full framework). The CHC framework is the most comprehensive taxonomy of cognitive abilities to date, influencing the construction of all contemporary IQ tests, including the latest edition of the Stanford-Binet, the second edition of the Kaufman Assessment Battery for Children, the third edition of the Woodcock-Johnson test of cognitive abilities, and the second edition of the Differential Ability Scales.[47] Even though other tests in use today weren't explicitly constructed based on CHC

FIGURE 2.2. CATTELL-HORN-CARROLL (CHC) THEORY OF COGNITIVE ABILITIES DEFINITIONS

Source: W. J. Schneider and K. McGrew, "The Cattell-Horn-Carroll Model of Intelligence," in *Contemporary Intellectual Assessment: Theories, Tests, and Issues*, ed. D. Flanagan and P. Harrison, 3rd ed., 99–144 (New York: Guilford, 2012). Adapted with permission.

theory, new statistical techniques have been used to map modern tests to CHC terminology, so everyone can speak the same language.

The following table is a list of some of today's most widely administered IQ tests, and what cognitive abilities they measure, using CHC terminology.[48]

Cognitive Ability Test	Publication Date	Age Range (Years)	Global IQ Label	Subtests with CHC Mapping
Cognitive Assessment System (CAS)	1997	5–17	Full Scale (FS)	*Gf*/Simultaneous *Gs*/Planning & Attention *Gsm*/Successive
Differential Ability Scales-II (DAS-II)	2007	2–17	General Conceptual Ability (GCA)	*Gf*/Nonverbal Ability *Gv*/Spatial Ability *Gc*/Verbal Ability *Gsm*/Working Memory *Gs*/Processing Speed
Kaufman Assessment Battery for Children, Second Edition (KABC-II)	2004	3–18	Mental Processing Index (MPI) Fluid-Crystallized Index (FCI)	*Gf*/Planning *Gc*/Knowledge *Gv*/Simultaneous *Glr*/Learning *Gsm*/Sequential
Stanford-Binet Intelligence Scales, Fifth Edition (SB5)	2003	2–85+	Full Scale IQ (FS IQ)	*Rq*/Quantitative Reasoning *Gc*/Knowledge *Gv*/Visual-Spatial Processing *Gf*/Fluid Reasoning *Gsm*/Working Memory
Wechsler Adult Intelligence Scale—Fourth Edition (WAIS-IV)	2008	16–90+	Full Scale IQ (FS IQ)	*Gsm*/Working Memory Index *Gf & Gv*/Perceptual Reasoning Index *Gc*/Verbal Comprehension Index *Gs*/Processing Speed Index

Cognitive Ability Test	Publication Date	Age Range (Years)	Global IQ Label	Subtests with CHC Mapping
Wechsler Intelligence Scale for Children—Fourth Edition (WISC-IV)	2004	6–16	Full Scale IQ (FS IQ)	*Gf & Gv*/Perceptual Reasoning Index *Gc*/Verbal Comprehension Index *Gsm*/Working Memory Index *Gs*/Processing Speed Index
Woodcock-Johnson III Normative Update (WJ III/NU)	2001, 2007	2–90+	General Intellectual Ability (GIA)	*Gf*/Fluid Reasoning *Gc*/Comprehension-Knowledge *Glr*/Long-term Storage & Retrieval *Ga*/Auditory Processing *Gsm*/Short-term Memory *Gv*/Visual Processing *Gs*/Processing Speed

Research on the practical utility of the CHC model is sparse, and the majority of the school or academic related CHC research has been conducted using the Woodcock-Johnson batteries. Nevertheless, a recent review by Kevin McGrew and Barbara Wendling on over twenty years of research conducted on the CHC framework suggests some important conclusions:[49]

- Most of the "action" is at the level of narrow abilities. It's these very specific skills—not global IQ scores—that have particular importance for understanding and developing interventions for reading and math.
- Professionals should adopt an intelligent testing approach and break the habit of "one complete battery fits all" testing: "The intelligent design of assessments does not come from a higher power—it comes from integrating the research synthesis presented here with professional and clinical experience."
- Different abilities contribute to achievement at different times during the course of development: "Before conducting assessments for

reading and math problems, practitioners need to ask the following questions when designing their initial assessment: What is (are) the subdomain(s) of concern? What is the age of the student? What CHC abilities does research suggest are most related to this (these) domain(s) at this age level?"

- There is a future to IQ testing. "Times and tests have changed during the past 20 years. . . . Contemporary intelligence tests should be viewed as valuable toolboxes, with each tool carefully selected by [an] intelligent craftsman to match the presenting problem. . . . We do not believe the current review is the end of the journey, but rather an important step toward a more complete understanding of the relationships between cognitive abilities and school achievement."

But have times really changed? Depending on whom you ask in the field, IQ tests are either really innovative or just the same old tests from the turn of the twentieth century repackaged. Undoubtedly we have come a long way in our society since the heyday of IQ test misuse and abuse. IQ tests aren't used for just any old purpose.

But is there *really* a futue for IQ tests? Can IQ tests—particularly the measurement of different CHC cognitive abilities in children—really predict student achievement and guide decisions about student placement? In this chapter I have tried to accurately represent the history of IQ testing and the development of IQ tests. I have immense respect for many modern-day IQ test theorists and constructors, and I believe they have the best of intentions. I also count many of them as my friends!

But that doesn't mean I blindly accept the relevance of their tests. In the next few chapters, let's scrutinize the use of IQ testing for sorting people into categories and assigning them different labels. First we'll look at the label "learning disabled" and then we'll look at the label "gifted." Scrutiny is essential, as hundreds of thousands, if not millions, of decisions are being made on a daily basis heavily informed by the results of these modern IQ tests. These decisions aren't trivial; they impact on people's chances of future success and the realization of their dreams.

Chapter 3

WHO IS LEARNING DISABLED?

1991

As I settle into my seat in the back of the classroom, I can't take my eyes off the perfect girl. She is the lead in every play, the soloist in every choir performance, and the winner of every writing award. Quite simply, she is the pride and joy of every teacher at the school. She also happens to be beautiful, and I am infatuated. I decide I'm going to talk to her after class. It's sixth grade and I'm back in the public school system. A fresh start. A new, improved—and I hope, suaver—me.

"Is Scott Kaufman here?" the teacher asks. My trance is interrupted. Without hesitation I raise my hand. "Can you come sit up front please?" she requests. Confused, I pick up my backpack and move down, inching closer and closer to the perfect girl, who is sitting in the front row. As I get closer, my heart starts beating faster. *Why am I being asked to move to the front? What if I have to sit next to her? What would I say? Walk smooth, Scott. Smooth.* I start to slow down. I put on a big, confident smile. Finally I reach my destination. The desk right next to hers.

She is writing in her notebook. Probably composing the next great sonata. I try to look cool. I nod my head a lot. I think that's a cool thing to do. The teacher seems impressed with my coolness, as she is smiling. She kneels down beside me and within earshot of the perfect girl, whispers, "Scott, your Mom requested that you sit at the front of the classroom since you have a serious learning disability. Thanks for changing seats."

The room starts to spin. *Did the perfect girl hear? She must have heard.* Humiliated, I sink down in my chair. I no longer feel cool. I feel trapped. It seems that no matter what I want to achieve, I am imprisoned by my label.

∽

As early as the nineteenth century in Europe, case reports of children with learning disabilities in reading, writing, and arithmetic cropped up.[1] Here's a description in 1896 from the physician W. Pringle Morgan of a 14-year-old named Percy F.: "I might add that the boy is bright and of average intelligence in conversation. . . . The schoolmaster who has taught him for some years says that he would be the smartest lad in school if the instruction were entirely oral."[2]

The history of learning disabilities is a tale of multiple conceptualizations, spanning several continents. In the United States, physician Samuel Orton studied children with reading disabilities who had at least average IQ scores.[3] Orton conceptualized language and motor disabilities as brain dysfunction in spite of normal or even above average intelligence. He believed that to adequately diagnose learning disabilities, it was important to combine a variety of sources of information, including IQ test scores, achievement test scores, family histories, and school histories. For those who then warranted the learning disability diagnosis, Orton believed the proper intervention consisted of directly targeting the specific area of weakness and using the child's "spared" abilities to help remediate the disability.

In Germany, the neurologist Kurt Goldstein studied the deficits of soldiers who sustained head injuries. His focus was on their deficits in visual perception and attention. Goldstein's student Alfred Strauss took this approach and studied adolescents with learning difficulties.[4] Along with educator Laura Lehtinen, they developed remediation techniques that involved providing students with a distraction-free environment and training perceptual deficits.[5] They merely inferred brain damage, though. They didn't actually peer inside the head.

The Goldstein-Strauss approach was widespread in the 1950s and 1960s. Thousands of children were identified as having "minimal brain dysfunction" by the use of a checklist, which included things such as academic difficulty, aggression, and "acting-out."[6] If a student exhibited 9 out of 37 possible symptoms, they received treatment, which typically meant they spent hours a day doing perceptual tasks such as connecting dots and learning how to distinguish between a foreground and background. Although a systematic review of 81 studies concluded that these techniques were useless,[7] many public schools in the United States continued to rely on perceptual training to remediate learning difficulties.[8]

In the 1950s and 1960s, a number of psychologists and speech and language specialists, including William Cruickshank, Helmer Myklebust, and

Doris Johnson, began focusing more on the specific cognitive processes relating to academic difficulties. Their focus was much more targeted on specific areas of academic weakness. But this hodgepodge of different approaches created much confusion in the schools, because children with distinctly different areas of academic weakness were lumped together, and no one knew what to call them. Children who were having difficulties learning in school were given a number of different labels, including "dyslexia," "learning disorder," "perceptual disorder," and "minimal brain dysfunction."

On Saturday April 6, 1963, parents and professionals met in Chicago to explore the "problems" of the perceptually handicapped child. All were struggling to integrate all of these various approaches. At this historic conference Samuel Kirk, professor of special education at the University of Illinois, coined the term "learning disabilities," noting, "I have used the term 'learning disabilities' to describe a group of children who have disorders in the development of language, speech, reading, and association communication skills needed for social interaction. In this group, I do not include children who have sensory handicaps, such as blindness, because we have methods of managing and training the deaf and blind. I also excluded from this group children who have generalized mental retardation.[9]

Professionals, educators, and parents rejoiced. Finally they had a single, unified label.

≈

Kirk's speech was highly influential on the first federal definition of learning disabilities: the 1969 "Children with Specific Learning Disabilities Act." Their definition was essentially Kirk's definition:

The term "specific learning disability" means a disorder in one or more of the basic psychological processes involved in understanding or in using language, spoken or written, which may manifest itself in imperfect ability to listen, think, speak, read, write, spell, or do mathematical calculations. The term includes such conditions as perceptual handicaps, brain injury, minimal brain dysfunction, dyslexia, and developmental aphasia. The term does not include children who have learning disabilities, which are primarily the result of visual, hearing, or motor handicaps, or mental retardation, or emotional disturbance, or of environmental, cultural, or economic disadvantage.[10]

Notice there's no actual mention of "intelligence" in this definition. There's the fuzzy term "basic psychological processes." The core of the definition is that those with a specific learning disability (SLD) show "unexpected" low achievement in a specific academic area that cannot be explained by other factors. This definition of specific learning disability remains in place today, virtually unchanged from its 1969 formulation, so it's important to understand its origins: *It was literally a definition created by a committee.*[11]

But defining the term was only the first step. Educators needed to know how they should *identify* children with a specific learning disability. Beginning with the "Right to Education for All Handicapped Children Act" of 1975, the following guidelines were included for identification:

- The child does not achieve commensurate with age and ability when provided with appropriate educational experiences.
- The child has a severe discrepancy between levels of ability and achievement in one or more of seven areas that are specifically listed (basic reading skills, reading comprehension, mathematics calculation, mathematics reasoning, oral expression, listening comprehension, and written expression).

The first guideline was intended to make sure that low educational achievement was due to an intrinsic characteristic of the student, and not just a reflection of bad teaching.[12] The second guideline was their attempt to measure "unexpected" low achievement. But they had a problem. There was no good way for educators to measure the "basic cognitive processes" mentioned in their definition. What were these mysterious processes? As you'll recall from Chapter 2, theory-based IQ tests, grounded in neuropsychological processes, hadn't yet arrived on the scene.

Their solution: use a "severe discrepancy" between IQ and achievement. This decision was largely based on the Isle of Wight studies conducted in the early 1970s.[13] Michael Rutter and William Yule found tentative evidence that there are meaningful differences between two different groups of poor readers—those whose low reading was unexpected based on their IQ ("specific reading retardation") and those whose low reading was "expected" based on their low IQ score ("general reading backwardness").* Rutter

---

*It's interesting to me how different psychologists conceptualize the term "underachievement." Statistically, it just means you're not achieving in line with your group prediction. In

and Yule concluded their study with the following: "The next question clearly is: 'do the two groups need different types of remedial help with their reading?' No data are available on this point but the other findings suggest that the matter warrants investigation."

But the U.S. government needed guidelines and couldn't wait for more research. So they left their guidelines open-ended, leaving it up to each state to decide what constituted a "severe discrepancy" between IQ and achievement. Of course, states differed quite a bit, creating a situation in which parents who wanted to gain a specific learning disability diagnosis for their child could pack up and move to a state whose guidelines required a smaller discrepancy! States also disagreed on which IQ test should be used and whether a global IQ score or subscale should be used. As we'll see, these aren't trivial differences.

Thus was born one of the most unintelligent methods of identifying learning disabilities ever invented.

~

Despite the high reliability of IQ test scores across most of the lifespan,[14] IQ testing is not an exact science. One of Binet's key insights is that you can't measure someone's IQ—or any psychological trait, for that matter—to the same level of precision as you can measure a person's height or weight (see Chapter 2). There are many reasons why a person's test score can change from one testing session to the next. One major source of IQ fluctuation is measurement error. Sometimes a score can be seriously underestimated because the test taker zoned out or temporarily became distracted. For instance, perhaps just before one IQ testing session, the test taker had a traumatic breakup that affects his or her concentration. It's also possible for a person's

---

1963 Thorndike argued that a better term for underachievement is "underprediction." That would be more technically correct. Lohman makes a good analogy to physical fitness. We know that height is strongly related to basketball performance, but we also know that some tall people are really terrible at basketball. We don't label all tall people who aren't in the NBA as "basketball underachievers." There are just so many other factors involved in basketball performance, including interest, athletic ability, specific basketball skills, and opportunity to practice. So why do we automatically label low-achieving individuals with a high IQ "underachievers"? Or put the other way, why do we view those who are achieving higher than their IQ "overachievers"? For more on this topic, see R. L. Thorndike, "Some Methodological Issues in the Study of Creativity," in *Proceedings of the 1962 Invitational Conference on Testing Problems* (Princeton, NJ: Educational Testing Service, 1963); and D. F. Lohman, "The Role of Nonverbal Ability Tests in Identifying Academically Gifted Students: An Aptitude Perspective," *Gifted Child Quarterly* 49 (2005): 111–138.

IQ score to be artificially inflated, which can happen with lucky guessing or cheating. There are some cases on record of parents feeding their children the answers ahead of time.

But the source of measurement error isn't always the test taker. There's plenty of room for administration errors, such as two different test examiners scoring answers differently, or one examiner making a clerical mistake and accidentally omitting the third digit in a child's IQ score. Just how prevalent are these errors? One study found that about 90 percent of examiners made at least one error, and two-thirds of the errors resulted in a different IQ score.[15] Also, despite IQ test administrators reporting confidence in their scoring accuracy, average levels of agreement was only 42.1 percent. As Kevin McGrew notes, "This level of examiner error is alarming, particularly in the context of important decision-making."[16]

To account for measurement error, most modern IQ tests provide an examiner with a confidence interval—the range of IQ scores that are likely to contain a person's "true" IQ. Of course, there is no such thing as a true IQ score. The only way we'd actually be able to find that out would be to give a person the same IQ test an infinite number of times. But it's clearly not feasible to give the same person the same test even a handful of times, so most IQ test manuals provide a *range* of IQ scores, leaving it up to the examiner to choose his or her confidence levels.

A commonly chosen confidence interval is 68 percent. Suppose you are trying to predict what an 11-year old child's IQ score will be at the age of 21 and you know that there's a .70 correlation in the general population between IQ measured at age 11 and IQ measured at age 21 (this correlation is at the upper end of what is typically found). Based solely on that information, what range of IQ scores can you expect he will obtain on his twenty-first birthday?

It depends how confident you want to be. If you are only 68 percent confident, you can expect that the child's true score is somewhere within 10 points of his 11-year-old score (in both directions—10 points higher or 10 points lower than his original IQ score). But that's with only 68 percent confidence. As Alan Kaufman notes, "I wouldn't cross a busy intersection if I had only a 65% to 70% probability of making it to the other side."[17]

For high-stakes decisions, test administrators have the option of increasing their confidence interval to 90 percent or even 95 percent. Of course, higher confidence comes at a cost: it widens the range of possible IQ scores. In the example of this 11-year-old boy, if you want to be 95 percent confident of what this child's IQ score will be at age 21, you'd have to expect a range of *20 points* in either direction.

Most contemporary IQ tests are a bit more reliable, but no test exists that is perfectly reliable. Even using the most reliable IQ tests available today, the expected spread is significant. Kevin McGrew reviewed IQ fluctuations among today's most frequently administered IQ tests and estimated that the full range of expected IQ differences for most of the general population is *16 to 26 points.*[18]

The problem gets even worse when you realize that those who are *most* impacted by high-stakes decisions—those at the extreme low and high ends of the bell curve—are also the ones who are most likely to show the largest test score fluctuations. The technical term for this phenomenon is "regression to the mean." Let's say you learn a new game, such as Scrabble, and the first time you play you do really great (beginner's luck). All else being equal, the next time you play you'll probably perform closer to average. Same thing if you performed really poorly the first time. Chances are, you'll perform better next time. This applies to any form of measurement. Sports rookies who have an amazing first year are rarely as hot the second year. Even the "linsanity" of Jeremy Lin cooled down. It's a statistical fact that initial expectations, based on a single number, can't be trusted.

But measurement error isn't the only culprit in IQ test score fluctuations. There are lots of other reasons why a person's IQ score might differ from one testing session to the next. One important (but often overlooked) cause is the format of the test. Different IQ tests measure a different mixture of cognitive abilities, and school psychologists often find different IQ scores if they administer more than one IQ test to the same person (even if the test manual says they are measuring the same skills).

Just how much can scores fluctuate from one IQ test battery to the next? During 2002–2003, as part of validation for their new IQ test, the KABC-II, Alan and Nadeen Kaufman looked at IQ test scores from a dozen children who were tested on three different contemporary IQ tests. Figure 3.1 shows the IQ profiles of a representative sample of those children, aged 12–13. The first thing to note is that those exposed to greater opportunities for learning (higher SES, based on parents' education) tended to score higher on IQ tests than those from lower-SES backgrounds. But even collapsing across SES, every single preadolescent had a different IQ score based on which test they took. The differences for the dozen children ranged from 1 to 22 points, with an average difference of 12 points. Leo earned IQs that ranged from 102 to 124. Brianna ranged from 105 to 125. In some districts, Brianna would have qualified as "gifted" based solely on her KABC-II score (see Chapter 4). But if the district looked at her WJ III score, she would be considered as

PARENTS' EDUCATION - COLLEGE GRADUATE OR HIGHER

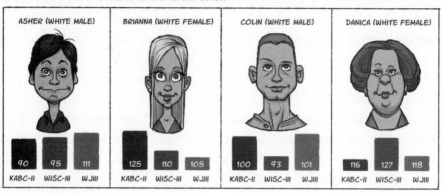

PARENTS' EDUCATION - SOME COLLEGE (1-3 YEARS)

PARENTS' EDUCATION - HIGH SCHOOL GRADUATE OR SOME HIGH SCHOOL

FIGURE 3.1.

Source: A. S. Kaufman, *IQ Testing 101* (New York: Springer, 2009). Adapted with permission.

having only average intelligence. Therefore, an ideal IQ score would be one that not only averages across multiple testing sessions but also uses multiple test batteries to get at what you are trying to measure and averages those scores as well.

But not all test score fluctuations are the result of measurement error or changes in test battery. Various school factors significantly influence IQ scores, such as quality of instruction, enriching classes and afterschool activities, entering school late, intermittent attendance, length of schooling, and summer vacations.[19] All of these factors influence *genuine* brain maturation.[20] An inconvenient truth for educators who employ rigid IQ cutoff scores when making important decisions is that the environment matters, and people really do grow at different rates.

There are also important personal factors that can affect IQ scores, such as changes in test anxiety (see Chapter 8) and test motivation. In a recent analysis of multiple studies based on 2,008 participants, Angela Duckworth and her colleagues found that offering material incentives increased IQ scores substantially (the effects ranged from medium to large).[21] The effect of incentives depended on the person's IQ score, however. Offering external rewards boosted IQ scores much more among those with below-average IQs than among those with above-average IQ scores.* These results don't mean IQ scores are meaningless as indicators of cognitive ability. It's pretty difficult to obtain a high IQ score based solely on passion. Indeed, IQ remained a significant predictor of life outcomes, even taking motivation into account, and IQ scores were a better predictor of academic achievement than test motivation.

Nevertheless, the study highlights the fact that motivation is an important contributor to IQ test performance. No test administrator knows all of the causes of a testee's low IQ score. Test examiners are trained to look out for signs of low motivation and high test anxiety, but they don't always take their qualitative observations into account when interpreting a child's score.

∽

If IQ is such a fallible measuring stick, can we really predict an individual's future level of academic achievement from their current IQ score? Averaging

---

*There could be multiple reasons for this finding, including the possibility that the kinds of puzzles included on IQ tests are intrinsically more rewarding for individuals who score higher on IQ tests.

over many students, we can. The most reliable IQ tests typically show correlations with academic achievement ranging from the mid-.60s to the mid-.70s.[22] These correlations offer some of the most reliable predictions in all of psychology.

But even with correlations this high, about 40 to 60 percent of differences in academic outcomes are *not* related to IQ scores. There are numerous factors that contribute to academic achievement (many of which we will review throughout this book). These include specific cognitive abilities, other student characteristics such as motivation, persistence, self-control, mindset, self-regulation strategies, classroom practices, design and delivery of curriculum and instruction, school demographics, climate, politics and practices, home and community environments, and, indirectly, state and school district organization and governance.[23]

In fact, the strength of the relationship between IQ and academic achievement depends heavily on just how you define "academic achievement." Consider two recent studies conducted by Angela L. Duckworth, Patrick D. Quinn, and Eli Tsukayama on middle school students.[24] They found that self-control predicted changes in report card grades better than IQ, whereas IQ predicted changes in standardized achievement test scores better than self-control. The teachers indicated that they factored in completion of homework assignments, class participation, effort, and attendance when determining report card grades. These results suggest that GPA highlights a broader range of key life skills than standardized test performance.

Even the very highest correlations between IQ and academic achievement leave plenty of room for error. Kevin McGrew found a correlation of .75 between IQ and standardized academic achievement test performance on a representative sample of the most recent edition of the Woodcock-Johnson tests of cognitive abilities and achievement.[25] Based on this correlation—which is on the very high end of what is typically found—just how well could he predict the academic achievement of those with IQs within the 70–80 range (those often labeled "slow learners")?

Figure 3.2 is a scatter plot of the relationship between IQ and academic achievement (averaged across tests of reading, math, and written language). Each little circle represents a real, live, breathing person. As you can see, even for individuals within that small range of IQ scores, expected achievement scores ranged quite a bit, from about 40 to 110. Half of the individuals within the 70–80 IQ range achieved at or below their expected achievement, but importantly, the other half scored at or *above* their predicted achieve-

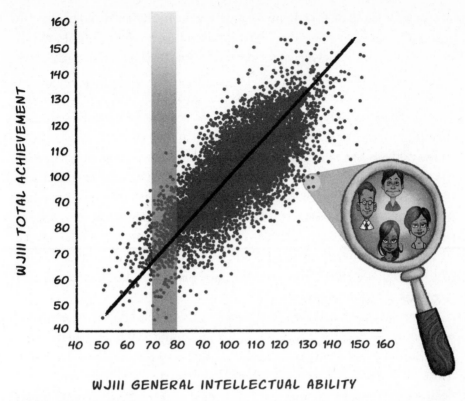

FIGURE 3.2.
Source: K. S. McGrew, *Expectations for Students with Cognitive Disabilities: Is the Cup Half Empty or Half Full? Can the Cup Flow Over?* (Synthesis Report 54) (Minneapolis: University of Minnesota, National Center on Educational Outcomes, 2004).

ment. This finding has some pretty striking implications! Back in 1937, Cyril Burt made his famous pint of milk analogy: "Capacity must obviously limit content. It is impossible for a pint jug to hold more than a pint of milk, and it is equally impossible for a child's educational attainment to rise higher than his educable capacity."[26]

McGrew concludes that the *correct* metaphor for the association between IQ and academic achievement is not that the jug can't hold more milk, but that the "cup can flow over." According to McGrew, "the carte blanche assumption that all students with disabilities should have an alternative set of educational standards and an assessment system is inconsistent with empirical data. . . . The current reality is that despite being one of the flagship developments in all of psychology, intelligence tests are fallible predictors of academic achievement."

McGrew's findings don't apply only to those with IQs in the 70–80 range. No matter what IQ band you pull out from McGrew's analysis, you'll find the same thing. In fact, a law emerges. Using the most reliable IQ tests available today, McGrew notes that "for any given IQ test score, half of the students will obtain achievement scores at or below their IQ score. Conversely, and frequently not recognized, is that for any given IQ test score, half of the students will obtain achievement scores at or *above* their IQ score."* Clearly a child's current discrepancy between IQ and achievement doesn't necessarily indicate a learning disability.

But perhaps the biggest flaw in the severe discrepancy method is that it's a fundamentally *unintelligent* method. It treats single IQ scores as the arbiter of truth, without looking at the person's history and understanding the numbers in context. Responsible and intelligent use of IQ tests require us to consider the student's overall pattern of strengths and weaknesses (not just on the IQ test but even more generally in terms of talents, and social and emotional functioning), life aspirations, developmental history, environmental circumstances, and opportunities to learn.

Robert Sternberg and Elena Grigorenko sum the situation up nicely: "The use of difference scores in diagnosing reading disabilities is analogous to the building of a house of cards. Millions of high-stake decisions are being made on the basis of a procedure that is flawed and greatly in need of modification."[27] You would think that every single school in the United States would have firmly placed the severe discrepancy method in the dustbin by now. Alas, this isn't the case. A recent survey by Perry Zirkel and Lisa Thomas found that the severe discrepancy approach remains a viable approach in the vast majority of states in the United States, with the decision to use the method left up to the local districts.[28] If you are one of those districts still relying on the severe discrepancy approach, you may want to seriously rethink your procedures for identifying learning disabilities.

~

---

*For readers interested in the statistics behind this statement, here is McGrew's elaboration: "This truism of prediction is reflected in the *Standard Error of the Estimate (SE_est)*. Given IQ and achievement tests on a scale with an $M = 100$ and $SD = 15$, and an IQ-Ach correlation of r, $SE_{est} = 15 \times SQRT\ (1 - r^2)$. If $r = .70$ and $SD_{ach} = 15$, then $SE_{est} = 10.7$. In real world terms, this means, that for any IQ score for this particular IQ test, the expected/predicted achievement (after accounting for regression to the mean effects) would be bracketed by ±10.7 points. That is, for any particular IQ score, 68 percent of the population would be expected to show a range of 21.4 achievement standard score points (half above and half below the predicted achievement score). Stated differently, for any given IQ score, the predicted/expected achievement score would be bracketed with a 'confidence of prediction band' of ±10.7 standard score points."

Psychologists quickly realized the flaws in the severe discrepancy model. Apart from all of these conceptual and statistical issues, the Isle of Wight studies—the bedrock on which the method was formed—were shown to be highly problematic. The researchers didn't exclude children with brain injury or intellectual disability.[29] The inclusion of these other special populations made it *appear* as though the children in the "generally reading backward" group were a qualitatively different kind of person. But newer, more sophisticated research shows this isn't so.

Looking at the combined effects of a number of different studies, researchers have found that there are no major differences in the behavioral, cognitive, and achievement characteristics or even long-term developmental reading outcomes of children who meet severe discrepancy criteria versus those who are just "low achieving."[30] Most troublesome from a practical perspective, severe discrepancies have been shown to be very weak predictors of actual treatment outcomes.[31]

After many years of fighting among psychologists, educators, and lobbyists, the Individuals with Disabilities Educational Improvement Act of 2004 (IDEA 2004) was enacted.[32] It included the same definition of SLD as prior definitions, but the guidelines for identifying SLD changed radically. Policy makers took the severe discrepancy model out of the recommendations. But what guidelines were put in its place? IDEA 2004 stated that schools must permit the use of a process based on the child's response to scientific, research-based interventions, but if a school decided they didn't want to use IQ tests for identifying learning disabilities, that was their prerogative. Educators were no longer *required* to use IQ tests.

The anti-IQ folks rejoiced in the streets, probably gathering to burn old editions of the Stanford-Binet. Cognitive assessment specialists, on the other hand, panicked that they would be out of jobs. The IQ test suddenly faced the very real possibility of becoming irrelevant. Before you make up your own mind on this matter, let's listen to the different sides in this heated battle. Trust me, there's no obvious solution here. Finding the most effective methods to identify learning disabilities is not a black-and-white, clear-cut issue. There are many complexities, and there are thoughtful researchers on all sides who are working hard to come up with the best procedures given the confines of the current educational system. Let's give both sides a fair hearing.

∿

First up is the response to intervention (RTI) approach. Those adopting this approach rely on the RTI delivery framework to identify learning disabilities.

The RTI framework is typically organized as a set of tiers. Tier 1 starts in the general education classroom. Students who don't show adequate progress in response to the standard curriculum are given some light research-based interventions. If that isn't adequate, then children can pass on to Tier 2, where they are given more intensive interventions. Children who are still struggling to learn after receiving multiple interventions pass on to Tier 3, where they are given a comprehensive evaluation and, if warranted, are eligible for special education.

If the child is designated as being at risk, the parents (who have been involved from the beginning of the process) are informed of the strategies the team will use to address the child's instructional needs. To inform their strategies, short assessments of specific academic skills predictive of academic achievement are administered to the student. In reading, this could include an assessment of oral reading ability for a short passage, in which the examiner counts the number of words read correctly in a minute. The team tracks these specific academic skills, and also collects information on what the teachers are doing and what seems to be working. Children who are making sufficient progress return to mainstream education.

Under this framework, inadequate response to instruction through direct assessment of academic and behavior skills meets the federal definition of SLD as "unexpected low achievement." IQ tests come into play only if there are concerns about an intellectual disability, autism, or other disorder. IQ tests aren't *automatically* administered.

A common misconception of RTI researchers is that they are less quantitative and assessment-oriented because they are more behavior focused. When I raised this point to Jack Fletcher, one of the world's most renowned experts on the RTI framework, he told me: "No, I think I'm very quantitative. I'm asking you where their data is, right? I'm not opposed to assessment. It's extensive assessments of cognitive skills that I don't think are supported. But we should be assessing achievement, instructional response, and other potential disabilities."

∾

Now let's consider the other side—which I'll describe as the cognitive pattern of strengths and weaknesses (COG-PSW) approach.* COG-PSW folks

---

*Although they focus on cognitive abilities, many COG-PSW researchers and practitioners do believe in the intelligent testing approach, where test scores are viewed in the context of the child's background and personality as expressed in the testing session (see Chapter 2).

aren't opposed to the RTI delivery framework. Quite the contrary, they believe that the RTI service is a necessary condition for identifying SLD. They just don't see it as a *sufficient* condition. They see the RTI's enormous potential to catch students at risk for low academic achievement, but they believe that the more difficulty the child has as he traverses the RTI tiers, the more data should be gathered to problem-solve and come up with a solution.

COG-PSW folks argue that many theory-based IQ tests grounded in the CHC model have come on the scene since the severe discrepancy approach was first proposed, and that these new tests can effectively be used to assess a child's pattern of cognitive-processing strengths and weaknesses. Here's Alan Kaufman, a major proponent of the COG-PSW method, summarizing their perspective: "Most advocates of IQ testing believe that psychologists should identify, rather than simply infer, the processing disorder in order to fulfill the true definition of SLD, and that today's theory-based IQ tests are the ideal tools to help identify the processing disorder."[33]

And here's Kevin McGrew and Wendling, further defending this position: "A number of today's CHC-based intelligence batteries include reliable and valid tests that can serve as psychometrically sound markers as articulated by RTI advocates. We believe that those who argue against the use of any cognitive ability tests in the new RTI environment (a) have failed to examine the abilities measured by many contemporary CHC intelligence batteries, (b) have not taken the time to do the RTI marker-to-CHC ability terminology 'crosswalk,' or (c) may have an agenda that is more sociopolitical than empirical."[34]

There are a number of different COG-PSW approaches, sometimes referred to as "third-method" approaches (severe discrepancy being the first method, and RTI being the second method).[35] Advocates of the COG-PSW approach believe that contemporary IQ tests can greatly help with accurate diagnosis by matching cognitive processing deficits with appropriate research-based intervention. To inform their interventions, COG-PSW folks draw on the latest scientific research showing correlations between different CHC cognitive abilities and specific academic outcomes. For instance, research shows that for children with deficits in short-term memory (*Gs*), it is helpful to keep oral directions short and simple, provide aids to help students compensate, keep lessons short, and allow for overlearning, review, and repetition.[36]

Accurate diagnosis is important to COG-PSW folks. Here's Dawn Flanagan, a major advocate of the third-method approach: "Although many children's academic needs can be well served through an RTI model, there continue to be children whose difficulties are neurologically based and who require specially designed instructions to overcome or compensate for their weaknesses or to make appreciable gains academically. Obscuring the differences among slow learners, individuals with general cognitive deficiencies (e.g., ID), and those with SLD does a disservice to all groups of students. A process that more discretely defines SLD and distinguishes it from other groups of low achievers will very likely increase the correspondence between SLD and treatment."[37]

This just may be the most striking difference between the two approaches. RTI folks do not believe cognitive ability test performance is directly related to intervention, so they focus on the direct assessment of academic and behavior skills. In contrast, those adopting the COG-PSW approach believe accurate diagnosis is necessary and that IQ scores are important in distinguishing between different kinds of learners.

According to Kenneth Kavale, a leading figure in the field of learning disabilities: "If a student is not an under-achiever, then the possibility exists that the student may fall into the category of 'slow learner' (i.e., students with IQs from 70 to 85). About 14 percent of the school population falls within this IQ range, but this status has never been associated with a special education category. A slow learner does not demonstrate unexpected low achievement but rather an achievement level consonant with IQ level. . . . What should *not* happen is that a designation of SLD be given to a slow learner."[38]

I admit the label "slow learner" makes me extremely uncomfortable. As we saw earlier in this chapter, half of children within the 70–80 IQ range achieve higher than expected. How do you know whether a child is capable of benefiting from a specific learning disability intervention if you don't give the child a chance? This mentality that people within the 70–80 IQ range are a qualitatively different kind of person than "normally abled" individuals seems very similar to the logic underlying the traditional severe discrepancy method.

To be fair, COG-PSW folks repeatedly argue that their method is *not* the same as the severe discrepancy method. For one, they deemphasize the use of global IQ scores in favor of patterns of scores for informing intervention, and some COG-PSW researchers, such as Dawn Flanagan, have attempted to carefully eliminate the attenuating influences of cognitive processing deficits on a child's overall cognitive ability estimate.[39] Nevertheless, the RTI folks still don't buy it. In a discussion with Fletcher, he rejected the COG-PSW approach, characterizing it as "essentially a psychometric extension of difference scores that's not really different from IQ-achievement discrepancy."

There are no easy answers here. I can understand the logic of COG-PSW researchers. How do you know what *specifically* needs remediation if a child has no cognitive deficit that stands out among the rest of their cognitive profile? But I can also appreciate and even personally resonate with the RTI perspective. Instead of being so concerned with finding the precise label for the child, shouldn't the emphasis be on directly addressing behaviors and getting the child back into the mainstream classroom as fast as possible?

While I think both sides have some valid points, I also think both perspectives are missing something really big. Despite all the talk of assessing patterns of cognitive strengths and weaknesses, COG-PSW researchers seem to have a disproportionate focus on the *weaknesses*. Also, even though the RTI folks are interested in moving the child as fast as possible into an intervention for the purposes of remediation, their focus is still on *remediation*.

In neither case are the psychologists using information about the child's *strengths* to help with remediation, or even to help the children feel good about themselves! In either approach, the child feels like a total loser. There had to be a bigger picture here. I mean, can't a learning disability sometimes be an *advantage*?

∽

In recent years, the "neurodiversity" movement has been gaining a lot of traction. The term is attributed to autism advocate Judy Singer, a sociologist with high-functioning autism whose own child has high-functioning autism. The term gained wide exposure in a 1998 article in the *Atlantic* written by Harvey Blume called "Neurodiversity." In the article, Blume remarked, "Neurodiversity may be every bit as crucial for the human race as biodiversity is for life in general. Who can say what form of wiring will prove best at any given moment? Cybernetics and computer culture, for example, may favor a somewhat autistic cast of mind."[40]

Today many different advocacy groups have joined the neurodiversity movement, including autism, schizophrenia, bipolar disorder, ADHD, anxiety disorders, intellectual disabilities, and dyslexia. At the end of the day, it's not all that surprising that such a movement would be popular. People who have been given these various labels want to be appreciated for who they are—quirks and all. They don't want to be defined by their deviation from normality. A major aim of the movement is to balance out the "disease" model of mental disorders by showing the upside of being different.[41]

Consider dyslexia—one of the most commonly diagnosed specific learning disabilities. As Brock Eide and Fernette Eide note in their recent book *The Dyslexic Advantage*, "Overlooking the talents that mature individuals with dyslexia characteristically display is like trying to understand caterpillars while ignoring the fact that they grow up to be butterflies."[42]

Without a doubt: for the 15 percent of the human population who have dyslexia, learning can be difficult, particularly when intensive and rapid reading is required. They require interventions and strategies, and thankfully many strategies out there have proven effective. But people with dyslexia are far from disabled as human beings. In fact, in some contexts they may even appear to be—dare I say—gifted.

Reading requires a complex integration of visual and auditory sensory processing. The reader must recognize letters and their combinations, convert them to speech sounds, and then extract meaning. Every step of the process is important, from the precognitive to the higher-level stages. Research shows that people with dyslexia are less aware of the sounds in words (phonological awareness) and have difficulties connecting visual and verbal information (rapid naming). But these learning difficulties may have some advantages in the visual domain.

In their 2003 paper in the journal *Brain and Language*, Catya von Karolyi, Ellen Winner, Wendy Gray, and Gordon Sherman argue that dyslexic individuals may excel at visual-spatial tasks that rely on the right hemisphere, because the right hemisphere tends to process information holistically.[43] To test their idea, they compared adolescents with and without dyslexia on a task requiring holistic inspection. People looked at line drawings of figures and indicated which ones represented possible objects and which ones were impossible. Impossible figures were objects that seem to be 3-D but could not actually exist in 3-D space. Examples can be found in M. C. Escher's paintings, such as his famous impossible staircase painting, *Ascending and Descending*. If you scan this painting bit by bit, without integrating the whole, you'll conclude that the figure is possible, but if you scan the picture holistically, you'll be able to see that the parts conflict.

They found that dyslexic individuals were significantly faster at recognizing impossible figures as impossible, and their faster speed didn't sacrifice accuracy. This suggests one upside of poor reading skills: rapid and accurate "holistic inspection." It appears dyslexics have a wider visual perceptual

BBS. I desperately want to be friends with them. Heck, I would be happy just to be associated with them. To enter their world.

They sit down at the table across from us, just as Mark gets up. "I'm gonna go get some more potatoes. I'll be back," he says. "Sure." I nod, even though I'm not listening to what he is saying. All I know is that the perfect opportunity to introduce myself to them has finally arrived. After all, they do know me. They just don't realize it.

I get up and walk over, plopping my sandwich down on their table. It explodes in a small eruption of meat. "Hey guys! Mind if I join ya'll?" I say confidently. A tall, lanky member of the group named Matt smiles. "Sure. What's your name?" "My name is Scaaa . . . ," I start, then stop. I think for a moment and decide to go for it. "I mean, I am . . . the Wizard," I say with a grin.

Suddenly the whole table is looking at me. "You're . . . the Wizard?" another kid named Matt asks. As I come to find out, there are three Matts at the table. *Must be a gifted name.* I reach into my bag and pull out my calculator. I turn it on and plop it on top of what is left of my sandwich. The group huddles around me and looks at the screen. They look astonished as a configuration of dots, which takes the form of the logo of my BBS, appears on the screen. "AWESOME!" the Matts say in unison.

Just then Mark returns with an overloaded plate of potatoes. He almost drops his plate when he sees me sitting with the gifted kids. He pauses and looks at us incredibly confused. "Mark!" I yell out and wave him over. "Come join me and my new friends!"

~

Who is worthy of the label "gifted"? For most of the twentieth century, only those scoring high on an IQ test were eligible for that nice-sounding label. And let's be honest: the label *does* sound nice. What would you rather get for the holidays, a gift or a learning disability? Given the choice, most of you would probably rather receive the gifted label!

Lewis Terman, the founder of gifted education in the United States, had very clear ideas about which children were gifted. It was Terman, after all, who decided to link high IQ scores on his test with "genius" in his classification scheme for the Stanford-Binet (see Chapter 3). Terman once explicitly remarked that from high-IQ children "and no where else, our geniuses in every line are recruited."[1]

mode than typical readers.[44] This way of seeing the world could make reading difficult for dyslexics because of their inability to perceive individual words without interference from the surrounding text.[45] Nevertheless, this can serve as an advantage in situations that require identifying information in the periphery.[46]

People with dyslexia also tend to have difficulty remembering words. Matthew Schneps and colleagues suggest that dyslexic individuals might use spatial learning strategies to compensate for difficulties in encoding memories phonologically.[47] To test their idea, they rounded up students who were enrolled in a remedial college for people with language-based disabilities who reported lifelong struggles with reading. They gave them a task especially suited to the strengths of dyslexic individuals. They predicted that advantages for spatial learning in dyslexia would be most prominent when their cognitive load is reduced by not requiring them to focus on the center. This would enable dyslexics to make good use of peripheral information, at which they excel. So the researchers blurred a set of photographs of natural scenes, reducing the high spatial frequency detail (making them "low-pass filtered"). They reasoned that this loss of spatial information would make it less likely for the participants to focus on the center, biasing spatial learning in favor of those with dyslexia. The researchers found that the students with dyslexia did indeed show advantages in memory for scenes, but only when the scenes were blurred.

This intriguing study suggests a trade-off between reading and visual cognition.[48] If you tend to have a narrower focus of attention, like many typical readers, you will be better at noticing small, isolated features near the center of gaze. In contrast, if you focus on the periphery, like some dyslexics, you will be more likely to notice the holistic patterns. Schneps and colleagues suggest that college students with dyslexia should be encouraged to enter careers in which sensitivity to low spatial frequency scenes is particularly valued, such as radiology, astronomy, cellular microscopy, and other scientific fields. Indeed, Nobel laureates with dyslexia include Carol W. Greider and Baruk Benacerraf. The researchers also suggest that spatial learning, which had already been an effective intervention for the elderly with nonspatial memory deficits, may also be an effective intervention for students with dyslexia.

People with dyslexia may compensate in many ways, sometimes developing enhanced communication skills, the ability to delegate responsibilities, or even the ability to read nonverbal facial expressions. These can be particularly important skills for entrepreneurship. Julie Logan investigated the coping strategies and business skills of a sample of 139 entrepreneurs and corporate managers in the United States.[49] She found a much higher incidence of dyslexia among the entrepreneurs compared to corporate managers and the general population.

While 15 percent of the general population has dyslexia, 35 percent of the entrepreneurs in her sample reported dyslexic characteristics. In contrast, less than 1 percent of the corporate managers reported dyslexic characteristics. Tellingly, people with dyslexia grew their own companies more quickly, and showed greater oral communication skills compared to those without dyslexia. Logan concluded that "dyslexic entrepreneurs may be more comfortable in a start-up or a serial entrepreneurial role so that they are able to do things in their own way."[50] Virgin Atlantic mogul Richard Branson has dyslexia, as does the CEO of Cisco Systems, John Chambers, who allegedly can't even read his own email.

The truth is that people with dyslexia thrive in many fields. Famous dyslexic artists include Pablo Picasso, Leonardo Da Vinci, Vincent Van Gogh, Michelangelo, Chuck Close, and Andy Warhol.[51] Famous designers include Tommy Hilfiger and Paul Smith. Sculptor John Mishler once wrote, "Being dyslexic has given me an enhanced imagination . . . in my head I see visual images that are often turned into sculptures without any drawings on paper. It took me a long time to realize that being dyslexic was a gift."[52]

Also, the written word need not always bar the dyslexic from achieving greatness. Many famous writers have not only compensated for dyslexia, but used their reading difficulty as a driving force. "In my day dyslexia didn't exist, merely stupid students," science fiction writer Piers Anthony told me. "I may have set a record for stupidity."[53] It took him three years and five schools to get through first grade. Other famous writers with dyslexia include Pulitzer Prize winner Richard Ford (*Independence Day*), novelist and screenwriter John Irving (*The Cider House Rules*), and Edgar Award winner Lynda La Plante (*Prime Suspect*). As Matthew Schneps notes, "We may be short-changing students who have reading difficulties. These students have strengths for visual learning that we could be building on." Perhaps instead of labeling dyslexics as learning disabled, we should call them *visually gifted*.

Chapter 4

WHO IS GIFTED?

1992

I open up my brown lunch bag and take out a meatloaf sandwich. *Again? Really?* I poke it just to make sure it's not still alive. "Hey man, wanna work on the BBS later today?" my best friend Mark asks as he sits down at the table. "Yeah, for sure," I respond. "We've got to work on advertising. We need more overseas users."

A few years ago, my parents bought me a brand new 80486 personal computer—my portal into a whole new world I could escape to whenever I came home. It wasn't long before I discovered bulletin-board systems (BBS). Anyone with a modem could dial in to another person's BBS and download the latest games and applications. I was instantly hooked and decided to start my own. Overnight I transformed myself from a 13-year-old kid in special education to "The Wizard," System Operator.

In only the past year my BBS has become immensely popular in Pennsylvania. This week, Wolfenstein 3-D is being downloaded like hotcakes. Mark is my co-sysop (sysop is short for system operator), helping to maintain the BBS, dealing with user complaints, and making sure the site is updated with the latest software. Mark is also in special education. That's where we met. We instantly bonded over our shared interest in computers and the fact that we both feel powerless in school. Our lives are completely consumed by the BBS: it's the only thing that makes us feel in control and good about ourselves.

I attempt to take a bite out of my sandwich when I hear laughing. I look up to see a group of kids walk past me. My heart skips a beat. There they are: *the gifted students*. Whenever I see them playing with their TI-81 calculators, I can hardly take it. I am dying to show them the applications I recently programmed on my own TI-81. Plus, I know some of them are users on my

Terman was fixated on precocity. In a 1917 paper he wrote an elaborate description of Francis Galton, incredibly impressed by his early accomplishments.[2] There's little doubt that Galton was precocious. We don't have to go much beyond a single example to determine that. Here's a letter the young Galton wrote to his sister (who served as his tutor) the day before his fifth birthday:

> My Dear Adele,
>   I am 4 years old and I can read any English book. I can say all the Latin Substantives and Adjectives and active verbs besides 52 lines of Latin poetry. I can cast up any sum in addition and can multiply by 2, 3, 4, 5, 6, 7, 8, [9], 10, [11].
>   I can also say the pence table. I read French a little and I know the clock.
>
> *Francis Galton,*
> *Febuary 15, 1827*[3]

Galton's only misspelling was the date! Apparently the young Francis felt he was claiming too much and decided to scratch out one of the numbers with a knife and paste paper over the other (that's why two of the numbers are bracketed). Terman used Galton's advanced development as proof of the validity of his IQ test, arguing that "a child of four years who is able to do the things characteristic of a child of seven or eight years is a genius of the first order."[4]

But Terman didn't stop there. He also noted the reverse: "The opposite error is no less common; that is, for a mentally retarded child in a grade far below his age to be considered perfectly normal and average in intelligence." He described the situation of a teacher who referred to a 12-year-old first-grader as "slow to learn." Terman suggested to the teacher that "in all probability the child was feeble-minded." The teacher assured Terman that the little girl was not feebleminded, was able to learn the work just fine, and even showed motherly instincts for her six-year-old classmates. So Terman ordered to have the child's IQ tested. Lo and behold, she was found on his test to have a mental age of about 6 years. His conclusion? "This child had been in school several years and had had every opportunity to learn, except the advantage of endowment. Experience has taught us that such a subject will never reach the mental level of seven years, however long she may live."

For Terman, the matter was settled! Terman's beliefs about his tests had direct practical implications. Here was Terman's proposed plan for identifying these budding geniuses: "Teachers should be better trained in detecting the signs of superior ability. Every child who consistently gets high marks in his school work with apparent ease should be given a mental examination, and if his intelligence level warrants it he should either be given extra promotions, or placed in a special class for superior children where faster progress can be made. The latter is the better plan, because it obviates the necessity of skipping grades; it permits rapid but continuous progress."[5]

I can't help but wonder a few things. First, what if a student has a high IQ but isn't getting stellar grades because she is bored and unchallenged? This "underachiever" would not get nominated, and thus wouldn't ever get the chance, to have a "mental examination." Or what if a child does get nominated because he is doing exceptionally well in school, but he doesn't score high enough on Terman's IQ test to qualify for gifted education? According to Terman's logic, these "overachievers" aren't really gifted, so they should just be thrown back into the regular classroom without any special resources. After all, no matter how well they are doing in school, they don't deserve the label "gifted" because they had to work hard to get the good grades. It didn't come *naturally*. Some of you may see problems with both of these scenarios.

But even if you don't agree these are thorny conceptual issues, there are the usual methodological problems. Many of the same problems that arise when identifying learning disabilities are equally problematic when trying to identify giftedness. One big issue for identifying both learning disabilities and giftedness is test format (see Chapter 3). Let's say you want to accurately measure fluid reasoning, but you don't want to discriminate against children with fewer opportunities to learn (such as lower-SES children) or children with limited English language proficiency. The typical response by educators is to use tests of "nonverbal" ability, as though that's some sort of panacea. Surely if you eliminate English from the test questions and instructions you can more accurately and fairly capture the child's fluid reasoning ability, right? *Wrong.*

It's a myth that "simplified," nonverbal instructions make the task less biased for non-native speakers. As psychologist Sandra Scarr has pointed out, sometimes understanding what you are supposed to do on a nonverbal IQ test is half the battle![6] Brief test directions with little chance for practice can lead the child down a dead end. This is especially problematic on group-administered tests, because there is no clinician present who can recognize that the student misunderstood the directions. Research shows that poor, bilingual, and minority children are *most likely* to be confused or adopt an oversimplified strategy to solving nonverbal test problems.[7]

There are a host of other problems with relying primarily on nonverbal tests of cognitive ability for making high-stakes decisions.[8] For starters, there is the very serious problem of "construct underrepresentation." If you only give children the chance to reason in a single symbol system (for instance, spatial), you have no idea how well they might be able to reason in a different symbol system, such as their native language. To capture the full range of fluid reasoning, it's crucial to include the full range of fluid reasoning *tests!*

There's also the real practical consideration: *What's the point of testing?* Is the point of testing to sort the "gifted" from the "ungifted," or is the point to use the test results to inform some sort of intervention? If the latter, then there are some more complicated decisions that ought to be taken into account. If a child struggles with the English language (for whatever reason), and you identify him as "gifted" on a test of nonverbal reasoning, you are going to stick that child into an even more challenging school environment heavily reliant on English (as well as quantitative) skills. The language difficulties will now become even *more* salient, and the child's self-esteem will drop even lower.

Indeed, research shows that nonverbal tests of cognitive ability are worse predictors of academic achievement than tests that also measure the ability to reason in the quantitative and verbal domains. In fact, once you've accounted for the overall composite score in an IQ test battery that contains verbal, quantitative, and figural reasoning, the figural reasoning battery has a *negative* correlation with success in verbally demanding courses.[9]

Another major issue with nonverbal tests is practice effects. You may intuitively think that nonverbal ability tests are more immune to enculturation and practice than tests of knowledge and vocabulary. But as Lohman and Gambrell note, "controlling for the effects of language does not control for the effects of culture."[10] Nonverbal tests of cognitive ability show large practice effects, and cultural influences can even be *larger* than on language-loaded tests.[11] As we'll see in Chapter 10, fluid reasoning test scores, which supposedly reflect skills that are independent from culture, showed *greater* increases over the twentieth century compared to tests that are supposedly more culturally based, such as general knowledge and vocabulary.

The choice of school norms is also crucial. As we saw in Chapter 3, your IQ score is technically nothing more than a percentile rank. But that rank depends on the nature of the population being sampled. This crucial point is often overlooked in the rush to place a label on a student. Most norms for nonverbal reasoning tests are outdated. Nonverbal reasoning performance has been increasing across generations (see Chapter 10), so comparing a child's performance with the performance of a child from a prior generation will overestimate that child's ability.

But even if norms are recent and properly computed, it is wrong to assume that all children have had equal opportunities to develop the particular skills that are required by the tests. There are significant cultural, ethnic, and SES differences on nonverbal tests of cognitive ability.[12] If you compare a minority student's test performance against the national average based on age and gender (which many schools do), you are likely *underestimating* the child's true score. This is why it's important to compare students with comparable opportunities to learn. This problem can be partly remedied by looking at the local norms of children who are all living in the same environment, as well as isolating particular variables that indicate opportunity to learn—such as number of years attending English-speaking schools, for native Spanish speakers.

These problems aren't merely hypothetical. As of this writing, New York City administrators have made the stakes as high as you can possibly get. As far as I'm concerned, their current procedure for identifying giftedness serves as a blueprint for test abuse, and their method is *indefensible*. Let's look at the New York City procedure:

1. Thousands of 4-year-old children who appear gifted have the pleasure of taking a 30-minute test that determines the fate of the rest of their schooling (and lives). Only children who match the teacher's preconceived notion of what a gifted child looks like will get nominated and have the opportunity to prove their worth. Of course, parents can also nominate their own child, but parents aren't nearly as aware of the child's inclinations in school as the teacher.

2. The primary test that is used to identify giftedness is the Naglieri Nonverbal Ability Test (NNAT-2).[13] This test has been advertised as "culture neutral," but there is no such thing as a culture-neutral test of cognitive ability. Carol Carman and Debra Taylor found that even after taking into account ethnic differences, children from low-SES

families were half as likely as other children to be identified as gifted on the first edition of the NNAT.[14]

3. Though the NNAT-2 is advertised as a measure of "nonverbal ability," it actually measures only a subset of nonverbal ability: *figural* nonverbal reasoning. Figural reasoning tests use arbitrary shapes such as triangles, circles, squares, and stars to measure nonverbal fluid reasoning. There are varied ways of measuring nonverbal fluid reasoning, however, including the use of artwork depicting objects other than spatial forms such as apples, soccer balls, shoes, hammers, and fire engine trucks. Therefore, not only does the NNAT-2 represent a subset of the total domain of fluid reasoning, but it also represents a subset of *nonverbal* fluid reasoning. In other words, it tests only a subset of the skills that contribute to school success, let alone real-world success.

4. The NNAT-2 is often measured in a group setting. Combine the high-stakes stress of the testing situation, the confusing nature of nonverbal test directions (despite being advertised as "simplified"), and the lack of a trained clinician who can form a personal connection with the child, and you have a recipe for disaster (particularly for children from a different culture). There's simply no opportunity for *intelligent* testing (see Chapter 2).

5. There are very few practice items on the test, so children who have prior experience with the structure of the test and the strategies that are important for performance are at a distinct advantage. Children who can afford prior practice materials will be at an advantage. Therefore, those who are already at a disadvantage in their opportunity to learn in school (such as lower-SES children) are even *further* disadvantaged in their opportunity to improve their test performance that could serve as a gateway to improved learning outcomes. *Catch-22*. To give you an idea, at Bright Kids NYC you can receive eight, 45-minute individual test prep sessions for $1,000; at NYC Gifted, you get 12-week sessions for $1,399.

6. Even if a student *does* qualify for gifted identification, she still may not be able to get into one of the five coveted gifted-and-talented schools in the city because she didn't win the lottery.

7. Have I mentioned yet that cognitive ability fluctuates most dramatically in youth, due to genuine brain maturation and enriching experiences (see Chapter 10)?

8. Did I mention these are *4-year-olds*?

NYC might want to seriously reconsider their approach to identifying gifted students!

~

Even if you are a school administrator and you are fully aware of these problems, your job is not done. You've still got to decide: *What IQ cutoff point should be used to identify giftedness?* This is not a trivial question. You've got to decide where on the IQ bell curve is "gifted." Which of course means you have to determine the point at which the individual suddenly becomes "ungifted." This isn't just difficult from a methodological viewpoint: the fact is, *there is no objective cutoff.* There's no objective commandment sent down from the sky that decrees a certain point on the bell curve as marking the split between the gifted and the ungifted.

Even if Moses did receive ten gifted commandments, we'd still be in trouble. As we saw in the previous chapter, IQ tests are fallible instruments. There are many reasons why someone's IQ score can change from one testing session to the next, and many of these reasons, including genuine brain maturation and intellectual development, have little to do with measurement error.

What makes problems even thornier is the fact that those with the most extreme scores obtained during a single testing session (both at the low and high ends of the IQ bell curve) are the *most* likely to score closer to average during the second testing session.

This puts a wrench in the notion "once gifted, always gifted." In their paper "Gifted Today but Not Tomorrow?," David Lohman and Katrina Korb note, "We speak of learning-disabled or gifted students as if there were sharp boundaries separating individuals in the categories from those outside of them. Even those who understand that the boundaries are arbitrary often think that if we agreed on the location of the category cut points and had perfectly reliable and valid measures, then category membership would remain constant over time."[15]

But is this assumption true? Lohman and Korb analyzed achievement test score changes among 6,321 students who were tested each year from third to eighth grade. To be consistent with commonly used cutoff points for gifted education programs, they estimated the percentage of students who scored in the top 3 percent in reading, language, and mathematics achievement. Just how many students who met the criteria for giftedness in Year 1 also met the criteria in Year 2? Only about half. By the eighth grade, only 35 to 40 percent of those scoring in the top 3 percent in grade 3 still scored in that range!

These individual effects occurred despite the fact that the overall correlation between third- and fourth-grade achievement scores was a whopping .91. In other words, even though there was extremely high stability among the rank ordering of achievement scores (those who were on top in the first year tended to remain on top the following year), there was still a large number of *individual* fluctuations that impacted on gifted education eligibility.

What can be done? Lohman and Korb argue that one can reduce the impact of these regression effects by retesting each child every year, averaging the test scores of multiple assessments taken on multiple occasions, and comparing student performance based on local norms, not national norms. But none of this will completely alleviate the fact that the more "gifted" a child is at initial testing, the *more likely* that child is to lose that qualification if they are retested. Lohman and Korb conclude that "instead of using terms that imply fixed categories, such as gifted, perhaps educators should use words that focus less on a fixed state and instead on current accomplishment, such as superior achievement or high accomplishment."[16]

We acknowledge problems with test format, and we accept that test score performance can ebb and flow. We're done, right? I'm afraid we're not. You have to decide what abilities should be used to identify giftedness in the first place! Even if we somehow managed to obtain an adequate reading of a person's current level of fluid reasoning, we still have to justify why we chose that ability among all the other characteristics of the child we could be assessing. What about the child's specific pattern of cognitive strengths and weaknesses (such as verbal, quantitative, spatial)? What about precocity in the arts and music? What about budding athletes and actors? Do interpersonal abilities count as gifts at all? What about characteristics such as creativity, leadership, motivation, self-control, and persistence? *What in the world counts?*

Both of these issues—*Is giftedness who you are or what you do?* and *Is giftedness singular or multiple?*—have been, and continue to be, the two most hotly debated issues in the field of gifted education. Let's see how we got here.

∼

The United States has always had a love/hate relationship with excellence.[17] For the first half of the twentieth century (despite Terman's best efforts), educators felt uncomfortable offering special educational resources to children deemed "gifted." In the 1950s and 1960s, however, the tide had turned and high ability became appreciated—even coveted. More articles were published on the gifted and talented in 1956–1959 than in the prior thirty years combined.[18]

It's no mystery why: America *needed* people with high ability, to compete. The launching of the Russian satellite *Sputnik* in 1957 set off fierce critiques of the U.S. education system, and gifted education in particular. The great talent hunt began. The father of the atomic submarine, Admiral Hyman Rickover, vehemently warned that if America wanted to compete, it had to overcome its guilt about singling out gifted children.[19] Efforts from nearly every level were made to identify and educate gifted children. Because the goal was to protect national security, most of the efforts during the early years of the Cold War were to find gifted scientists, which was considered the most worthy form of giftedness.

But as far as the pendulum swung toward excellence during the *Sputnik* era, it swung just as far back toward egalitarianism during the 1960s and 1970s. The pressing need for international dominance and security receded, and humanitarian national issues rose to prominence. People became much more interested in civil rights, freedom, school integration, special education, and equality for all. Giftedness—particularly *scientific giftedness*—became suspect. Thousands of disenchanted youths espousing peace, unity, and equity during the Vietnam War focused their efforts on improving society to combat social injustice. The underrepresentation of minority and female students in gifted education programs—whose sole criteria for entrance was high IQ—added even more justification to those who had already made up their mind about the inequality of giftedness. Gifted education lost much of its funding and much of its momentum.*

A big boost to gifted education came in 1972 when U.S. Commissioner of Education Sidney P. Marland Jr. wrote the groundbreaking report that bears his name.[20] Marland estimated that only a small percentage of the 1.5 to

---

*Historical reviews of giftedness often treat this time as anti-excellence. As I see it, the emphasis had just shifted away from scientific forms of giftedness to more humanitarian forms of giftedness. Certainly, the Vietnam protestors wouldn't have explicitly stated it in those terms, but isn't that what they were really doing? War activists were recruiting compassionate, egalitarian peers to rally together for a cause larger than them. In a sense, they were identifying and selecting for high levels of civic engagement. If you conceptualize advocacy as a form of giftedness (which I do!), then giftedness wasn't *entirely* lost during this era.

2.5 million U.S. gifted children were benefiting from special education, and he emphasized that gifted education had deteriorated. The Marland report greatly increased public awareness that the needs of gifted children were being neglected.

But the most influential aspect of the report is that it broadened—for the first time—the definition of giftedness beyond high IQ. Gifted and talented children were defined as those who demonstrated achievement and/or potential ability in any of the following areas, singularly or in combination:

1. General intellectual ability
2. Specific academic aptitude
3. Creative or productive thinking
4. Leadership ability
5. Visual and performing arts
6. Psychomotor ability

For the most part, this federal definition has remained unchanged, although psychomotor ability was eventually dropped from the list. Note that, like the federal definition of learning disabilities (see Chapter 3), IQ doesn't explicitly appear in the definition. Nevertheless, in the Terman tradition, "general intellectual ability" was interpreted by most schools as an IQ score in the top 3 to 5 percent.[21]

The Marland report was influential, fueling the first legislative action for the gifted and talented, contributing to the allocation of $2.56 million of federal money in 1974 for the improvement of gifted education in America, and spurring the creation of the National Office of the Gifted and Talented. The definition also strongly influenced a wave of research-based, multidimensional definitions of the gifted and talented.

In his 1978 article "What Makes Giftedness?," psychologist Joseph Renzulli argued that the federal definition left out motivational factors, and mixed together specific domains of accomplishment (academic, arts, and so on) and abilities that cut across all domains (creativity, leadership).[22] He also pointed out that even though the Marland definition said that children could display any of the six categories in combination, in practice many educators ended up treating the categories as mutually exclusive. According to Renzulli, "many people 'talk a good game' about the six categories but continue to use a relatively high intelligence or aptitude score as a minimum requirement for entrance into a special program."[23]

In its place, Renzulli proposed his three-ring conception of giftedness. Based on his review of the characteristics of accomplished adults, he argued that giftedness consists of the interaction among three clusters of traits: well-above-average ability, task commitment, and creativity. Renzulli distinguished between *schoolhouse giftedness* and *creative-productive giftedness*, arguing that kids who demonstrate schoolhouse giftedness are excellent consumers of knowledge, whereas those who show high levels of creative-productive giftedness are superior producers of knowledge. As he notes, "History tells us it has been the creative and productive people of the world, the producers rather than consumers of knowledge, the reconstructionists of thought in all areas of human endeavor, who have become recognized as 'truly gifted' individuals. History does not remember persons who merely scored well on IQ tests or those who learned their lessons well but did not apply their knowledge in innovative and action-oriented ways."[24]

Allowing an opportunity for other abilities to shine, Renzulli broadened the notion of ability, defining "well-above-average ability" as either general ability that can be applied across all domains or specific ability, consisting of the ability to perform at a high level within a specific domain. He also lowered the ability identification threshold, defining above-average ability as that possessed by individuals performing in the top 15 to 20 percent in any socially valued domain. This differed significantly from the cutoff point most schools used for IQ tests: top 3 to 5 percent.

According to Renzulli, no one trait—general ability, task commitment, or creativity—is enough to warrant the label "gifted." Instead, Renzulli argued, giftedness emerges from the interaction of all three traits. This was quite a departure from the predominant view at the time. Instead of giftedness as the enduring essence of a person, Renzulli argued that giftedness is an *outcome*, defined by characteristics that contribute to real-world achievement. He also emphasized that each trait is an "equal partner" in contributing to giftedness. His intention was to allow for creativity and task commitment to play a greater role in conceptualizations of giftedness. As he lamented, "A sad but true fact is that special programs have favored proficient lesson learners and test takers at the expense of persons who may score somewhat lower on tests but who more than compensate for such scores by having high levels of task commitment and creativity."[25]

Renzulli's conception of giftedness was only the first of many broadened conceptions of giftedness. In the 1980s and 1990s (and still to a large extent today), the phrase "multiple intelligences" became a major buzzword. Two major pioneers in this regard were Howard Gardner at Harvard and Robert Sternberg at Yale. While both Gardner and Sternberg initially proposed broadened conceptions of intelligence, and not of giftedness per se, their theories were embraced by many in the field of gifted education (and criticized by just as many intelligence researchers—see Chapter 10).

In his 1983 bestseller *Frames of Mind: The Theory of Multiple Intelligences*, Howard Gardner stressed the need for educators and psychologists to broaden their definition of intelligence as well as their methodologies.[26] Relying on a number of criteria—including an identifiable core set of mental operations, brain damage, distinct developmental and evolutionary history, and special populations such as prodigies and savants (see Chapter 11)—he argued that there are seven independent intelligences: logical-mathematical, linguistic, spatial, bodily-kinesthetic, musical, interpersonal, and intrapersonal. More recently he added naturalistic intelligence. Gardner argued that schools tend to overemphasize logical-mathematical and linguistic intelligence to the exclusion of the other intelligences.

In 1984 Sternberg published *Beyond IQ: A Triarchic Theory of Human Intelligence*.[27] Sternberg argued that if you want to understand intelligence, you must take into account the particular abilities a culture values (contextual subtheory), the degree of novelty of the task (experiential subtheory), and the cognitive processes necessary to solve a task (componential theory). More recently, Sternberg transformed his triarchic theory into the theory of "successful intelligence."[28] Sternberg took his three subtheories and made them much more user-friendly for educators. He referred to the componential component as *analytical intelligence*, the ability to solve problems and judge the quality of ideas. The experiential component became *creative intelligence*, the ability to find problems in the first place and novel solutions to those problems. Finally, the contextual theory became *practical intelligence*, the ability to use the ideas and analysis in an effective way in one's everyday context. Sternberg argued that all three forms of intelligence, in combination, are important for achieving one's goals in life.

Even more recently, Sternberg embedded his theory of successful intelligence into an explicit theory of giftedness, called the Wisdom, Intelligence, and Creativity Synthesized (WICS) model of giftedness.[29] Sternberg defined wisdom as the balance of self-interest (intrapersonal interests) with the interests of others (interpersonal interests) while taking into consideration the context in which one lives (extrapersonal interests). Sternberg argued that without wisdom, the gifted individual can apply his or her intelligence to achieve selfish and socially destructive goals. Recognizing that a person can be gifted in any combination of the three components, he argued a person isn't worthy of the label "gifted" unless he or she synthesizes all three abilities. He argued that without all three components, one can be a decent contributor to society but never a *great* contributor.

The broadened theories of Renzulli, Gardner, and Sternberg were influential in expanding our conceptualizations of giftedness. But you may have noticed that their theories are static: we are simply told that various abilities and traits are important, but we aren't told how they actually develop across the life span. How do ability and motivation get converted to real-world achievement? Are environmental factors important, or does it all come from within? These issues were taken up by the next hottest trend in gifted education: *talent development*.

By the end of the 1980s, the notion of giftedness as a global, enduring essence of a person was in serious trouble. The work of a number of psychologists, including David Henry Feldman, Benjamin Bloom, John Feldhusen, Abraham Tannenbaum, Francois Gagne, and Mihaly Csikszentmihalyi, were all conceptualizing giftedness as talent in a *particular* domain (such as academics, art, music, vocations, social) and *developmental* across the life span. Research shifted away from a focus on the person to the many different ways the person interacts with the environment to achieve in a particular field.[30] *Talent development* became the buzzword in academia.

In 2011, Rena Subotnik, Paula Olszewski-Kubilius, and Frank Worrell proposed a Talent-Development Mega-Model, "a model integrating the most compelling components of already-established models, intended to apply to all domains of endeavor."[31] Drawing on research in human development, expertise, creativity, motivation, and optimal performance, they argue that giftedness is a developmental process that is domain specific and malleable.

They note that prior models haven't been able to predict who achieves eminence, suggesting that there is "a much larger base of talent than is currently being tapped."[32] To overcome these problems, they cast a very wide net of talent domains, including exemplary performers such as singers, instrumentalists, dancers, actors, and athletes, and producers, such as composers, choreographers, writers, and scientists. They point out that there are differences in how performers and producers are identified and developed.

In summary, their model is grounded in five main principles:

1. Abilities, both general and special, matter and can be developed.
2. Domains of talent have varying developmental trajectories.
3. Opportunities need to be provided to young people and taken by them.
4. Psychosocial variables, such as handling setbacks, adjusting anxiety levels, and so on, are determining factors in the successful development of talent.
5. Eminence is the intended outcome of gifted education.

They argue it's important to view the talent development process in stages. Early on, giftedness is determined by potential, whereas the markers for identification turn more to achievement in more advanced grades, and then eventually to eminence in adulthood. They define eminence by how much a person moves the field forward. They also argue that at every stage there are important transitions, where abilities are developed into competencies, competencies are developed into expertise, and expertise is developed into eminence.

But the most controversial aspect of their theory, by a *long shot*, was their proposed goal of gifted education: "increasing the number of individuals who make pathbreaking, field-altering discoveries and creative contributions by their products, innovations, and performances."[33] The implication here is that at some point in development, giftedness becomes what you do, not who you are. This means, of course, that people can flow in and out of giftedness throughout the course of their lives. These authors' paper was really just the zenith of a trend that started in the late 1970s—a trend to open giftedness up to all people, not just the chosen few displaying precocity.[34] This new conception of giftedness as domain-specific and developmental is reflected in the current U.S. federal definition,[35] is the official position of the U.S. National Association for Gifted Children, and is embraced by many psychologists.

But not everyone is on board with a focus on achievement.[36] In his recent book *Serving the Gifted*, Steven Pfeiffer, a psychologist and counselor who has worked with many gifted and talented children over many years, sounds a cautionary note about focusing on achievement: "Potential can become a terrible burden for some children of high ability. We certainly don't want parental thoughts about potential to slip from 'possibility' to 'expectation.' . . . Many children of uncanny ability may decide—and should be encouraged by their parents to decide—to follow their hearts, wherever their life journey may take them."[37]

The shift to a focus on achievement also angered and alienated a whole other cross section of the gifted community, including teachers, parents, counselors, school administrators—even gifted adults—who were quite content with viewing giftedness as *who you are*. As gifted counselor Linda Silverman has noted, "In forsaking the term, gifted, we seem to have abandoned much more than a name. We have chosen to ignore the rich, deep internal milieu from which moral sensitivity and higher level value systems emerge. We have forgotten the Self or soul of the child. This does not appear to be a wise trade."[38]

Let's hear their story next.

Chapter 5

GIFTED SOULS

Spring 1995

I stare at the history exam. With intense effort, I pick up my pencil to fill in the rest of the answers. I hesitate and put the pencil back down on the desk. I know the answers. I can go through the motions. But what's the point? They have given me as much time as I want to complete this test. I have the rest of my life to finish this test. If I ace the test now, or ace it when I'm 40, what's the difference? It's the start of ninth grade, and I'm still in special education. I yearn for more of a challenge. So much more.

I peer out the cracked door into the main corridor. Directly across the hall is the advanced biology classroom, and I can see my friends from the gifted classroom. I feel a sudden impulse to get their attention. I desperately want to say hi. Then it hits me: *I'm saying hi from the resource room.* I still haven't told them I'm in special education. I'm afraid of what they would think of me if they found out.

I've got to hide. I slump down in my seat and put my head down on the table. My heart beats fast. I feel anger, frustration, and anxiety. I start fighting back tears. But I accept my fate.

After a few minutes, I sense that I am being watched. I raise my head and find today's resource room teacher standing across from me. She is looking at me quizzically. While I think she is a special education teacher at our school, I have never seen her before. She smiles, and starts walking toward me. I panic. *Am I in trouble? Am I not acting learning disabled enough?*

"Can we talk outside please?" she asks, as she approaches my desk. We step outside the classroom, and I make sure to stand closest to the door, so she will block me from being seen by my friends across the hall.

For the first time, I look her in the eyes. Almost immediately, I am put at ease. My heartbeat calms down. Something about her demeanor and tone is soothing. She isn't condescending or judgmental. She is different. I can tell she is choosing her words very carefully. "I have been watching you and I can tell you are very bored," she begins. "You don't seem to belong in this classroom. Why are you here?"

I'm taken aback. No one has ever asked me anything like this before. It has not even dawned on me to ask myself that question! I start to open my mouth, and quickly close it. I realize I don't have a good answer. A surge of excitement runs through me. I suddenly realize what I must do. Something I've wanted to do for a long time, but just couldn't. Until now.

I politely excuse myself and start walking toward the school pay-phone. Of course, at this moment, my gifted friends look up and see me walking by. This time, I don't hide. I immediately wave to them. They wave back.

My mom answers the phone. "Why am I still in the resource room?" I ask with urgency. Silence. "I'm not sure," she says finally. "I guess your father and I wanted to make sure you wouldn't be too challenged." My heart starts racing. "But why?" "Well, once you outgrew your childhood hearing difficul-ties, you developed a lot of anxiety and self-doubt. The school administra-tion recommended that you receive more one-on-one support." I clench my fists, as she continues. "Honey, where are you calling from?" I look around and scramble for an answer. The world suddenly clicks. "Well, I was in the resource room," I say. "But not anymore."

That night at dinner, I announce my intention to leave. My parents set up a big meeting with me, my parents, the special education team, and some of the school administration. After much deliberation, they decide I am ready to take on a regular course load—on a "trial basis."

I'm out. I'm free. But I'm also on my own. No more crutches. From now on I will be held to the same standards as the rest of the students. While I'm both elated and terrified, the support for my decision from my parents and administrators gives me strength. I'm done with the anxiety and self-doubt. In fact, I've never been so sure of anything in my entire life: *I'm ready.*

~

Leta Stetter had a traumatic childhood growing up in DeWitt, Nebraska.[1] Her mother passed away immediately after giving birth to Margaret, Leta's youngest sibling. First Leta was raised in a log cabin by her grandparents, and then she was forced to move in with her alcoholic father and stepmother.

Around the age of 10, she decided she was ready to skip right to adulthood. "I decided to grow up then and there, solemnly renouncing the rest of childhood," she later wrote in a letter to her husband.[2]

Writing in her journal, Leta described the pain she felt as beyond "mere emotion," and felt as though her life was a "fiery furnace." When she was only 14, she described her incredibly intense emotions in the touching poem "Lone Pine":

High up, on the peak of the hill-top,
Where the tempests meet in strife,
Thro' the night and the storm and the
darkness
It stands like a lonesome life.

Beaten and scarred and crippled,
By the winds and rain made old,
While the pine trees down in the valley
Are sheltered from storm and cold.

From a barren rock on the summit
Of the hill it lifts its form,
Alike to the warm spring sunshine
And the fury of the storm.

Silent and uncomplaining.
Except when the sad winds moan
Thro' its broken and battered branches,
The tale of a life, alone.

High up where the world may see it,
Sharp outlined against the sky.
While its brothers down in the valley
Unnoticed are all passed by

And the Lone Pine standing patient,
Where the wild winds wage their strife,
Beaten and scarred and crippled,
Like a broken, lonely life,

Is telling again the story,
As the winds thro' its branches moan,
Of a soul lifted high o'er its brothers
That must bear the storm alone.
—L.S.H.[3]

Clearly having a way with words, at the age of 16 the precocious Stetter entered the University of Nebraska, where she gained accolades for her poignant creative writing. It was there that she met her future husband, Henry Hollingworth, who described her as "small, lithe, and graceful, with a lively gait and a characteristic lilt to her gestures . . . she was full of enthusiasm and animation, unpretending and friendly."[4]

Leta and Henry soon became engaged. Unfortunately, just as soon they were forced to separate. Henry graduated before Leta and moved to New York City to enter a graduate program at Columbia University. A few years later he received an assistant professorship at Barnard College: with more money in hand, he invited her to join him in the city. In 1908, the year they married, Leta stepped foot in the Big Apple. She arrived with a BA, a state teacher's certificate, and experience as an assistant principal of a high school in Nebraska, but she was unable to secure any teaching position. Not only that, but when she tried to obtain funding for graduate education in literature, she was denied a number of scholarships.

The problem seemed to be her marital status: married women were just not expected to leave the household and create a unique identity for themselves. Undoubtedly this experience contributed to her deep sense of injustice and belief that all people should have the opportunity to succeed. So she turned her energies to the field of education. Soon after obtaining a master's in education at Columbia University, an opportunity arose to work part-time at the Clearing House for Mental Defectives administering the Binet-Simon scale to individuals with mental disabilities. She observed that many of the so-called mentally defective children had quite normal intelligence but were having difficulty adjusting to adolescence. She would eventually publish three books on the topic, including *The Psychology of the Adolescent*, which became one of the most prominent textbooks in the field.[5]

In 1914 Hollingworth became the first psychologist ever to enter the civil service in New York City.[6] Working at Bellevue Hospital administering tests, she quickly gained a reputation as a stellar examiner. While still at Bellevue, she also completed her PhD at Columbia under the supervision of Edward Thorndike. She used her doctoral studies as an opportunity to challenge the prevailing dogma of the time about the nature of women.

With doctorate in hand, in 1916 she accepted a professor position at Teachers College, Columbia, a post she would hold until her death. This year, 1916, which was also when Terman introduced his revision of the Binet-Simon scale (see Chapter 2), would change Hollingworth's life. Taking over a course on mentally disabled children from her predecessor Naomi Norsworthy (the course was called "Inheriting"), she decided to provide an example to her students of the contrast between the extreme ends of the bell curve.

Hollingworth asked teachers to nominate an exceptionally intelligent individual. A child at the nearby Horace Mann School was brought forward. To her shock, the 8-year-old scored an IQ of 187. She became fascinated with "Child E" (as she would refer to him). At the time, no provisions were in place for children who scored so high on an IQ test. Her deeply ingrained sense of injustice was on high alert as she wondered: What were the unique emotional needs of these children?

Unlike others at the time, who were mostly concerned with stamping a label on the high-IQ child's forehead, Hollingworth took the time to really get to know children with high IQs, including their backgrounds, families, personalities, and physical and social needs. Through her investigations with high-IQ children, Hollingworth observed that adults ignored these children because they assumed they would achieve on their own, without any assistance. She also noted that children with high IQ scores often faced social isolation.

Many of the children she studied also displayed heightened levels of solitary play (skating, swimming, horseback riding, running, reading, collecting objects, and so on), and many also invented imaginary friends and lands because of their difficulty relating to peers of their own age. In addition, some of the children who were accelerated were frequently terrorized by their older classmates. Hollingworth pointed out that "the more intelligent a person is, regardless of age, the less often can he find a truly congenial companion."[7]

Hollingworth was a strong believer that highly gifted children have special emotional needs because of their early advanced cognitive ability—having to navigate their worlds with "the intelligence of an adult and the emotions of a child"—which put them out of sync with their peers. She argued that one of the symptoms of a heightened intellect is an early interest in "origins" and "destinies": "The higher the IQ the earlier does the pressing need for an explanation of the universe occur, the sooner does the demand for a concept of the origin and destiny of the self appear."[8]

Hollingworth found that children scoring in the 125–155 range on the Stanford-Binet were confident, outgoing individuals. She argued, however, that not all gifted students are alike, with moderately and extremely gifted children having different developmental needs. She observed that those with an IQ above 180 (1 in a million) displayed the most severe adjustment problems because they were not being challenged. In her posthumously published book *Children above 180 IQ*, she presented case studies of 12 children with IQs of about 180, who mostly came from the Speyer School in Harlem.[9] Based on her observations, she posed the following question: "In the ordinary elementary school situation, children of IQ 140 waste half their time. Those above IQ 170 waste practically all their time. With little to do, how can these children develop power of sustained effort, respect for the task, or habits of steady work?"[10]

Hollingworth set up full-time, self-contained classes where these high-IQ children experienced challenging, fast-paced instruction, with classroom discussion, group projects, and self-directed learning. Children with high IQs learned about a wide range of disciplines, including history, biography, literature, and foreign languages. She had a special curriculum called "Evolution of Common Things," where children learned about practical matters such as food, shelter, clothing, transport, tools, time keeping, and communication. Hollingworth felt this form of learning was more beneficial to gifted children than forcing them to take advanced college courses. She also taught them other important skills, such as how to handle the foolishness of others with patience and love, balance candor with tact, and engage in masterful argumentation and public debate.

What Hollingworth discovered delighted and vindicated her: when children were grouped with children of similar ability, many of their earlier vulnerabilities disappeared. A three-year follow-up found that children in her program developed a love of learning, were happy, and were thankful to finally find true peers who shared their intellectual interests. Much longer follow-ups showed that her program had a lifelong influence on the students' friendships, values, and achievement.[11]

In 1938, over a four-month period, Hollingworth watched 2 of the 12 high-IQ children in her study pass away. These were children she knew very well, whom she had taken the time to get to know fully. But for ten years Hollingworth had been secretly battling her own physical illness, not even telling her husband about her suffering. Less than a year after the death of "Child F," Hollingworth passed away of abdominal cancer, the very same calamity that claimed Child F's life. Hollingworth's work was left unfinished.

Nevertheless, her legacy continues. Leta Stetter Hollingworth was a seminal early figure in psychology, and an inspiration to many women. She was listed in *American Men of Science* and was one of only fourteen women to be included in Watson's *Eminent Contributors to Psychology*. Hollingworth's influence on parents, practitioners, and counselors runs deep. If Terman was the godfather of gifted child identification, Hollingworth was the godmother of gifted child *understanding*. She practically invented the child-centered approach to giftedness. According to psychologist Barbara Kerr, Hollingworth is the "first and greatest counselor to the gifted and talented."[12]

∼

The year of Hollingworth's death, Annemarie and George Roeper arrived in New York City. As Holocaust survivors, they were excited to start life anew. They came with a purpose: to ease the pain and suffering of children. After a few years they founded the Roeper City and Country School in Bloomfield Hills, Michigan. Their mission was to create an environment where children could be free of hostility and bullying.

Like Hollingworth, they became aware of the emotional characteristics and educational needs of the academically advanced children.[13] Roeper urged people to custom tailor the curriculum to the inner, emotional lives of these gifted children: "It is this inner self, the unique self of each human being that is the central point of their lives."[14] Roeper believed that the emotional, intellectual, and physical realms could not be viewed in isolation.

By 1956 the Roeper School officially became a school for the gifted. All new applicants were evaluated by the use of a combination of IQ tests, observations, and interviews. Annemarie and her husband would often estimate the applicant's IQ score, and she noted that their assessment would almost always be in agreement with the score. But she also recalled that sometimes their intelligence assessment was higher than the child's IQ score, and on occasion even the child herself felt as though the test score didn't fully capture her intelligence. As Roeper recalls, "It became more and more clear that the IQ test gave us only a partial answer, namely, one that revealed the cognitive but not the emotional and spiritual characteristics of the gifted."[15]

Roeper and her husband also founded *The Roeper Review*, an academic journal with the purpose of presenting research on the emotional and social needs of gifted children. When they retired in 1983, they moved to California and opened the Roeper Consultation Service for the Gifted, where they developed and put into practice the Method of Qualitative Assessment (QA): "If we are to understand children and their behavior, we must honor their inner world, relate to the unconscious as well as the conscious, and to the emotional as well as the cognitive. Education needs a clinical and developmental approach to assessment."[16]

Roeper's approach was a call for practitioners to incorporate empathy and intuition into the assessment process, as well as their knowledge and experience of the characteristics of gifted children. Roeper argued that the gifted child exhibits a number of characteristics, including heightened empathy, a strong sense of justice, perfectionism, acute sensitivity, intensity, and an all-encompassing passion. The QA technique was designed to provide a safe environment for the children to express themselves through mutual understanding and trust, without expectations for any particular performance. According to Roeper, "The goal is not for children to show how much they know or how bright they are, but to show who they are."[17]

The centerpiece of the QA technique is the interview with the child. During the course of the interview, the evaluator observes the child's manner, personality, and style of answering questions. Afterward a careful report is prepared by the examiner, in which a large amount of information is taken into consideration, including the child's characteristics and thoughts, as well as family and developmental background. This method sounds very similar to Alan Kaufman's intelligent testing approach (see Chapter 3), but without the use of the IQ test.

According to Roeper, "Evaluators need to look at the whole process like a piece of art that is created by the encounter of the family, especially the child, with the evaluator. By the end, something new has been created—a dance, a work of art, a symphony. In the process, the soul of a child gets recognized, and the degree of giftedness of the child gets understood."[18]

What is this soul she speaks of? Roeper herself was not sure. Nevertheless, she noted, "In the 40-plus years I have worked with gifted children, I have seen more than a thousand of them. I continue to be in awe of each young soul whom I am privileged to get to know. I have learned a great deal about each Self. I've experienced their emotions, anxieties, joys, passions, and ambitions, and I see that each Self is perfect in itself. It is only when we start comparing them to each other that we begin to see imperfection."[19]

Like many who adopt a person-centered approach today, Roeper firmly believed that children should not be seen for their potential but who they are as a person. "Do we want to use the child for our own purposes, using his talents for ourselves? Or do we want to help him find a place for his sacred Self in this world?"[20]

~

By the early 1990s there was a growing unrest among a certain segment of the gifted community over the talent development approach to giftedness. A number of gifted counselors and psychologists—who were deeply influenced by Hollingworth and Roeper—gathered at a conference in Ohio to discuss the work of Polish psychiatrist Kazimierz Dabrowski. Many in the gifted community felt that his Theory of Positive Disintegration—which focuses on levels of intensity—perfectly described the emotional characteristics of gifted children.[21]

Dabrowski believed that emotional development is the most important dimension of life and that intensity represents the potential for further growth. Figure 5.1 is a description of Dabrowski's five forms of "psychic overexcitability" by gifted advocate Michael Piechowski.[22]

Some researchers in the gifted community have attempted to quantitatively measure Dabrowski's overexcitabilities using various methods, such as self-report questionnaires, teacher ratings, interviews, case studies, and neurological testing. So far the only group of individuals that consistently report high levels of Dabrowski's intensities are creative adults, particularly artists (see Chapter 12). For children and adults with high IQs the results are much more mixed.[23]

One recent study found that high-IQ adults scored higher only on "intellectual overexcitability," and the accuracy of prediction based on group membership (gifted/nongifted) was only 60.4 percent.[24] Clearly more research needs to be conducted on this important topic, and one must be careful not to assume that intensity will be an automatic consequence of having a high IQ score. People all across the IQ spectrum experience Dabrowski's overexcitabilities. Nevertheless, some people in the gifted community have found that these intensities accurately describe the characteristics of the children they have personally worked with.

PSYCHOMOTOR OVEREXCITABILITY

THE MANIFESTATIONS OF PSYCHOMOTOR EXCITABILITY ARE ESSENTIALLY OF TWO KINDS: SURPLUS OF ENERGY AND NERVOUSNESS. IN NERVOUSNESS, THE EMOTIONAL TENSION IS TRANSLATED INTO PSYCHOMOTOR ACTIVITY SUCH AS TICS, NAIL BITING, OR IMPULSIVE BEHAVIOR. THE SURPLUS OF ENERGY CAN BE OBSERVED IN ANIMATED GESTURES AND TAKING ON SELF-IMPROVEMENT TASKS.

SENSUAL OVEREXCITABILITY

SENSUAL OVEREXCITABILITY IS EXPRESSED IN HEIGHTENED EXPERIENCING OF SENSORY PLEASURES AND IN SEEKING SENSUAL OUTLETS FOR INNER TENSION. OTHER MANIFESTATIONS OF SENSUAL OVEREXCITABILITY INCLUDE MARKED INTEREST IN CLOTHES AND APPEARANCE, FONDNESS OF JEWELRY AND ORNAMENTS.

INTELLECTUAL OVEREXCITABILITY

THE MANIFESTATIONS OF INTELLECTUAL OVEREXCITABILITY ARE ASSOCIATED WITH AN INTENSIFIED AND ACCELERATED ACTIVITY OF THE MIND. ITS STRONGEST EXPRESSIONS HAVE MORE TO DO WITH STRIVING FOR UNDERSTANDING, PROBING THE UNKNOWN, AND LOVE OF TRUTH THAN WITH LEARNING PER SE OR ACADEMIC ACHIEVEMENT.

IMAGINATIONAL OVEREXCITABILITY

THE PRESENCE OF IMAGINATIONAL OVEREXCITABILITY CAN BE INFERRED FROM FREQUENT DISTRACTION, WANDERING ATTENTION, AND DAYDREAMING. THESE OCCUR AS CONSEQUENCE OF FREE PLAY OF THE IMAGINATION. HERE, TOO, BELONG ILLUSIONS, ANIMISTIC THINKING, EXPRESSIVE IMAGE AND METAPHOR, INVENTION AND FANTASY.

EMOTIONAL OVEREXCITABILITY

AMONG THE FIVE FORMS OF PSYCHIC OVEREXCITABILITY, THE MANIFESTATIONS OF EMOTIONAL OVEREXCITABILITY ARE THE MOST NUMEROUS. THEY INCLUDE CERTAIN CHARACTERISTIC AND EASILY RECOGNIZABLE SOMATIC EXPRESSIONS, EXTREMES OF FEELING, INHIBITION, STRONG AFFECTIVE MEMORY, CONCERN WITH DEATH, ANXIETIES, FEARS, FEELINGS OF GUILT, AND DEPRESSIVE AND SUICIDAL MOODS.

FIGURE 5.1. DABROWSKI'S OVEREXCITABILITIES

Source: M. M. Piechowski, "Developmental Potential," in *New Voices in Counseling the Gifted*, ed. N. Colangelo and R. T. Zaffrann, 25–57 (Dubuque, IA: Kendall Hunt, 1979).

When people gathered at the conference on Dabrowski in Ohio, the talent development model of giftedness was in full swing, and a large number of practitioners felt that the focus on achievement was ignoring the emotional needs of gifted children. Writer and gifted advocate Stephanie Tolan, who was living in Columbus, Ohio, at the time, recognized this growing unrest and invited a small gathering of folks to meet at her house after the conference for discussion.[25]

The meeting took place in Tolan's living room. In attendance were five women, all of whom had extensive experience working directly with gifted children and their families. In addition to Tolan herself, they were Linda Silverman, Kathi Kearney (who was working on her PhD at Columbia University under the advisement of James Borland), gifted educator Dr. Christine Garrison (who is now Christine Neville), and Martha Morelock, who was working on her PhD in child development at Tufts under the advisement of David Henry Feldman, a world-renowned expert on child prodigies (Morelock was also well published by this point).

One thing they all agreed on immediately was their disdain for the talent development model of giftedness that was so popular in academic circles. In discussing the commonalities of the children they worked with, they noted that the children appeared out of sync with expectations, norms, and averages, making them appear many ages at once. They felt this left these children vulnerable, giving them special emotional and social needs. They tried to come up with a new definition of giftedness to adequately capture these characteristics.

After many hours of discussion, they decided "asynchronous" was a good word for what they were trying to describe. They couldn't find it in a dictionary, so they called the Columbus Public Library's research division and found out that the word was not in use outside of a computer context. So they adopted the word and decided on "asynchronous development." After many more hours of discussion, they crafted the following definition of giftedness:

Giftedness is asynchronous development in which advanced cognitive abilities and heightened intensity combine to create inner experiences and awareness that are qualitatively different from the norm. This asynchrony increases with higher intellectual capacity. The uniqueness of the gifted renders them particularly vulnerable and requires modifications in parenting, teaching and counseling in order for them to develop optimally.[26]

Morelock volunteered to write the first official article presenting the definition to the world. Their only problem: they had to figure out how they were going to cite the definition. They recognized that they weren't academics with impressive credentials and were in danger of being personally attacked by academics for their definition. After someone mentioned the quote "It is amazing what you can accomplish if you do not care who gets the credit," they decided to remain anonymous. Since Morelock's article would be released during the 500th anniversary of Columbus's discovery of America, and the meeting was taking place in Columbus, Ohio, they decided to refer to themselves as the Columbus Group.

In January 1992, Morelock's article "Giftedness: The View from Within" was released, including the anonymous citation of the Columbus Group.[27] As predicted, their definition of giftedness made a big splash among a wide cross section of the gifted community, including parents, counselors, and teachers. The emphasis on the child's emotional needs resonated much more among those who worked personally with this special population of children than did the talent development approach, which emphasized the development of talent for the use of society.

The Columbus definition highlighted something very real: children who are out of sync with expectations are vulnerable in a number of ways, particularly to bullying.[28] In fact, people who lie outside the norm on *any* trait often feel misunderstood in school, at work, in the larger community, and sometimes even in their own families.

∾

We've been through quite a journey so far. We've reviewed the identification of learning disabilities (Chapter 3), the talent development approach to giftedness (Chapter 4), and the person-centered approach to giftedness. Along the way we reviewed different conceptualizations of giftedness, expanding not just the abilities spectrum but also the emotional spectrum. But at no point did I actually tell you about the current state of affairs in the United States. With all the heated debates, where are we *really*? Has anything actually changed since the Terman days?

To see where we're at, Mary-Catherine McClain and Steven Pfeiffer recently conducted a national survey of current state policies and practices to assess how states define giftedness, identify giftedness, and accommodate gifted minority students.[29] Nearly all U.S. states (48 out of 50) today have established definitions of giftedness. The two exceptions are Massachusetts and South Dakota, who have no current definition for gifted and talented students.

Even so, states differ quite a bit in how they define giftedness. Some states stick with the label "gifted," whereas others use more expansive definitions, including "gifted and talented" or "high ability students." Also, 24 states explicitly changed or modified their definition of giftedness over the past decade. For example, Indiana's definition changed from "gifted and talented" to "high ability."

What areas of giftedness are included in state definitions? *Intelligence* and *high achievement* are still two of the big winners. Forty-five state definitions (90 percent) include intelligence as an area or category of giftedness, and 39 include high achievement. Interestingly, 27 states include creativity (54 percent). Twenty-eight states include a specific area of giftedness, and 15 states include leadership skills. Motivation and the performing arts are seriously lacking in definitions of giftedness, with only three states thinking either of these were an important aspect of giftedness.

There have been some changes in the past ten years, but these changes don't necessarily indicate progress. More schools now include intelligence in their definition of giftedness, and fewer schools view creativity as a form of giftedness. Also, since 2000, New Jersey, New Hampshire, and Minnesota developed state definitions for giftedness, Maryland added the category "leadership," and Georgia removed "leadership" and "artistic" from their state definition.

So that's how states *define* giftedness. What methods do they use to identify giftedness? Do they practice what they preach? Again, the clear winners for identifying giftedness are the use of IQ global scores and standardized achievement tests. The biggest losers are tests of creativity, teacher rating scales, indicators of actual performance, and the use of behavior checklists. Teacher nominations came in third place, and *no state in the United States included any form of motivation whatsoever as a required identification method.* Compared to earlier reports, there was only a small overall change nationwide with respect to how states identify gifted students. Of particular note, no state reported using a single IQ score alone to determine whether a student is gifted. This is actually a pretty big deal, and a huge change from just twenty years ago and certainly a change from the Terman era.

Instead, most states (54 percent) use a *multiple cutoff* or *averaging approach*. The multiple cutoff model requires that students score above a set score on two or more different measures. The averaging approach is similar to the multiple cutoff approach, but the student doesn't have to show the same level of threshold across different domains. Seven states (14 percent) use a *single cutoff: flexible* model, in which only one outcome is considered, but school districts can be flexible in terms of which test and threshold is allowable. Sixteen states (32 percent) report that they do not require, recommend, or adhere to any one specific criterion for identifying gifted students. Most states (64 percent) do not use specific tests or cutoff scores for gifted eligibility in their state. With that said, 18 states *do* use a specific cutoff on IQ tests, with 15 of those 18 using specific cutoff scores on standardized tests of achievement and 10 of the 17 using cutoff scores in one or more specific areas of academic ability.

What about minority students? It is no secret that minority students are seriously underrepresented in gifted education programs in the United States.[30] About half of the states recognize that some groups of students are less likely to do as well on traditional methods of gifted identification and would benefit from flexible and nontraditional gifted identification procedures. Twenty-six states have specific policies for identifying culturally diverse students, and the remaining 24 states have no specific cultural diversity mandates. To give an example of such a mandate, Georgia allows educators to use a measure in any area of giftedness when there is clear evidence of culture, language development, disability, or economic disadvantage and the initial test score is within one standard error of measurement or standard deviation of the qualifying score.

Let's reflect on all this for a moment. Even with all the nuanced debates and expanded definitions of "learning disabilities" and "giftedness," *no one* is winning. Not the multiple intelligence folks, not the talent development folks, and certainly not the child-centered folks. No one. Strict IQ cutoffs are still used on a regular basis all around the globe. Global IQ scores still take precedence over the many specific CHC cognitive abilities and nonacademic talents (such as music, art) on offer. Testing is still a one-shot deal—either you were born gifted or you weren't. Morality, intensity, sensitivity, compassion, creativity, and leadership are almost completely absent from both the stated definitions of giftedness and the actual identification procedures. And perhaps the *most* striking absence from any state definition of giftedness is motivation and engagement. They aren't even on the radar. Looks like we still have a long way to go.

Chapter 6

PASSION

The first summer after I leave the resource room, I take a course in non-Western history so I can start catching up to my peers.

Summer 1995

"We are one of the best orchestras in the state." We are supposed to be doing group work, but I am far more interested in hearing about the school orchestra from one of their leading violinists. "So, let me get this straight," I say, focusing intensely on her. "You get to take trips around the country, and perform in front of sold-out audiences?" She nods. Images from my early childhood flash into my head. The Philadelphia Orchestra. The Academy of Music. Loud applause. Standing ovations. The music. The rush. My grandfather smiling at me from the stage.

Immediately after class, I find my way to the orchestra room. I enter the room, and find the conductor alone in the room, tuning a violin. "Can I sign up for your orchestra?" I mumble. "What instrument do you play?" he asks me. Fair question. Apparently I hadn't thought this whole thing through.

"I don't play anything yet, but I will play cello in time for the start of the school year," I say decisively, regaining my composure. He has a quizzical look on his face. "Who's your teacher?" he asks. Without skipping a beat, I say the name of my grandfather: "Harry Gorodetzer." He pauses for a moment, scratches his head, and says, "OK. Go ahead, sign up."

∾

I ring the doorbell to my grandparents' house. I look through the window of my grandfather's practice room and see his hands gliding across his cello in that familiar way I have seen so many times on stage. My grandmother lets me in and tells me to interrupt him to tell him the good news. "Ever since he retired from the Orchestra, he doesn't know what to do with himself," she says. "He will be so pleased to teach you."

As I approach his study, I hear the same sequence of notes played repeatedly. I am hesitant to disturb his practicing, but I can't wait to tell him. "So, I was thinking of learning the cello," I announce as I enter the room. He looks up with an expression of intense concentration and puts down his bow on the music stand. He motions for me to sit on the sofa next to him.

"That's wonderful. When would you like to begin?" he asks. I look at his cello. He sees me looking at his cello. I suddenly feel an overpowering urge to play it. To just take his bow and do exactly what he does.

"Go ahead," he says, motioning me to sit down. I feel giddy. He moves out of the way, and I take a seat in this great musician's chair. I place the cello between my legs and pick up the bow. I scratch the bow against the first string. I take a finger and put it on the string and move the bow again. I remove the finger and put the finger back. I repeatedly do this, alternating where I place my finger on the first string. With each step, I get more and more immersed in what I'm doing, and start to forget where I am. It feels so natural. Something about the instrument, and the classical music structure, seems to gel with me. My heart is racing, and I feel intense excitement over the new object of my exploration.

After about fifteen minutes, I snap back to reality. I look up to see a full smile across my grandfather's face. "Scott, that is incredible," he says, breathless. "You just learned how to play the A, C, and E major scales on your own." I can barely contain my excitement. "The what scales?" I respond. He laughs. "Don't worry, I'll teach you. You may just be ready for the school orchestra in time for the school year after all."

∾

Go to virtually any preschool or elementary classroom, and you'll witness something rare: *excitement.* Whether it's engagement in painting, make-believe games, or learning why the moon disappears, there appear to be very few young children with deficits in motivation. Children love learning. They *want* to figure out what this new, shiny world of theirs is all about.

Contrast this with a typical middle school or high school classroom. They can't wait to get done with school and go on to "after-school" activities. You ask them what they think of school, and many will say it's dull, boring, and dry. Systematic studies show that intrinsic motivation decreases steadily starting from about third grade.[1] What explains this motivation epidemic?

Over the past half century, researchers from the "social cognitive" perspective have shown us the dynamic, multifaceted, and contextual nature of motivation. As Elizabeth Linnenbrink and Paul Pintrich put it, "social cognitive models stress that students can be motivated in multiple ways and the important issue is understanding how and why students are motivated for school achievement. This change in focus implies that teachers or school psychologists should not label students as 'motivated' or 'not motivated' in some global fashion."[2]

To understand how motivation works, it's helpful to get under the hood and consider the neurotransmitter dopamine. Dopamine is an ancient molecule, but it plays a unique role in humans, fueling some of our most uniquely human cognitive abilities, including working memory, cognitive flexibility, abstract reasoning, and creativity. Indeed, Fred Previc has argued that the human cultural flourishing seen about 70,000 years ago was due to an expansion of our dopaminergic system.[3]

Dopamine also plays a crucial role in motivation. Dopamine has activating effects on cognition and behavior, pulling us to engage in the world and with ideas. While dopamine is often mentioned in association with pleasure, this is actually a very common misconception. Although we typically enjoy emotions such as pleasure and satisfaction, dopamine does not, in fact, arouse these emotions.

Instead, its primary role is in making people *want* things. Dopamine arouses emotions such as desire, excitement, and hope. The dopaminergic system goes crazy when there is a *possibility* of a big payoff, especially when the risk is high (as in casinos). But once you obtain the object of your desire, dopamine offers no guarantee that you will necessarily *like* what you obtained. So while dopamine *can* make us feel good, it doesn't *necessarily* make us feel good. Because of these features of dopamine, Kent Berridge argues that dopamine's primary role in behavior is "incentive motivation," influencing our attention and making things that are relevant to our personal interests more salient than other things.*[4]

The fact that wanting and liking are different systems in the brain can lead to all sorts of seemingly irrational behavior, such as wanting things you

---

*Technically, Berridge is referring to the mesolimbic dopaminergic system, which has projections to areas of the brain associated with emotion and the learning of reward values, including the medial prefrontal cortex, nucleus accumbens, amygdala, and hippocampus. Note there are other dopaminergic pathways in the brain involved in motor behavior and working memory. I discuss some of these pathways in Chapter 12.

don't currently expect to like, wanting things you consciously remember you hated, and wanting things you *know* you won't like once obtained. Drug users show increased production of dopamine when they see any cue relating to drugs, even if they don't actually enjoy being addicted. The dopamine pathway can cause two people to anticipate passionate sex at the slightest cue of each other, even if they can't stand each other as people. Dopamine also explains why people frequently experience separation anxiety when separated from their iPhones, even if they despise being a slave to the machine.

Our knowledge of dopamine helps us understand motivation in a number of ways. For one, there is research showing that some people are more willing to put in a greater effort to accomplish a dull task, and these people show increases in dopamine production when the potential monetary payoff is high.[5] Therefore, individual differences in dopamine production relate to decision making and motivation.

But I believe the most important take-away message from the inner workings of dopamine for our understanding of motivation is just how much engagement is based on prior learning experiences—both positive and negative—and the expectations that are learned based on those experiences. Rather than focus on how to make people more motivated for the possibility of *external rewards* (such as money, grades), we should focus, instead, on creating the learning conditions, experiences, and positive expectations that will make it more likely that students will both *want* and *like* to engage in school and the world.

∾

One of the most prominent and well-studied factors influencing intrinsic motivation—going all the back to John Dewey and Jerome Bruner—is the decontextualization of learning and instruction.[6] As students get older, instruction is increasingly stripped of its real-world context. But context sometimes makes all the difference.

In one pathbreaking set of studies, Stephen Ceci and Urie Bronfenbrenner asked 10-year-old children to predict the destination of a shape on a computer screen by using a joystick to move the cursor to the predicted location.[7] The shape took the form of either a square, a circle, or a triangle, and the objects had different sizes and color. The underlying rules of movement were quite simple. Squares always went up, circles always went down, and triangles always remained horizontal. Large objects moved right, small objects moved left, dark-colored objects traveled a wide distance, and light-colored objects moved a only short distance. After 750 chances, the children couldn't predict the direction of the objects better than chance, only getting it right 22 percent of the time.

Then the researchers turned the task into a game. Triangles, circles, and squares became birds, butterflies, and bumblebees. Rather than being asked to point to the location they thought an object would move to, they were asked to move a cursor resembling a butterfly net to "capture the prey." Children were rewarded points for each correct capture, and sound effects were added to indicate that the child had earned points. In this context, virtually *all* of the children learned the rules perfectly within the first 400 trials. In another study, they made the rules even more complex, and again found a substantial improvement when the game was put within the context of a motivating video game. Ceci notes, "These data would seem to dispel the belief that young children are . . . incapable of grasping more complex, multiplicative models. Had the children been tested in only the disembedded laboratory context (squares, circles, etc.), a vastly underrated estimation of their competence would have resulted."[8]

In a 1994 comprehensive review of research spanning continents, social classes, and levels of formal education, Ceci and Antonio Roazzi concluded that the context in which learning occurs has an enormous influence on the manifestation of a person's intelligence by influencing the person's interpretation of the task, and activating specific knowledge representations and strategies that are not activated when the task is decontextualized.[9] "Neither context nor cognition can be understood in isolation; they form an integrated system in which the cognitive skill in question becomes part of the context. To try to assess them separately is akin to trying to assess the beauty of a smile separately from the face it is part of."[10]

Contextualized tasks can lead to a greater sense of competence, but that's only one fundamental human psychological need. According to Edward Deci and Richard Ryan's self-determination theory (SDT), tasks that are intrinsically motivating satisfy the basic human psychological needs for competence (the desire to feel capable of mastery and accomplishment), autonomy (the desire to feel in control of one's decisions), and relatedness (a desire to feel a sense of connections with peers).[11] A number of studies show that tasks that satisfy all three of these basic strivings lead to the highest levels of intrinsic motivation.

Consider a series of studies conducted by Maarten Vansteenkiste and colleagues on the importance of autonomy among a diverse sample of preschool teachers in training, college students majoring in marketing, and high school students.[12] They found that students tended to show better learning outcomes when the material was framed in terms of intrinsic goals (such as personal growth, health, or community contribution) rather than extrinsic goals (such as money, an attractive image). What's more, they found an increase in learning outcomes when the students were made to feel as though they had choice over their actions (for instance, using phrases such as "you can" and "if you choose" in the instructions) rather than being made to feel as though they were being controlled (using phrases such as "you must" and "you have to" in instructions). Importantly, there was an interaction: intrinsic goals and autonomy worked synergistically to produce lower levels of superficial processing of the material, more deep processing, greater persistence, and higher levels of performance.

Bringing these various threads together, Diana Cordova and Mark Lepper designed a clever experiment to investigate the effects of contextualization, personalization, and choice on intrinsic motivation.[13] They presented fourth- and fifth- grade schoolchildren with a game that taught arithmetical and problem-solving skills, such as the hierarchy of the order of operations and the proper use of parentheses in arithmetic expressions.

While all of their experimental conditions involved the same instructional content, they added various elements to the other conditions. In one condition they added the element of fantasy. For instance, in "Space Quest" students were encouraged to imagine themselves as commanders of a space fleet with the mission of saving the Earth from an energy crisis by traveling to a faraway planet in search of an alternative energy source. In another fantasy context called "Treasure Hunt," children were encouraged to imagine themselves as the captain of a ship in search of an ancient treasure buried on a deserted island.

In another condition they personalized aspects of the game (such as including the participant's name and birthday) based on background information they obtained from the students before the experiment. And in another condition they gave participants choices over instructionally irrelevant aspects of the fantasy, such as choosing icons that best represented themselves and their computer, as well as naming their characters and their opponents' characters. A week after the games were played, the students who were in the conditions explicitly designed to increase intrinsic interest showed greater learning and retention of the abstract mathematical material using standard written tests administered outside of the computer context.

They also found effects on various indices of intrinsic motivation, including more deep involvement in the activities, the use of more complex operations, and the reporting of higher levels of interest, enjoyment, and perceived competence compared to those who took part in the decontextualized version of the game, removed of any fantasy. The *biggest* increases in intrinsic motivation, however, were found when personalization or personal choice was added to the fantasy context. What is so striking about this study is that such effects on intrinsic motivation were found despite the fact that all of the students received the same exact instructions and the same exact problems across all of the conditions. The only difference was the enhancement of contextualization, personalization, and choice.

Another incredibly important, but often overlooked, activator of intrinsic motivation is *inspiration*. Inspiration awakens us to new possibilities by allowing us to transcend our ordinary experiences and limitations. Inspiration propels a person from apathy to possibility, and transforms the way a person perceives of his or her own capabilities. Inspiration may sometimes be overlooked because of its elusive nature. Its history of being treated as supernatural or divine hasn't helped the situation. But a number of recent studies suggest that inspiration can be activated, captured, and manipulated, and has a major effect on engagement and achievement.

Todd Thrash and Andrew Elliot note three core aspects of inspiration: evocation, transcendence, and approach motivation.[14] First, inspiration is evoked spontaneously and without intention by some force—whether it's a sudden insight that comes from within or an encounter with an inspiring person such as a role model. Inspiration is also transcendent of our more self-serving concerns and limitations. Such transcendence often involves a moment of clarity and awareness of new possibilities. "The heights of human motivation spring from the beauty and goodness that precede us and awaken us to better possibilities."[15] This moment of clarity is often vivid, and can take the form of a grand vision or a "seeing" of something that one has not seen before (but that was probably always there). Finally, inspiration involves approach motivation, in which the individual strives to transmit, express, or actualize a new idea or vision. According to Thrash and Elliot, inspiration involves both being inspired by something and acting on that inspiration.

As a first pass to capture inspiration in the laboratory, Thrash and Elliot developed the "Inspiration Scale," which measures the frequency of experiencing inspiration.[16] They found that inspired people were more intrinsically motivated and less extrinsically motivated. Inspired people were also more open to new experiences and reported more absorption and flow in their activities (see Chapter 12). Inspired individuals also reported having a stronger drive to master their work, but were less competitive. Inspiration was least related to variables that involve agency (such as conscientiousness) or the enhancement of resources, consistent with the transcendent nature of inspiration. Inspired people also reported higher levels of psychological resources, including belief in their own abilities, self-esteem, and optimism. Inspired people also viewed themselves as more creative and showed actual increases in self-ratings of creativity over time. Patent-holding inventors reported being inspired more frequently and intensely than did those who did not hold patents, and the higher the frequency of inspiration, the higher the number of patents held.

Inspiration is also important for making progress toward goals. In a recent study conducted by Marina Milyavskaya and her colleagues, college students were asked to report three goals they intended to accomplish during the semester, and then they reported on their progress three times a month.[17] Those who scored higher on the Inspiration Scale displayed increased goal progress, and their progress was a result of setting more inspired goals. These results held even after taking into account other personality traits. Importantly, the relationship between inspiration and goal progress was reciprocal: goal progress also predicted future goal inspiration. Noted the researchers, "This suggests that goal progress and goal inspiration build on each other to form a cycle of greater goal inspiration and greater goal pursuit."[18]

While these studies focused on inspiration as a stable trait, other studies show that inspiration is also a *state of being* that can be turned on and off by an inspiring memory, role model, or story.[19] One study found that the state of inspiration predicted the creativity of writing above and beyond sheer effort and SAT verbal scores.[20] Taken together, these findings support a clear conclusion: engagement matters, and it can be activated by a clear set of conditions. But what happens when mere engagement becomes a *passion*?

∽

When Robert Vallerand and his colleagues started their research on passion in the late 1990s, they didn't have much to build on. While philosophers, such as Spinoza, Descartes, and Hegel, engaged in passionate debates about the merits of passion, the existing psychological research was focused mainly on romantic passion.[21] Of course, there was a growing literature on intrinsic motivation, but they felt as though ephemeral, fleeting interests weren't quite the same thing as a sustained love for an activity. People can have intrinsic motivation for an activity without a deep internalization of the activity into the core essence of their being. Vallerand and his colleagues were grasping for something, well, more passionate.

To address this gap in the literature, they proposed a new theory, grounded in self-determination theory. They argued that everyone has a preference for some activity, but the reason an activity is preferable and enjoyable is because it satisfies the basic human needs for autonomy, competence, and relatedness. Over time these activities can eventually become a central part of a person's identity. For instance, while intrinsic motivation involves feeling joy from playing basketball, passion involves *being* a basketball player.[22]

Vallerand and colleagues defined passion as "a strong inclination toward an activity that people like, that they find important, and in which they invest time and energy."[23] They also made a crucial distinction between two different flavors of passion: harmonious and obsessive. The defining difference is how the person's activity has been internalized into their identity. People who are obsessively passionate have lost control of their activity. They feel pressure to engage in their activity either because of contingencies such as social acceptance or self-esteem, or because of an uncontrollable urge. They often can't disengage until the compulsion runs its course. What's more, their activity has not been well integrated into their overall self-concept. Their ego is dependent on the activity, and their rigid persistence frequently conflicts with other aspects of their lives.

In contrast, harmonious passion stems from a sense of freedom. The person feels in control of their activity, able to freely choose when and where they will engage in the activity with no contingencies attached. They rarely feel an uncontrollable urge to engage in their activity. While the activity forms a core of their identity, it doesn't overpower the other aspects of their ego. Their activity is so well integrated into their authentic self that it is in harmony with the other aspects of their lives, and they are flexibly able to engage with the various activities and people that make life meaningful to them.

To measure their conceptualization of passion, Vallerand and colleagues came up with a "Passion Scale," which includes the following items:

Harmonious Passion

1. This activity allows me to live a variety of experiences.
2. The new things that I discover with this activity allow me to appreciate it even more.
3. This activity allows me to live memorable experiences.
4. This activity reflects the qualities I like about myself.
5. This activity is in harmony with the other activities in my life.
6. For me it is a passion, which I still manage to control.
7. I am completely taken with this activity.

Obsessive Passion

1. I cannot live without it.
2. The urge is so strong, I can't keep myself from doing this activity.
3. I have difficulty imagining my life without this activity.
4. I am emotionally dependent on this activity.
5. I have a tough time controlling my need to do this activity.
6. I have almost an obsessive feeling for this activity.
7. My mood depends on me being able to do this activity.[24]

They administered their scale to 539 college students, asking them to fill it out in reference to an activity "that was very dear to their heart." Every single person reported some activity, and 84 percent reported that the activity was a passion for them. Over 150 different activities were mentioned, including physical activities (such as cycling, jogging, swimming), team sports (basketball, hockey), passive leisure (listening to music, watching movies), active music (playing the guitar), reading (novels, poetry), active arts (painting, photography), work/education (part-time work, reading in area of study), and interpersonal relationships (hanging out with friends or family).

The students reported that they engaged in their activity for about 8.5 hours a week on average and had engaged in the activity for about six years. Importantly, for most of the students the activity started around adolescence, which is a crucial period for forming an identity.[25] The researchers were excited: they hadn't merely captured some fleeting, whimsical interest but something that really was personally meaningful to the individual.

Both harmoniously and obsessively passionate individuals reported they were passionate about their activity, placed a high value on their activity, and considered the activity an important part of their identity. But this is where the similarities ended.

Taking into account the overlap between the two forms of passion, harmonious passion was positively correlated with positive emotions, flow, concentration while engaging in the activity, and continued positive emotions and lack of negative emotions after engagement. Harmonious passion was unrelated to negative feelings, flow, and concentration when the participants were prevented from engaging in their activity.

In contrast, obsessive passion was unrelated to positive emotions but was positively correlated with negative emotions such as shame during engagement in the activity. After engagement, and when prevented from engaging in the activity, the obsessively passionate folks continued to experience negative emotions, including shame and anxiety, and showed rumination about the activity. Obsessively passionate individuals also persisted on tasks even when it was no longer adaptive to persevere. None of this was found for harmoniously passionate individuals.

The different shades of passion were also associated with different physical and psychological outcomes. Elderly individuals who were harmoniously passionate scored higher on various indicators of psychological adjustment, such as life satisfaction, meaning in life, and vitality, while they reported lower levels of negative indicators of psychological adjustment such as anxiety and depression.[26] In contrast, the obsessively passionate elder participants reported higher levels of anxiety and depression, lower levels of life satisfaction, and there was no relationship between obsessive passion and vitality or meaning in life.

The positive benefits of harmonious passion can be explained by the repeated engagement in positive emotions. Barbara Frederickson and her colleagues have conducted an impressive amount of research showing that positive emotions lead to an "upward spiral" of adaptive behaviors and better psychological adjustment.[27] In contrast, the negative psychological adjustment associated with obsessive passion can be explained through a combination of rigid persistence in activities that provide negative returns and the fact that their object of passion forms an overriding part of their identity.

This may explain why so many child prodigies fizzle out later in life—regardless of their talent (see Chapter 11). By being obsessively attached to their domain, they are increasing their chances of burning out. This is why it's so important that we foster a climate of harmonious passion in all students.

Consider a recent study by Jennifer Fredricks and colleagues, in which they conducted in-depth interviews with gifted and talented adolescents.[28] Their "gifted" sample consisted of college students aged 17 to 21 who were identified as gifted by their elementary school and were also in the top 25 percent of GPA. These college students were asked to recollect on their high school experiences in gifted education. In contrast, their "talented" sample included students who were perceived (by themselves and by parents and teachers) as being highly competent in at least one nonacademic activity, who valued engagement in that activity, and who spent considerable time in the activity. They selected adolescents in grades 9, 10, and 12 who participated in their activity after school. Nonacademic domains included sports, instrumental music, vocal music, drama, and dance.

The researchers found striking differences in the responses between the two groups. The students in the talented sample reported a great love for their domain, a strong sense of identity, more frequent flow experiences, and the desire to engage in their domain all the time. In contrast, the gifted sample didn't appear to be nearly as wrapped up in academics as much as the talented adolescents were in sports and the arts.

The researchers speculate that there was more passion for nonacademic domains because individuals' need for challenges, autonomy, competence, and relatedness were more likely to be met in athletics and the arts than in academic domains. Youth in the talent sample talked more about having opportunities for making choices, receiving public recognition for their ability, and being supported and encouraged by teachers and peers. Tellingly, the researchers found that when students in the gifted sample were given greater freedom of course selection, they reported greater enthusiasm.

This study raises an important point: passion isn't an automatic consequence of performing well on an IQ test or getting good grades in school. Passion is activated by a clear set of conditions, and these rules apply to everyone; no one is immune. We're all human, with fundamental needs, even if we may differ in our level of development in any one slice in time.

But passion isn't the whole story. How we interpret our experiences, and integrate our activities into our identities, strongly influences the strength of our drives. In fact, as we'll see next, mindset and engagement are *inseparable*.

Chapter 7

MINDSET

Fall 1995

"Hi, I'm Scott!" I say, plunking myself down in the back of the cello section. It's the first day of orchestra, and I can't wait to begin. "Hey," the female cellist next to me responds flatly. I reach into my bag and pull out the special arrangement of the orchestral piece my grandfather made for me. She looks at it quizzically. "It's to help me keep up," I say. She shrugs and continues practicing her full version of the piece.

The conductor steps up to the podium and an erratic buzz fills the room as everyone tunes their instruments. Then the conductor juts his baton forward, and the music begins. I slide my bow across the strings just like I have been practicing. My own special arrangement has me playing the starting note of every measure. As we continue into the piece, I can't believe I am keeping up. It's exhilarating. The beautiful sound of the instruments in harmony with one another rushes over me and swells in the room. I can't believe I am contributing to what I am hearing.

I get so engrossed in the overall sound of the orchestra that I start to fall behind. The cellist to my right shows me a look of disapproval. The old me would have run away and hid. Escaped the possible feeling of embarrassment and failure. But not this time. Instead, I feel even more driven to get rid of these crutches and master this challenge. I wait a few measures and get back in the zone.

For the next few months all I do is practice cello. I practice in the orchestra room during lunch period. I receive extra lessons from the conductor on how to read music and rhythm. And every day after school, I have lessons with my grandfather that last for hours.

These were wonderful experiences. My grandfather told me all sorts of riveting stories about his time in the Philadelphia Orchestra and all the enchanting people he met. He told me about the Orchestra's famous 1973 tour of the People's Republic of China, in which they were the first Western symphony orchestra to visit in decades. He also told me about his experiences playing under Leopold Stokowski in the 1940 Walt Disney movie *Fantasia*. Every now and then, my mom or grandmom would pass by the room and scream, "Harry, he's here to have a lesson, not chat!" We just laughed, and continued our conversations. After my lessons, I came home and practiced until bedtime. Morning, noon, and night—cello.

It paid off. A few weeks into the semester, we had a seating test. This test involved private auditions with the conductor that determined our placement. The slots ranged from last chair to first chair. The first cellist is the most prestigious position and something I dreamed of attaining.

Finally I found a test I could pass. After this first seating test, I ended up second-to-last chair, placing better than the cellist who on the first day had wondered why I wasn't playing the regular version of the orchestral piece. Although now I was no longer playing the abbreviated version my grandfather arranged. The crutches were off.

Spring 1996

As I sit on the bleachers during gym class, I stare at Kobe shooting baskets on the main court. I admire Kobe and his work ethic. I frequently see him in the gym practicing the same move over and over again until it is perfect. I see the fire in his eyes. I can tell he really wants to succeed. I have a feeling he will be very successful someday.

It's one of the last classes of the semester and everyone is clearing out their lockers. We are free to play on our own. I get a sudden urge to test my limits. I always loved basketball when I was younger. I wondered whether I could beat the high school star. I run down to the court.

"Wanna play a game of P-I-G?" I ask Kobe with enthusiasm. Kobe nods and agrees to a match. "No dunking?" I ask. "Alright," he mumbles, not seeming to care nearly as much about this competition as I do. He lets me go first, and the game begins.

Something extraordinary happens. I am making shots. He is missing shots. I put my full gusto into the game. I look at Kobe and realize he's not trying nearly as hard, but I just ignore that detail. After a few more back-and-forths, somehow I become one shot away from beating him. I look up and realize the entire class has their eyes on our game. I throw the ball to Kobe for his one last chance.

Suddenly his facial expression changes. His eyes narrow. I know what is coming next. I take a deep breath as Kobe soars high above me and completes a dazzling dunk. *I think I'll stick to the cello.*

~

In the 1980s Carol Dweck wondered why some students seemed to welcome challenges, whereas others saw obstacles as a huge burden. She thought perhaps children differ in the goals they bring to the table. Along with her colleague Elaine Elliot, they identified two different goals: learning and performance.[1]

People with learning goals are all about increasing their skills, whereas those with performance goals are all about winning, and looking smart. Because people with performance goals intentionally avoid negative outcomes that may make them appear dumb, they miss out on potential opportunities for growth. To be sure, both goals can contribute to achievement: we have many different motives, including the need to be validated as well as the need for growth. As Dweck notes, the ideal situation is one where students can achieve both goals at the same time—pursuing tasks with the aim of constant improvement while being able to earn positive praise along the way.[2]

Unfortunately, learning and performance goals often come into conflict with each other, and frequently the kind of tasks that offer the greatest opportunity for growth are the ones that offer the most challenges and require many stumbles along the way. When things are out of alignment, and there is too much of a focus on performance goals, then there is a real risk for stagnation. The question that interested Dweck and her colleagues was how students respond when both goals are pitted against each other.

In one of their studies, Dweck and Elliot randomly assigned fifth-graders to one of two conditions. In the performance goal condition, students were told that they would be evaluated on the task, whereas students in the learning goal condition were told that the task would offer them the opportunity to learn something valuable. They then gave all students the same task.

When the problems were easy, there was little difference between the groups in performance. When the problems got difficult to solve, however, many of the students who were given performance goals showed a "helpless-oriented" pattern of thinking, chastising their own ability and giving up. In contrast, most of the students who were given learning goals displayed a "mastery-oriented" pattern of thinking, staying focused on the task, maintaining the same strategies they used earlier.

They also told some children at the start of the experiment that they had the ability to do really well on the task, whereas they told others that their ability was not as good. The students with performance goals who were told they had high ability persevered in the face of difficulty, but the ones that were told they had low ability slipped into a helpless-oriented mode of thought. For those with learning goals, however, there was no difference in performance based on what they were told about their ability. This provides further evidence that people with learning goals are not about proving their smarts, but instead are more interested in learning and growth.

~

Since this pioneering work, researchers have clarified and added further nuance to achievement goal theory. A major pioneer in this regard has been Andrew Elliot, who with his colleagues has integrated past research on motivation with more contemporary work on achievement goals.[3] The "classical" achievement motivation literature goes back to the work of Kurt Lewin, David McClelland, and John Atkinson. In 1951, McClelland proposed that "there are at least two kinds of achievement motivation, one of which appears to be oriented around avoiding failure and the other around the more positive goal of attaining success."[4]

While Dweck and her colleagues originally grounded their work in this classical approach, Elliot and Judith Harackiewicz note that they abandoned the approach/avoidance distinction.[5] To bring this important distinction back into the picture, they argue for a tripartite division of learning goals— *mastery, performance-approach,* and *performance-avoidance.* Both mastery and performance-approach goals are forms of self-regulation that involve positive expectancies, whereas performance-avoidance goals are a form of self-regulation involving the potential for negative outcomes. Under their framework, performance-avoidance goals are a separate motivational tendency that activates self-protective functions such as anxiety, a fear of failure, and an intense self-focus that can interfere with achievement.

There are important implications here for intrinsic motivation. In 1999 Laird Rawsthorn and Andrew Elliot presented their analysis of 23 separate experiments—going back to 1971—on the link between intrinsic motivation and achievement goals.[6] Overall, they found that the adoption of performance goals was associated with less intrinsic motivation and enjoyment in a task compared to the pursuit of mastery goals. Crucially, they found that experiments that focused on the possibility of a negative performance outcome, thereby activating a performance-avoidance goal, had a damaging effect on all of their measures of intrinsic motivation. This included reduced persistence when given a choice, as well as reduced levels of reported task interest and engagement.

In contrast, performance goals involving an approach motivation did not produce a decrease in intrinsic motivation, and in fact showed the same levels of intrinsic motivation as those adopting mastery goals. Therefore, the link between achievement goals and intrinsic motivation appears to be robust, with the strength of the relationship becoming more obvious when people encounter tasks that give them the opportunity to perform poorly.

There are also implications for temperament. Approach and avoidance are two fundamental temperaments.[7] Children high in *approach temperament* tend to experience positive emotions more frequently, and smile, laugh, and talk more often. They also tend to be more impulsive, show a higher rate of approaching objects, experience more pleasure in high-intensity situations, and find social interactions more rewarding. Although these children are at risk for developing externalizing problems such as aggression, they are less likely to develop internalizing problems such as low self-esteem and depression. According to Jeffrey Gray's biopsychological theory of personality, approach behavior is driven by the Behavioral Activation System (BAS), which is highly sensitive to the possibility of reward.[8] The approach temperament is primarily associated with the adult personality trait extraversion but also shows a positive relationship with openness to experience.[9] This temperament is associated with functioning of the dopaminergic neurotransmitter system.

In contrast, children high in *avoidance temperament* tend to show higher levels of discomfort, fear, and sadness, and lower levels of activity, impulsivity, and aggression. They also tend to have lower positive expectations for reward, which puts them at higher risk for developing depression. Children who are high in approach *and* low in avoidance are at particular risk for developing behavioral problems due to their heightened impulsivity unbridled by fear. The avoidance temperament is driven by Gray's Behavioral Inhibition System (BIS), which is sensitive to the presence of threats, punishment, intense stimulation, and fear.[10] Among adults, the avoidance temperament is related to neuroticism. This temperament is associated with functioning of the serotonin neurotransmitter system. Both temperament systems—approach and avoidance—are constantly interacting and frequently competing with each other for the control of attention and behavior.

Over the course of seven careful experiments, Andrew Elliot and Todd Thrash examined the connection between temperament and achievement goals.[11] They found that extraversion and positive affect were consistently related to mastery and performance-approach goals but were unrelated to performance-avoidance goals. In contrast, neuroticism and negative emotions were consistently linked to performance-approach and performance-avoidance goals but were unrelated to mastery goals. All of these findings held even after taking into account the gender of the participants and their SAT scores.

Do these findings mean that you're destined to adopt a particular achievement goal depending on your temperament? No. Even though personality traits tend to remain stable across different contexts, specific situations do matter.[12] Introverts can appear quite engaged if you give them something that intrinsically interests them, and extroverts can appear introverted in environments that do not provide high levels of social engagement.

Even though the approach and avoidance temperaments are fundamental across a wide range of animals,[13] we are unique in our flexible pursuit of goals. We don't have rigid dispositions, but context-dependent contingencies. Those with an avoidance predisposition aren't destined to adopt performance-avoidance goals across the board, but can choose to override their predisposition and adopt an approach orientation.

That's why intervention is so important.

~

In 1992 Carole Ames published a series of papers describing how classroom learning environments can be structured to make different learning goals salient.[14] These key structures form the acronym TARGET:

> T is for how learning activities are designed.
> A is for how much a lesson plan gives children autonomy.
> R is for how children are rewarded.
> G is for how children are grouped together.
> E is for how children are evaluated.
> T is for the timing and pacing of instructions and assignments.

In a recent intervention Paul O'Keefe and colleagues investigated the effects of a TARGET classroom environment on achievement goal orientations and self-worth.[15] They followed a group of high-ability adolescents over the course of nine months, surveying the students before, during, and after their participation in a three-week summer program. The students—who were in grades 8 through 10—were required to score 500 or higher on either the math or the critical reading section of the SAT for entrance into the program.

The summer program was intentionally designed with TARGET principles in mind. The goal was to simultaneously create a mastery goal environment while deemphasizing performance goals. They went about this in a number of ways. They planned social activities that provided opportunities for students to interact with their peers and build friendships, and activities were intentionally designed to offer just the right level of challenge for each student. They also gave students enough time to learn the information, and they emphasized intellectual risk-taking, self-directed learning, and treatment of fellow summer students as colleagues, not competitors.

Compared to students' incoming levels, the researchers found a significant increase in students' mastery goal orientations and a decrease in their performance-approach and performance-avoidance goal orientations during participation in the program. They also found a significant decrease in levels of self-worth being contingent on outperforming others (such as "Doing better than others gives me a sense of self-respect"). Crucially, changes in both performance-approach and performance-avoidance goal orientations were linked to these changes in self-worth.

What happened after the students left the program and returned to their prior learning conditions? The effects of the mastery learning environment on mastery goal orientations were sustained six months after the students returned to their prior learning environments. Unfortunately, the same couldn't be said for performance goals. While performance-approach and performance-avoidance goal orientations decreased throughout the summer program, both performance orientations returned to prior levels when the students went back to their more traditional educational settings.

These researchers argue that the mastery goal orientation may have been sustained because mastery goal orientations are not linked to the desire for normative success (outperforming others), allowing them to exist in a variety of environments that are not as dependent on context. In contrast, environments that emphasize competition and social comparison are likely to shape both forms of performance goal orientations.

These findings show that mastery goal orientations are susceptible to environmental influence regardless of the goals a student brings to the table. Environments that are intentionally structured to be high in mastery and low in performance, and which minimize the availability of information about relative ability and social comparison, *can* have an impact. Regardless of the direction a person's mindset starts out in any particular situation, we can help point it in the most productive direction.

~

After her early research on learning goals, Dweck wondered: Why are some students who are performance-oriented so concerned about their level of ability? It occurred to her that maybe it has to do with the way students think about ability more generally. After all, if intelligence is fixed at birth and can't be developed, then what's the point of persevering when the road gets bumpy?

Dweck and colleagues identified two different mindsets that students carry around with them: a *fixed* mindset in which intelligence is thought of as set in stone at birth, and a *growth* mindset that views intelligence as dynamic and capable of improvement. She set out to investigate how these different mindsets affect performance.[16]

In one study, Dweck and Ellen Leggett asked eighth-grade students how much they agreed or disagreed with statements such as these:

> *Your intelligence is something about you that you can't change very much.*
>
> *You can learn new things but you can't really change your basic intelligence.*
>
> *You have a certain amount of intelligence and you can't really do much to change it.*

Then students were given the option of engaging in a variety of different tasks, which differed in how much they involved performance versus mastery goals. For instance, a task that involved a performance goal was described as "easy enough so you won't make mistakes" whereas a task that involved a mastery goal was described as being "hard, new and different—you might get confused and make mistakes, but you might learn something new and useful." The more students held a fixed mindset, the more likely they were to choose a task involving a performance goal, whereas the more they held a growth mindset, the more likely they were to choose a task involving a learning goal.

The self-defeating nature of a fixed mindset has recently been tracked in the brain. Jennifer Mangels, Dweck, and colleagues used event-related potentials (ERPs) to investigate how different mindsets influence the processing of information.[17] While students answered general information questions, their brain activity was monitored. Then they received feedback about whether their answer was correct. Afterward they took a surprise retest that included all of the questions they answered incorrectly.

While those with a growth mindset attempted the same number of questions and performed just as well as those with a fixed mindset, those with a growth mindset corrected more errors, suggesting they benefited more from the feedback. In terms of brain waves, participants with a fixed mindset showed an enhanced response in the frontal pole region to negative feedback about their ability. Because this area of the brain is associated with increased attention (see Chapter 10), it appears that the fixed theorists were more focused on what they got wrong than what they could do to improve.

Those with a fixed mindset also appeared to engage in less sustained and deep encoding of the information as reflected in the duration of activation of the inferior frontal-temporal region, a region known to play a role in the activation of preexisting knowledge in memory. In contrast, the brain activity of those with a growth mindset suggested they paid attention to the feedback and were more deeply engaged in processing that feedback. This learning strategy paid off: those with a growth mindset performed better than those with a fixed mindset on the surprise retest. The researchers suggest that these differences in the processing of information may explain why people with a growth mindset are better able to rebound following failure.

Additional studies—conducted on a range of age groups—suggest that mindset isn't just *related* to performance, but that the link is *causal*. When students encounter instruction that induces a fixed mindset, they are more likely to focus on performance goals, and when they are taught in a way that brings out growth mindset, they are more likely to focus on learning goals.[18] Importantly, mindset impacts on achievement in both the short term and the long term.[19]

∽

To be sure, Dweck's research is about *beliefs* about intelligence, not about how intelligence actually develops. But as I pointed out in Chapter 1, it's not an either/or proposition: traits are simultaneously influenced by genes *and* must be developed. What's potentially problematic is that children who are stamped with an enduring label are being fed a fixed theory of intelligence, which dramatically influences their motivation, how they approach learning, and how they handle setbacks. Many important skills aren't being developed because we are cultivating erroneous beliefs about how abilities develop.

Even the most well-intentioned teachers can send damaging messages to their students.[20] Dweck and colleagues found that praising the ability of students after doing well on a test promoted a fixed view of ability, whereas praising the effort that contributed to the performance led to a growth mindset.[21] This mattered. Those who were praised for their ability showed a drop in intrinsic motivation, confidence, and performance when they later encountered difficult problems whereas those praised for their effort maintained their levels of motivation and performance when the road got bumpy.

In a more recent study, Aneeta Rattan, Catherine Good, and Carol Dweck found that teachers who held a fixed theory of intelligence were significantly more likely to diagnose a student as having low ability based upon a single, initially poor, performance.[22] They were also more likely to "comfort" students for their low ability, saying things like "It's OK—not everyone can be good at math," which did in fact reduce student engagement with school subjects. Also disconcerting, students who were exposed to comfort-oriented messages reported less motivation, expected lower final grades, and viewed their professors as having lower engagement in their learning.

These results are startling, especially considering that many of the instructors with a fixed mindset of math ability most certainly *believed* they were considering the students' best interests. In reality their fixed view led them to express their support and encouragement in unproductive ways that ultimately backfired. As the researchers note, "the popular practice today of identifying weaknesses and turning students toward their strengths may be another self-esteem-building strategy gone awry, and one that may contribute to the low numbers of students pursuing math and science."[23]

There are important implications here for putting labels on students. After all, labels imply a fixed ability. According to Dweck, "The term 'gifted' conjures up an entity theory. It implies that some entity, a large amount of intelligence, has been magically bestowed upon students, making them special. Thus, when students are so labeled, some may be over concerned with justifying that label and less concerned with seeking challenges that enhance their skills. . . . They may also begin to react more poorly to setbacks, worrying that mistakes, confusions, or failures mean that they don't deserve the coveted label. If being gifted makes them special, then losing the label may mean to them that they are 'ordinary' and somehow less worthy."[24]

The effects of labeling can be just as damaging for students who are labeled "learning disabled." Our society has clear expectations about these students. In a 2004 national survey reported in *Education Week*, 84 percent of 800 surveyed special and general education teachers did not believe that students in special education should be expected to meet the same set of academic standards articulated for students without disabilities.[25] In other research, Nancy Hertzog interviewed 50 college students about their prior experiences in gifted programs and the impact of the programs on their lives.[26] In nearly every interview, the students said that teachers who taught the gifted classes were better teachers and more enthusiastic about teaching compared to the "nongifted" classes. The students said that teachers of the gifted classroom treated them with more respect, and the expectations were higher. The students also noticed that their peers in the general education classes appeared much less motivated than the students in their gifted classes, and they think this might have played a role in the teachers' lower expectations.

These expectations are important, as they guide policies that determine whether students with disabilities will receive the same opportunities to flourish as everyone else receives. Most troubling, research shows that expectations can *create* outcomes. When we expect something to happen, we (often unconsciously) behave in a way that actually makes it a reality. Sociologist Robert Merton first coined the term "self-fulfilling prophecy" in the late 1940s to describe this phenomenon.[27] Educational psychologists first labeled this the "Pygmalion effect" after the pathbreaking study by Robert Rosenthal and Lenore Jacobson in the 1960s.[28] In 18 classrooms, they told teachers that some of the children showed "unusual potential for intellectual gains." In reality they singled out students at random. Eight months later, these "unusual" children actually *became* unusual, showing significantly greater gains in IQ than the rest of the children.

The Rosenthal and Jacobson findings were a bit more complicated and nuanced than their portrayals in the media,[29] but a number of more recent studies on "expectancy effects" confirm that self-fulfilling prophecies are very real. In one study, Elisha Babad found that teachers' expectations had systematic effects on their grading as well as on students' performance on standardized achievement tests.[30] Similarly, Kathleen Cotton reported that teacher expectations affected students' achievement and attitudes, including offering fewer opportunities to learn new material, insincere praise, providing less stimulating and lower-level cognitive questions, and providing less effective but time-consuming instructional methods.[31] Peer expectations also played an important role, as children with disabilities were very sensitive to the overt and covert signals they were receiving from their friends. Also, despite a teacher's best effort to suppress their expectations, communication "leakage" often still came through loud and clear. Jan Pieter Van Oudenhoven and Frans Siero reported that even though teachers gave twice as much verbal praise to students they thought were learning disabled, they also displayed more negative nonverbal feedback such as discouraging head movements.[32]

Implicit signals can have a big impact on the brain, which of course is reflected in actual behavior. In a recent study Kenneth Kishida and colleagues had people take an IQ test alone and then in a group setting.[33] In the group situation, the participants received their score and were told their rank in the group. In this situation, in which implicit signals of social status were broadcast to everyone in the group, everyone performed worse. Those who suffered the most, however, were those who were told they were the "low performers." Not only was their IQ score lower than their earlier performance, but they also showed brain changes in areas associated with fear and working memory (amygdala, dorsolateral prefrontal cortex, and nucleus acumbens), suggesting that such lowered expectations brought about anxiety that prevented them from showing their true colors. Low expectations shut down their brains.

Just how prevalent are expectancy effects? Researchers have reported that of all students treated with high expectations, about 10 percent demonstrated substantial improvement.[34] Any other large-scale social program that could move 10 percent of the below-average students into higher achievement levels would be heralded as a success. Many significant public and social policy decisions have been based on relationships lower in magnitude than expectancy effects! Here are some examples, with effect sizes in parentheses:[35]

- Effect of sugar consumption on the behavior and cognitive processes of children (.00)
- Aspirin and reduced risk of death by heart attack (.02)
- Chemotherapy and surviving breast cancer (.03)

- Calcium intake and bone mass in premenopausal women (.08)
- Coronary artery bypass surgery for stable heart disease and survival at five years (.08)
- Impact of parental divorce on child well-being (.09)

Of course, expectancy effects will vary by individuals, and some children with severe disabilities need alternative strategies to meet goals and standards. But many children with disabilities are being denied the right to appropriate and demanding expectations.[36] As far as I'm concerned, stereotyping students with disabilities on the basis of a disability label or standardized test score is not only unsupported by the best evidence from the field of psychological and education measurement, but it's also just plain discrimination!

As a result of these lowered expectations, students with learning disabilities frequently develop motivational and social problems due to their inaccurate belief that their difficulties are stable and can't be overcome. They adopt self-defeating behaviors, such as not working as hard and giving up quickly when a task becomes difficult. As Kevin McGrew notes, "The early years of academic learning are critical; once a specific domain of academic self-efficacy beliefs are developed, they can be difficult to change."[37]

Students with learning disabilities frequently compare themselves to their "nondisabled" and even "gifted" peers, and this can profoundly affect their self-concept. Sometimes referred to as the big-fish-little-pond effect, such comparisons often lead to a decline in the academic self-concept of students who are grouped together according to their ability.[38] Recent research suggests that ability grouping doesn't have to be harmful. Matthew Makel, Seon-Young Lee, Paula Olszewski-Kubilius, and Martha Putallaz measured changes in academic self-concept among a group of over 2,000 predominantly white, high-SES, high-ability students with aspirations of attaining an advanced degree.[39] They measured the students' academic self-concept before, at the end of, and six months after they left their regular school environment to participate in an enriched three-week intensive summer program. Crucially, the summer program fostered mastery goals and minimized performance goals. (In fact, the study included the same summer program that was evaluated by O'Keefe and colleagues described earlier in this chapter.)

They found that children who participated in this mastery-oriented summer program maintained their already high levels of academic self-concept throughout the program. This suggests that ability grouping doesn't inevitably lead to a decline in academic self-concept. They also found increases in several aspects of the students' nonacademic self-concept, including physical attractiveness, behavioral conduct, close friendship, social acceptance, and global self-worth (although some of these improvements declined once the students went back to the regular classroom). Because the high-ability students already entered the enrichment program with extremely high levels of self-concept, the effect of the program was most likely underestimated among these students. This leads me to believe that students with learning disabilities, who have lower levels of self-concept to begin with, may benefit even more from such an enriched program that increases their competence while minimizing comparisons.

When students are lower in abilities relative to their peers, there is an increased probability they will avoid putting effort into challenging tasks. But people who are low in ability and fed a fixed mindset on a regular basis (for instance, constantly being told they are "learning disabled") are *particularly* prone to viewing effort as risky, as it can only reinforce the belief that they really are disabled.

～

Labeled children aren't the only ones who are vulnerable to expectations. In fact, there can be drastic effects on performance for *any* socially stigmatized group that repeatedly finds itself negatively stereotyped. In a groundbreaking 1995 paper, Claude Steele and Joshua Aronson investigated the impact of "stereotype threat" on performance.[40] They defined stereotype threat as a "predicament" in which a student's self is threatened by being evaluated for an ability that has a relevant negative cultural stereotype.

To test this notion, they gave black and white college students a thirty-minute test of difficult verbal GRE items that only 30 percent of pretest participants solved correctly. Then they randomly assigned participants to one of three conditions. In the stereotype-threat condition, the test was described as diagnostic of intellectual ability, whereas in the non-stereotype-threat condition the test was simply described as a laboratory problem-solving task. They also included another nondiagnostic condition in which participants were encouraged to view the test as a challenge. After taking preexisting ability (verbal SAT scores) into account, they found that black participants in the stereotype-threat condition performed significantly worse than black participants in the other two conditions. Black participants also performed worse than white participants in the stereotype-threat condition. The presence of the stereotype had little effect on the white test-takers.

These influential studies led to a flurry of research on stereotype threat. Over 200 studies from different research teams have now been conducted on stereotype threat, spanning a wide range of groups (including African American and Hispanic test takers, and female math test takers) and situations (including applying for a job, playing chess, and driving a car).[41] Essentially any situation in which a stereotype can be relevant to performance can produce stereotype-threat effects.

To be sure, no single factor has yet been found that reliably completely alleviates the black–white gap in IQ and academic achievement.* It's unlikely that any single factor will be found. The causes of the black–white achievement gap are most certainly multifaceted, involving an interconnected web of societal factors (see Chapter 13). In a recent review, Nicholas Mackintosh carefully considered a wide range of factors that influence the gap. After a balanced weighing of the evidence he concluded that there is no really convincing evidence for the genetic view, but "rather good evidence that a variety of environmental factors have contributed to the differences in average test scores."[42]

In my view, the most telling research comes from a look at human development. Research shows that white Americans and African Americans do not differ in "information processing" in infancy.[43] By early childhood there *are* significant differences in IQ. As developmental psychologist Joseph Fagan noted in a recent chapter in *The Cambridge Handbook of Intelligence*, the most parsimonious explanation for these findings is that "later differences in IQ between different racial-ethnic groups spring from differences in cultural exposure to information past infancy, not from group differences in the basic ability to process information."[44]

Just how strong are these multiplier effects? By the age of 4, the average black–white gap in the United States widens to about 5 IQ points, and continues to widen steadily across development by about 2.5 points a year, leading to a 17-point gap by the age of 24.[45] While these findings from 2002 are

---

*Although in some individual studies, researchers have been able to completely eliminate the gap. Ryan Brown and Eric Anthony Day found that African Americans underperformed whites under high-threat instructions while taking the Raven's Advanced Progressive Matrices Test, one of the best measures of "general intelligence" (see Chapter 10). But under low-threat instructions, the gap completely evaporated. See R. P. Brown and E. A. Day, "The Difference Isn't Black and White: Stereotype Threat and the Race Gap on Raven's Advanced Progressive Matrices," *Journal of Applied Psychology* 91 (2006): 979–985.

a significant improvement compared to the IQ gap in 1972, they are still worrisome, and suggest we still have a long way to go before there is equality of opportunity in the United States across all ethnic groups, and stereotype threat can play an important role.

How much does stereotype threat matter? In a recent review, Hannah-Hanh Nguyen and Anne Ryan looked at over ten years' worth of experimental research on the effects of race-based and gender-based stereotype threat on test performance.[46] Overall, they found a small but significant effect size of .26—which is consistent with prior reviews of the literature. They also found considerable variability in the strength of the effect across studies. In fact, one-fourth of the studies showed no effect whatsoever or even a *positive* effect of stereotype threat!

Part of the problem is that different studies go about activating stereotype threat in different ways, and there are nuanced effects depending on gender and ethnicity. Nevertheless, the researchers "suggest treating the phenomenon as if it were a real occurrence (e.g., a nonzero effect size), as most mean effects were suggestive of the existence of stereotype threat effects, and a substantial proportion of the data tends to align with the theory."[47]

To put the effect size in perspective, if a minority student took the SAT and his or her cognitive ability were at the national average, the researchers estimate that he or she could underperform by about 50 points due to subtle stereotype threat cues. Other researchers have also shown that a stereotype threat effect as small as .20 in the context of high-stakes testing can still translate to an additional 5.9 percent of women failing to achieve a passing score for calculus.[48] Therefore, stereotype threat is a real phenomenon that interferes with the ability of affected groups to express their intelligence in the real world.

~

If we really want to translate these research studies into meaningful interventions, we must peer underneath the hood and see how stereotype threat really works. What are the real mechanisms driving stereotype threat? In their initial paper, Aronson and Steele presented a number of different possibilities as to how stereotype threat exerts its effects on performance, including distraction, narrowed attention, anxiety, self-consciousness, withdrawal of effort, and over-effort. They conclude that their best assessment is that stereotype threat causes an "in-efficiency of processing much like that caused by other evaluative pressures."[49]

Since their initial speculation, a large number of studies have been conducted on the mechanisms of stereotype threat. Looking at the big picture, it appears that there are multiple paths to stereotype threat and the phenomenon involves a complex interaction of cognition and affect.[50] Anne Krendl and colleagues found that women experiencing stereotype threat displayed greater activation in the ventral cingulate cortex compared to those in a control condition.[51] This brain region has been linked to social evaluation and emotion regulation. Activation in the same region was found by Mary-jane Wraga and colleagues, after activating stereotype threat in women about their spatial abilities (the brain activation differences were significantly different between men and women).[52]

Along similar lines, Chad Forbes, Toni Schmader, and John Allen investigated the neurological effects of stereotype threat among a group of 57 minority undergraduates (46 Latinos and 11 African Americans).[53] The researchers randomly assigned participants to either a control condition in which the task was described as a pattern recognition task or a condition in which the task was described as diagnostic of intelligence. Then they had participants complete a reaction-time task while their brain activity was recorded. In particular, they were interested in activity in the anterior cingulate cortex (ACC) of the prefrontal cortex 50 to 100 milliseconds after participants made an error on the task. They focused on the ACC because this area of the brain has been linked in prior research to the monitoring of one's environment for goal conflict.

The pattern of brain activity (larger error related negativity, or ERNs) indicated that those who assigned a greater value to their performance (e.g., "being good at academics is an important part of who I am") showed heightened vigilance, monitoring, and attention to the errors made during the task when they were led to believe the task was diagnostic of their intelligence compared to the control condition. This suggests that those whose identity was threatened showed increased motivation to excel so they could disprove the stereotype.

But this presents a puzzle: Shouldn't the higher motivation of the threatened individuals lead to *better* performance, not worse performance? The answer lies in understanding the effect of stereotype threat on working memory. Explicit, conscious reasoning requires focused attentional resources (see Chapter 10). There's only so much information one can hold in his or her memory at one time while processing other information.

In a clever series of studies, Toni Schmader and Michael Johns showed how working memory and stereotype threat are connected.[54] They selected females whose math SAT scores were greater than 500 and who were aware of the stereotype that women are worse than men in math. Before taking a test of working memory, some females were told by a male experimenter that performance might be related to underlying gender differences in "quantitative capacity." Females who were given this framing of the task showed reduced working memory performance, assessed by the number of words they were able to recall compared to females who were just told the test was a measure of working memory. Their second study found similar results among a Latino population, and their third study found that the reduced working memory of women under threatening situations was the *key factor* explaining their reduction in math performance.

There are a number of ways in which stereotype threat can sap important working memory resources. One way is through rumination and concerns about failure. As Steele, Spencer, and Aronson note, stereotype threat can lead to "concerns about how one will be perceived, doubts about one's ability, and thoughts about the stereotype."[55] In support of this notion, Mara Cadinu and colleagues found that women who were told that women perform worse than men in logical-mathematical tests showed poorer performance, lower expectations, and more negative math-related thoughts while completing a difficult math problem compared to women who were not threatened.[56] These negative thoughts partially explained their lower levels of performance.

Other research shows that stereotype threat occurs because people are actively trying to regulate the negative thoughts and feelings that have been activated by the stereotype.[57] Because the experience of threat activates a goal to avoid confirmation of the stereotype, and the experience of self-doubt or anxiety is often interpreted as a sign of failure, efforts are made to detect and suppress these negative thoughts and feelings and push them out of mind. This suppression is mentally taxing and relies on the same working memory resources necessary to solve the problem.

Importantly, the effect of stereotype threat depends on the task. Sian Beilock and colleagues looked at golf putting, a task that is harmed when too much attention is allocated to performance and not when working memory is impaired.[58] They found that well-learned golf putting is susceptible to stereotype threat, but that distracting expert golfers away from the behavior (having them land a ball on a target rather than in a hole) eliminated the harmful impact of negative stereotype activation.

This suggests that performance degradation under threat can occur when too much attention is allocated to processes that usually run more automatically. In well-learned skills that do not rely heavily on working memory, stereotype threat harms execution by inducing too much attention to execution rather than too little. Increased vigilance is not always a good thing—especially when it pays to perform more automatically.

These results have broad practical implications. As the researchers note, for any skills that are highly proceduralized, such as sports, medical routines (like surgery), or musical performances, diverting attention to another task (for instance, by having the subject count backward during performance) in threatening situations may prevent unwanted thoughts and feelings. This research is consistent with other research on "choking under pressure" conducted by Beilock and colleagues.[59]

Taken together, these intriguing results suggest that when people are faced with threatening situations, their confidence can drastically drop, lowering the working memory resources they can bring to the task at hand. Fortunately there are interventions to curb this threat.

One way to combat stereotype threat is to reduce the likelihood that such threatening cognitions get activated in the first place. This can happen in a number of ways. Research shows that the direct training of implicit stereotypes can boost women's working memory and increase their math performance even under stereotype threat.[60] Other studies have shown effects of the presence of role models, mentioning other good qualities of one's group, increasing a sense of belonging to a domain, strengthening one's confidence in a domain, affirming one's values, and reminding people of the complexity of their self-concept.[61] Additionally, pioneering interventions designed by Joshua Aronson, Catherine Good, and colleagues to change stereotyped students' responses to a threatening situation have also borne fruit.*[62] All of this research suggests that it is possible to nip in the bud the "downward spiral" of self-blame, anxiety, and underperformance that many adolescents experience on a regular basis.

---

*Historical note: These interventions by Joshua Aronson and colleagues were the first to use the term "mindset" in the context of beliefs about intelligence. Prior to these studies, Carol Dweck made the distinction between fixed and incremental "theories of intelligence," not fixed and growth mindsets.

Another way to combat stereotype threat is through interventions that can facilitate more effective ways of coping with the threat. As we saw, making a conscious effort to suppress the negative emotions and thoughts is not an effective technique to curb the effects of stereotype threat, as it will only further tax working memory. A better method is *reframing* negative feelings in a more positive light. Studies have found that people who view math test anxiety as a response to challenge instead of response to a threat show stronger physiological response to the testing situation (salivary cortisol), which leads them to *better*, not worse, performance.[63] Similarly, Schmader and colleagues found that anxious arousal predicted *higher levels* of working memory under stereotype threat when people were primed with confidence or already had a general tendency to reappraise negative emotions in a more positive way.[64] Jamieson and colleagues found that simply telling people that physiological responses typically related to anxiety (such as increased heartbeat) are beneficial to reasoning led to improved test performance under stressful conditions.[65]

Sometimes even just making people aware of the relationship between anxiety and stereotype threat helps. One study found that women who were taught about stereotype threat's effect on anxiety and performance performed just as well on a math test as males, and significantly better than women who were told the math test was "diagnostic" of their math ability.[66] It seems that reframing the anxiety as a response to stereotype threat instead of an indicator of one's innate ability allows the person to distance themselves from the negative feelings and actually improve ability. When it comes to stereotype threat, knowledge really is power.

Improving basic numerical and spatial competencies has also been shown to reduce the detrimental effects of math anxiety.[67] This is why it's really important to identify students at risk for low school performance as early as possible before the anxiety develops and becomes strong. Learning how to regulate and control negative emotions—even before a math test begins—can also enhance math performance for the already math anxious. When anticipating a math test, math-anxious individuals who show activation in brain regions associated with the control of negative emotions perform nearly as well as their nonanxious counterparts on a difficult math test.[68]

One way to regulate negative emotions is through expressive writing. One study asked people to write freely for ten to fifteen minutes about their emotions regarding an upcoming task. Writing alleviated the burden that negative thoughts placed on working memory by allowing people an opportunity to reevaluate the stressful experience in a matter that reduced the necessity of worry. Ramirez and Beilock showed that having highly test-anxious high school students write about their worries prior to an upcoming final exam boosted their scores from B– to B+, even after taking into account their prior grades.[69]

What should be quite clear from this wealth of research is that mindset matters, playing a crucial role in engagement. Mindsets are highly sensitive to environmental expectancies. What's more, self-regulation plays a critical role in preventing the negative emotions from spiraling out of control. Because self-regulation is such an essential skill, it's worth taking a closer look at it next.

Chapter 8

SELF-REGULATION

1997

There she is: the gatekeeper of the gifted class. From the end of the corridor I watch her class file out. As the last gifted kid leaves the room, the teacher stands outside alone. I decide it's time. I had fought my way out of my learning disability, my label, and special education. I've decided it's time to be gifted. *Go Scott, go!*

Heart pounding, I thrust my chest out, put on my smartest facial expression, and start walking toward her. She greets me with a welcoming smile. "Hi, I'm Scott, and I think I may be gifted," I blurt out. I pause, surprising myself. *Where did that come from?*

I look up and notice the teacher didn't run away. Good sign. "Great! How are your grades?" she asks me. I think about this. "I'm getting straight A's in challenging classes." She gives me a warm smile. "Splendid! You certainly sound gifted . . . ," she begins, to my immense delight. *Yes, I did it! All of the hard work paid off!* I think about doing a break-dancing move on the concrete floor to celebrate.

Then she finishes her sentence. ". . . but to be formally added to my roster, the school psychologist has to make sure your IQ score meets the eligibility requirement." I almost have a heart attack. It feels like one of those movies where the person mouths "Nooooooo . . ." in superslow motion.

～

I burst into the school psychologist's office. I am promptly removed from the school psychologist's office. But I have an appointment! Upon my return, the psychologist motions for me to sit down. *Great. I'm going to have to sit down for this news.*

"So, I've been reviewing your charts," he says, seemingly nervous. Which makes me even more nervous. He takes out a piece of notebook paper and a pen, and robotically draws me a diagram. "This is you," he says as he pushes up his horn-rimmed glasses and points to the left side of what looks like the outline of a camel's hump. "And this," he says, moving his finger toward the far right of the hump, "is gifted."

Leaning forward, I patiently explain to him that maybe that was my IQ score at age 11, but six years later, it no longer defines me. I am getting straight A's, I tell him. "Isn't that enough to be gifted?" I ask calmly, masking the tension bubbling inside. I sit back in my chair trying to calm myself. I explain how I have finally caught up to the rest of the kids and, as my grades now clearly show, I am ready for the challenging resources of gifted education. He doesn't seem to be that interested. I take a deep breath and politely excuse myself.

I decide to take a different approach. After school I dash off to the local library and find a book about human intelligence. I flip through the pages and come face to face with a terrifying chart. At the top is listed the average IQ of PhDs. I am way lower than this number. Tentatively, I go down the list. College graduate? Closer, but still no cigar. My blood pressure is rising. Semiskilled laborer? In my dreams. After some time, I finally find my range: "Lucky to graduate high school," it says.

In a fit of panic, I throw the intelligence book as far as I can with an audible "F**k!" Unfortunately the librarians don't appreciate such passionate displays and start running toward me.

The next day I walk into the gifted classroom and solemnly tell the teacher that I don't qualify for gifted education. We stand in silence. After a few moments, a flash of excitement spreads across her face. "I have an idea!" she exclaims. "Why don't you just unofficially come join my classroom this year?" I think about this for a moment. *Unofficially gifted? Close enough. I'll take it.*

~

As college application season begins, I wonder about my options. Over the past few years I have rapidly moved up the seating ranks in the orchestra and become heavily involved in choir and school musicals. I can see myself pursuing music as a career, but I also really want to study cognitive science and learn more about human intelligence.

To help with my college decisions, my parents take me to a college consulting service. In a meeting with my parents and the head of the counseling center, the director asks me where I would like to go to college. Without skipping a beat, I say "Yale," picking the most prestigious name that comes to mind. "Surely they have good programs in music and cognitive science?" I ask. He nods politely and asks me to join him in the other room.

We sit down, and he starts reading from a paper. "OK, Mary bought 27 items in the supermarket, but accidentally left 3 items at the checkout line. How many items were in her car?" I stare at him. "Really? Are you seriously giving me an IQ test right now?" I ask. He doesn't blink. "Yes. It will help me gauge what schools you can realistically attend" is his response.

A jolt of anxiety surges through me. I feel like I'm 11 years old again. The self-doubt comes flooding back. *OK, let's see. Why did Mary leave the items at the checkout line in the first place? Maybe she had a very good reason. And about the car thing—maybe the cashier at the register noticed Mary left some items and ran out and put them in her car. So maybe all the items are there in her car. This has got to be a trick question. Or am I way overthinking this?*

As before, I don't do so well on the test. Also, confirming the counselor's expectations, my SAT scores aren't even close to Yale's level. Or any top school's level, for that matter. One night at the dinner table, I propose an idea to my parents. By this point I have set my sights on Carnegie Mellon University, because they have world-class programs in both music performance and cognitive science.

"Why don't I start majoring in voice performance at CMU, and then add a major in cognitive science once I demonstrate I am capable of getting good grades?" I propose. "Maybe my talent is good enough to get me in based on my voice alone." My parents think the idea is brilliant. So does my voice teacher, who is also extremely supportive.

And that's exactly what happened: I am accepted to Carnegie Mellon University's music department for voice performance, while being rejected from Carnegie Mellon University's cognitive science department. One way or another, I am still determined to make my way in.

∼

In the late 1960s and early 1970s, Walter Mischel and colleagues set out to find out how people exert willpower in the face of temptation.[1] One by one, they brought over 500 preschool children into a "game room" at the Bing Nursery School at Stanford University. Scattered across a table were a variety of delectable treats, including marshmallows and cookies. The child was asked to pick a treat and was then offered the following choice: either (a) eat one treat right away or (b) wait a few minutes and get *two* treats. Then the experimenter left the room, leaving the child to face the temptation alone. *What would you do?*

Mischel and colleagues found large individual differences among the children. Some stuffed their faces right away, whereas others were far more patient. While it seemed like all the children had the same impulse to eat the treat, they differed in their strategies to avoid the temptation. Those who were particularly successful in delaying the gratification were really good at shifting their focus of attention away from the sweet, chewy taste of the treat to nondelectable aspects of the delight such as its shape.

While the study wasn't originally designed to follow up the preschool children, the researchers wondered if any of the participants would respond to mailings ten years after their initial testing. To their delight, over a third of the once-preschoolers responded! So they conducted some follow-up studies.

The 4- or 5-year-old preschoolers who waited for a larger reward tended to have higher SAT scores in adolescence.[2] They were also rated by their parents as more academically and socially competent, verbally fluent, rational, attentive, planful, and able to deal well with frustration and stress.[3] Following them up even further to adulthood, the researchers found that early willpower predicted higher educational achievement, greater levels of self-worth, better ability to handle stress, and less cocaine/crack use especially among participants at risk for psychological maladjustment.[4]

While those who are able to delay an immediate award in the service of a bigger payoff later do tend to have higher IQ scores,[5] there is suggestive evidence that when analyzed independently of IQ, self-discipline predicts academic achievement *better* than IQ. Angela Duckworth and Martin Seligman put eighth-graders in a number of situations in which they would experience conflicting desires and impulses.[6] They found that self-discipline predicted most indicators of academic achievement at least twice as well as IQ.

They also found that self-discipline, but not IQ, predicted improvement in grades over the course of the year.*

In recent years researchers have begun to understand the mechanisms underlying self-regulation. According to Clancy Blair and Adele Diamond, self-regulation "refers to the primarily volitional cognitive and behavioral processes through which an individual maintains levels of emotional, motivational, and cognitive arousal that are conducive to positive adjustment and adaptation, as reflected in positive social relationships, productivity, achievement, and a positive sense of self."[7]

Self-regulation is critical to success! Which is why it's so crucial to target these skills as early as possible. Blair and Diamond argue that school readiness requires the integration of the emotionally reactive brain areas and the cognitive control brain areas—not dominance of one system over the other. From their perspective, the ideal learning environment is one that supports active engagement in learning and facilitates a sense of agency and self-efficacy in the school environment.

Consider the child who enters first grade with a decreased ability to concentrate on material that doesn't interest him in the least, and who has difficulty regulating his urge to do something that does interest him. Because the child *expects* school to be uninteresting, he does not engage and is not motivated to apply himself to school tasks. To the extent that his preferred activities interfere with schoolwork, the child is at risk of being reprimanded and obtaining poor grades. This creates a feedback loop. The child starts to expect school *failure*, so avoids challenging work and engages in other areas

---

*However, Paul Sackett, Matthew Borneman, and Brian Connelly point out that Duckworth and Seligman's conclusion was based on a restricted sample of already high-IQ participants. Correcting for this range restriction, Sackett and colleagues found that the correlation of .49 between IQ and GPA was larger than the uncorrected value of .32 reported by Duckworth and Seligman. While this corrected correlation remained lower than the .67 correlation between self-discipline and GPA, Sackett and colleagues point out that Duckworth and Seligman's conclusion that self-discipline accounted for *twice* as much variation in GPA than IQ no longer holds. They also applied corrections to the other outcomes of academic achievement and found that IQ had a slightly *higher* corrected negative correlation with procrastination (−.28) than self-discipline (−.26). They conclude: "Whereas Duckworth and Seligman made a strong case for the value of studying self-discipline as an additional predictor of academic outcomes, a clear picture of the relative value of self-discipline and IQ requires careful attention to range restriction." See P. R. Sackett, M. J. Borneman, and B. S. Connelly, "High-Stakes Testing in Higher Education and Employment," *American Psychologist* 63 (2008): 215–227.

in life—which can include crime and delinquency—that provide an alternative means to self-esteem and confidence.

In contrast, consider the child who enters first grade with higher levels of self-regulation. She can concentrate on the teacher's instructions without any intrusive thoughts. She is also studious and hardworking. Because she is a dream to teach, she receives praise from her teachers, which motivates her to study and work harder. Almost immediately, she is branded "gifted" by all her teachers and carted off to a special classroom where she receives even more challenges. The gap between her abilities and those of the child who has been carted off to a classroom for students with "behavioral problems" or "learning disabilities" grows stronger and stronger, confirming the teacher's initial expectations.

This is not merely a hypothetical scenario. These results have dramatic implications, considering that many children begin school with under-developed executive functions and poor self-regulation skills, and the gap widens every passing school year.[8] As a result, those with the less-developed self-regulation skills fall farther and farther behind.[9] This matters, as these skills are predictive of emerging skills in mathematics and literacy as early as preschool.[10]

But the importance of self-regulation goes beyond school performance. Terrie Moffitt and colleagues looked at data on a group of 1,037 children born in one city in a single year who were followed from birth to age 32.[11] Poor childhood self-control predicted substance dependence at age 32, including alcohol and drug problems. Poor childhood self-control also predicted lower adult socioeconomic status and income, even taking into account social class and IQ. By the age of 32, 47 percent of the participants had become parents, and childhood self-control predicted whether their children grew up in one-parent or two-parent households.

Those with poor childhood self-control were also less likely to save money for the future, were perceived by others as poor money managers, and were struggling financially in adulthood. They reported more money-management problems and accumulated more credit problems. Again, poor childhood self-control was a better predictor of these financial outcomes than the social class they grew up in or their IQ scores. In terms of crime, 24 percent of all participants had been convicted of a crime by the age of 32. Children with poor self-control were more likely to be convicted of a criminal offense.

The researchers also collected data at the ages of 13, 15, 18, and 21 and found that children with poor self-control were more likely to make mistakes as adolescents, which resulted in "snares that trapped them in harmful life-styles."[12] Children with low levels of self-control began smoking by the age of 15, left school early with no educational qualifications, and became un-planned teenaged parents. In fact, the lower their levels of self-control, the more "snares" they experienced, and the more likely they were as adults to have poor health, less wealth, and criminal conviction.

The researchers wondered what would happen if they were able to inter-vene and improve self-control. To determine this, they focused on the chil-dren who changed their rank in their levels of self-control from childhood to young adulthood. After all, the correlation between childhood self-control and adult self-control was only .30—statistically significant but clearly leav-ing plenty of room for changes in self-control across the life span. They found that those children who improved their self-control from childhood to young adulthood had better outcomes by age 32, even after taking into account their initial levels of childhood self-control. "Interventions that achieve even small improvements in self-control for individuals could shift the entire distribution of outcomes in a salutary direction and yield large improve-ments in health, wealth, and crime rate for a nation."[13]

This bears repeating. Interventions, whether in early childhood or in adolescence, can improve the health, wealth, and public safety of the general population. Interventions that mitigate the consequences of teenagers' mis-takes might help them overcome their mistakes. But more importantly, early intervention might also *prevent* these outcomes from occurring in the first place.

Fortunately, such effective interventions exist.

∼

The Tools of the Mind curriculum, developed by Elena Bodrova and Debo-rah Leong, is based on the sociocultural perspective of Russian develop-mental psychologist Lev Vygotsky.[14] The underlying principle is that success is most likely to occur when people engage in environments in which they are active participants in the learning process, and are challenged and sup-ported. The Tools curriculum emphasizes the teacher's role in "scaffolding" learning—guiding and supporting the child in learning.

The core of the curriculum is forty activities designed to promote self-regulation. These activities are interwoven into almost every classroom activity throughout the day. Consider the activity "Buddy reading," which uses concrete, external aids. In this activity, children pair up and take turns telling a story from a picture book. The teacher gives one child a drawing of lips and the other child a drawing of an ear, noting that "ears don't talk; ears listen." The listener is expected to ask the reader a question about the book. This exercise promotes the ability to inhibit talking, wait their turn, and listen. Children then swap roles. After a few months, children no longer need the pictures to wait for their turn; the external aids have become internalized.

Or consider the use of mature, dramatic play. Children are encouraged to plan out the play scenario together. After the scene is agreed upon, they act it out. The teacher offers guidance by approaching the children as they are playing and encouraging discussion of who will do what next. This role-playing allows engagement in what Vygotsky referred to as "thinking as they are talking." Indirectly, this task facilitates the development of inhibition (for instance, children must inhibit behaviors inconsistent with their role) and self-regulation (for example, using the initial plan instead of being driven by the most attractive toy that is available but not related to the scene, or impulsively grabbing the other person).

In 2007 Adele Diamond and her colleagues W. Steven Barnett, Jessica Thomas, and Sarah Munro published their evaluation of the Tools curriculum in the prestigious journal *Science*.[15] In total, their evaluation consisted of 147 preschoolers (with an average age of 5) from low-income families who all came from the same neighborhood. The children received either the district's standard literacy curriculum or the Tools curriculum for one or two years. Both programs covered the same academic content, but the literacy curriculum didn't address the development of self-regulation. All of the classrooms received the same resources, teacher training, and support.

The results were so striking that after the first year, educators in one school using the Tools curriculum halted the experiment so that the students receiving the standard curriculum could get the same benefits! On tasks involving cognitive inhibition, children experiencing the Tools curriculum outperformed those receiving the standard curriculum. On tasks requiring multiple "executive functions"—working memory, inhibitory control, and mental flexibility—roughly twice as many students who had the Tools curriculum scored better than 75 percent correct as compared to children taught the standard curriculum.

Another program that is similar to the Tools curriculum is Montessori education. More than 5,000 schools in the United States currently use the

Montessori program.* A large number of these programs include multi-age classrooms, student-chosen course content, collaboration, the absence of grades and tests, and individual and small-group instruction in both academic and social skills. Like the Tools program, Montessori has also been found to be effective in improving school readiness.[16] According to Diamond, the Tools curriculum and the Montessori programs share the following features:[17]

1. They help children exercise their executive functions and constantly challenge them to do so at higher levels.
2. They reduce stress in the classroom.
3. They rarely embarrass a child.
4. They cultivate children's joy, pride, and self-confidence.
5. They take an active and hands-on approach to learning.
6. They easily accommodate children progressing at different rates.
7. They emphasize character development as well as academic development.
8. They emphasize oral language.
9. They engage children in teaching one another.
10. They foster social skills and bonding.

In recent years many interventions have specifically targeted social-emotional competence in young children (typically between the ages of 3 and 6), including school enrichment add-ons such as the PATHS,[18] CSRP,[19] and the Research-Based, Developmentally Informed (REDI) Head Start curriculum.[20] These programs work on a number of skills, such as self-regulation, awareness of feelings, identification of emotions, perspective taking, affective self-monitoring, managing feelings, the empathic realization of the effects of one's behavior on others, and adaptive problem solving. These programs have shown improvements not only in behavioral and social outcomes, but also in more traditional academic outcomes, such as emerging language and literacy skills.

Psychologists have also become increasingly aware of the importance of pretend play as a vital component to the normal cognitive and social development of children. Systematic research has shown clear benefits of children's engagement in pretend games from the age of about 2½ through age

---

*It should be noted that there is a wide range of Montessori models of education and intense debate over which models can rightfully claim the Montessori mantle.

6 or 7.* Studies have demonstrated cognitive benefits such as increases in language usage, including subjunctives, future tenses, and adjectives. The important concept of "theory of mind," an awareness that one's thoughts may differ from those of other persons and that there are a variety of perspectives of which each of us is capable, is also closely related to imaginative play.[21]

Psychologist Sandra Russ identified a number of different cognitive and affective processes that are associated with pretend play.[22] Her research dealing with play involves fantasy, make-believe, symbolism, organization, cognitive integration of seemingly separate content, and divergent thinking (the ability to come up with many different ideas, story themes, and symbols). Pretend play allows the expression of both positive and negative feelings, the modulation of affect, and the ability to integrate emotion with cognition.[23]

Other research suggests that make-believe games directly impact self-regulation, reducing aggression and increasing delay of gratification.[24] When children use toys to introduce possible scenarios or friends, the representation of multiple perspectives occurs naturally. Taking on different roles allows children the unique opportunity to learn social skills such as civility, communication, problem solving, and empathy.[25]

An important benefit of early pretend play may also be its enhancement of the child's capacity for cognitive flexibility and, ultimately, creativity (see Chapter 12). For example, Sandra Russ found in longitudinal studies that early imaginative play was associated with increased creative performance years later.[26] Michele and Robert Root-Bernstein's research with clearly creative individuals such as Nobel Prize winners and MacArthur Foundation "genius" grant awardees, indicated that early childhood games about make-believe worlds were more frequent in such individuals than in control participants in their fields.[27]

---

*I should note that the precise causal route from pretend play to the outcomes discussed in this section is not clear. In a recent review of the impact of pretend play on child development, Angeline Lillard and colleagues concluded that "existing evidence does not support strong causal claims about the unique importance of pretend play for development and that much more and better research is essential for clarifying its possible role" (1). While I wholeheartedly agree that there needs to be more research to determine the features of play that are particularly important for child development, the high-quality research I present in this section does highlight the incredible value of pretend play regardless of its precise causal agency. See: A.S. Lillard, M.D. Lerner, E.J. Hopkins, R.A. Dore, E.D. Smith, and C.M. Palmquist, "The Impact of Pretend Play on Children's Development: A Review of the Evidence," *Psychological Bulletin* 139 (2013): 1–34.

What environments and interactions promote early and frequent imaginative play? Research has demonstrated that parents who talk to their children regularly, explaining features about nature and social issues, or who read or tell stories at bedtime, seem to be most likely to foster pretend play.[28] A school atmosphere in which pretend games are encouraged, or even just tolerated in the curriculum or in children's recess play, has been shown to lead to even greater amounts of imaginativeness and enhanced curiosity, and to learning skills in preschoolers and children in the early grades.[29] Indeed, educators are using pretend games to teach math and reading.[30]

A key question that arises from the literature is how parent and teacher training in "guided play" may influence literacy. Dorothy Singer and colleagues conducted a series of studies on the effectiveness of Learning Through Play, an intervention program designed to teach parents and educators how to engage in learning-oriented, imaginative play games with children.[31] In the initial evaluation of the program, kindergarten children of low-SES parents who participated in the intervention showed greater gains on an academic readiness assessment than those whose parents did not participate. Modest improvements were found in subcomponents of the test, including vocabulary, knowledge about nature, general information knowledge, and knowledge about manners.

Perhaps the idea of a built-in "pretend play recess" during the regular school day—where children can get together and explore an unlimited number of possible combinations of ideas, emotions, and perspectives—will one day be just as acceptable as traditional, but no less important, forms for recess and play. Of course, pretend play is a vital cognitive process for people of every age. Play is possible in virtually any domain of human functioning, from video games (the gamification of learning[32]) to painting to music performance to sexual expression in adults (e.g., BDSM[33]). The centrality and importance of pretend play goes well beyond early childhood. Arguably, it is intrinsic to nearly all imaginative play for all human beings.

Other social-emotional interventions have been found to work on children across a wide range of ages. One study found that adolescents in a two-year emotional intelligence training program in Spain increased their skills in perceiving, facilitating, understanding, and managing emotions. Importantly, these effects persisted six months after the program concluded.[34] Another intervention, by Mark Brackett and colleagues, consisted of a thirty-week social and emotional learning curriculum for fifth- and sixth-graders in fifteen classrooms.[35] They used the RULER curriculum, which is designed to help students understand *feeling words*—words that include the full range of human experience, such as excitement, shame, alienation, and commitment. Those in classrooms using the RULER curriculum scored higher in year-end grades and teacher ratings of social and emotional competence, such as leadership, social skills, and study skills, compared to students who didn't receive the program.

There is also a growing recognition for the need for social-emotional learning (SEL) programs among special education students. Students in special education classrooms are at higher risk of developing emotional and interpersonal problems, considering they have to deal with the frustration of experiencing learning difficulties, and they are more likely to be rejected by their schoolmates.[36] As a result, children with learning disabilities are at increased risk for depression and suicide.[37] Therefore, interventions are *crucial* for this population.

So far, the results are promising. In one study, Chi-Ming Kam, Mark Greenberg, and Carol Kusche investigated the effects of the PATHS curriculum on 133 elementary school students with disabilities.[38] Eighteen special education classrooms were randomly assigned to either the intervention group or the control group. The classification breakdown was as follows: 53 children had learning disabilities, 23 had mild mental disabilities, 31 had emotional and behavioral disorders, 21 had physical disabilities or health impairments (such as ADHD), and 5 had multiple handicaps. Most of the students were in self-contained classrooms. Those involved in the intervention experienced sixty lessons throughout the course of a year that included units on self-control, emotions, and problem solving.

The researchers found that the PATHS curriculum was effective, reducing levels of teacher-reported externalizing and internalizing behaviors as well as reductions in self-reported levels of depression among the children. Both the teachers and the children recognized these changes, and the decreases remained two years after the intervention. In contrast, children in the control group showed a continual increase in both externalizing (e.g., aggression) and internalizing (e.g., depression) behaviors. Additionally, the PATHS curriculum led to significant improvements in knowledge of both comfortable and uncomfortable feelings, as well as a greater fluency in understanding emotions and recognizing cues in other people, and a greater ability to provide nonconfrontational solutions to situations, indicating improved self-control.

Another intervention that shows great promise is Project Bright IDEA.[39] Funded by the U.S. Department of Education (the Javits Education Program),

Project Bright IDEA was built around the assumption that all children of all ages can benefit from gifted curriculum. A major aim was to nurture and develop the interests and abilities of children in underrepresented groups, including children whose limited English proficiency, cultural backgrounds, economic disadvantages, educational disadvantages, disabilities, or other differences make it difficult for them to show their brilliance on traditional methods required for entrance into gifted and talented programs.

The latest phase of the program (Project Bright IDEA-2) focused on K–2 instruction and targeted a wide range of "gifted intelligent behaviors" that help students "as they are challenged by problems, dilemmas, paradoxes, and enigmas for which the solutions are not immediately apparent."[40] Teachers underwent an extensive training procedure to learn how to teach the following "gifted behaviors": persisting, listening with understanding/empathy, thinking flexibly, thinking about thinking/metacognition, questioning and posing problems, applying past knowledge, thinking and communicating with clarity and precision, creating, imagining and innovating, taking responsible risks, finding humor, and remaining open to continuous learning.

The results of the program, based on over 10,000 students, 225 educators, thirty schools, and five years of research in North Carolina, are striking (importantly, the program was evaluated by an outside investigator). Before the project was implemented, virtually none of the students that were nominated to Gifted and Talented programs came from underrepresented populations. After the program was implemented in these schools, one in four (24 percent) of the second-graders who participated in Project Bright IDEA-2 were identified for Gifted and Talented programs! But even those who weren't officially identified as gifted still showed a significant improvement in their gifted behaviors, as well as in their performance on more traditional academic outcomes. One principal showed that nearly every single Bright IDEA-2 student in K–2 classrooms scored 50 to 100 percent higher than students in regular classrooms on *every single academic assessment given*!

Importantly, the project also found a profound change in teachers' beliefs about race/ethnicity and the need to form a partnership with parents. Teachers also increased their understanding of how to teach math and complex concepts to young children and how to increase challenges in the curriculum and differentiate strategies for diverse learners. Currently the program directors are working with five school districts in North Carolina to expand the project to K–12, and they are in the process of developing a project in

Virginia. Project Bright IDEA is a terrific example of what is possible when we hold high expectations for all children.

Other interventions that have been effective at improving self-regulation include interactive computer games, aerobic exercise, music training, traditional tae-kwon-do training (but not competitive modern martial arts), yoga, and mindfulness meditation.[41] While this may seem like a broad range of activities, *that's the whole point*. Diamond argues that the most successful programs will be the ones that address the "whole child"—that reduce stress, improve the ability to handle stress, increase joy, improve physical fitness, increase feelings of social belonging and support, and build confidence, pride, and self-efficacy. Counterintuitively—and contrary to the practice of most schools—the most efficient and cost-effective route to obtaining the best academic outcomes for all students is *not* a narrow focus on content but a focus on the whole child, including their social, emotional, and physical development.[42]

High-quality early interventions don't just pay in terms of social gains. The economist Raj Chetty and colleagues looked at the life trajectories of nearly 12,000 children who were part of a large-scale education program in the 1980s based in Tennessee called Project Star.[43] Although they found that the effect of good teaching, as measured by test scores, almost completely disappeared by junior high, a different story emerged when they checked in on the study participants as adults (age 30).

Those adults who did better in preschool were more likely to go to college and to attend a higher ranked college, were less likely to be single parents, and were more likely to save for retirement than those with similar backgrounds who did not do as well in preschool. Some people would say these outcomes are more important than test scores. Teaching quality turned out to be a particularly important factor in preschool performance: students who had more-experienced teachers had higher earnings as adults. Factors such as class size and the socioeconomic status of peers had an effect on preschool performance, but neither of these factors explained differences in preschool performance as much as good teaching. One of the authors of the study, Emmanuel Saez, estimated that a terrific kindergarten teacher is worth about $320,000 a year, if you consider the additional monetary value a full class of students with a good preschool teacher can expect to earn throughout their careers.[44] This figure doesn't even take into account social gains, such as better health and less crime.

None of these interventions are magic, nor do they replace the need for quality course content.[45] What they suggest, however, is that even small changes in the environment can significantly affect a person's motivation, mindset, and self-regulation. The more we address the whole child, the more likely we are to see that child flourish.

But is this the whole story? We've tackled the early years, but now it's time to leave school behind and see how ability operates in the real world. After all, most people don't stay in school their whole lives! It's time to move on and look at what it takes to perform on the stage of *life*.

Chapter 9

DELIBERATE PRACTICE

Spring 2000

I eagerly turn the page of my cognitive psychology textbook. I get to the section on multiple intelligences, and a surge of excitement shoots through me. *This is amazing! This is exactly what I want to be studying!* I flip back to the inside cover and see "Robert J. Sternberg, Yale University." I immediately remember the time in high school I told the SAT prep director I wanted to go to Yale. He didn't seem to think it was too realistic back then. *Has anything changed? Is the dream still possible?*

A few days later I meet with the professor of my cognitive psychology class, Anne Fay. "So, I love this class. I think I found my calling," I tell her. She thanks me and encourages me to continue in the field. She asks how she can help. "I'd really like to study intelligence with Robert Sternberg at Yale," I say excitedly. "Do you think there's any chance that's possible?" Without skipping a beat she replies, "Of course! You are one of my best students. Let's properly prepare, though. Want to do directed readings one-on-one with me next semester? We can come up with a plan." I am absolutely flabbergasted. *She is actually taking my dream seriously.*

I get approval from the psychology department to major in psychology, and change my music performance major to a minor. Thankfully, all they looked at were my college grades, not my SAT scores from high school. The following semester I read everything Dr. Fay assigns me on the topics of intelligence and expertise. Once a week we meet and discuss the readings, while also systematically coming up with a plan to conduct the research that will give me a fighting chance for Yale's PhD program in cognitive psychology.

November 17, 2000

"Go ahead, try it," Herbert Simon says as he points to the puzzle on his desk. I look at the three wooden pegs, with three discs of varying sizes sitting on the first peg. This puzzle is called the Tower of Hanoi puzzle, and we just learned about it in Simon's graduate class on thinking and problem solving. I am one of only a few undergraduates in his course. Every single lecture, I hang on every word of this famous psychologist. The Tower of Hanoi task is discussed in many of our psychology courses, and I have already mastered—with lots of practice—the ins and outs of this puzzle. I grin. Three discs is nothing.

I approach the puzzle and quickly shuffle the discs around in robotic fashion. I can do this in my sleep. I look over to Simon and see him smiling. "Very nice. You did that in the minimal number of moves. Want me to add some discs?" he asks. "Maybe some other time," I reply. This wasn't the reason why I'm in his office. Instead, I want his advice.

We sit down, and discuss many topics. I find out he plays the violin. I tell him I play cello. We discuss what is takes to reach the highest levels of expertise. I ask why he became a cognitive psychologist, and he tells me it's the only profession that allows him to engage so many of his interests at the same time. I consider that response, and decide that it *is* pretty cool being a cognitive psychologist. I can integrate all my interests—music, theater, intelligence, expertise, whatever. Throughout the conversation, I can't take my eyes off his Nobel Prize, lying modestly on the top shelf of one of his filing cabinets.

I leave the meeting in a state of wonder. When I'm far enough away from his office, I pull my electronic dictionary out of my backpack and look up a few words he used in our conversation that were unfamiliar to me. After committing the new words to memory, I put the dictionary back in my bag. As I walk off to my next class, I realize I have never been more inspired.

～

As a doctoral student at the University of Stockholm in Sweden in the mid-1970s, K. Anders Ericsson was fascinated by the work of Herbert Simon and Allen Newell on problem solving.* For good reason: Simon and Newell's

---

*Much of K. Anders Ericsson's history is taken from his manuscript "Exceptional Memory and Expert Performance: From Simon and Chase's Theory of Expertise to Skilled Memory and Beyond," in *Expertise and Skills Acquisition,* ed. J. Staszewski (Abingdon, Oxon, UK: Taylor & Francis, forthcoming).

theory, presented in their 1972 book *Human Problem Solving,* was ground-breaking.[1] Steeped in the new digital computer metaphor, Simon and Newell proposed that problem solving is a matter of information processing.

They even specified the cognitive landscape, complete with a central processor and memory systems, and limits for storage capacity and how fast information can be processed. According to their theory, "well-defined" problems have a clear starting point and end goal. During the course of problem solving, problem solvers use their information-processing capacities to search through the "problem space," reducing the distance between the start and goal states. This discrepancy is reduced when the problem solver chooses "operators" that draw from a tool kit of general problem-solving strategies ("heuristics") likely to work across a wide variety of problems.

Take the Tower of Hanoi task. The problem solver is given three pegs, with a certain number of discs of varying sizes circling the first peg. The goal is to move all the discs from the first peg to the middle peg. Only one disc can move at a time, but a disc can't be placed on top of a smaller disc. With this kind of task, it's possible to define the problem space for any number of discs, with the problem space getting increasingly complex as the number of discs increases. Figure 9.1 shows the most efficient solution path for three discs.

In 1959 Simon, Newell, and J. C. Shaw built a computer program called the General Problem Solver (GPS) that was capable of solving this puzzle, among other well-defined problems.[2] Though their computer program was rudimentary by today's standards and had major limitations in solving many real-world problems, their program was landmark at the time and helped kick off the artificial intelligence and cognitive science revolution.

In their theory, a particularly troublesome bottleneck in information processing was short-term memory (STM). In 1957 George Miller proposed that our short-term memory can only hold 7 meaningful "chunks" of information, give or take a few.[3] He cheekily called this a "magic number."* What makes Miller's paper so historic is not the precise number—current estimates place the magic number closer to 4.[4] What was so important was his

---

*Miller has pointed out that he never meant for his "magic" number to be taken too seriously. He was preparing an upcoming lecture, and it was mainly a rhetorical device he used to tie together the different strands of his research. See his "George A. Miller," in *A History of Psychology in Autobiography,* ed. G. Lindzey (Stanford: Stanford University Press, 1989), 8:391–418.

1.

5. FROM TOWER A TO TOWER B

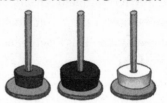

2. FROM TOWER A TO TOWER B

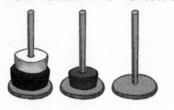

6. FROM TOWER C TO TOWER A

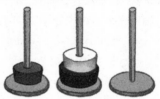

3. FROM TOWER A TO TOWER C

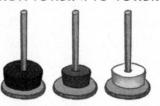

7. FROM TOWER C TO TOWER B

4. FROM TOWER B TO TOWER C

8. FROM TOWER A TO TOWER B

FIGURE 9.1. TOWER OF HANOI

demonstration that we can far surpass our fundamental human memory capacity by grouping multiple symbols together in meaningful ways.

For example, give yourself fifteen seconds to memorize the following 23 letters:

CI AFB IKG BDN ABD C UKC NNU SA

Now try to recall as many as you can. You probably won't be able to memorize more than a handful of these digits. Now give yourself fifteen seconds to memorize this list:

CIA FBI KGB DNA BBC UK CNN USA

I guarantee you improved your memory performance by leaps and bounds. Of course, they are the same exact letters, just grouped differently. The meaningful grouping makes the task a breeze, while the arbitrary grouping taxes your short-term memory. Chess experts are well aware of this memory loophole. In the 1930s, chess master and Dutch psychologist Adriaan de Groot set out to experimentally find out what separated the very best chess players from the rest.[5] He watched games between chess masters and identified chess positions he could use in his experiment. Then he presented these chess positions to a new batch of chess players with differing levels of expertise and asked them to think aloud as they selected the best next chess move for the current position. He found that the best players consistently selected the best next move, instantly recognizing the structure of the chess position, and the meaningful relations between the pieces. The best players considered moves that some of the weaker players never considered—even after much deliberation.

But de Groot wasn't done. He also had the chess players examine a position for a few seconds and then try to reconstruct the entire chessboard from memory. Beginners could recall only a few details, whereas grandmasters could recall virtually all of the chess pieces—sometimes more than twenty—in only a few seconds! Importantly (and often overlooked), de Groot found that less-skilled chess players benefited from studying the chess master's move selections, and could even reconstruct the details of a chess position if given more time—about ten to fifteen minutes.

These influential studies suggested that chess experts might have enhanced memory. How else could they go so far beyond normal human information-processing limitations? In 1973 Simon and William Chase decided to get to the bottom of this mystery.[6] They brought chess players into their laboratory, and showed them chess positions for five seconds. Like de Groot, they found that experts were able to recall the positions, whereas beginners could recall only about four or five pieces. Also consistent with de Groot's analysis, they found that the better players recognized more chunks, instantly seeing the complex relationships among a large number of previously encountered positions. In contrast, beginners relied more on the locations of individual pieces.

But they added a crucial tweak: in addition to familiar chess positions, they also presented the chess experts with *randomly* arranged pieces. This had a huge effect. Suddenly chess experts were at no significant advantage in remembering the positions over less-skilled players.* This suggested that the grandmaster advantage was very specific to chess pieces. What separated the best from the rest? Whatever it was, it wasn't an innately superior short-term memory capacity.

To explain the chess master advantage, Simon and Chase proposed that chess expertise involves the accumulation of chunks acquired through many years of engagement in the domain.[7] Just how many chunks does this amount to? They estimated that "very roughly . . . a master has spent perhaps 10,000 to 50,000 hours staring at chess positions, and class A players 1,000 to 5,000 hours."[8] They argue that these hours are comparable to the amount of time people have spent reading by the time they become adults. Just as adults have a reading vocabulary of about 50,000 words, chess masters have a "chess vocabulary" of about 50,000 patterns stored in memory, with grandmasters having an even larger vocabulary.

Their conclusion? Superior chess skill is a matter of pattern recognition; no special general memory ability required. Just how many years of engagement is required to store all these chunks? Simon and Chase proposed about ten years ought to do the trick, noting: "There are no instant experts in chess—certainly no instant masters or grandmasters. There appears not to be on record any case (including Bobby Fischer) where a person has reached grandmaster level with less than about a decade's intense preoccupation with the game."[†]

Their findings have been replicated in chess and have also been found in other domains that rely heavily on procedural knowledge (knowing how to do things), such as basketball, bridge, and GO, although the effects are smaller in these other domains than they are for chess.[9] But Chase and Simon's theory wasn't complete. What was missing was a mechanism to explain *how* expert chess players were able to form chunks so quickly. A number of studies found that expert chess players were able to store large amounts of related and even unrelated chess pieces after only a few seconds of exposure. Even when the chess masters were distracted by the experimenters, or were blindfolded, their performance was hardly affected. They could

---

*Note that they studied only three chess players. Later studies have found an advantage, albeit a small one, for skilled chess players even for random positions.

†Although they didn't deny a role for talent: "Clearly, practice also interacts with talent, and certain combinations of basic cognitive capacities may have special relevance for chess." They also leave open the possibility that "World Championship caliber grandmasters may possess truly exceptional talents along certain dimensions" (403).

follow chess games in their mind's eye just by hearing descriptions of sequences of moves and still reproduce the position, and could play multiple games at the same time, maintaining multiple chess positions in their minds.

It seemed as though increased chess skill was related to a more efficient way of encoding and manipulating mental representations in the service of planning future moves. This requires both retrieval and manipulation of long-term memory. But if not solely short-term memory or long-term memory, what was the mechanism? Enter Ericsson.

∼

When Ericsson first arrived on Carnegie Mellon's campus in July 1977 to work on a postdoctoral fellowship, he spent much of his time in the library. He was looking for a topic to study that gelled with the work of his mentors, Simon and Chase. In particular he searched for a topic that related to the structure of short-term memory but also relied on the analysis of verbal reports ("protocol analysis"). So he dug into a century's worth of studies.

One day he came across a study from 1929 conducted by Pauline Martin and Samuel Fernberger that showed that after fifty training sessions, two students increased their recall dramatically.[10] One student went from 9 digits to 13 digits, and the other went from 11 digits to 15 digits. This suggested that people were capable of circumventing their limited-capacity short-term memories. Ericsson was intrigued.

Ericsson approached Chase and asked him if he was interested in replicating the finding. Excited about the project, Chase recruited lanky, 6-foot-3 work-study student Steve Faloon to be a participant. The experiment would count as part of his job. Steve, an undergraduate at CMU, has been described as a "Bruce Springsteen fan, a joker and an extracurricular dynamo."[11] He was also an accomplished long-distance runner. In high school he helped his track team win the city championship, and then he attended the Community College of Allegheny County because it had one of the nation's very best college marathon teams. Eventually Steve made his way to CMU and their track team. According to an article in the *Pittsburgh Post-Gazette*, Steve's coaches at CMU believed that "it wasn't natural talent but his overwhelming desire that made Steve Faloon outrun so many."[12]

Before the memory experiment began, Ericsson and Chase interviewed SF (as Steve would affectionately become known in the psychological literature) to make sure he was just a "typical CMU [Carnegie Mellon University] student without any special cognitive abilities."* In the summer of 1978, training began. Ericsson, Chase, and SF got together for an hour a day, three to five days a week, for twenty months. This tallied more than 230 hours of time in the laboratory! Ericsson would read a list of arbitrary numbers at the rate of about one second per number while Chase checked the accuracy. Then SF would offer his thoughts about what was going through his head as he tried to remember the numbers. If SF got all the numbers correct, they would add one in the next set, but if he missed even a single digit, they reduced the length of the list by one.

The first few sessions weren't extraordinary. SF's short-term memory was only a bit higher than 7 digits, within the perimeter of Miller's magic number. SF's initial strategies were no different from those of the typical college student. By the fourth testing session, SF felt that he was pushing up against his limits and didn't think he could improve much more. Then, during the fifth testing session, something changed. SF recalled an average of about 10 numbers, which suddenly took him outside the range of the average college student. How was this possible?

SF reported that for the first time, he noticed that some groupings reminded him of familiar running times for different races. So he decided to encode 3- and 4-digit groupings as running times. This is known in the psychological literature as "elaborative encoding." For instance, he would see "3492" and think something along the lines of "That's close to the world-record running time for a mile—3 minutes, 49.2 seconds." Early on in his training, he only recognized a few of these times, so his learning strategy was a mixture of elaborative encoding and raw rehearsal.

Over the course of training, Ericsson and Chase devised all sorts of different experiments to better understand the mechanisms that allowed SF to perform such memory feats.[13] If they presented SF with a number that couldn't easily be converted into a running time, his performance would drop to close to his beginning level of performance. For instance, the number 672 is hard to convert into a mile time because there's no such thing as 72 seconds. SF was clearly clever, and within the first four months he came up with other methods of elaborative encoding that better accommodated the digits, such as using ages of people (for example, 893 was translated to

---

*Although I can assure you that the typical CMU student is far from the typical university student! K. A. Ericsson, "Exceptional Memory and Expert Performance: From Simon and Chase's Theory of Expertise to Skilled Memory and Beyond," in Expertise and Skills Acquisition, ed. J. Staszewski (Abingdon, Oxon, UK: Taylor and Francis, forthcoming).

"89.3 years old, a very old person") and dates (1944 was "near the end of World War II"). Once he started using a mixture of different mnemonics, he'd get over his hump.

SF would constantly come up against brick walls and would devise more clever strategies to overcome his seeming limitations. After some training, SF started memorizing a list by encoding groups of 3 and 4 digits as running times, ages, and so on, and rehearsing the very last 5 or 6 digits presented at the end of the list. But this didn't always work out so well, as he would get confused and recall the groupings in the incorrect order. So what did he do? He *created an even more elaborate mental structure*. For instance, if he was given 30 digits to memorize, such as the sequence

$$8\ 8\ 7\ 4\ 3\ 3\ 7\ 4\ 3\ 5\ 7\ 4\ 8\ 3\ 7\ 0\ 5\ 5\ 4\ 7\ 1\ 2\ 0\ 4\ 3\ 1\ 0\ 5\ 3\ 7$$

SF would split up the first 16 digits into four groups of four (8874 3374 3574 8370), and cluster that entire grouping together into a "supergroup" consisting of two old ages (88, 74), a record-setting mile (3 minutes 37.4 seconds), another record-setting mile (3 minutes, 57.4 seconds), and another two old ages (83, 70). Then he would cluster together the next three groups of three (554 712 043) into another supergroup. Finally, he would link the two supergroups together into an even higher-level grouping that could cue the lower-level groupings. During recall he could visualize the structure in his head and spatially see where all the groupings were located. Once he located in his mind a super-grouping, he would be able to retrieve each group of numbers within that grouping. SF rehearsed the last five digits (10537) so he didn't have to slot them anywhere and could immediately recall them.

If this all seems complex, that's because *it is*. Perhaps even more remarkable than SF's ability to memorize so many numbers was his ability to construct such a complex mental structure on the spot! This is a point I'll return to in Chapter 10. At no point did Ericsson or Chase coach SF on how to improve his memory: "He was highly motivated and constantly tried different methods to improve his span. His skill was thus self-taught."[14] SF rediscovered, all by himself, one of the most ancient and effective memory techniques of all time.

∿

According to folklore, the fifth-century BCE poet Simonides of Ceos had an epiphany one evening as he was standing in front of a collapsed banquet hall, the sole survivor of an ill-fated dinner. After being asked who were in attendance, he closed his eyes and was able to visualize every last guest who perished, based on where they were seated. He realized that this technique could apply to remembering virtually anything.

Simonides' technique—the "method of loci"—became very popular and was used by orators to memorize speeches, and was even taught in schools as an essential part of the curriculum. In a pre-Internet, pre-mass-information consumption era, an exceptional memory was considered one of the highest virtues. The technique was in such wide use that Cicero didn't even see a need to write it down. The first-ever mention of the technique was included in the Latin textbook on rhetoric and persuasion called *Rhetorica ad Herennium*, anonymously written sometime in the 90s BCE.

Even today, the method of loci is the primary technique used by memory experts. There are national and international memory championships where top memorizers from all around the world come together to memorize all sorts of things in a very limited time span. It's essentially a mental decathlon, with ten events, including an event for the memory of names and faces, and an event involving the memorization of the order of a shuffled deck of playing cards. In his recent book *Moonwalking with Einstein: The Art and Science of Remembering Everything*, journalist Joshua Foer described how he entered the inner world of these memory experts and, by learning these techniques, became champion of the 2006 USA Memory Championship.[15]

You, too, can use the method of loci to memorize virtually anything. You're really only limited by your imagination. The more memorable you make something, the better the chances you'll be able to recall it, because it will stand out in the sea of memories. The whole point is to make boring information come alive, so it really stands out in your mind when it's time to retrieve the memories. Take a random series of numbers, letters, or even lines of abstruse poetry, and make it sing. No, really, I mean *really make it sing*. If you're trying to remember to buy spaghetti, visualize a life-size spaghetti monster belting out a high note telling you to get your behind to the grocery store and buy some spaghetti. If you're trying to remember to buy a tie, really visualize that tie tying itself in knots, getting stuck, and cursing in frustration. It also helps to mix senses, as that just adds more retrieval cues. So if you can try to smell the tie, and imagine it smells like burnt marshmallows (since in your imagination you accidentally dropped it in the bonfire last weekend), that will add an extra dimension that will make it more likely you'll remember it later.

Also, it's really important to use a location that you are intimately familiar with, so you can effortlessly navigate every last corridor, cabinet, and nook and cranny in your mind. Then sprinkle the content. When I walk through the door in my mind, the opera-singing spaghetti monster greets me with a reminder to buy more spaghetti. As I walk to the couch, I see a frustrated tie tying himself into knots. I suddenly get a whiff of burnt marshmallows and remember nearly burning my entire tie in the bonfire, which reminds me of the next word on the list, fire . . . and so on. Using this technique, and a big enough "memory palace," you can remember virtually anything. There's research suggesting that the method of loci may tap into the natural human ability to use spatial context as a way to learn information by recruiting the right hippocampus.[16]

Steve Faloon was eventually able to achieve a memory span of 82 digits—leaving Miller's magic number in the dust. Tellingly, his "natural" short-term memory stayed the same. His mnemonic groupings and the number of groups in each supergroup never exceeded four (which as noted earlier is closer to the real magic number). He also rarely rehearsed more than six digits at the end of the list. And when Ericsson and Chase tested him on other kinds of information, such as letters, he couldn't go beyond six.

Nevertheless, SF's memory feats were certainly impressive. After 100 hours of practice, he was also able to cut in half the time required to memorize 50 digits—even to the point where he could remember numbers presented at 5 numbers per second (the fastest that could be read aloud by the experimenter) for shorter lists of around 11 digits. He was also able to accomplish the very same memory feats that were once thought to only be reserved for gifted mnemonists such as the famed subject S. In the 1960s, the neuroscientist Alexander Luria investigated the memory of newspaper reporter S. V. Shereshevskii (S) over the course of a twenty-year period. S demonstrated an uncanny ability to memorize random bits of information, such as nonsense syllables, complex mathematics formulas, and poems in foreign languages. In one paper, Luria described S's ability to recall the details of a matrix of 50 digits after looking at it for only three minutes.

Soon Ericsson and his colleagues branched out and tested others students—including another graduate student at CMU and a student at the University of Colorado. Three students eventually attained a digit span of over 18 digits. One student, "DD," was able to get to a digit span of 106 after four and a half years of training! He was also able to do the same task as Luria's subject S.

Other researchers in other laboratories also found that they could train people to overcome their natural memory "limitations."

Ericsson and colleagues even tested famous memory experts, including Guinness Book of World Records holders for the most digits of pi memorized—including Chao Lu (67,890 digits), Hideaki Tomoyori (40,000 digits), and Rajan Mahadevan (31,811 digits). They all (with the possible exception of Mahadevan) appeared to be using elaborative encoding methods, with no extraordinary natural memory. For instance, Masanobu Takahashi and colleagues estimate that Tomoyori spent about 9,000 to 10,000 hours memorizing to accomplish his feat.[17] Now *that's* devotion!

After Steven Faloon completed the experiment and then graduated from CMU, he took up jobs in Pittsburgh teaching high school psychology, sociology, and health. He launched a boys and girls' track team, a girls' basketball team, and a drama class, encouraging kids who had never taken the stage before to join. On May 14, 1981, just a few years after his extraordinary memory feats, 23-year-old Steve Faloon's life was taken by a rare disease that attacked his bone marrow. Just a few years later, in 1983, Bill Chase passed away while jogging at the age of 43.[18] Having inspired a whole new generation to believe in the power of their minds, they were gone, but certainly not forgotten.

The methodology that Chase and Ericsson used to train memory quickly spread through the research community as researchers attempted to reverse-engineer the mind of the expert. Many different forms of expertise were investigated, including chess, bridge, physics, computer programming, typing, juggling, music performance, political science, sales, medical diagnosis, sports, games, and dance. In their 1991 edited volume *Toward a General Theory of Expertise*, Ericsson and Jacqui Smith brought together various psychologists to present their findings.[19] The book showed that the same methodologies used to study the nature of human thinking and reasoning in the tightly controlled laboratory setting could also be applied to real-life forms of expertise. They came up with a name for this new paradigm: *the expert performance approach*.

The approach goes like this: Find a group of people who are consistently good at something—whether it's selecting the best next chess move, playing a rapturous violin concerto, making an accurate medical diagnosis, or predicting a soccer player's next move—and design representative tasks that can be administered in the laboratory. Bring people with differing levels of expertise into the lab and try to figure out what cognitive processes separate the experts from the novices by employing a variety of experimental techniques, including verbal reports, reaction times, and eye tracking. Aspects of the stimuli—whether it's a musical note, or a 30-digit number—can be manipulated to see how experts respond.

Based on a rigorous experimental procedure, researchers can come up with theories of what they think is really going on, instead of relying on reports from the performers themselves and the performers' mentors, family, and friends. Through many years of research, it has become clear that experts don't just know more about their specific domain of expertise.[20] Crucially, their knowledge is better organized, with richer networks of information and connections between their networks.

Experts also have more sophisticated mental representations that allow them to anticipate the next move, control the aspects of performance necessary to achieve at higher levels, and evaluate many different alternatives quickly before making the next move. This allows them to work forward from a given problem instead of shooting in the dark and working backward from the goal. Experts are quicker at recognizing the relevant information because they have many strategies stored in their densely connected forest of information.

In 1995 Ericsson and Kintsch proposed a cognitive mechanism that gives experts their advantage: long-term working memory (LTWM).[21] It's not quite short-term memory, the simple maintenance of information or chunks in a temporary state. It's also not just working memory, which requires the simultaneous maintenance and manipulation of information, or even long-term memory, the retrieval of permanent memories. Instead, LTWM is a hybrid of working and long-term memory, and involves deep encoding of information temporarily held in working memory based on the storehouse of knowledge held in long-term memory. Experts use their LTWM to anticipate future moves and construct their more elaborate representations and schemas.

Multiple threads of research demonstrate the incredible potency of expertise, sometimes trumping IQ in predicting complex reasoning.[22] Studies show that poor, uneducated children can solve problems when the task allows them to draw on their expertise, but that they may fail when presented with abstract versions of the same problem.[23] Similar results have been found for adults who can do quite complex reasoning within their area of expertise but do poorly operating on content that is not within their area of expertise—from bartenders remembering drink orders to expert grocery shoppers doing mental arithmetic.[24]

After conducting numerous studies in the real world, Gary Klein and colleagues concluded that expertise is related to recognition of a situation that had been encountered previously, and the automatic retrieval of schemas that match the situation.[25] Along similar lines, Valerie Reyna argues that experts acquire knowledge that allows them to make fast, intuitive, and effective decisions whereas novices need to rely on deliberate, effortful reasoning.[26] Timothy Wilson and Jonathan Schooler have also shown the importance of automatic processing in decision making—demonstrating that when making a decision that is complex and multi-attributed, people sometimes do better when conscious deliberation is intentionally prevented.[27]

Expertise isn't infallible, however. From the expert performance perspective, the phrase "expert performance" has a very precise scientific definition. It means *reproducibly superior performance*. As Ericsson and colleagues have repeatedly pointed out, just because someone is subjectively given the label "expert" doesn't make that person an expert. As the comedian Steve Martin once noted, "It was easy to be great. Every entertainer has a night when everything is clicking. These nights are accidental and statistical: Like lucky cards in poker, you can count on them occurring over time. What was hard was to be *good*, consistently good, night after night, no matter what the abominable circumstances."[28]

If we rely too much on expertise, we can become inflexible and unable to make reliable decisions. Therefore, one of the greatest aspects of expertise—instant pattern recognition—can also be its greatest downfall when context is ignored. Indeed, research on a range of experts—from psychotherapists to forecasters to wine-tasters—frequently fails to demonstrate consistent superior performance.[29] As Christopher Chabris and Daniel Simons point out in their book *The Invisible Gorilla: How Our Intuitions Deceive Us*, various real life "illusions" can lead us astray when we place too much confidence in our capacities for attention and rapid impressions.[30] They report that even expert chess players make better decisions when they are given more time to analyze their next move.[31] As Chabris and Simons wisely conclude in their book, "The key to successful decision-making, we believe, is knowing when to trust your intuition and when to be wary of it and do the hard work of thinking things through."[32]

A distinguishing characteristic that appears to separate the mere expert from the eminent performer is not just the ability to occasionally think things through, but to consistently put in a very specific sort of mental effort. Enter *deliberate practice*.

∽

After a large (but certainly not exclusive) review of research findings on the determinants of elite performance, Ericsson, Ralf Krampe, and Clemens Tesch-Römer concluded that the search for the genetic basis of characteristics that predict or account for superior performance of eminent people has proven largely unsuccessful.[33] They propose an alternative explanation for the development of elite performance: *deliberate practice*.

They distinguish deliberate practice from other activities such as work and play. They point out that deliberate practice is not mere repetition of an activity: "When laboratory training is extended over longer time periods, studies show that providing a motivated individual with mere exposure to a task does not ensure that the highest levels of performance will be attained."[34] Instead, deliberate practice is a highly structured activity that has been explicitly designed to improve a person's current level of performance.

Those who engage in deliberate practice engage in activities that allow them to attend to critical aspects of performance and incrementally improve performance in response to knowledge of results, feedback, or both from a teacher or mentor. While the activity itself may be inherently enjoyable (indeed, that's probably why the person was attracted to the activity in the first place), and the final achievement (such as performing at Carnegie Hall in front of thousands of adoring fans) can be immensely rewarding, the researchers emphasize that the actual *act* of deliberate practice is not fun. Deliberate practice requires intense effort and concentration.

What distinguishes mere mastery from eminence? Ericsson and colleagues argue that eminence is the result of ten years of incremental, sustained, deliberate practice in a domain. In support of the "ten-year rule," Ericsson and colleagues cited studies on chess (including the classic study by Simon and Chase I discussed earlier), music, mathematics, tennis, swimming, and long-distance running. They described a study by John R. Hayes, who analyzed the career trajectory of 76 classical composers and observed that their first notable compositions typically didn't appear until at least a decade after the composer began acquiring expertise in the domain (more on that study later).[35] They noted that "Long periods of necessary preparation can also be inferred for writers and scientists, although the starting point of their careers is more difficult to determine."[36] The idea of a ten-year rule can actually be traced back to the much earlier work of William Bryan and Noble Harter.[37] In July 1897 they proposed that it takes more than ten years of professional experience to "make a thoroughly seasoned press despatcher."[38] They go on to speculate that their theory may also pertain to "chess, geometry, chemistry and the like."[39]

To test the ten-year rule, Ericsson and colleagues asked violinists from the Music Academy in West Berlin to keep detailed diaries about their practice regime for a full week. They were asked to record at the end of the day all of their activities with their start and end times, and to recall the complete sequence of activities they engaged in during the day. They analyzed the duration and regularity of activities that they judged to be forms of deliberate practice and compared the different levels of deliberate practice between elite performers with promise as international soloists with the less accomplished performers.

All of the expert musicians spent about the same amount of time on music-related activities during the week—about 50 to 60 hours. But mere participation wasn't what differentiated the best from the rest. The two most accomplished groups of expert musicians spent more than twice the time in solitary practice during the week (25 hours) than the least accomplished group of experts (10 hours). The best violinists spent about 4 hours a day (including weekends) in solitary practice. The experts wrote that during these practice sessions they concentrated on improving very specific aspects of their performance as instructed by their music teacher in their prior lesson.

Ericsson and colleagues also asked all of the violinists to estimate the average number of hours of practice alone with the violin per week for each year since they started playing the violin. According to these estimates, the most elite violinists accumulated about the same number of hours of deliberate practice (about 7,410 hours) by the age of 18 as professional middle-aged violinists belonging to international-level orchestras (about 7,336 hours)! By the age of 20, the most accomplished musicians estimated they spent over 10,000 hours in deliberate practice, which is 2,500 and 5,000 hours more than two less accomplished groups of expert musicians or 8,000 hours more than amateur pianists of the same age. Figure 9.2 is a graph of the results.

Ericsson and colleagues argue that these results provide support for their theory. In their view, once individuals have begun the long, winding road to elite performance, deliberate practice leads to acquired skill and characteristics that enable even higher levels of performance. Over time, these built structures cause the maximal amount of possible practice time to increase.

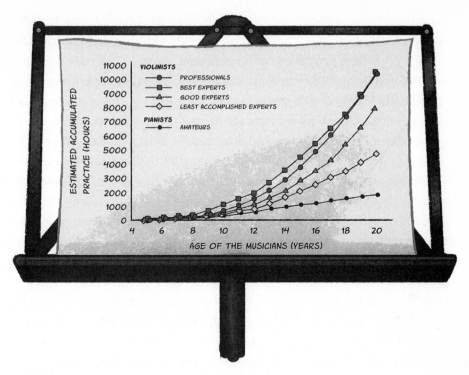

FIGURE 9.2.
Source: Data is from K. A. Ericsson, R. T. Krampe, and C. Tesch-Romer, "The Role of Deliberate Practice in the Acquisition of Expert Performance," *Psychological Review* 100 (1993): 363–406. Figure adapted with permission from K. A. Ericsson, R. A. Roring, and N. Kiruthiga, "Giftedness and Evidence for Superior Performance: An Account Based on the Expert Performance Framework," *High Ability Studies* 18 (2007): 3–56.

They argue that the very best performers start practice at earlier ages and maintain a higher level of daily practice.

Ericsson and colleagues acknowledge the possibility that innate talent might influence performance by allowing people to complete the same activity for longer times with the same amount of effort, but they dismiss the currently available evidence for this possibility. For one, they argue that once individuals have started deliberate practice, it is virtually impossible to distinguish innate talent from acquired characteristics. They also argue that deliberate practice is not a matter of merely "doing more of the same" but involves effortful engagement in an activity with full concentration designed to improve performance.

They don't completely rule out the influence of personality factors, such as "activity levels" and "emotionality," early in the process. But with the exception of height, they argue that eminent performers acquire virtually all of their distinguishing characteristics through deliberate practice, and they "reject any important role for innate ability" in constraining adult performance. Instead, they believe *perceptions* of innate talent play a crucial role: "We also recognize that being told by parents and teachers that they are talented, that is, genetically endowed with unusual gifts, most likely increases motivation, boosts self-confidence, and protects young performers against doubts about eventual success during the ups and downs of the extended preparation."[*,40]

Ericsson and colleagues do make it clear that their rejection of innate limits on acquired performance does not mean that elite performance is *easily* acquired. They point out that many elite performers have overcome multiple constraints, such as investing enormous amounts of time and energy, generating the motivation necessary to sustain this concentration, gaining access to important resources, receiving supports from their environment, and avoiding exhaustion, disease, injury, and failure. In their closing paragraph, Ericsson and colleagues conclude that "by viewing expert performers not simply as domain-specific experts but as experts in maintaining high levels of practice and improving performance, we are likely to uncover valuable information about the optimal conditions for learning and education."[41]

In recent years, the deliberate practice approach has been integrated into a number of related research programs. Let's consider some of these new, exciting lines of research.

∽

In a 2007 paper, Angela Duckworth and colleagues set the popular media on fire when they proposed a new psychological construct: *grit*.[42] They defined grit as "perseverance and passion for long-term goals" and cited a classic study by noted developmental psychologist Benjamin Bloom on the development of world-class pianists, neurologists, swimmers, chess players, and sculptors.[43] After extensive interviews, Bloom concluded that "only a few of [the 120 participants] were regarded as prodigies by teachers, parents, or experts."[44] Bloom observed that in every field the most accomplished individuals demonstrated a strong interest in their field, a desire to rise to the top of their field, and a willingness to put in the time and effort required to succeed. The most accomplished individuals were the ones who worked hard every single day, for at least ten or fifteen years.

---

*What a contrast from a growth mindset (see Chapter 7)!

Duckworth and colleagues distinguished grit from conscientiousness and self-control, arguing that the defining feature of grit is "long-term stamina rather than short-term intensity." They also distinguished grit from a need for achievement, defined by David McClelland as a drive to complete manageable goals that allow for immediate feedback.[45] People high in a need for achievement typically don't pursue goals that take them out of their comfort zone, and the need is often unconscious. In contrast, gritty people intentionally set challenging long-term goals and stay the course even in the absence of immediate rewards.

To test their ideas about the uniqueness of grit, Duckworth and colleagues constructed a brief self-report questionnaire, which they call the "Grit Scale." The scale measures the ability to persevere amongst setbacks as well as the ability to maintain interests over time. Here is the scale (test yourself!):

Consistency of Interests

I often set a goal but later choose to pursue a different one.

New ideas and new projects sometimes distract me from previous ones.

I become interested in new pursuits every few months.

My interests change from year to year.

I have been obsessed with a certain idea or project for a short time but later lost interest.

I have difficulty maintaining my focus on projects that take more than a few months to complete.

Perseverance of Effort

I have achieved a goal that took years of work.

I have overcome setbacks to conquer an important challenge.

I finish whatever I begin.

Setbacks don't discourage me.

I am a hard worker.

I am diligent.

As expected, Duckworth and colleagues found that their scale was highly related to the personality trait conscientiousness. While the correlations weren't as strong as with conscientiousness, gritty folks also tended to be less neurotic, more agreeable, more extraverted, and more open to new experiences. Crucially (in terms of their argument that grit is a distinct construct), they found that grit predicted a number of outcomes above and beyond these personality traits. This included higher undergraduate GPA (despite lower SAT scores), summer retention and cadet quality at West Point (as assessed by a committee), and a higher ranking in the Scripps National Spelling Bee.

In a more recent study, Duckworth teamed up with Ericsson (as well as other colleagues) to integrate the grit and deliberate practice approaches.[46] They found that National Spelling Bee participants who engaged in more solitary study of word spellings and origins (their measure of deliberate practice) were more likely to attain a higher level of performance, and this activity was a better predictor of performance than other activities such as verbal leisure activities (for instance, playing word games) and preparation (for instance, being quizzed by another person or a computer program).

They also found that competitors who scored higher on the Grit Scale engaged in more deliberate practice than their less gritty competitors, and total hours of deliberate practice explained the association between grit and spelling performance. Intriguingly, they also found a *negative* association between openness to experience and spelling bee performance. This suggests that openness and curiosity may get in the way of the deliberate practice required to succeed in some highly disciplined activities such as learning how to spell words (more on openness to experience in Chapter 12).

While the grit research program holds a lot of promise, the jury is out on whether grit really is a different trait than conscientiousness. Grit and conscientiousness consistently demonstrate very high correlations.[47] It also remains to be seen whether grit is more trainable than IQ and other personality traits. Nevertheless, I remain optimistic that grit is trainable: we've already seen in prior chapters that motivation and self-regulation are malleable and highly dependent on context. A number of researchers, myself included, have further interventions under way on grit, and I look forward to the results.

∼

The early work of Albert Bandura, written in the 1960s, also shares some conceptual similarities to the deliberate practice approach. Bandura rejected the view that learning is passive. Instead he emphasized the importance of the active use of strategies.[48] Extending this research in 1986, Barry Zimmerman and Martinez Pons published a paper that helped spur an entire new field of study on *self-regulated learning strategies* (SRL).[49]

Zimmerman and Pons interviewed 40 tenth-grade students who were on a "high achievement track" and compared their responses against those of 40 tenth-graders who were in "lower achievement tracks." Specifically, they asked the students about the learning strategies they used to participate in class, study, and complete their assignments. Through the course of their interviews, they identified fourteen self-regulated learning strategies. They found that the high-achieving students differed from the low-achieving students in regard to whether they used these strategies, how much they used the strategies, and their consistency in using the strategies.

Over the past few decades there have been many studies based on the self-regulated learning strategies approach, including recent integration with the expertise performance approach.[50] In one recent study, Kiruthiga Nandago-pal and Ericsson investigated the use of self-regulated learning strategies among advanced undergraduate bioscience majors.[51] Because these students "made active decisions to embark on the road to acquiring expertise in the biological sciences," they met the expert performance approach criteria.[52]

Adopting one of the key methodologies of the expert performance approach, they analyzed student diaries over the course of three weeks, estimating the presence, frequency, and duration (in terms of total number of hours) of self-regulated learning strategies. They grouped fourteen self-regulated learning strategies into six main categories: *self-regulating* (self-assessing, goal-setting, planning, and so on), *organizing, seeking information, mnemonic usage, seeking social assistance* (for instance, seeking assistance from peers, tutors, and professors), and *reviewing* (reviewing prior problems, notes, textbook, and such). Then they compared the diary responses among the following three groups of achievers based on their GPA before entering the course: high-achieving students (GPA > 3.7), average-achieving students (GPA ≥ 3) and low-achieving students (GPA < 3).

Unsurprisingly, students engaged in organizing, transforming, and reviewing notes more frequently and for longer stretches of time during the midterm week than other weeks. But the really informative results came from comparing the diary responses of the different groups of achievers. The high-achieving students reported employing a larger number of different strategies. Timing was also important: high-achieving students sought more assistance from their peers and spent more time studying during midterm weeks compared to low-achieving students. In contrast, low-achieving students engaged in these strategies more than average-achieving students toward the *end* of the semester. High-achieving students also spent more time overall in study-related activities earlier in the semester compared to average and low-achieving students, whereas there was no such difference between the groups later on in the semester.

While the correlation between SAT scores and prior GPA was significant, once SRL strategies were considered, SAT scores didn't explain any additional variation in GPA. Interestingly, only their diary method differentiated between the three groups; interviews did not. Because the diaries assessed day-to-day strategy use, these results suggest that the effectiveness of strategies is highly contextual and dependent on the specific time point in the course.

Another recent study further supports the importance of cognitive strategies for predicting long-term achievement. Kou Murayama and colleagues investigated the simultaneous prediction of motivation, cognitive strategies and IQ for explaining the long-term growth in mathematics achievement from Grades 5 to 10 among a sample of German students.[53] Their measure of math achievement tested competencies such as arithmetic, algebra, and geometry. At the start of their study, IQ, motivation, and cognitive strategies significantly predicted math performance, with motivation and cognitive strategies adding additional prediction above IQ.

A different story emerged, however, once they looked at the predictors of long-term growth. IQ was not related to growth after taking into account demographic information. In contrast, *perceived control* (e.g., "When doing math, the harder I try, the better I perform"), *intrinsic motivation* (e.g., "I invest a lot of effort in math, because I am interested in the subject"), and *deep learning strategies* (e.g., "When I study for exams, I try to make connections with other areas of math"), significantly predicted growth of mathematics. What's more, *surface learning strategies* ("For some math problems I memorize the steps to the correct solution") *negatively* predicted mathematics growth. The researchers relate their findings to the Matthew Effect (see Chapter 1): those with high intrinsic motivation and effective cognitive strategies will tend to increase their ability, while those without those characteristics will tend to decrease their ability. Over time, the gap between those with higher ability and those with lower ability will widen. Which is all the more reason why we ought to set up the right conditions for engagement (see Chapter 6), and teach people the proper strategies for success.

It seems a marriage of the self-regulated learning and deliberate practice approaches can be fruitful for our understanding of effective learning, as well as long-term growth and development.

$\sim$

Another crucial concept related to deliberate practice is hope. In 1991, positive psychologist Charles Snyder and colleagues came up with "hope theory."[54] According to their theory, hope consists of agency and pathways. The person who has hope has the will and determination to achieve goals and a set of various strategies at their disposal to reach their goals. Put simply: *Hope involves the will to get there and different ways to get there.*

Both are important. Life is difficult. There are inevitable obstacles. Having goals is not enough. One has to keep getting closer to those goals amid all the inevitable twists and turns of life. Hope allows people to approach problems with a mindset and strategy set suitable to success, thereby increasing the chances they will actually accomplish their goals. Studies conducted by Gabriele Oettingen, Peter Gollwitzer, and colleagues have shown that both *mental contrasting* and *implementation intentions* are important for achieving goals. Mental contrasting involves comparing your dreams about the future with the realistic reflection of the obstacles that may prevent their realization. Implementation intentions involve coming up with a detailed plan that makes it clear when, where, and how you will take practical action and make the realization of your dreams more likely.[55]

A recent study by Duckworth, Heidi Grant Halvorson, Benjamin Loew, Oettingen, and Gollwitzer asked a group of high school students preparing for the high-stakes, standardized Preliminary SAT (PSAT) to complete a thirty-minute written intervention that involved mental contrasting (vividly imagining the goal and writing down possible obstacles) with implementation intentions (coming up with two if-then contingency plans if an obstacle presents itself). They found that students undergoing the intervention completed more than 60 percent more practice questions on the PSAT compared to a placebo control group who were instead asked to write about an influential person or event in their life.[56]

These results suggest that hope, as defined by Snyder and colleagues, is not just a feel-good emotion, but a dynamic cognitive motivational system. According to hope theory, emotions follow cognitions, not the other way around. Hope-related cognitions are important: Snyder and his colleagues proposed that a person's level of hope leads him or her to choose learning or performance goals.[57] According to their theory, those lacking hope typically adopt performance goals and choose easy tasks that don't offer a challenge or opportunity for growth. When they fail, they quit. They act helpless and feel a lack of control over their environment. They don't believe in their capacity to obtain the kind of future they want. In other words, *they have no hope.*

Science is on the side of hope. Snyder and his colleagues came up with a way of measuring hope, both as a stable trait of an individual and as a state one can be in at any time. "The Hope Scale," which has been translated into more than twenty languages, includes items relating to *agency* (such as "I energetically pursue my goals") and *pathways* (such as "There are lots of ways around any problem").

Whether measured as a trait or as a state, hope is related to positive outcomes. In one study, researchers looked at the impact of hope on college academic achievement over the course of six years.[58] Hope was related to a higher GPA six years later, even after taking into account the original GPA and ACT entrance examination scores of the participants. High-hope students (relative to low-hope students) were also more likely to have graduated and were less likely to be dismissed from school due to bad grades. Researchers have also looked at the role of hope among athletes. In one study, athletes had higher levels of hope than nonathletes.[59] Hope also predicted semester GPAs, overall GPAs, and overall self-worth. Among a group of female cross-country athletes in particular, the state of having hope predicted athletic outcomes beyond training, as well as self-esteem, confidence, and mood.

In more recent research, Liz Day and her colleagues found that hope was related to academic achievement above and beyond IQ, divergent thinking (the ability to generate a lot of ideas), and conscientiousness.[60] In that study, hope was measured as a trait. In a recent undergraduate thesis study, Rebecca Görres found that *situational* hope was related to divergent thinking.[61] In her study, participants who were instructed to think hopefully (e.g., "What motivates you to pursue your goal?," "What are your alternative pathways to reach your goal?") were better at making remote associations, generated a higher quantity of ideas, and added more details to their ideas compared to those who weren't instructed to think hopefully.

The link between hope and divergent thinking makes sense, considering that divergent thinkers are good at coming up with lots of different ideas (see Chapter 12) and hope involves coming up with a number of different strategies for obtaining a goal. In terms of practical implications, Görres notes: "It seems that performance can be enhanced in the short term by reminding people that they have the motivation and the means to pursue a goal. This 'situational hope' could potentially be useful in the future as a means of short-term intervention to enhance performance. By reminding people before tests or situations in which performance and achievement are required that they have the will and the ways to do well, possible potential can be better utilized."

Hope can be distinguished from other psychological resources, such as self-efficacy and optimism. Self-efficacy refers to your belief that you can master a domain. Optimism refers to a general expectation that it'll all just "be all right." Hope, self-efficacy, and optimism are all important expectancies and contribute to the attainment of goals. Even though they all involve expectations about the future, they are subtly, and importantly, different from each other. People with self-efficacy expect that they will master a domain. Optimism involves a positive expectancy for future outcomes without regard for one's personal control over the outcome.

In contrast to both self-efficacy and optimism, people with hope have both the will *and* the strategies necessary to achieve their goals. So how does hope stack up against other psychological resources? Philip R. Magaletta and J. M. Oliver measured hope, self-efficacy, and optimism and found that hope stood head and shoulders above the other vehicles.[62] They also found specific effects: The *will* component of hope predicted well-being independent of self-efficacy, and the *ways* component of hope predicted well-being independent of optimism. In another study, Kevin Rand and his colleagues found that hope, but not optimism, predicted grades in law school above and beyond LSAT scores and undergraduate grades.[63] Interestingly, LSAT scores were not a significant predictor of law school GPA. It appears that law school performance might be better predicted by a twelve-item measure of hope than completion of a standardized entrance exam! Additionally, both hope and optimism uniquely predicted greater life satisfaction at the end of the first semester.

It looks like hope—with its will and ways—is an important characteristic contributing to deliberate practice.

∾

Other recent research shows the tight linkages among passion, mindset, self-regulation, and deliberate practice. In a recent paper Jeni Burnette and colleagues reviewed a number of articles that report on the relationship between mindset (fixed vs. growth mindset) and various self-regulatory processes.[64] There's so much meat in their paper, but here are three take-away messages:

1. Mindsets matter for the goals we set (goal setting), the ways we try to achieve our goals (goal operating), and how we assess progress (goal monitoring).
2. The relationships between mindset and these three self-regulatory processes[65] are nuanced. For instance, the connection between mindset and self-regulation is particularly strong following setbacks, when the ego is threatened.
3. The most important impact of mindset on achievement is through the monitoring process. People with a growth mindset are better at regulating their emotions and expectations in the face of setbacks, and this helps them to achieve their goals.

Another recent set of studies shows the tight link between passion and deliberate practice. Vallerand and colleagues investigated the role of passion among 143 Canadian students enrolled in a specialized course for the dramatic arts.[66] These students aspired to be television, film, and theater actors and comedians. The researchers found that both harmonious and obsessive passion positively predicted the amount of deliberate practice, and deliberate practice in turn positively predicted the instructor's ratings of performance. Only harmonious passion was related to life satisfaction, however.

The researchers also looked at the role of passion among 130 undergraduate students enrolled in a selective psychology course. They found a direct path from harmonious passion to deliberate practice: the students who were more harmoniously passionate about their work were more likely to engage in deliberate practice. They also found a direct path from mindset to deliberate practice: a mastery mindset directly predicted deliberate practice, and deliberate practice and performance-approach mindsets predicted performance. Performance-avoidance goals did not influence performance.

But the researchers also found indirect pathways. Harmoniously passionate students were more likely to engage in their studies for mastery, and this growth mindset predicted higher levels of deliberate practice. In contrast, obsessive passion was more of a mixed bag, predicting all three mindsets: mastery, performance-approach, and performance-avoidance. Harmonious passion was positively related to subjective well-being, whereas obsessive passion was negatively related to subjective well-being. Similar findings have been demonstrated in subsequent research among high school basketball players, synchronized swimming and water-polo players, and classical musicians.[67]

This research suggests that there are at least two different passionate paths to high performance. The first road—the *harmoniously passionate road*—is the most direct and psychologically healthy. It's paved with a focus on the goal of mastery and growth, not looking good or outcompeting others. This path is fueled by feelings of positive emotion, enjoyment, and vitality. The second road—the *obsessively passionate road*—is way more winding. While it is paved with goals that can be adaptive for performance, it is also paved with other goals that can be detrimental to performance, such as the avoidance of challenges that could lead to further growth. This path is also driven by low levels of subjective well-being.

Therefore, passion influences deliberate practice, but not all passionate paths are fueled by the same mindset.

∼

These studies are exciting, because they all converge on the importance of passion, growth mindset, perseverance, and deliberate practice for attaining your goals. But is this the whole story of high performance? Are we done? Not yet. Few researchers doubt the importance of deliberate practice. What is still in dispute is whether it's *sufficient* for high performance. In recent years, a number of studies have cropped up suggesting that more nuance is in order. For one thing, it is becoming increasingly clear that the ten-year rule is not a fixed threshold, but an average with a great amount of variation. People differ greatly in their *rate* of expertise acquisition.

Dean Keith Simonton noted that the classic study by Hayes on the ten-year rule among classical composers omitted some key methodological details and also made some jarring mistakes.[68] For instance, Hayes wrote: "Albeniz's first masterwork was written in the 72nd year of his career."[69] But this can't be true. Albeniz's *last* major work was *Iberia*, which appeared somewhere between his forty-sixth and forty-ninth birthday. Since Albeniz passed away at the age of 49, it's difficult to imagine how he could have composed his *first* masterwork at the age of 72! This casts doubt on the rest of Hayes's analysis.

So Simonton decided to conduct a study of his own. He included a larger sample of 120 classical composers.[70] Only 100 composers account for nearly all the major works in the classical repertoire, so this assured that no composer worthy of study was excluded. Simonton found support for the importance of deliberate practice: very few composers launched their careers by composing a masterpiece. Some preparatory period was required. On average, notable compositions weren't created until 17 to 22 years after the first formal lessons, and 10 to 14 years after the first compositions.

But Simonton wasn't done. He observed that these averages masked considerable individual differences. Some composers only took two years to contribute to the classical repertoire, whereas others took decades. What's more, composers with accelerated accomplishments tended to have the largest lifetime output of masterpieces, were the oldest when making their last notable compositions, and displayed the greatest lasting reputation in the world of classical music.

Other departures from the ten-year rule have been found in other domains across the arts and sciences.[71] Not all fields show an early advantage, however. James C. Kaufman (no relation) and Claudia Gentile looked at the relationship between age at first publication in creative writing and career productivity (number of works produced) and success (winning a Nobel or Pulitzer prize).[72] While they found a significant relationship between an early debut in poetry and increased productivity, they did not find an early advantage when it came to career *success*. Also, there was no early advantage in fiction when looking at productivity or success.

More recently, I teamed up with James to investigate how long it took a contemporary sample of 215 of the most accomplished fiction writers (as judged by *Salon*) to publish their most revered work.[73] We found it took the fiction writers *on average* 10.6 years between their first publication and their best publication. This suggested that there may be two phases among eminent creative writers: a first phase of preparation leading up to initial publication and another phase leading to greatness. In other words, ten years appears too brief to account for creative writing greatness!

But consistent with the work of Simonton, we also found substantial variation. The first work was also the best work, for 17 percent of the writers in our sample. Such first-hit wonders include Allan Gurganus (*Oldest Living Confederate Widow Tells All*), William Gibson (*Neuromancer*), and Joseph Heller (*Catch-22*). Such precocity wasn't necessary though: we found that individual cases were all over the place. In fact, most writers (53 percent) produced their masterpiece eight or more years after their debut publication.

For instance, Norman Mailer took 11 years to produce his best work, John Irving took 16 years, and Don DeLillo took 26 years. One writer even took 45 years! Clearly, later blooming is possible.

~

Another thread of research that has added further nuance to the deliberate practice approach are studies looking at the relationship between cognitive ability and the acquisition of different forms of knowledge. A common criticism of the expertise performance approach is *restriction of range*: by focusing on already-established experts in a field who are all quite similar to each other, the full range of traits that were crucial to their development won't be discovered.

But even within a restricted range, cognitive ability may still be significantly correlated with the acquisition of expertise. Ericsson and colleagues investigate a wide variety of domains that differ in their demands for procedural knowledge (knowledge of how to do something) and declarative knowledge (factual information stored in long-term memory). Some characteristics may contribute more heavily to the acquisition of declarative knowledge than procedural knowledge.[74] This is important, because by focusing on deliberate practice *in general*, Ericsson may be missing out on important characteristics that distinguish experts *across* domains.

Phillip Ackerman's research suggests that cognitive abilities, interests, and personality develop in tandem. In an impressive review of the literature, Phillip Ackerman and Eric Heggestad integrated multiple strands of research by showing the substantial overlap among *cognitive*, *affective* (e.g., anxiety and motivation), and *conative* (e.g., self-control, directed effort) traits.[75]

They found that neuroticism and test anxiety have pervasive *negative* correlations with abilities, whereas extraversion had pervasive *positive* relationships with abilities. This is highly consistent with what we saw in Chapter 7—positive emotions propel engagement, whereas negative emotions impede engagement. Additionally, the researchers identified four clusters of traits ("trait complexes"):

- **Social cluster:** social and enterprising interests, extroversion, social potency (the ability to influence others), and well-being; ability test scores were *irrelevant* to this cluster.
- **Clerical/Conventional cluster:** perceptual speed abilities, conventional interests, conscientiousness, and traditionalism.

- **Science/Math cluster:** math reasoning ability, spatial ability, and realistic and investigative interests.
- **Intellectual/Cultural cluster:** verbal reasoning ability, ideational fluency, absorption, typical intellectual engagement (a person's typical level of intellectual engagement in their daily lives), openness to experience, as well as artistic and investigative interests.

These clusters are informative in our understanding of how ability, interest, and personality are inextricably linked across domains. But what is the relationship between these traits and the actual acquisition of declarative knowledge in these domains? In a more recent study, Ackerman investigated the relationship between knowledge across eighteen domains of human achievement and ability, personality, and interests among 228 educated adults 21 to 62 years of age.[76] Ackerman administered tests of nonverbal fluid reasoning to measure "fluid intelligence" and vocabulary, general cultural knowledge, and verbal fluid reasoning to measure "crystallized intelligence" (in Chapter 10 you'll see why I put these terms in quotes). Here is what he found:

Domain of Knowledge	Correlation with Fluid Intelligence	Correlation with Crystallized Intelligence	Age
Chemistry	.516	.385	−.240
Physics	.568	.515	−.136
Biology	.409	.397	−.202
Psychology	.361	.391	−.099
Business/Management	.352	.395	.083
Astronomy	.440	.518	.014
Electronics	.347	.451	.200
Technology	.410	.510	.030
Economics	.397	.501	.082
Law	.188	.379	.189
Geography	.320	.525	.150
Music	.269	.527	.297
American Government	.317	.583	.218
Art	.168	.468	.224
World Literature	.253	.600	.248
American History	.226	.582	.345
Western Civilization	.232	.588	.277
American Literature	.156	.574	.357
Fluid intelligence		.589	−.388
Crystallized intelligence	.589		.143

One notable aspect of this data is the age trends. Consistent with many prior studies, fluid intelligence tended to *decrease* with age, whereas crystallized intelligence tended to *increase* with age.[77] Surely the decrease in fluid reasoning as we age has some impact on our acquisition of expertise. If anything, it can make it more difficult for us to form strategies to solve novel problems (see Chapter 10). For instance, Paul Baltes and Reinhold Kliegl found that after numerous training sessions, older participants showed sizable deficits compared to younger adults in their ability to use the method of loci technique to aid themselves in encoding and retrieving a new list of words.[78] They argue that as we age, we suffer a loss in the production and use of the mental imagination necessary for operations of the mind.

But don't give up on adults just yet. Ackerman also found that with the exception of the sciences, there was a trend for domain-specific knowledge across all of the domains to *increase* with age. Ackerman makes the distinction between "intelligence-as-process," which is what is primarily measured by fluid reasoning tests, and "intelligence-as-knowledge," which consists of the important forms of expertise that we acquire throughout the life span.[79] As Ackerman points out, many intellectually demanding tasks in the real world require a vast repertoire of declarative knowledge and procedural skills. Under his framework, "knowledge does not compensate for a declining adult intelligence, it *is* intelligence!"[80]

That doesn't mean that individual differences in cognitive ability across the life span are irrelevant. As you can see, for the entire sample there was a pervasive influence of fluid and crystallized intelligence test scores across all domains of knowledge. But there were also important patterns. Domain-specific knowledge across the domains was much more strongly correlated with crystallized than with fluid intelligence. The crucial exception was the science domains: fluid intelligence was a particularly strong predictor of knowledge in chemistry, physics, and biology. In contrast, social sciences showed roughly equal correlations with fluid and crystallized intelligence, and arts and humanities and civics showed the greatest relationship to crystallized intelligence relative to fluid intelligence. Also note that both fluid and crystallized intelligence were correlated with each other .589, suggesting there may be some skill or set of skills in common across different measures of cognitive ability (much more on that in Chapter 10).

Nevertheless, fluid and crystallized intelligence accounted for at most only 50 percent of the differences in all eighteen domains of knowledge, with some domains accounting for much less. For instance, fluid and crystallized intelligence accounted for only 23.5 percent of the differences in business/law knowledge. Personality and interests added additional predictive value. Typical intellectual engagement contributed to prediction in every domain of knowledge except for business/law. Investigative interests were strongly correlated with knowledge in science, and artistic interests were strongly correlated with knowledge in the humanities. Interestingly, those with enterprising, social, and conventional interests tended to have *less* science knowledge, and lower fluid and crystallized test scores. But do we want to call individuals with interests in these domains of knowledge less *intelligent*?

Taken together, these results suggest that personal characteristics—including cognitive skills, personality, and interests—are significantly related to the acquisition of a variety of forms of expertise. The correlations were far from perfect, and there was still a lot of variation left unexplained, but some of the correlations were moderate. On the one hand, there was support for Ericsson's theory: cognitive ability didn't *determine* the acquisition of expertise; there was plenty of room for error among the correlations. But on the other hand, they did tell us an important story about the kinds of minds that are attracted to acquiring particular domains of knowledge, and how ability, personality, and interests develop in tandem.

In my view, although there has been a great and very important integration in recent years among the many drivers of success (passion, mindset, self-regulation, grit, hope, deliberate practice, and so on), there are still multiple areas of research that are ripe for integration. In the next few chapters, let's improve this integration by coming to a deeper understanding of the true mechanisms that lie beneath the psychologists' labels "general intelligence," "talent," and "creativity."

Not only might we see a more nuanced picture of deliberate practice, but maybe we'll also come to a more complete understanding of human intelligence.

Chapter 10

g

Fall 2001

"I'm going to email him," I tell my friend. She looks at me like I am crazy. I am starting to get used to this reaction. "Scott, you can't just randomly email the head of the Cambridge Psychology Department! Who does that?" I sit down and think this through. I really want to step into the lion's den and learn everything there is to know about intelligence. I need a mentor. I also am rather scared to stay in the country at the moment due to recent attacks. Which is why I searched online for intelligence experts in England. I came across Professor Nicholas J. Mackintosh, an expert on IQ and human intelligence. Since he was at Cambridge University, I dreamed of spires, ivy, and stained glass windows. Images of the prep school I was denied access to as a child came flooding back. "What do I have to lose?" I told my friend. "I'm gonna do it."

To my surprise, Professor Mackintosh is very welcoming, and happy for me to work with him. Carnegie Mellon grants me a one-semester, six-month leave of absence. To work out the details, I fly to England to have a chat with the professor. In one of the most surreal moments of my life, I find myself sitting in the waiting area to see the head of the Cambridge University Department of Experimental Psychology. My heart and mind race. *What if I'm not smart enough for this? This is Cambridge, for heaven's sake. What if he gives me an IQ test?* Then, the door opens.

"Mr. Kaufman?" I stand up and find myself face to face with a distinguished-looking elderly man. His smile puts me immediately at ease. "Come inside." I walk into his office and look around the room. Lots of books with the word "intelligence" on the cover. I feel a tingle. Am I finally going to be able to solve the mysteries of intelligence that brought me so much pain and anxiety as a child?

"So let me get this straight," he says, scratching his gray hair. "You'd like to take six months off from your American University and learn everything there is to know about intelligence from me?" I nod, just as a tall, middle-aged woman enters the room. "This is Sheila," he says, beckoning her to sit down next to me. "She teaches at a local Sixth Form College, which is the equivalent of an American High School. We're working on a study investigating differences in spatial intelligence. We would more than welcome your help. Is this the sort of thing you'd like to be involved with?"

I can barely contain my excitement. The room starts spinning. He continues: "I think we'd be able to set you up in King's College for the duration of your stay as a Visiting Scholar. You could engage in the social life of the College. It's a wonderful place. I'll give you a tour later today."

Now I can barely breathe. Cambridge consists of thirty-one colleges, in which the students live and work. King's is one of the oldest (founded in 1441) and arguably the most beautiful, most noted for its magnificent late-Gothic perpendicular chapel. I look up at Professor Mackintosh, then over to Sheila. Feeling as though the room is spinning, I muster just enough strength to respond: "I'm in."

So my journey to master the science of intelligence began. As I learned everything I could about measuring intelligence—keeping my own past a secret—I encountered many surprises. What surprised me most was the disconnect between two worlds—clinicians interested in the practical application of IQ and research scientists interested in understanding the nature of human intelligence. Over the past 100 years, the majority of scientists who studied intelligence weren't interested in IQ, per se. For them, IQ was just a proxy for something called g (general intelligence factor)—which many of them conceptualized as the essence of human intelligence. In fact, the first scientific study to discover g was published a year before the first IQ test appeared.

I realized that if I *truly* wanted to understand the foundation upon which modern IQ tests were constructed and eventually applied, I had to tame g.

$\sim$

At the turn of the twentieth century, the British psychologist Charles Spearman made a startling discovery. He went to a few local British schools in the nearby village and collected student grades, teacher ratings, and scores on tests of sensory discrimination. He then ranked each child's performance relative to his or her peers on this assortment of outcomes, and calculated by hand the strength of the relationship among the different outcomes. This is what he found among six areas of school performance:

	Classics	French	English	Math	Pitch	Music
Classics	—					
French	.83	—				
English	.78	.67	—			
Math	.70	.67	.64	—		
Pitch	.66	.65	.54	.45	—	
Music	.63	.57	.51	.51	.40	—

Each number represents the strength of the correlation between each set of tests, ranging from .40 to .83. These results surprised Spearman. Some relationships made good sense, such as the high correlation between classics and French (.83). They both, after all, involved facility with languages. But some correlations had a less obvious explanation, such as the relation between math grades and pitch discrimination, as rated by their school music teacher (.45).

In fact, the most unexpected finding of them all was that *every single correlation* was positive. You would expect that the more time a student puts into one area of study, the more performance in other areas suffer. But that wasn't the case. Students who performed well in one school subject tended to perform well in other school subjects. Spearman referred to this phenomenon as the *positive manifold*.

Based on the patterns of student performance, Spearman was able to rank all of the students on a single dimension, which he called the *g* factor, and showed that performance in each class was related to this factor to a varying degree. For instance, classics was correlated with this factor (.95) much more than music (.65), but all subjects were still positively related to this factor. Spearman also showed that each subject also had its own unique set of skills (for instance, classics involves learning how to conjugate Latin verbs), which he labeled *s* for "specific." In his groundbreaking 1904 paper "General Intelligence, Objectively Determined and Measured," Spearman proposed that the cause of the *g* factor (or *g*, for short) was a general cognitive ability he called "general intelligence."[1]

Spearman presumed that the *g* factor—which explained the largest source of differences in performance across all school subjects—represented something we would want to refer to as "general intelligence." It is important to recognize, however, that this was Spearman's decision, to label the factor "general intelligence." To derive g, Spearman used a statistical method called factor analysis, which is a potentially useful way of telling a story with data. The technique simplifies a large number of correlations by finding common sources of variation. Using factor analysis, you can come up with a manageable number of factors instead of having to deal with the unwieldy correlations among the tests. But as is the case even to this day, it is entirely up to the psychologist to label the factors.

If Spearman wanted to be really descriptive, he could have just labeled the factor "general test-taking ability," or "the general ability to quickly choose the response deemed correct by the psychologist," but that wouldn't have made for such a sexy journal article title. And it certainly wouldn't have sounded as scientific—Spearman was proud that he "objectively" discovered "general intelligence," as though he discovered a law of human nature akin to any other physical law of nature.

With that said, some frequent criticisms misrepresent Spearman's position. In *The Mismeasure of Man,* the late Harvard paleontologist Stephen Jay Gould accused Spearman of reifying g (that is, treating g as though it really exists).[2] While this is certainly a fair charge against some modern-day intelligence researchers (see Chapter 13), a close reading of Spearman suggests he knew better. He understood the difference between the g factor and "general intelligence," which he proposed is the psychological ability that causes the g factor to emerge.

Remember, Spearman *discovered* the positive manifold. It didn't have to be the case—and certainly wasn't expected—that all his variables would positively correlate with one another. It's the positive manifold that needs explaining: Why do people who do well on one cognitive test tend to perform well on all the others? Spearman argued that general intelligence was an innate general "mental energy" that pervaded performance on all tests of cognitive ability. This was just a hypothesis; he knew it would require further testing.

∼

Spearman's g didn't go unchallenged.[3] An American psychometrician, Louis Thurstone, showed that his battery of tests formed clear clusters of abilities.[4] For example, his spatial tests were more strongly related to each other than to the verbal tests. Using a different method of factor analysis than Spearman, he argued that g doesn't exist. Instead, he argued that we differ from each other on seven *independent* primary mental abilities: verbal comprehension, verbal fluency, number facility, spatial visualization, associative memory, perceptual speed, and inductive reasoning.

Both Spearman's and Thurstone's theories were heavily influenced by their authors' own psychological stances on pressing issues of the time. Spearman shunned "faculty" psychology that attempted to decompose the mind into distinct faculties. Thurstone, on the other hand, embraced the compartmentalization of the human mind and strongly believed that human intelligence is the result of a number of independent components.

But who was right? No matter how hard Spearman tried to sweep the importance of Thurstone's primary mental abilities under the rug, they kept cropping up whenever he analyzed sufficiently large batteries of tests. At the same time, no matter how hard Thurstone tried to make *g* disappear through his own special method of factor analysis ("rotation to simple structure"), individual cognitive abilities still tended to correlate positively.[5]

Again, some critics miss this fact. Gould argued that whether or not *g* appears depends on your method of factor analysis. But this is not correct. Today there are formulas available to mathematically transform the *g* calculated by one method of factor analysis into the *g* calculated by a different method of factor analysis.[6] In fact, this is a story that is repeated over and over again in every generation. In the 1960s, Raymond Cattell and his student John Horn argued that "fluid" and "crystallized" intelligence are independent abilities.[7] They claimed that "fluid intelligence" is influenced by biology and independent of education and experience, whereas "crystallized intelligence" is influenced by learning and experience, and involves accumulated knowledge and skills. They quickly realized, however, that all of their tests positively correlated with each other. By the 1990s their model of intelligence included nine to ten different positively correlated cognitive abilities.[8]

Eventually a compromise was made, based on a grand synthesis. In 1993 John Carroll published his monumental analysis of over fifty years of factor analytic research.[9] He analyzed over 400 datasets—including some of the very same datasets used by Spearman and Thurstone. He looked at a wide (but certainly not all-inclusive) range of cognitive ability tests, including language, reasoning, memory, learning, visual perception, auditory perception, idea production, cognitive speed, and psychomotor abilities. Not all of the tests included abilities explicitly taught in school, not all were timed, and not all were administered in a paper-and-pencil format. Nonetheless, despite this diversity of cognitive ability tests and testing formats, *g* still emerged.

Based on a careful analysis, Carroll argued for a hierarchical model of intelligence, which he called the "Three Stratum Theory." At the top of the hierarchy ("Stratum III") is *g*—the common factor among all the diverse tests. This stratum is the most abstract, and doesn't represent any *actual* cognitive ability. *g* strips all of the specificity out of each test and represents solely what they all have in common. At "Stratum II" are eight broad abilities, each one varying in its relation to the *g* factor at the topmost level: fluid intelligence, crystallized intelligence, general memory and learning, visual perception, auditory perception, knowledge retrieval ability, cognitive speediness, and decision speed.

At the lowest level of the hierarchy is "Stratum I"—sixty-nine narrow abilities that make up the eight broad abilities. For instance, "fluid intelligence" is made up of nonverbal, verbal-deductive, and quantitative forms of fluid reasoning, and "crystallized intelligence" is made up of a cluster of narrow abilities such as reading comprehension, inferring the meaning of peculiar words from their context, reading decoding, reading speed, spelling ability, writing ability, lexical knowledge, listening ability, and phonetic coding. As we saw in Chapter 2, Carroll's model of cognitive abilities strongly influenced the CHC theory of cognitive abilities, which greatly informed the construction of numerous contemporary IQ tests (see the Appendix).

Rightly so, Carroll's massive synthesis garnered immense respect from his colleagues. Horn referred to Carroll's book as a "tour de force summary and integration" comparable to "Mendeleev's first presentation of a periodic table of elements in chemistry."[10] Most can only dream of such recognition among colleagues!

At last, all seemed to be resolved. The field now had a road map—a taxonomy of patterns of covariation among a wide-ranging (but still limited) set of cognitive abilities. While there's still some disagreement today as to the precise structuring of the levels of the hierarchy, new, more sophisticated statistical techniques have confirmed that the hierarchical structure fits the data the best.[11] What's more, you'd be hard-pressed to find a taxonomy of individual differences in cognitive abilities in which *g* doesn't sit securely at the top. But just how general is *g*?

∽

Alfred Binet succeeded in devising a test that is highly relevant to school performance: *g* is substantially correlated with concurrent academic achievement, and also does a good job of statistically predicting future academic performance. Ian Deary and colleagues gathered data on over 70,000 British school students who had taken the Cognitive Abilities Test (CAT), which measures verbal, quantitative, and nonverbal fluid reasoning abilities.[12] They found positive correlations between the CAT's g factor assessed at age 11 and standardized achievement test performance on all twenty-five individual school subjects at age 16, though the strength of those correlations varied.

The highest correlations were with mathematics (.77), science (.68), and English (.67), and the lowest was in art and design (.43). Nevertheless, all the correlations were medium to high. Even physical education (.55), drama (.47), religious education (.52), and business (.56) were moderately related to g. From a *practical* perspective, g accounted for about 65 percent of the total variation in total educational achievement, which leaves about 35 percent of the differences in student achievement unexplained. For some school subjects, such as art and design, over 80 percent of the variance was unexplained. This certainly leaves plenty of room for academic achievers who exceed statistical predictions based on their g ranking (see Chapter 3). This also leaves plenty of room for other factors to influence academic achievement, such as specific cognitive abilities, motivation, mindset, self-regulation, environmental support, and so on. Nevertheless, from a *scientific* perspective, these correlations are impressive, and do suggest that g is relevant to learning a wide range of material.

Not only does g pervade learning across a wide range of subjects, but many different standardized tests may be measuring the very same g—or at least very close. Wendy Johnson and her colleagues found that the g extracted from one diverse IQ test battery is almost perfectly correlated with the g extracted from a different IQ test battery.[13] What's more, two tests used in the United States for college admissions—the SAT and ACT—are correlated with g about .91, and with each other almost perfectly, once you correct for the reliability of each test.[14]

Recently I teamed up with Matthew Reynolds, Xin Liu, Alan Kaufman, and Kevin McGrew to see whether the g factor extracted from IQ tests is the same as the g factor extracted from standardized tests of academic achievement.[15] To find out, we looked at two large, nationally representative data sets with over 7,000 participants in total, and two independent individually administered sets of test batteries. Cognitive g was measured by the use of IQ test batteries that measure the CHC domains (see the Appendix), and academic achievement g was measured by standardized tests of reading and writing and quantitative knowledge. We found that cognitive g and academic achievement *g* were not identical (there was still a significant amount of variance unexplained), but the relationship was really close. While the correlations generally increased with age, the range of correlations across age groups (spanning ages 4 to 19) was .77 to .94, with an average correlation of .83.

g also pervades reasoning about content that goes beyond school subjects. As part of my doctoral dissertation I teamed up with Colin DeYoung, Deidre Kolarick, and Jeremy Gray (my primary PhD advisor) to look at the role of *g* in reasoning across different kinds of content.[16] In particular, we looked at *contextualized* deductive reasoning, which involves if-then reasoning situated in real-world contexts. We looked at three types of problems: social exchange problems, precautionary problems, and arbitrary-rule problems. *Social exchange* problems concern the mutual exchange of goods or services between individuals, and involve detecting whether one party might be taking a benefit without fulfilling an obligation ("If you borrow my motorcycle, then you have to wash it"). *Precautionary problems* involve rules relating to avoiding potential physical danger ("If you surf in cold water, then you have to wear a wetsuit"). Finally, *arbitrary-rule problems* involve rules that are contextualized in realistic scenarios but are arbitrary ("If the soda is diet, then it has to be in a purple container").

We found that precautionary and social exchange reasoning problems were solved more frequently and more quickly, on average, than reasoning about arbitrary rules. This suggests that reasoning about contextualized and familiar real-world scenarios does facilitate reasoning. Nevertheless, looking at individual differences in deductive reasoning, we found that all seventy problems—regardless of content—were substantially positively correlated with each other. In fact, the reliability of all seventy problems was .88. What's more, this deductive reasoning common factor was significantly correlated (.45) with the *g* factor extracted from other well-known tests of verbal, spatial, and fluid reasoning. This suggests that covariation between people on these three forms of reasoning—even though they were contextualized in real-world scenarios and involved reasoning on different content—were not completely independent of each other.

How does *g* fare among the multiple intelligences that have been proposed in recent years? Have any of them dethroned *g*? Consider Howard Gardner's theory of multiple intelligences (see Chapter 4). Gardner explicitly states that his eight intelligences are independent of each other. He argues that schools tend to overemphasize logical-mathematical and linguistic intelligence to the exclusion of spatial, bodily-kinesthetic, musical, interpersonal, intrapersonal, and naturalistic intelligence.

In a paper called "Beyond g: Putting Multiple Intelligences Theory to the Test," Beth Visser, Michael Ashton, and Philip Vernon constructed a test to measure Gardner's eight intelligences, selecting two paper-and-pencil tests for each intelligence.[17] Lo and behold, a positive manifold emerged—all the tests were positively correlated with each other. But once again, not all tests were *equally* related to g. Linguistic, spatial, and logical/mathematical reasoning tests were most strongly related to g. Nevertheless, even measures of interpersonal and naturalistic intelligence (ability to classify one's surroundings) were moderately related to g.

Some tests, however, were much less related to g: bodily-kinesthetic intelligence, tonal and rhythmic music ability, and intrapersonal accuracy (knowing thyself) were least related to g. Visser and colleagues point out that some of the lower test correlations with g were most likely due to the unreliability of the tests. They also argue that the overall pattern of findings makes sense because they consider these tests less "cognitive" in nature.

In his response, Gardner argued that "while the intention is praiseworthy, the actual effort recreates the very conditions that I had sought to challenge."[18] While Gardner admitted that g "regularly emerges whenever a battery of tests is administered," he argued that we still have little understanding of what the positive manifold actually is.[19] Gardner went on to argue for the use of "intelligence-fair tests" that assess his multiple intelligences through methods other than a paper-and-pencil test and attempt to eliminate, as much as possible, linguistic or logical components.

Gardner gave an example of measuring spatial intelligence by seeing how people can navigate an unfamiliar terrain, or measuring interpersonal intelligence by examining how people negotiate with other people in the real world. These points are certainly worth considering, but they are problematic upon further examination. In reality, it's very difficult to develop tasks that completely isolate a single cognitive process and entirely eliminate the use of logic and/or language. Also, while Gardner doesn't mention it, Carroll did find that the ability to navigate unfamiliar terrains was significantly related to g. So although Gardner's proposal to construct fairer tests for people to fully express themselves is a worthy one, the positive manifold still exists. And from a scientific perspective, this still requires explaining.

What about other theories of intelligence that attempt to go beyond g? Again, the same story emerges. If you look closely at the research, you'll see that Sternberg's tests of his three so-called intelligences—analytical, creative, and practical—are moderately correlated with each other, and with traditional measures of intelligence.[20] The same with emotional intelligence. Tests of the four branches of "emotional intelligence"—perception, facilitation, understanding, and management—are also moderately correlated with each other and with traditional measures of intelligence.[21] Although to be fair, neither Sternberg nor the originators of the theory of emotional intelligence—Peter Salovey and John Mayer—claimed that emotional intelligence is completely independent of g. Only Gardner has made that strong claim.

None of these findings suggest that attempts to go beyond g are fruitless. On the contrary, they highlight the diversity and richness of human intelligence. Each additional form of intelligence deserves appreciation, predicting important life outcomes above and beyond g.[22] But out of the hundreds and hundreds of studies conducted on cognitive abilities measured by brief, reliable tests in a laboratory setting, it is difficult to find a single one where the positive manifold is completely absent. The positive correlations among diverse tests of cognitive abilities is such a robust finding that the psychologist Christopher Chabris referred to it as the "Law of General Intelligence."[23]

No doubt, if Spearman were alive today, he'd be happy to hear his initial findings have become a law! More than 100 years ago, Spearman proposed that the precise makeup of the cognitive test battery shouldn't matter, calling this the "indifference of the indicator." He argued that you could substitute one cognitive test for another, and you would still find positive correlations among all the tests in the battery. According to Spearman, all that matters is that the substituted test has the same level of difficulty, and the battery is diverse enough that any characteristics unique to any one test will wash out. This is how David Wechsler, who spent a few months working with Spearman, conceptualized global IQ scores on his test (see Chapter 2). Although Wechsler created "verbal" and "performance" subscales, he believed that all "the subtests are different measures of intelligence, not measures of different kinds of intelligence."[24]

But what, *really*, is this elusive, seemingly pervasive g? Does it really represent a source of human variation we'd want to label "general intelligence"? Is Gardner right that we still have little understanding of what causes the positive manifold to emerge? Now that I've defended the existence of the positive manifold against nearly every attempt to challenge it over the past 100 years, it's time to get to the bottom of g.

∼

In *The Mismeasure of Man*, Gould rightly noted the limitation of correlations. Just because two tests are highly correlated—say, that between mental rotation and vocabulary—doesn't necessarily mean that the two tests are measuring the same psychological process. There are numerous alternative explanations for the positive manifold. For one thing, it's possible that those who have a large vocabulary may also be good at mental rotation—not because those two tests are measuring the same mental process, but simply because we live in a society that encourages the development of vocabulary (English class) and spatial abilities (geometry class) in school.

Another possibility was pointed out to Spearman in 1916 by fellow Englishman Godfrey Thomson.[25] Using keen mathematical proofs, Thomson showed that g could theoretically arise through a large number of independent "bonds" or associations between basic processes. For instance, let's assume that the mind consists of 500 basic processes. If two tasks each depend on 250 of those processes, there is a good chance that about half, say 125 of them, will be engaged by both tasks, producing a sizable correlation of .50. According to this account, a single psychological process common among all the tests is not necessary to produce g. All that's needed is a partial overlap between processes engaged by different tests.

For example, consider the task of building a house. Even though making a bed, a wall, and a garden shed are vastly different tasks, people will generally most likely use a ruler in all three tasks, and a hammer in two of the tasks. So it's almost impossible to study one cognitive process ("hammer") in isolation, because whatever task you develop (building a shed) will also recruit other abilities shared in tasks where you aim to measure something else (a steady hand).

Thomson's point still holds water. In their 2009 paper, David Bartholomew, Ian Deary, and Martin Lawn showed that there is no *statistical* way of deciding whether Spearman's view or Thomson's view is correct.[26] So how are we ever to get at the truth? To attempt to get to the bottom of this mystery, we'll investigate the issue at multiple levels of analysis, including the behavioral, biological, and cultural.

As a first pass to help us wrap our heads around g, let's look at the features of cognitive tests that are *most strongly* correlated with g, and try to figure out what task demands they have in common. Imagine a bunch of cognitive tests spread around a circle. The closer to the center, the better the test measures g. The more the test falls off to the periphery, the less related it is to g. Figure 10.1 shows what that looks like in one study.[27]

What can we glean from this? One thing we notice is that processing speed tasks lie at the periphery of the circle. While still on the g map, if we

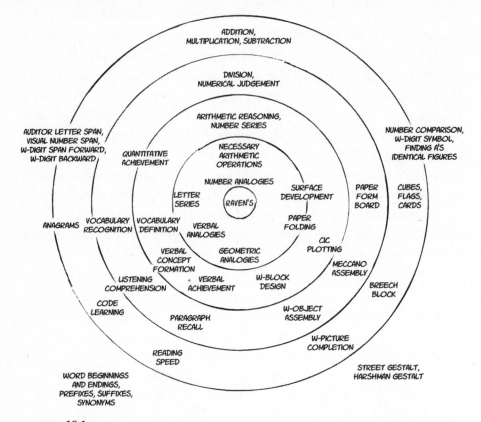

FIGURE 10.1.

Source: R. E. Snow and D. F. Lohman, "Implications of Cognitive Psychology for Educational Measurement," in *Educational Measurement*, ed. R. Linn, 3rd ed., 263–332 (New York: American Council on Education/ Macmillan, 1989). Adapted with permission.

Note: "W" indicates a subset of the Wechsler Adult Intelligence Scale.

want to understand *g*, sheer speed of basic information processing is not going to be the magic bullet.[28] Let's get closer. Surrounding the center of the circle are a bunch of tests that appear different on the surface. Each test differs in its content: verbal, quantitative, and spatial. Some involve rotating images in your mind, others involve mentally manipulating mathematical operations, and still other tests involve conceptual reasoning. As you can see, there are also quite a number of tests that involve analogical reasoning across different content (numbers, words, geometric forms). It's almost as if figuring out what all of these seemingly diverse tests have in common is an IQ test in itself!

Let's zoom in right to the very center, to the very heart of *g*. Here we find the Raven's Progressive Matrices Test, or Raven's for short. On each Raven's question, you are presented with a 3x3 matrix and you have to identify the missing piece that completes the pattern (see Figure 10.2 for an example).

What does it take to do well on this test? It turns out there are only a handful of rules required to solve all the items on this test. The easier problems require you to apply a single rule—such as adding or subtracting a single attribute (such as a line). But the harder ones require combining multiple rules, and juggling multiple attributes (such as shapes, sizes, and colors). The difficulty in solving the Raven's items is that you have to sort out the relevant attributes from the irrelevant attributes and hold the rules in your mind while testing them. And when some rules don't work out, you have to know when to stop going down that path and start over. This task—which requires the ability to discover the abstract relations among novel stimuli—is a good measure of *nonverbal fluid reasoning*.

Note that I said fluid reasoning, not fluid *intelligence*. In recent years Wendy Johnson and Thomas Bouchard Jr. have shown that the traditional distinction

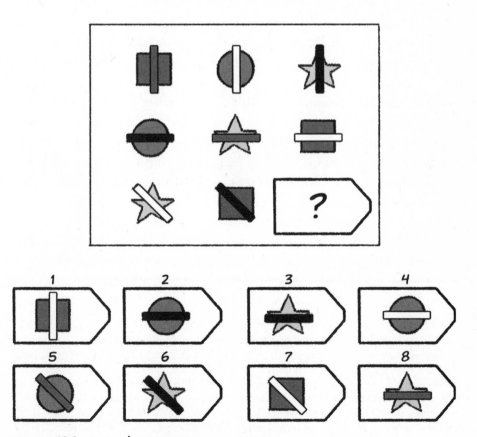

FIGURE 10.2. RAVEN'S PROGRESSIVE MATRICES

between "fluid" and "crystallized" intelligence is misguided. Through rigorous statistical testing, they found that cognitive tests of ability tend to covary depending on whether they are verbal or nonverbal,* *not* by how much they are influenced by culture.[29] As we saw in Chapter 4, this has important implications for assessing giftedness. It is incorrect to assume that tests of nonverbal fluid reasoning are somehow measuring intelligence in its "purest" form, completely divorced from experience and culture. Likewise, just because a test measures vocabulary or general knowledge doesn't mean it doesn't place demands on fluid reasoning. Vocabulary tests often require choosing the right meaning for infrequent words. That requires quite a bit of inference and deduction. Both verbal and nonverbal tests of cognitive ability involve fluid reasoning, and fluid reasoning skills in turn are influenced both by genes *and* culture (which are always interacting with each other; see Chapter 1).[30]

Fluid reasoning is not just any kind of reasoning, however. Tasks that engage a well-organized knowledge base place fewer demands on fluid reasoning. Fluid reasoning involves inferring underlying patterns based on minimal evidence. This requires concentration, planning, breaking the task down into subgoals, and managing these problem-solving goals in working memory.[31]

If you recall from Chapter 9, the human working memory capacity limit is on average about four chunks. This is the number of meaningful bits of information that can be held in consciousness at any point in time. People differ in capacity, however, with the typical range being two to six chunks.[32] And even within this small window, variation in working memory is significantly related to variation in fluid reasoning performance. Consider a commonly administered working memory task called the reading span test:

INSTRUCTIONS: *I will present a series of five sentences one at a time. Read each sentence and remember the last word of the sentence. When you see the word "RECALL" you should recall the last words of all the sentences.*

---

*Technically, Johnson and Bouchard distinguish between "verbal" and "perceptual" abilities. Because the term "nonverbal reasoning" will be more intuitive to readers, I decided to replace "perceptual" with "nonverbal." Also, as Colin DeYoung has noted, given that nonverbal memory and perceptual fluid reasoning tasks were both included in the perceptual factor identified by Johnson and Bouchard, "nonverbal" is sensible as an inclusive label for the factor. I should also note that Johnson and Bouchard also discovered a smaller third factor representing mental rotation skills. See C. G. DeYoung, "Intelligence and Personality," in *The Cambridge Handbook of Intelligence*, ed. R. J. Sternberg and S. B. Kaufman 711–737 (New York: Cambridge University Press, 2011).

1. The hunter chased after the man on horseback.
2. After a time, the correspondent looked around.
3. The children ate the cake with a spoon.
4. Helen is expecting tomorrow to be a bad day.
5. The ship left with a noise and went up into space.

RECALL

ANSWERS: Horseback, around, spoon, day, space

Most people can't go beyond five sentences without getting a serious headache! Daneman and Carpenter found a correlation of .50 between this task and SAT verbal scores, and they found even higher correlations with tests of reading comprehension.[33] They found much lower correlations between fluid reasoning and versions of a memory task that only required remembering words.

It seems it's the dual requirement of remembering the last word of each sentence while processing the sentences that makes it a test of working memory. To illustrate, consider this lovely passage from Proust:

> On the occasion of this first call which, after leaving Saint-Loup, I went to pay on Mme de Villeparisis following the advice given by M. De Norpois to my father, I found her in a drawing-room hung with yellow silk, against which the settees and the admirable armchairs upholstered in Beauvais tapestry stood out with the almost purple redness of ripe raspberries. . . . Mme de Villeparisis herself, wearing an old-fashioned bonnet of black lace (which she preserved with the same shrewd instinct for local or historical colour as a Breton innkeeper who, however Parisian his clientele may have become, thinks it more astute to keep his maids in coifs and wide sleeves), was seated at a little desk on which, as well as her brushes, her palette and an unfinished flower-piece in water-colour, were arranged— in glasses, in saucers, in cups—moss-roses, zinnias, maidenhair ferns, which on account of the sudden influx of callers she had just left off painting, and which gave the impression of being arrayed on a florist's counter in some eighteenth-century mezzotint.[34]

If you made it all the way through without your brain short-circuiting, try answering some questions about what you just read: Why was Mme de

Villeparisis wearing a black bonnet? Why would the innkeeper dress his maids in coifs and wide sleeves? Why did Mme de Villeparisis stop painting?

And this passage is only two sentences long! Comprehending complex passages such as this one is difficult in large part because it requires holding in memory the gist of prior sentences while reading new sentences, and then integrating the meaning of all of the sentences to form a coherent narrative. The more sentences you have to read, and the longer each sentence, the greater the demand on working memory. At the same time, task-irrelevant information, such as the humming of the radiator, or wandering thoughts about the big party Saturday, must be ignored.

For this reason, psychologists make an important distinction between short-term memory and working memory.[35] Some researchers argue that the reason working memory and fluid reasoning are so strongly correlated with each other is because they both require the control of attention.* Today there is widespread evidence and acknowledgment among intelligence researchers that although working memory is not the same as fluid reasoning, it is indeed an important piece of the g puzzle.[36]

Cognitive psychologists made headway using their behavioral tests, but once new neuroscience techniques came along they were eager to see what pattern of brain activations were associated with cognitive performance. Of course, any one person's IQ score is the result of multiple cognitive processes. The human brain is massively interconnected, with many specialized regions contributing to performance on every single cognitive task. To perform even the simplest tasks, such as quickly matching up letters with symbols, requires the activation of many brain regions, including regions associated with concentration, vision, sensory motor functions, and semantic retrieval. The key

---

*It should be acknowledged that working memory tests are more strongly related to fluid reasoning that match their content (e.g., spatial working memory is more strongly related to spatial reasoning than verbal reasoning, and verbal working memory is more strongly related to verbal reasoning than spatial reasoning). See P. Shah and A. Miyake, "The Separability of Working Memory Resources for Spatial Thinking and Language Processing: An Individual Differences Approach," *Journal of Experimental Psychology: General* 125 (1996): 4–27; N. J. Mackintosh and E. S. Bennett, "The Fractionation of Working Memory Maps onto Different Components of Intelligence," *Intelligence* 31 (2003): 519–531; S. B. Kaufman, "Sex Differences in Mental Rotation and Spatial Visualization Ability: Can They Be Accounted for by Differences in Working Memory Capacity?," *Intelligence* 35 (2007): 211–223.

question is this: *What brain regions are consistently associated with differences in performance across diverse cognitive tests?*

In one of the earliest neuroscience studies of *g*, neuroscientist John Duncan and colleagues found that spatial, verbal, and perceptual-motor tasks that correlated more strongly with *g* recruited the lateral prefrontal cortex (located just behind the forehead in the outermost region of the brain) much more than tasks that had low correlations with *g*.[37] This study was important, because it was one of the first studies linking the prefrontal cortex—particularly the lateral region—to fluid reasoning.

Of course, the lateral prefrontal cortex doesn't contribute to fluid reasoning in isolation. This brain region is heavily connected to other cortical and subcortical brain structures in the right and left hemispheres and recruits these areas depending on the content (verbal, spatial, etc.) and task requirements (number of dimensions, number of distractors). Nevertheless, further research on both humans and monkeys suggests that cells in the lateral prefrontal cortex are critical for maintenance of diverse content in working memory.[38]

Consider a study by Jeremy Gray, Christopher Chabris, and Todd Braver.[39] They gave 48 university students the Raven's Matrices test to solve as well as a measure of working memory called the *n*-back working memory test. The *n*-back task requires people to view a sequence of items presented once every 2.36 seconds and indicate whether the current item is the same as or different from the item presented a certain number of steps back in the sequence. So on a one-back task, all you'd have to do is indicate if an item is the same as that presented on the immediately preceding presentation. Easy. But it quickly gets more difficult. The three-back requires thinking three items back. Still seems easy in theory, but trust me, it's *hard*. This requires fast and constant online updating of the sequence in memory.

Gray and colleagues used words and faces in two separate three-back tasks. They also made the task even more difficult by presenting "lures," which were stimuli that matched a stimulus that was seen recently, but not exactly three back. They included lures that were a two-back, four-back, or five-back match. These interfering lure trials placed a higher demand on attentional control mechanisms. Figure 10.3 shows an example of the different kinds of trials on the three-back task, using faces as stimuli.

They found that subjects who scored highest on the Raven's test were better at the working memory task and showed more neural activity in the lateral prefrontal cortex and parietal lobe regions (located at the top of

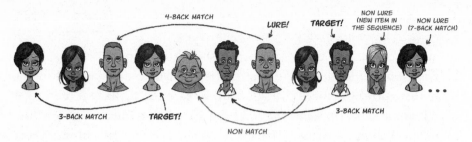

FIGURE 10.3.

the head toward the back) associated with sensory integration. What's more, brain activity differences in these regions were most pronounced on lure trials, in which interference was high and attentional control was particularly necessary. This study suggests that fluid reasoning tasks recruit areas of the lateral prefrontal and parietal cortices to maintain focus on a goal to inhibit distractions, and rapidly update the contents of working memory.*

By 2007 a number of studies on the neuroscience of cognitive ability had accumulated. Rex Jung and Richard Haier reviewed thirty-seven neuroimaging studies that were then available, using a variety of methodologies (PET, fMRI, MRI spectroscopy, structural MRI imaging), and concluded that a specific network of brain regions is critical for cognitive test performance across different content.[40] According to their Parieto-Frontal Integration Theory of Intelligence (P-FIT), different brain regions play a role at different stages of information processing.

In the first few stages, the brain's temporal regions (located behind the ears) and occipital regions (located in the back of the head) process basic sen-

---

*These aren't the *only* functions of the lateral prefrontal cortex. Activation of the dorsal (top) region of the lateral prefrontal cortex has also been associated with such diverse cognitive processes as pain modulation and mastication (chewing hard gum)! Nevertheless, this does not negate the relationship with fluid reasoning. As Rogier Kievit notes, "Functional heterogeneity should not be construed as a failure of cognitive neuroscience but rather as an inherent property of brain function and organization" (76). What this *does* mean is that we shouldn't point to the lateral prefrontal cortex as the fluid-reasoning area of the brain, or attempt to use lateral prefrontal cortex activation as a measure of fluid-reasoning performance. See R. A. Kievit, J.-W. Romeijn, L. J. Waldorp, J. M. Wicherts, H. S. Scholte, and D. Borsboom, "Mind the Gap: A Psychometric Approach to the Reduction Problem," *Psychological Inquiry* 22 (2011): 67–87; J. Lorenz, S. Minoshima, and K. L. Casey, "Keeping Pain Out of Mind: The Role of the Dorsolateral Prefrontal Cortex in Pain Modulation," *Brain* 126 (2003): 1079–1091; T. Takahashi, T. Miyamoto, A. Terao, and A. Yokoyama, "Cerebral Activation Related to the Control of Mastication during Changes in Food Hardness," *Neuroscience* 145 (2007): 791–794.

sory information, and the parietal cortex integrates this information. Then, the next "hypothesis testing" stage involves higher levels of abstraction and requires efficient information flow between the frontal and parietal regions, with white matter helping to reliably move information across the frontal parietal network. (White matter consists of axons surrounded by a fatty insulation called myelin that helps different gray matter regions of the brain communicate with each other. The prefrontal cortex and parietal cortex are gray matter.) Then once the best solution is determined, the anterior cingulate is recruited to select the appropriate response and inhibit alternative responses.

The P-FIT theory is not without its critics. One criticism is that Jung and Haier based their theory on individual differences at multiple levels of analysis: brain structure, function, and task comparisons (for instance, differences between high g and low g tasks). While these questions are all interesting, they are very different questions, and results from one level don't necessarily apply to results at the other level.[41] Another criticism is the consistency of the brain regions: only a few brain areas showed activations by more than 50 percent of the studies.[42] Part of the problem may have been that the studies included in the review differed in the assortment of cognitive tests they administered to participants. Remember, Spearman argued that to properly measure g, you must administer a wide variety of cognitive tasks, or else you're more likely to measure domain-specific skills.

Although these criticisms are certainly valid, since Haier and Jung's 2007 paper numerous studies have consistently shown that communication between the lateral prefrontal cortex and posterior regions of the parietal lobe is related to differences in cognitive test performance across a range of tasks.[43] The most striking evidence comes from a growing number of large-scale lesion studies that have all implicated the prefrontal parietal network as crucial for fluid reasoning.[44]

In one recent large-scale lesion study, Aron Barbey and colleagues obtained access to a remarkable sample of 182 Vietnam veterans with highly localized brain damage due to penetrating head injuries.[45] Consistent with the P-FIT theory, they found that damage to specific areas of the lateral prefrontal and parietal cortex impaired the integration and control of a distributed pattern of neural activity throughout the brain. They found that the tests of g and executive function that were *most* affected by prefrontal and parietal damage involved verbal comprehension, working memory, mental flexibility, and attentional control. The researchers argue that the prefrontal parietal network is at an "ideal site" in the brain to support goal-directed behavior because of its tight connections and broad access to perceptual and motor representations.

They found that a major player in the prefrontal parietal network was the frontal pole, an area at the very front of the prefrontal cortex, just above our eyes. There is evolutionary significance of this brain region. Compared to other species, we don't have the largest brains; sperm whales and elephants beat us on that front. We don't even have a larger prefrontal cortex overall. We do, however, have a larger frontal pole and inferior parietal lobe compared to macaques and apes.[46] Intriguingly, a recent analysis of Albert Einstein's brain shows that although the overall size and shape of his brain weren't abnormal, he did have unusual frontal and parietal lobes (among other unusual brain regions), with the frontal pole being *particularly* unusual within his prefrontal cortex.[47]

What are the functions of the frontal pole? Answering that question may help us understand some of the most uniquely human aspects of human intelligence. But the matter isn't so simple. According to cognitive neuroscientist Paul Burgess and colleagues, the study of the functions of the frontal pole "presents one of the greatest scientific puzzles to cognitive neuroscience."[48] The frontal pole has been linked to a diverse range of cognitive processes, including fluid reasoning, relational complexity (the number of interdependent items that must be simultaneously considered in working memory), abstract integration during analogical reasoning, semantically distant mapping during creative analogical reasoning, abstract mental flexibility, evaluation of creative ideas, memory retrieval, moral decision making, "reality monitoring" (the ability to judge whether an event was imagined or actually occurred), and metacognition (the ability to think about one's own cognition).[49]

Because g, reality monitoring, and metacognition are all at least partially distinct sources of human variation, this suggests that the frontal pole serves functions that go beyond fluid reasoning.[50] So what is the common theme of the frontal pole, if there even is one? Accumulating research suggests that the frontal pole sits at the top of a hierarchy in the prefrontal cortex that monitors the current contents of consciousness to make sure the larger goal is maintained, and helps integrate the prior stages of cognitive processing.[51] Surely more research is needed on this fascinating area of the brain, but it is becoming increasingly clear that the frontal pole is a critical team player in the prefrontal parietal network.

Based on their lesion mapping results across all of their tests of g and executive function, Barbey and colleagues put forward an integrative archi-

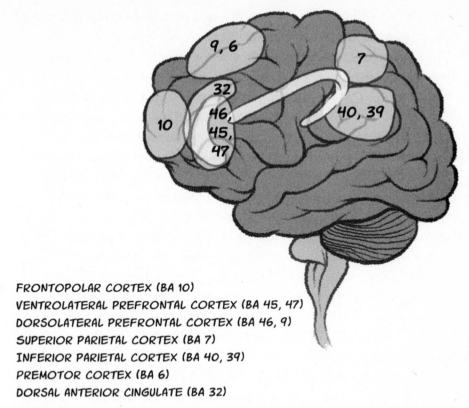

FRONTOPOLAR CORTEX (BA 10)
VENTROLATERAL PREFRONTAL CORTEX (BA 45, 47)
DORSOLATERAL PREFRONTAL CORTEX (BA 46, 9)
SUPERIOR PARIETAL CORTEX (BA 7)
INFERIOR PARIETAL CORTEX (BA 40, 39)
PREMOTOR CORTEX (BA 6)
DORSAL ANTERIOR CINGULATE (BA 32)

FIGURE 10.4. INTEGRATIVE ARCHITECTURE FOR GENERAL INTELLIGENCE AND EXECUTIVE FUNCTION
Source: A. K. Barbey, R. Colom, J. Solomon, F. Krueger, C. Forbes, and J. Grafman, "An Integrative Architecture for General Intelligence and Executive Function Revealed by Lesion Mapping," *Brain* 135 (2012): 1154–1164. Adapted with permission.

tecture for general intelligence and executive function critical for novel, goal-directed problem solving. Consistent with the P-FIT theory proposed by Jung and Haier, this architecture involves strong communication between specific areas of the lateral prefrontal cortex and posterior parietal lobe. The critical brain regions involved in this neural architecture, along with the white matter tract binding these regions together into a coordinated network, are shown in Figure 10.4.* Note that although the regions in this prefrontal parietal network are distributed, they aren't *everywhere*. As the researchers note, "Despite its distributed nature, the neural substrates of

---

*Technically, this particular white matter tract is called the superior longitudinal/arcuate fasciculus. Say that ten times real fast.

g and executive function were remarkably circumscribed, concentrated in the core of white matter and comprising a narrow subset of regions."[52]

This is worth emphasizing. For one thing, *g* should not be equated with the entire prefrontal cortex. The prefrontal cortex consists of billions of nerve cells linked together by trillions of connections. All areas of the prefrontal cortex are massively connected with each other (and with many other areas of the brain), but *g* appears to be primarily associated with broad brain activation in the *lateral* prefrontal cortex, the outermost part of the brain. Barbey and colleagues didn't measure the self-regulation of emotions, the learning of reward values, daydreaming, creative improvisation, emotional intelligence, or social reasoning. If they had, they would most likely have found additional recruitment in *medial* regions of the prefrontal cortex (which reside in the center of the brain) along with connections to subcortical areas of the brain associated with emotional functioning (see Chapter 12).[53]

Also, *g* isn't equally related to all executive functions. There are a variety of executive functions in humans, including working memory, mental flexibility, and inhibition. While these various executive functions are significantly correlated with each other, they also show diversity in their functions.[54] A striking demonstration of this can be found at the developmental level of analysis. Naomi Friedman and colleagues found that the development of *better* behavioral restraint across four testing periods (ages 14, 20, 24, and 36 months) was accompanied by the development of *worse* mental flexibility.[55] Out of the entire suite of executive functions, *g* appears to be most strongly associated with working memory-related functions.[56]

Nevertheless, the discovery of the prefrontal parietal network gives us insight into the information processing critical for novel, goal-directed problem solving. Barbey and colleagues argue that a major function of the prefrontal parietal network is the manipulation, integration, and control of distributed patterns of neural activity throughout the brain, including lower-level sensory and motor modules. We've already discussed some of these prefrontal parietal network functions (such as goal maintenance, attentional control, updating information in working memory, ignoring distractors, relational complexity), but I believe one of the *most important* functions of the prefrontal parietal network for understanding *g* is often overlooked.

∾

In his recent book *The Ravenous Brain*, neuroscientist Daniel Bor argues that consciousness is a form of information processing.[57] In particular, Bor argues that consciousness processes information that is useful and relevant to a particular goal and that captures some pattern in the world. In formulating his cogent argument, Bor links the prefrontal parietal brain network, and its associated working memory and attentional control functions, with consciousness. While attention and consciousness are certainly not the same, Bor argues that attention, as a way of selecting content and attending to stimuli, is a necessary aspect of consciousness.

But Bor doesn't stop there. He cites numerous studies showing that *chunking* heavily activates the prefrontal parietal brain network, sometimes *more so* than working memory.[58] Consider one elegant study conducted by Bor and Adrian Owen.[59] They asked participants to memorize novel verbal and numerical double-digit sequences. Critically, the information was either randomly arranged or structured. For instance, 57 68 79 90 is a structured sequence because each number goes up by 11, but 31 24 89 65 is an unstructured sequence because you can't readily apply a chunking strategy to organize it more easily in memory. They also had a mnemonic condition in which participants could apply phone extension numbers they memorized earlier. What did they find?

Unsurprisingly, participants performed better when the information was structured compared to unstructured, as it allowed them to reorganize and chunk the information into more efficient forms. Also, consistent with prior research, the prefrontal parietal network (consisting mainly of communication between the dorsolateral prefrontal cortex and the posterior parietal lobe) lit up more brightly during the structured and mnemonic conditions than during the completely unstructured condition where chunking wasn't possible.* Most interestingly, the prefrontal parietal network was consistently *most* active during the structured trials compared with the unstructured and mnemonic sequences.

This is interesting because the unstructured sequences were more difficult to memorize and placed a higher demand on working memory than the structured trials did. According to Bor, these findings suggest that "the prefrontal parietal network will activate for many complex tasks, but it will be

---

*Additionally, structured mathematical sequences more robustly activated the prefrontal parietal network compared to a control condition in which participants performed equivalent mental calculations without any chunking component. The same goes for the mnemonic sequences when compared with the same level of memory recall, but with still no chunking aspect. Therefore, it appears that the prefrontal parietal activation wasn't due just to mental arithmetic or memory recall but was specific to the act of chunking.

most excited when subjects are actively searching for and finding entirely new patterns."[60] Bor raises the intriguing possibility that chunking is one of the most central functions of the prefrontal parietal network and may have evolved to provide innovative solutions to complex or novel problems.

Even though Bor doesn't explicitly make the connection, I believe his theory may help us better understand g. Perhaps one of the fundamental characteristics of individuals who rank high on g is their ability—when given an explicit goal—to quickly focus on the relevant aspects of the task, ignore the irrelevant aspects, and find efficient means of organizing the information in working memory. This would free up important resources for fluid reasoning. Spearman's hypothesis was that the best measures of g are those that require grasping relationships, inferring rules, spotting similarities and differences, and "educing" (Latin for "drawing out") the relevant relations within a complex pattern. Fluid reasoning tasks do seem to be measuring these skills. But fluid reasoning also places a heavy burden on working memory, because you have to conduct all the reasoning in your head with no external aids and often with a timer counting down! Those who have better cognitive strategies for lessening the cognitive load will be at a distinct cognitive advantage in this testing environment. If true, I think these findings allow for a tighter integration between the scientific study of g (which emphasizes cognitive efficiency) and the expertise performance framework (which emphasizes efficient chunking strategies).

I witnessed the importance of cognitive strategies firsthand during a study I conducted for my doctoral dissertation.[61] I measured g by administering three highly correlated tests of cognitive ability: Raven's, verbal analogical reasoning, and mental rotation. I found that working memory, processing speed, and the deliberate learning of complex associations were each significantly and independently related to g. During the interviews at the end of the experiment, some participants told me they tried coming up with elaborate mnemonic strategies to memorize the list of words on the tests of associative learning. At the time, I just filed this away as interesting.

More recently I came across a study by Kiruthiga Nandagopal, Roy Roring, K. Anders Ericsson, and Jeanette Taylor that had twins think aloud during measures of associative learning, working memory, and processing speed— the same skills I measured in my study.[62] They found that performance on all three cognitive tests was heavily influenced by strategies. Most compellingly, differences in strategy use on the associative learning task (which was most amenable to the use of strategies) explained a significant amount of the genetic influences on performance. Their study is the first to demonstrate that the heritability of performance on cognitive tasks is due, in part, to the use of specific cognitive strategies.

The use of strategies to facilitate performance is consistent with studies linking *g* with neural efficiency. Cognitive effort consumes a lot of glucose in the brain. As tasks become more automated, we require fewer cognitive resources. A number of studies suggest that people who do well on IQ tests are faster at recruiting the right brain resources for the right task. Consider an earlier study by Haier and colleagues using PET. They had 8 participants practice the video game Tetris for fifty days.[63] At the time of the study, Tetris had just been introduced in the United States and the participants weren't familiar with it. The researchers found that the highest scorers on the Raven's matrices test showed the largest *decreases* in brain activity with practice, particularly in the prefrontal and cingulate cortical areas.

Newer studies using fMRI generally support the notion that people who do well on cognitive tests use fewer brain resources to solve novel and complex problems.* But while these findings are generally expressed in terms of "intelligent people" having more "efficient brains," I think a more precise framing is that people who are "good at fluid reasoning" are "faster at freeing up expensive brain resources through the use of efficient cognitive strategies." I concede it's more of a mouthful, but I think it's more precise.

Importantly, different people can solve the same problem using different strategies.[64] For instance, some people may rely more on their verbal strengths to solve verbal and spatial problems, while others may use a spatial strategy across the board. There is evidence that this is the case. On a test of verbal processing speed, Erik Reichle and colleagues found that the use of verbal strategies produced more brain activation in language-related cortical areas (such as Broca's area), whereas the use of visual-spatial strategies produced more activation in visual-spatial areas (such as the parietal cortex).[65] Also, those with better verbal working memory skills showed less activation in the language-related regions when using the verbal strategy, and those with better mental rotation skills showed less activation in visual-spatial brain regions when they used the visual-spatial strategy. The researchers concluded

---

*Provided that the task is difficult enough—but not so difficult that even high IQ test scorers (on average) have to recruit all of their brain resources or people with lower IQs (on average) quit out of frustration; I. J. Deary, L. Penke, and W. Johnson, "The Neuroscience of Human Intelligence Differences," *Nature Reviews Neuroscience* 11 (2010): 201–211.

that cognitive strategies are useful because they help minimize cognitive workload.

If people can recruit different brain regions to solve the same novel or complex problem, it might not make sense to ask "Where is *g* in the brain?"[66] A recent study by Rogier Kievit and colleagues illustrates this point.[67] They administered tests of verbal comprehension, perceptual organization, working memory, and processing speed. They also gave participants MRI scans and estimated their level of white matter, gray matter density, and brain volume in eight brain regions of interest that have shown correlations with *g* in prior studies. They found that people could arrive at a similar *g* score with a very different neural composition. These findings are important because they suggest that studies that average over many different brains mask the fact that every single person may arrive at the same *g* score via different neural pathways.[68]

Additionally, Kievit and colleagues found that individual differences in brain structure *jointly* determined individual differences in *g*. In other words, *g*, like consciousness, was an *emergent* property of the brain, not a single feature. This finding is consistent with a number of other recent studies that suggest that the positive manifold is largely the emergent result of overlap between multiple specialized brain regions.[69] As Cristina Rabaglia (who is currently conducting research on this topic with Gary Marcus and Sean Lane) told me, "to the extent that individual cognitive tasks each require a particular, unique set of neural resources drawn from a common pool that is reused across tasks, individual differences in performance on those tasks will be correlated—even if particular neural resources have prescribed functions."

Although these findings don't negate the existence of the positive manifold (those who do well on one IQ test item are statistically more likely to do well on the other items), they do suggest that to measure *g*, it's best to measure a diverse range of cognitive skills, not look at any individual's brain and attempt to predict their *g* ranking (or IQ score, for that matter).

These findings are also consistent with recent work by Han van der Maas and colleagues.[70] According to their dynamical model of intelligence, *g* is an emergent property of a number of independent mental processes that beneficially interact and mutually reinforce each other throughout the course of development. This research is exciting because it shifts our level of understanding from individual differences to the development of intellectual skills across an individual's life span.

~

In childhood and adolescence, brain maturation is particularly vulnerable to plasticity and change. The relation between brain size and IQ is lower in children than in adults, and IQ is related to brain development in complex ways. One study followed 300 children up to early adulthood.[71] At age 7, the higher IQ children (IQ > 120) tended to have less cortical thickness. Soon after, however, the high-IQ children showed a rapid increase in cortical thickness, overtaking the other children and peaking at age 11 to 12 before slowly declining to about the same level as the others. The researchers concluded, "'Brainy' children are not cleverer solely by virtue of having more or less gray matter at any one age. Rather, intelligence is related to dynamic properties of cortical maturation" (678).

To be sure, genes substantially influence the development of brain structure.[72] But the relation between genes and cortical maturation need not be direct. Higher IQ children, due to their prefrontal parietal brain wiring, may act differently in the world and elicit different reactions from others, which in turn sculpts their brains. A number of studies across various domains show the importance of experience on both gray and white matter structures in the brain.[73]

People learning to juggle over the course of three months showed increased gray matter volume in brain regions associated with visuomotor coordination, reaching, and grasping.[74] In fact, brain plasticity in gray matter was observed after only seven days of juggling training! After three months of juggling, changes were also seen in the organization of underlying white matter pathways. Likewise, research among expert taxi drivers has found enlargement in the volume of the posterior hippocampus, an area of the brain crucial to spatial navigation, and mindfulness meditation training has been found to alter cortical representations of interoceptive attention (attention turned inward).[75]

Multiple studies have also found significant brain plasticity among people engaging in music.[76] Expert musicians display greater gray volume matter and cortical thickness in auditory, somatosensory, and motor cortices, with the effects increasing as a function of years of musical practice. There are also important effects of early ability. In one study, skilled string players showed neurological differences in the area of the cortex associated with the representation of their left hand, and these differences were significantly correlated with the age at which they first started playing the instrument.[77]

There even appear to be very *specific* age effects: Sara Bengtsson, Fredrik Ullén, and colleagues identified several brain regions where white matter was directly related to the amount of piano practice during particular periods in childhood and adolescence.[78] Along similar lines, Krista Hyde and colleagues identified numerous changes in brain structure among 5- and 6-year-olds who engaged in keyboard training thirty minutes every week for a year.[79]

Recent research has also demonstrated the plasticity of brain regions associated with cognitive ability. Hikaru Takeuchi and colleagues found that working memory training resulted in measurable changes in the structural connectivity critical for working memory performance, including areas of the parietal lobe and the anterior part of the body of the corpus callosum.[80] In another recent study, Allyson Mackey, Kirstie Whitaker, and Silvia Bunge found plasticity in the white matter structure of the frontal and parietal lobes after just three months of reasoning training among a sample of participants enrolled in a course to prepare for the Law School Admission Tests (LSAT).[81]

Besides brain changes, there are also behavioral changes. Multiple studies suggest that working memory training programs produce reliable short-term improvements in working memory skills, and there's accumulating evidence that fluid reasoning training can also result in short-term improvements in fluid reasoning skills. Some of the strongest results have come from Cogmed computer-based training and interactive games.[82]

Transfer effects appear to be limited, however. Training children in working memory improves performance on other working memory tasks, but the evidence is mixed on whether it improves fluid reasoning.[*,83] Vice versa, fluid reasoning training has been found to improve untrained fluid reasoning performance but doesn't appear to improve working memory or processing speed. Also, unsurprisingly, considering that g reflects variation in a variety of cognitive skills, there's little evidence that working memory training changes people's ranking on g.[84]

Clearly, the picture is muddled at the moment, and we will have to wait for more research to clarify it. In the meantime I have a few suggestions that

---

*Interestingly, some working memory tasks, such as the *n*-back task, do seem to transfer to fluid reasoning more reliably than other measures of working memory, although training on the *n*-back task doesn't necessarily improve performance on other working memory tasks even if it does improve fluid reasoning!

might help bring things into focus. I think it's worth keeping in mind that working memory may serve a domain-independent function for fluid reasoning across multiple forms of content (verbal, nonverbal, mental rotation, and so on), but it surely isn't *emotion*-independent. As we've seen throughout this book, stress, anxiety, and stereotype threat can significantly impact working memory and can cause a person's prefrontal parietal brain network to shut down (see Chapter 7). This is probably one of the reasons the most widespread gains in brain training come from programs that simultaneously address *multiple aspects of a person*, such as traditional martial arts training and enriched school curricula.[85] I believe *g* researchers underestimate the extent to which multiple aspects of development—cognitive, physical, social, and emotional—all feed off each other.

A related consideration is individual differences in response to training. One recent study found that variation in a gene that codes for dopamine transportation was related to improvements in working memory and fluid reasoning in preschool children following training.[86] While the results certainly require replication (the sample size was small, and the effects did not remain significant after correcting for multiple comparisons), the results suggest that dopamine may play an important role for cognitive performance and brain plasticity (see Chapters 6 and 12 for more on the role of dopamine in motivation and cognition).

Another recent study found effects of personality on cognitive training.[87] Conscientious participants were better than other participants on working memory training, but their improvement in working memory didn't transfer to a measure of fluid reasoning. In contrast, participants scoring higher in neuroticism (a proxy for anxiety) showed lower training scores on a difficult version of a working memory task, but showed more gains on an easier version. It seems that in the easier version, higher levels of emotion may have been an advantage, allowing them to maintain their concentration and vigilance, whereas on the more difficult version of the task they became overwhelmed. Therefore, personal characteristics should be taken into account when considering the effectiveness of cognitive training.

Another thing to keep in mind is that those who need the training the most are the ones who are most likely to benefit.[88] In recent discussions with neuroscientist Silvia Bunge, she noted that most reasoning tests only require the ability to maintain and manipulate a few bits of information in working memory. So training working memory among those who are already at the minimum necessary to solve the task won't improve reasoning performance.

Individuals with low working memory who have difficulty keeping a few things in mind and integrating, comparing, or sequencing them are more likely to show meaningful improvement in training, because for them working memory serves as a bottleneck. This is why it's important we teach all people the importance of strategies to relieve the mental burden.

According to Philip Johnson-Laird and his colleagues, people solve syllogisms (a form of deductive reasoning) by constructing a *mental model*—an internal representation of the premises.[89] The juggling of mental models in your mind places a very heavy burden on working memory. That's why it's important to *choose your mental models wisely*. For instance, Johnson-Laird and Mark Steedman asked people to describe their mental models for the following syllogism:[90]

> All of the artists are beekeepers.
> Some of the beekeepers are clever.
> Are all artists clever?

One participant remarked, "I thought of all the little . . . artists in the room and imagined they all had beekeeper's hats on."[91] You may have relied on an altogether different mental model. How you represented the problem, however, strongly determined how well you were able to reason with the information. If you started with an inaccurate representation, you were more likely to overburden your working memory and end up with an inaccurate answer, regardless of the level of syllogistic reasoning you are actually *capable* of attaining.

People can be taught to improve their reasoning by learning how to draw diagrams to represent a problem.[92] Even blind people can create spatial mental models.[93] When Kenneth Gilhooly and his colleagues presented syllogisms orally, it placed a higher demand on working memory, as participants had to store the premises in their head.[94] But when the syllogisms were presented with all the premises remaining on the projector screen, people performed better because they could unload the premises from their working memory and free up limited resources to construct efficient mental models.

Over the past decade John Sweller and colleagues have designed instructional techniques that relieve working memory burdens on students and increase learning and interest.[95] Drawing on both the expertise and working memory literatures, they match the complexity of learning situations to the learner, attempting to reduce unnecessary working memory loads that may interfere with reasoning and learning, and optimize cognitive processes most relevant to learning.

Finally, it's important to consider length of training. In a recent *New York Times* Op-Ed called "IQ Points for Sale, Cheap," David Z. Hambrick notes his skepticism that a few hours of working memory training can create long-lasting and meaningful improvements in IQ.[96] He makes an important point that such increases aren't likely without substantial commitment of resources. Hambrick points to a few kindergarten after-school programs that involve substantial enrichment and support but don't demonstrate a large increase in IQ scores, and whatever increases are found don't sustain in the long-term.[97]

If the skills that determine someone's IQ test score operate by the same developmental principles as any other abilities, then why would we expect them to be radically improved through enrichment programs that may last no more than sixty hours, let alone working memory training that lasts only a few hours? As Michael Howe notes in his book *IQ in Question*, "If we start by assuming that the skills that contribute to a person's IQ score have no special or unlearned status, and are acquired by processes that are similar to the ones involved in the acquisition of other kinds of mental expertise, then it makes sense to ask how much time is typically needed in order to gain those mental abilities that are acknowledged to be acquired through learning."[98]

Howe suggests that the amount of training would be at least as large as the time necessary to acquire high levels of expertise in music, chess, and sports. After all, IQ tests sample an assortment of mental forms expertise. Therefore, to build up the high levels of mental expertise required to do well on IQ tests would require *thousands* of hours, not just a couple.

This doesn't mean that there are no biological contributions to the acquisition of cognitive expertise. There are biological contributions to the acquisition of *any* forms of expertise (see Chapter 11). Some children from a very early age, due to their prefrontal parietal brain wiring, may gain a greater reward from engaging in fluid reasoning and so become more motivated to engage in intellectually demanding activities. All those hours of continual intellectual engagement add up (see Chapter 1). In recent years psychologists—including Robert Sternberg and David Lohman—have begun to view IQ test scores at any single point in time as a measure of developing expertise or ability.[99]

From this perspective, we also shouldn't be surprised that IQ gains don't last very long after an intervention is over. We certainly wouldn't expect people who stop practicing music or Spanish or chess to maintain the same levels of expertise across their life span. Repeated practice and challenge are crucial.[100]

But increased IQ test scores may not even be the most practically meaningful outcome of interventions for all children. As we saw in Chapter 8, there are successful interventions that improve multiple aspects of self-regulation—skills that may be more important for people in reaching their own personal goals.

Nevertheless, this shift in conceptualization of g from "mental energy" to various forms of cognitive expertise serves a real practical purpose. Instead of focusing so much on how people differ from one another on tests that place heavy demands on working memory, it shifts the focus to what people can actually achieve if we really give them the chance. A truly potent demonstration of this isn't even found in the *current* generation.

The twentieth century witnessed a dramatic increase in IQ scores, as much as 3 points per decade. This phenomenon is dubbed "The Flynn Effect."[101] Not all IQ subtests showed the same level of increase, however. As we saw earlier, all tests of cognitive ability involve at least some fluid reasoning and prior knowledge, but some tests are better measures of fluid reasoning than others. The most dramatic increases in the twenty-first century were found on those that made the strongest demands on fluid reasoning. Tests of vocabulary, short-term memory, and general knowledge showed much smaller increases. But what caused these increases?

In his book *What Is Intelligence? Beyond the Flynn Effect*, James Flynn offers a plausible account of the rise in fluid reasoning.[102] According to Flynn, our ancestors thought very differently about the world. The Industrial Revolution brought to prominence a particular type of thought—scientific abstract thought. People back then didn't receive the same scientific instruction we do today. Once the Industrial Revolution brought with it a different set of demands, abstract thinking flooded the classroom curriculum, and the average person became much more comfortable at hypothetical thinking and making abstract generalizations.

Today, with more opportunities for educating the scientific mind, more people hold a ticket that gives them the chance to properly develop their abstract reasoning ability. According to Flynn, many people may have been smart back in the day, and may have been *capable* of answering the IQ items requiring abstract generalizations, but may have found the items so foreign and absurd that they may have answered the test questions with a certain habit of mind that wouldn't have earned them a high score.

Let's take an example of an actual IQ testing session from the early part of the twentieth century:

IQ TEST EXAMINER: All bears are white where there is always snow; in Novaya Zemlya there is always snow; what color are the bears there?

SOVIET UNION PEASANT: I have seen only black bears and I do not talk of what I have not seen.

IQ TEST EXAMINER: But what do my words imply?

SOVIET UNION PEASANT: If a person has not been there he can not say anything on the basis of words. If a man was 60 or 80 and had seen a white bear there and told me about it, he could be believed.

This peasant, hailing from a remote area of the Soviet Union, was interviewed by the psychologist Alexander Luria. It turns out that this peasant's way of thinking was quite common back then. This type of thinking involves reasoning based on personal experience and reference to the concrete, functional use of objects. As Flynn notes, "You are just not supposed to be preoccupied with how we use something or how much good it does you to possess it."[103]

A recent paper supports the notion that abstract reasoning comes more naturally to people who grow up in scientifically advanced cultures. Mark Fox and Ainsley Mitchum conducted an analysis of how test takers of different cohorts solve problems on the Raven's test.[104] As we saw earlier, performance on the Raven's test involves high levels of relational abstraction. The important aspect of the task isn't the figures themselves, but how they relate to each other. Multiple attributes of the figures have to be integrated in working memory to spot the pattern.

Fox and Mitchum classified all of the Raven's items in terms of their amount of relational abstraction and found that individuals tested in 1961 were less likely to map objects at higher levels of relational abstraction than individuals tested in 2006. It's not that those tested in 1961 were incapable of solving the problems; they were just not as accustomed to this way of thinking. When given the Raven's test, they became so fixated on the literal appearance of the figures, it didn't occur to them to apply more abstract strategies. The researchers argue that today's test-takers have a qualitatively different strategy to responding to test items: they know to search for the analogical relations among information when the initial interpretations do not automatically lend themselves to such a strategy.

The Flynn Effect raises a number of important issues. For one, it supports the findings from the behavioral and biological levels of analysis that *g* consists of multiple, interacting, cognitive mechanisms. The Flynn Effect clearly shows that the various cognitive abilities that form *g* can come apart across generations.

The Flynn Effect also highlights the important influence of cultural priorities on the development of specific forms of cognitive expertise. As an analogy, consider sports. There's evidence that many of today's world records are at least 50 percent superior to those of a century ago.[105] Accomplishments for such events as the marathon and swimming have increased so much that the gold medal winners of the early days of the Olympics would barely meet today's requirements for entrance into high school swimming teams.[106] Officials almost banned the double somersault in dives during the Fourth Olympic Games in 1908 because they believed they were too dangerous and impossible to achieve. Today, *triple* somersault dives are part of the standard repertoire of competitive divers! But if you go to any high school gym class *within* a generation and measure performance across various tests of physical fitness, a general physical fitness factor will most likely emerge.[107]

Likewise, within a generation, people who tend to do well on one test of cognitive ability do tend to do well on other tests causing a cognitive *g* factor to emerge. But *across* generations, tests placing heavy demands on fluid reasoning have increased the most, because culture has placed greater emphasis on this type of thinking, compared to short-term memory, vocabulary, and general knowledge—all tests that have not increased nearly as much throughout the generations. According to Flynn, we have to face a different set of problems today that were unheard of to our ancestors. Today, we take such thought for granted. But that doesn't necessarily make us *smarter* than prior generations.

Flynn's explanation of the Flynn Effect is just one of many "social multipliers" that have been proposed to explain the rise in fluid reasoning. According to Dickens and Flynn, a social multiplier is any societal factor that can multiply through the generations, causing large effects.[108] In addition to increased scientific spectacles, other factors undoubtedly played a role, including increased nutrition, increased literacy, increased test familiarity, video games, complexity of TV shows and movie plotlines, modernization, decreased prevalence of infectious disease and parasites, and more.[109]

Surely a combination of factors contributed to the rise in fluid reasoning. Regardless of the specific causes, the Flynn Effect serves as a reminder that when we give people more opportunities to prosper, more people *do* prosper.

~

So have we tamed *g?* Even though many issues remain unresolved and require further research, I think we can at least wrap our head around the phenomenon. In Thomson's time, they didn't yet have a language for talking about cognitive processes. That's why Thomson had to rely on his abstract, theoretical notion of "bonds." But modern cognitive science suggests that the truth is somewhere between Spearman's and Thomson's extreme positions. There appears to be a manageable number of cognitive processes available for use in any given cognitive task, with each cognitive test engaging a different—but overlapping—subset of human cognition. These processes are related to each other, and to *g*, but there is no reason to believe they are the same mental "energy."

An important implication of these findings is that although *g* is a real statistical phenomenon that emerges when we examine performance on a diverse range of cognitive ability tests across a large number of diverse individuals, *g* does not exist within any *single* individual. IQ test scores are probably best thought of as the summary of a restricted but important range of cognitive forms of expertise, involving fluid reasoning, abstract integration, working memory, short-term memory, cognitive strategies, mental rotation, verbal comprehension, vocabulary, and processing speed. Of course, which particular subset of these skills is being measured depends on the IQ test battery (see Chapters 3 and 4).

Importantly, not all test items equally measure *g*. Multiple threads of research suggest that when a large and diverse-enough battery of cognitive tests is administered, the very best measures of *g* will tend to involve a high amount of on-the-spot manipulation, integration, and control of cognitive processes in working memory (although all indicators of *g* require these skills to some degree). When tasks place such a heavy demand on working memory, the prefrontal parietal regions of the brain play an important role in helping us find efficient cognitive strategies to chunk the material and reduce the mental burden. People can draw on different strategies, however, to achieve the same *g* score, and there is accumulating evidence that the skills that are most strongly related to *g*—working memory and fluid reasoning—can be trained. Although evidence for transfer is mixed, I've highlighted the need for long-term cognitive training interventions to simultaneously target multiple cognitive mechanisms as well as social and emotional functioning.

Though *g* describes the common variance between individuals on tests of cognitive ability, *g* doesn't capture all the richness of human intelligence. In fact, there is accumulating evidence that at the upper end of IQ scores the positive manifold starts to break down, and scattered cognitive profiles become more prominent. In 1925 Spearman published a paper in which he compared the performance of 78 "normal" and 22 "defective" children on a battery of twelve cognitive tests.[110] He found that the positive correlations among the tests were much higher among the "defective" group. He labeled this discovery the Law of Diminishing Returns. Modern-day researchers have confirmed Spearman's initial findings, but refer to it as the *differentiation hypothesis*, since cognitive abilities tend to become more differentiated as *g* increases.[111]

On this point, we may have finally found some common ground. Let's end our long survey of *g* by considering two viewpoints from two intelligence researchers who come from vastly different time periods and appear to be completely at odds in their conceptualization of human intelligence: Charles Spearman and Howard Gardner.

First, here's Spearman in his 1925 paper:

At the extreme ends of the distribution will lie a very small number of performances for which the person is, on one side a genius, and on the other an idiot. Every normal man, woman, and child is, then, a genius at something as well as an idiot at something. It remains to discover *what*—at any rate in respect of the genius. (439)

Now here's Gardner, as quoted in a 1995 interview with Daniel Goleman:

The time has come to broaden our notion of the spectrum of talents. The single most important contribution education can make to a child's development is to help him towards a field where his talents best suit him. . . . We should spend less time ranking children and more time help-ing them to identify their natural competencies and gifts, and cultivate those. There are hundreds and hundreds of ways to succeed, and many, many different abilities that will help us get there.[112]

Maybe they aren't all that different after all.

Chapter 11

TALENT

Fall 2002

As I stare at the computer screen, I watch the seconds count down. I feel the sweat dripping from my brow. I look around the room, and everyone else looks equally frustrated. *OK, Scott, focus. You can think analytically. You can do this. You aren't going to let this single test get in the way of all you've worked for over the years.* I revisit the GRE problem on the screen with a newfound determination:

> Six people are sitting around a circle. One person is bald. The person to the left of the bald person is overweight. The person to right of the bald person is smelly. The person sitting to the right of the smelly person is bored. The person to the right of the bored person is excited. The bald person has now put on his hat because all this attention is making him uncomfortable. Which of the following is an accurate description of the person sitting two places to the left of the smelly person?*
>
> (a) bald
> (b) overweight
> (c) bored
> (d) smelly
> (e) cannot be determined

---

*Note that this is not an *actual* problem from the old GRE Analytical Reasoning section. But to the best of my memory, this is an example of the kind of problem you would have found on the analytical portion of the test before it was changed to the Analytical Writing section.

I try to visualize the entire circle of smelly, obese people in my head but quickly get overwhelmed. My mind wanders. I think about Michael Jordan's lackluster return to basketball. I think about how much the Phillies went down the drain since 1993. I think about that girl in my human computer interaction class who may or may not know I exist. Before I know it, time is up.

I get the results back and am surprised to discover I scored nearly 0 percent on the Analytical Reasoning section. I know I did badly, but I didn't realize I did *that* bad! With my Yale future in doubt *once again* due to a single test, a miracle occurs: a few weeks later, the folks at the College Board replace the Analytical Reasoning section with the Analytical *Writing* section. When I retake the test, it's like night and day. I express myself more fully on the writing section, weighing the debates analytically and critically. I feel like a completely different person. I get nearly a perfect score.

As I sit there with both test scores in front of me, I reflect on my existence. *Which is it? Am I one of the worst analytical thinkers in the history of humankind or am I actually a pretty good analytical thinker? The College Board says that both tests measure the same analytical thinking skills. Well, it doesn't matter. Yale only needs to know about that last score. Thankfully, I never have to tell anyone about that other score!*

Spring 2003

"How do I look?" I ask my family before I step into the interview for the Gates Cambridge Scholarship. This scholarship would offer full tuition to do graduate study at Cambridge University. My grandmother adjusts my tie. "There. Perfect. Go knock their socks off!" I take a deep breath and push open the door.

I see a big table with three British-looking people on the other side. The interviewer on the right is dressed in full barrister attire, complete with gray wig, black robe, and white flap collar. They motion me to sit down all alone on the other side of the table, with nothing to console but a single glass of water.

"We have been reviewing your life history," they note. I see a binder in front of them labeled "Scott Kaufman." I take a few more deep breaths. "Professor Mackintosh tells us you are a fine scholar . . ." the interviewer on the left says. The barrister-looking British man on the right completes the sentence, ". . . but the Gates Cambridge Scholarship is based on more than just scholarly activity. We are looking for people with the potential to improve the lives of others." Ahhh, this is the bad cop. Got it. "How will you change the world?" the barrister-looking British guy asks.

I take a sip of the water and make a loud, audible gulping sound. "Ummm . . . yea. I don't think I alone can change the world. But I wouldn't mind the chance to be able to work with others on that." The one in the middle writes something down in the binder. I can't tell if they like my answer. The interviewer in the middle narrows his focus on me, and takes up the next question. "You say you want to come up with a new theory of human intelligence. Why?" he asks with a tinge of skepticism in his voice. I scan all three of them as I search for my answer. I decide to just be honest. "Well, I don't think any of the current theories are complete."

After months of agonizing, my graduate school decisions start trickling in. I get accepted to the doctoral program at Harvard Graduate School of Education to work with Kurt Fischer and Howard Gardner. I also receive the Gates Cambridge Scholarship to work with Mackintosh on a master's degree. But still, no Yale. Every day that goes by, it feels more and more unlikely that my dream will come true.

One day I open my email inbox and see an email from Robert Sternberg. I look up and say a little prayer before reading the email. Sternberg starts off by telling me he wants to break the news before the official letter arrives. He notes that there was some disagreement on the committee over whether I could handle graduate work at Yale, considering my less-than-stellar GRE scores. He goes on to tell me that he successfully made the case, however, that I have potential for graduate work based on the quality of the work I did with him a few summers ago during an internship. His conclusion? *The committee has decided to accept me to the Yale PhD program.*

Nearly falling out of my chair, I run into the corridor and scream *YES!!!!!*, as I well up with tears.

~

Prodigies dazzle us with their virtuoso violin concertos, seemingly prescient chess moves, and vivid paintings. Their work would be enough to impress us if they were 40, but prodigies typically reach adult levels of performance *before the age of 10*. The new YouTube series "Prodigies" from THNKR TV shows a sampling of the prodigy phenomenon (see Figure 11.1).[1]

It's easy—perhaps *too* easy—to dismiss cases like these as just more exaggerated stories of ambitious parents pushing their children to excel, but this would deny the existence of many children who experience the world in the same way, and have throughout history. Historical examples include the

VICTORIA AND ZOE YIN ARE SISTERS WHO ARE BOTH ART PRODIGIES. ZOE, AGE 11, STARTED DRAWING WHEN SHE WAS ONLY ONE YEAR OLD. HER WORK IS DESCRIBED BY HER MOTHER AS "PASSIONATE," "MODERN," AND "VERY HAPPY." ZOE ESTIMATES SHE HAS SOLD ABOUT 20 PIECES SO FAR. VICTORIA, AGE 15, HAD HER FIRST INTERNATIONAL EXHIBITION WHEN SHE WAS 10 AFTER SHE WAS DISCOVERED BY HER CURRENT AGENT. HER PAINTINGS SELL FOR UPWARDS OF $30,000. HER WORK IS DESCRIBED BY HER FATHER AS MORE "RATIONAL AND PRECISE" THAN HER SISTER. HER STUNNING DISPLAYS HAVE BEEN COMPARED TO MATISSE. ZOE NOTES THAT IT'S "REALLY AN HONOR TO BE CALLED A PRODIGY, BECAUSE WHEN WE FIRST STARTED PAINTING IT WAS FOR ENJOYMENT."

GAVIN GEORGE, AGE 9, IS A PIANO PRODIGY. HE CAN ALREADY PLAY SOME OF THE MOST DIFFICULT PIECES EVER WRITTEN FOR PIANO. HIS PIANO TEACHER REMARKS THAT "THERE JUST AREN'T ENOUGH HOURS IN A DAY FOR HIM TO LEARN ALL THE PIECES HE WANTS TO LEARN." GAVIN'S MOM NOTES THAT "MUSIC SINCE A YOUNG AGE HAS BEEN A PASSION FOR GAVIN. IT'S IN HIS MIND ALL THE TIME. IT'S PART OF WHO HE IS. GAVIN IS MUSIC." ONE CHRISTMAS WHEN GAVIN WAS VERY YOUNG, HIS PARENTS GOT HIM A MUSIC DVD. HE TOOK TO IT IMMEDIATELY, CONDUCTING AND JUMPING ON THE COUCH. ABOUT A HALF A YEAR LATER, HE STARTED FORMAL TRAINING AT THE PIANO. GAVIN'S PIANO TEACHER NOTES THAT SHE TOOK GAVIN AS A STUDENT WHEN HE WAS 5, AND HE WAS "PLAYING QUITE WELL THEN. BUT HIS RATE OF PROGRESS IS TREMENDOUS. EACH MONTH IT SEEMS HE HAS PROGRESSED ANOTHER YEAR." SHE ALSO OBSERVES THAT GAVIN HAS AN "AMAZING MEMORY. HE CAN LEARN THOSE NOTES OVERNIGHT, JUST ABOUT." GAVIN CONFIRMS THIS, NOTING THAT "ONCE I'VE MEMORIZED A SONG, IT'S JUST IN MY HEAD. I KNOW IT'S THERE. I DON'T HAVE TO MEMORIZE NOTES." HIS MOTHER, WHO HAS A MASTER'S DEGREE IN GIFTED EDUCATION, GAVE UP HER JOB ONCE SHE SAW HOW PRECOCIOUS HER SON WAS AT LEARNING. HER MOTHER NOTES THAT "FROM A YOUNG AGE, HE'S BEEN VERY SENSITIVE. HE FEELS EMOTIONS, I THINK, DEEPER, THAN A LOT OF PEOPLE. I JUST REALLY THINK PLAYING MUSIC ALLOWS HIM TO EXPRESS THEM." GAVIN SAYS "ONE REASON I LOVE PLAYING THE PIANO IS BECAUSE WHEN I PLAY IT, IT MAKES ME HAPPY, AND THEN I KNOW IT MAKES OTHER PEOPLE HAPPY." HE ADDS: "I REALLY DREAM TO BE A CONCERT PIANIST. I THINK THAT WOULD BE A DREAM COME TRUE. MUSIC A SPECIAL GIFT TO GIVE TO PEOPLE."

FIGURE 11.1.
Source: THNKR, "Prodigies" series on YouTube, http://www.youtube.com/playlist?list=PLB1860C67A2998C0B.

biblical David, Jesus of Nazareth, Joan of Arc, Christian Frederich Heineken, Blaise Pascal, and Wolfgang Amadeus Mozart.

About 50 prodigies have been studied worldwide. One striking pattern is the child's chosen domain. Prodigies tend to gravitate toward highly structured and rule-based domains of knowledge, including oral language, reading, religion, mathematics, biology, physics, chess, realistic and schematic art, music composition and performance, tennis, bridge, gymnastics, skating, and swimming.[2] Prodigies have also been discovered in creative writing (poetry, fiction), although this is a more recent phenomenon.

Precocity tends to display itself early, and learning proceeds rapidly. According to Ellen Winner, precocious children tend to "march to the tune of their own drummer," needing little explicit instruction and teaching themselves the rules of the domain. Precocious children also tend to display an intense intrinsic interest. When they are engaged in their domain, they focus like a laser beam, entering the psychological state of "flow"—a state of concentration that is enjoyable and effortless, where time recedes into the background (see Chapter 12).

The performance of prodigies is hard to explain solely through the lens of the deliberate practice perspective. For one thing, the flow experience that prodigies frequently experience appears to be at odds with the concept of deliberate practice, which involves intense effort and, as Ericsson argues, is distinct from a state of play. Also, although it's true that many prodigies receive support, resources, and encouragement from parents and coaches early on, their support is typically the result of a demonstrated "rage to learn," as one father of an academic prodigy referred to his son's precocious development.[3] *Why* prodigies are so driven to deliberately practice in their domain, and then proceed to learn so rapidly in their chosen symbol system, requires explaining.

Traditional explanations of prodigies have appealed to supernatural forces, prophesy, reincarnation, sorcery, and astrology. With the emergence of psychology came a more systematic look. Binet and other psychologists studied a few prodigies between 1909 and 1930. But for whatever reason, there was a major lull in the investigation of prodigies between 1930 and 1986. A major resurgence came in 1986 with the publication of *Nature's Gambit: Child Prodigies and the Development of Human Potential*, by David Henry Feldman and Lynn Goldsmith.[4] The researchers reported on their careful, detailed analysis of six child prodigies, which covered the domains of chess, violin, writing, and mathematics/science (they also studied an "omnibus" prodigy).

Based on detailed interviews with the children and their family members, Feldman and Goldsmith concluded that the phenomenon of the prodigy is domain-specific and cannot be captured by global IQ scores or any single factor. Instead, they argued that the prodigy phenomenon is the result of a lucky "coincidence" of factors, including the following: the existence of a domain matched exceptionally well to the prodigy's proclivities and interests, availability of the domain in the prodigy's geographical location, healthy social/emotional development, family aspects (birth order and gender), education and preparation (informal and formal), cultural support, recognition for achievement in the domain, access to training resources, material support from family members, at least one parent completely committed to the prodigy's development, family traditions that favor the prodigy's development, and historical forces, events, and trends.[5]

According to Feldman, while the feats of prodigies are certainly unusual for their age, their explanation doesn't have to lie outside the confines of science and nature. To Feldman, prodigies are just extreme variations of dimensions that are part of all of us (talent, personal qualities, family traditions and their coordination), which play out in culturally important domains over a shortened period of time. "With a prodigy, we see nature and culture and tradition in one of their most successful joint efforts."[6]

In more recent years there have been a number of investigations of the mind of the prodigy. Consider a recent study by psychologist Joanne Ruthsatz and violin virtuoso Jourdan Urbach. They administered the latest edition of the Stanford-Binet IQ test to eight prominent child prodigies who have all been featured on national and international television programs.[7] Most of the children reached professional-level performance in their domain by the age of 10, and their chosen domains were notably rule-based. There was one art prodigy, one math prodigy, four musical prodigies, one prodigy who switched from music to gastronomy, and another prodigy who switched from music to art.

They found some telling patterns. There was a wide range of IQ scores—from 108 to 147. Consistent with the earlier work of David Henry Feldman, Lynn Goldsmith, and Martha Morelock, it appears that a high IQ score is not necessary to be a prodigy.[8] More telling, however, were the subtest scores. All of the prodigies showed uneven cognitive profiles. In fact, one prodigy obtained a total IQ score of 108 and a visual spatial IQ score of 71, which is worse than 97 percent of the general population. That didn't prevent him from winning a prestigious award for his violin jazz improvisational abilities, becoming the youngest person ever to perform with Wynton Marsalis at Lincoln Center! He also scored three films *without any formal composition lessons*. These findings are also consistent with prior research showing that balanced cognitive test profiles are more the exception than the rule among academically precocious students as well as students who are precocious in art and music.[9]

Even though the prodigies showed quite a bit of scatter in their abilities, there were some striking commonalities. Every single prodigy scored *off the charts* in working memory—better than 99 percent of the general population. In fact, six out of the eight prodigies scored at the 99.9th percentile! This may explain their ability to maintain practice for extended periods of time without distraction. Consistent with these findings, David Z. Hambrick and colleagues found that working memory is correlated with a number of "complex tasks," including piano sight-reading performance. While deliberate practice explained far more of the performance outcomes than working memory, working memory performance was still correlated with these tasks even among individuals with high levels of specific experience and knowledge for the domain.[10]

Superior working memory was only part of the story among the prodigies. About one in every 88 children in the United States is diagnosed with autism.[11] But *four out of the eight prodigies* in the sample had family members who either had an autism diagnosis or had a first- or second-degree relative with an autism diagnosis. Additionally, three of the prodigies had already been diagnosed with autism, and *as a group* they showed higher levels of autistic traits compared with a control group consisting of people who weren't prodigies (but they scored only slightly higher than those with high-functioning autism).

One particular autistic-like trait stood out among the prodigies: *attention to detail*. These results are intriguing and suggest that a deeper understanding of the autistic mind may shed light on talent and the genesis of some of humanity's most profound achievements.

∾

Autism spectrum disorder (ASD) is a wide spectrum, ranging from those with severe disabilities to highly functioning autism, or Asperger's syndrome (AS). In reality, all of us are somewhere on the autism spectrum, and there are multiple subtypes of autism. Nevertheless, people who are diagnosed with ASD are typically characterized by their early language delays, atypical social behavior, obsessive narrow interests, and repetitive routines.

Let's first consider social behavior. It's true that the social behaviors of people with ASD are *different*. They typically include lack of eye contact and lack of spontaneous greetings and farewells, limited use of facial expressions and gestures, and speech that is flat in affect, unusual in rhythm, and often described as "robotic."[12] People with ASD report less interest and intrinsic enjoyment in engaging in social activities, and they are also less likely to care about managing their social impressions.[13] One study found that people with ASD were less likely to laugh with other people for the purposes of facilitating social bonding, although they were just as likely as controls to spontaneously laugh at their own inner thoughts—which can come across as inappropriate in social situations.[14]

But what are we to make of these findings? Some researchers focus on impairment, arguing that the atypical social behaviors among people with ASD are due to a lack of social motivation, empathy, or the ability to take the mental perspective of others (theory of mind).[15] But I don't believe these explanations tell the full story. The Austrian physician Hans Asperger noticed among his patients with ASD many years ago that they had a "surprisingly accurate and mature observation about people."[16] More recent research confirms that people with ASD do not differ from typically developing individuals in the intensity of their emotional reactions in response to the emotions of others (for instance, as when seeing a picture of an upset woman in a hospital room).[17] Research also suggests that people with ASD are just as able as typically developing individuals to recognize basic facial expressions and reason about social information.[18]

Also, multiple autobiographical accounts from people with high-functioning autism reveal feelings of loneliness and a strong desire to make meaningful friends.[19] Many of these individuals work in occupations that require high levels of empathy and social connection, such as occupational therapy, nursing, general medical practice, and teaching and caregiving.[20] While people with ASD do tend to report less interest in engaging in superficial social activities, their attachment system and sex drive are intact.[21] A recent study found that college students with "autistic-like traits" tended to report lower interest in short-term sexual liaisons compared to a group of students with high-functioning schizophrenia, who showed *greater* interest in short-term sexual liaisons (see Chapter 12). Instead, students with autistic-like traits were much more interested in partner-specific investment and commitment to long-term romantic relationships.[22] Therefore, people with ASD may just be more interested in forming meaningful, long-lasting relationships than fleeting flings.

When it comes to the "disorder" part of autism spectrum disorder (ASD), it seems there's more going on than meets the eye.

∿

An alternative perspective, which has gained a lot of research support in recent years, is that autism is merely a different way of processing incoming information.[23] Individuals with ASD have a greater attention to detail and tend to adopt a bottom-up strategy—they first perceive the parts of an object and then build up to the whole.[24] As Uta Frith puts it, people with autism have difficulty "seeing the forest for the trees." There is neurological evidence that the unique mind of the person with ASD is due in part to an excessive number of short-distance, disorganized local connections in the prefrontal cortex (required for attention to detail) along with a reduced number of long-range or global connections necessary for integrating information from widespread and diverse brain regions.[25] As a result, people with high-functioning autism tend to have difficulty switching attention from the local to the global level.[26]

This sometimes plays itself out in social communications. People with ASD focus on details in the environment most people find "irrelevant," which can lead to some awkward social encounters. When people with

are shown photographs with social information (such as friends chat-
) or movie clips from soap operas, their attention is focused much less
on the people's faces and eyes than the background scenery, such as light
switches.[27] Differences among toddlers in attention to social speech is a robust predictor of ASD, and social attention differences in preschool lead to a
deficit in theory of mind.[28] This is important, considering that an early lack
of attention to social information can deprive the developing child of the
social inputs and learning opportunities they require to develop expertise in
social cognition.[29] It's likely that from multiple unrewarding social interactions during the course of development, people with ASD *learn* that social
interactions are unrewarding, and retreat even further into themselves.

Kate O'Connor and Ian Kirk argue that the atypical social behaviors
found in people with ASD are more likely the result of a processing difference than a social deficit, and may represent a strategy to filter out too much
sensory information.[30] Indeed, people with ASD often report emotional
confusion during social interactions, in which they interpret expressions,
gestures, and body language to mean something different from or even the
opposite of what the other person intended.[31] Many people with ASD report
that the eye region is particularly "confusing" and "frightening."[32]

Indeed, the eye region is very complex, transmitting a lot of information
in a brief time span. For one thing, it's always in motion (blinking, squinting,
saccadic movement, and so on). But the eye region also can depict a wide
range of emotions in rapid succession. It's likely that over the course of many
overwhelming interactions with people in the context of other sensory information coming in from the environment, people with ASD learn to look less
at the eye region of faces.[33] People with ASD do frequently report being distracted by sensory information in the environment, including background
noise, fluorescent light, shiny objects, body movement, and smells.[34]

Compellingly, recent studies have found that social skills can be significantly increased among people with ASD by giving them explicit instructions
to pay attention to social information, increasing the relevance of social information, and increasing their motivation to pay attention to social information.[35] In their book *The Unwritten Rules of Social Relationships*, Temple
Grandin—a highly accomplished professor of animal science who has autism
spectrum disorder*—and journalist Sean Barron argue that it's possible for

---

*Recently Janet Lainhart, Jason R. Cooperrider, and colleagues at the University of Utah
have studied Grandin's brain. Most strikingly, her left lateral ventricle is significantly larger

people with ASD to learn strategies they can apply across a wide range of social situations.[36] They note the following ten "unwritten rules of social relationships":

1. Rules are not absolute: They are situation-based and people-based.
2. Not everything is equally important in the grand scheme of things.
3. Everyone in the world makes mistakes. It doesn't have to ruin your day.
4. Honesty is different from diplomacy.
5. Being polite is appropriate in any situation.
6. Not everyone who is nice to me is my friend.
7. People act differently in public than they do in private.
8. Know when you're turning people off.
9. "Fitting in" is often tied to looking and sounding like you fit in.
10. People are responsible for their own behaviors.

There's even evidence (although it's highly tentative) that administration of the neuromodulator oxytocin can increase performance on a range of social cognitive tasks among people with ASD.[37] As Coralie Chevallier and colleagues note, "the underlying competence to process social stimuli may be more spared than previously thought and atypical performance can be accounted for by differences in spontaneous attentional patterns."[38]

In recent years researchers have developed strength-based models of autism spectrum disorder to stand alongside and complement the traditional deficit model.[39] *Both approaches are important*: people with ASD deserve the right to receive the resources they require to thrive, but they also deserve to be appreciated for their many strengths. One robust finding is that people with ASD have enhanced perceptual functioning.[40] People with ASD tend to perform better than people without ASD symptoms on IQ subtests that

---

than her right, an asymmetry that existed to a substantially lesser degree in the control group. The increased ventricular volume in her left hemisphere could be indicative of some developmental damage to parenchymal tissue that resulted in passive ventricular expansion. Compensation by the right hemisphere for diminished function in the left hemisphere could be a major contributing factor to her exceptional abilities. Grandin scored high on tests of spatial reasoning, spelling, and reading, and scored perfect on the Raven's matrices test, an excellent measure of nonverbal fluid reasoning (see Chapter 10). She performed poorly on a test of verbal working memory, however.

involve nonverbal fluid reasoning and the segmentation and reconstruction of novel visual designs.[41] Individuals with ASD also perform better than controls on the Embedded Figures Task (EFT), which requires quick detection of a target within a complex pattern.[42] The ASD tendency to see patterns as collections of details instead of as wholes helps people with ASD to segment and chunk visual information, freeing up visual working memory resources and allowing them to handle a higher perceptual load than typical adults.[43]

This enhanced attention to detail also manifests itself in restricted interests. Tony Attwood found that all-consuming special interest areas are "a dominant characteristic, occurring in over 90 percent of children and adults with AS."[44] While most people may find it difficult to understand why anyone could possibly be so intensely fascinated with yellow pencils, pinball machines, paper bags, globes and maps, industrial fans, and the buttons on shoes, special interest areas have an immense emotional impact on people with ASD and form a core of their identity. It just so happens that these individuals often find themselves in a culture that doesn't value their highly specialized passions. As Uta Frith points out, "A child who talks about electricity pylons all the time is more likely to be thought oddly fixated than one who talks about horses or football teams."[45]

Mary Ann Winter-Messiers recently explored the impact of special interest areas (SIAs) among children with Asperger's syndrome.[46] She defined special interest areas as "passions that capture the mind, heart, time, and attention of individuals with AS [Asperger's syndrome], providing the lens through which they view the world."[47] Her research team interviewed 2 girls and 21 boys with Asperger's syndrome (aged 7 to 21) about their special interest areas. All of the participants talked enthusiastically about their areas at length and displayed extensive professional knowledge of their area that went way beyond what would be expected based solely on their ages. Major themes included transportation, music, animals, solitary sports (such as swimming), video games (such as role-playing games), fantasy motion pictures (Star Wars, vampire movies), woodworking, and art (Anime, Manga, sculpting). Many children used video games as a way to socially bond with others with similar interests.

As the researchers conducted their interviews, it became clear that the SIAs of people with Asperger's were inextricably linked to their self-images. While the participants reported having a negative self-image in virtually every other area of their lives, they said that when they engaged in their special area they felt positive emotions, including enthusiasm, pride, and happiness. They also reported feeling more competent, in control, and self-confident. At the same time, the participants were hesitant about telling others about their area of interest out of fear of rejection, and many of the participants expressed frustration at being misunderstood. As one participant noted, "Well, if they're not interested, I don't really talk about airplanes at all . . . I just wish they'd think planes were cool."[48]

The researchers also noticed a distinct shift in speech patterns—including affect and animation—when participants shifted from any topic to talking about their special interest area. They noted a marked increase in the complexity of their responses and the sophistication of their vocabulary, word order, and syntax. For example, one participant named Charlie responded to general questions with "Uh, I don't think so, just whatever," but when he was asked about his favorite thing to play with, he suddenly became alive: "My favorite is a Yu-Gi-Oh! Card that combines with three Blue-Eyed White Dragons, and due to polymerization it forms those three into a three-headed dragon."[49]

In fact, the research team consistently observed that many of the so-called "impairments" of the participants diminished considerably when they talked about their SIA, including significant reductions in stress, self-stimulation, distraction, and body movement. They also observed heightened sensitivity to subtle social cues, eye contact, and expressive gestures. For instance, one participant only gave monosyllabic and repetitive answers to questions, but when the interviewer acknowledged his interest in trains, he suddenly made direct eye contact and came alive. The interviewer wrote that "he got so excited that you could barely understand his excited and hurried words."[50]

Also, while many of these children were thought to be "severely challenged" by intense sensory stimulation, they were able to persevere for hours at a time in their interactions with model airplane glue, modeling clay, horse manure, goat odors, sawdust, sweat, sticky or dirty hands, drum beats, and the bright lights, rapid movements, and loud, startling sounds of video games.

Winter-Messiers concluded that parents and educators should be more welcoming and encouraging of special interest areas because they form such a vital part of the self-image and motivation of children with Asperger's. She notes that students can benefit from engagement of their special interest to deal with negative emotions, reduce anxiety, and calm themselves in stressful situations. She made a call for educators to finally take special interest areas (SIAs) seriously and see them "for the gold mine they are in helping our students progress toward their academic, social, emotional, communication, and behavioral goals."[51]

Winter-Messiers and colleagues argue that the first step toward increasing engagement is for teachers to discover their students' areas of academic strength and consider how the curriculum can be modified to incorporate the student's special interest area. For math, this can be as easy as placing stickers on a worksheet or working their area of interest into story problems. According to these researchers, "there is no limit to what they can accomplish when they are appropriately encouraged to use their SIAs [special interest areas] to improve their academic and social pursuits."[52]

They also point to crucial applications at home, in the community, and in the workforce. Again, Asperger was well ahead of his time when he noted that "we can see in the autistic person, far more clearly than with any normal child, a predestination for a particular profession from earliest youth. A particular line of work often grows naturally out of his or her special abilities."[53] Temple Grandin and Kate Duffy echo this sentiment: "Society loses out if individuals with autism spectrum disorders are not involved in the world of work or make other kinds of contributions to society."[54]

This research clearly shows that ability can grow out of seeming *disability*. In fact, those who appear to be the most severely disabled often demonstrate the highest levels of performance. Nowhere is this more evident than with savants. As scientist Allan Snyder told me, "savantism is autism in its purest form, uncontaminated by other disorders."[55]

～

There's a scene in the 1988 movie *Rain Man* in which Raymond Babbitt (played by Dustin Hoffman) recites a waitress's phone number. Naturally the waitress is shocked. Instead of mental telepathy, Raymond had memorized the entire telephone book and instantly recognized the name on her nametag.

Hoffman's character was heavily influenced by the life of Kim Peek, a real memory savant who recently passed away. Peek was born without a corpus callosum, the fibers that connect the right and left hemispheres of the brain. He was also born missing parts of the cerebellum, which is important for motor control and the learning of complex, well-rehearsed routines.*

---

*Interesting tidbit: Some researchers have argued that throughout the past million years of human evolution, the prefrontal cortex coevolved with brain support systems—such as the cerebellum—to help store, implement, and smooth out tried and true routines and solu-

When Peek was 9 months old, a doctor recommended he be institutional-ized due to his severe mental disability.[56] By the age of 6, when Peek had already memorized the first eight volumes of the family encyclopedia, an-other doctor recommended a lobotomy. By 14, Peek completed a high school curriculum.

Peek's abnormal brain wiring certainly came at a cost. Though he was able to immediately move new information from short-term memory to long-term memory, there wasn't much processing going on in between. His adult fluid reasoning ability and verbal comprehension skills were on par with a child of 5, and he could barely understand the meaning in proverbs or metaphors. He also suffered deficits in the area of self-care: he couldn't dress himself or brush his teeth without assistance.

But what Peek lacked in brain connections and conceptual cognitive functioning, he more than made up for in memory. He had the extraordi-nary ability to memorize any text in just one sitting. With two pages in front of him, he had the uncanny ability for each eye to focus on a different page. His repertoire included the Bible, the complete works of Shakespeare, U.S. area codes and zip codes, and roughly 12,000 other books. He was known to stop performances to correct actors and musicians who had made a mistake! He could also tell you what day of the week your birthday fell on in any year. Toward the end of Peek's life, Peek showed a marked improvement in his engagement with people. He also began playing the piano, made puns, and even started becoming more self-aware. During one presentation at Oxford University, a woman asked him if he was happy, to which he responded: "I'm happy just to look at you."[57]

The trade-off between memory and meaning is common among savants. The purpose of memory is to simplify experience.[58] We didn't evolve mem-ory to be precise. Instead, we extract meaning wherever we can so that we can organize the regularities of experience and prepare for similar situations in the future. But without the imposition of meaning, savants can focus on literal

tions. This offloading would have given much needed relief to an overburdened working memory. It has even been suggested that the increased cultural demands in only the past 10,000 years have put such an extraordinary burden on our working memory that it has driven an expansion of the cerebellum relative to the neocortex. See J. H. Balsters, E. Cus-sans, et al., "Evolution of the Cerebellar Cortex: The Selective Expansion of Prefrontal-Projecting Cerebellar Lobules," *NeuroImage* 49 (2010): 2045–2052; L. R. Vanderbelt, "The Appearance of the Child Prodigy 10,000 Years Ago: An Evolutionary and Developmental Explanation," *Journal of Mind and Behavior* 30 (2009): 15–32; L. Vandervert, "The Evolu-tion of Language: The Cerebro-Cerebellar Blending of Visual-Spatial Working Memory with Vocalizations," *Journal of Mind and Behavior* 32 (2011): 317–332.

recall. Some savants even have *hyperlexia*, which is the opposite of dyslexia.[59] They are precocious readers, but have no comprehension of what they are reading.

Descriptions of savant syndrome first appeared in the scientific literature as early as 1789. In 1887 the British doctor J. Langdon Down (who discovered Down syndrome) described 10 people with savant syndrome and coined the term "idiot savant" (which is no longer used, because of its pejorative connotation). Today, one in ten people with autism have savantism, although only half of the documented savants are autistic. The rest have some other kind of developmental disorder.

Savantism disproportionately affects males, with about five male savants for every one female, and the syndrome generally occurs in people with IQs between 40 and 70. Like others with ASD, when savants take IQ tests they tend to score higher on nonverbal problems than verbal problems. As Darold Treffert, a world-renowned expert on savant syndrome, observes, "IQ scores, in my experience with savants, fail to adequately capture and reflect the many separate elements and abilities that contribute to 'intelligence' overall in everyone."[60]

Like others on the autism spectrum, savants display a narrow repertoire of skills, which tend to be highly structured, rule-based, and nonverbal. Common savant domains include music, art, calendar calculating, lightning calculating, and mechanical/visual spatial skills. Most musical savants are blind and have perfect pitch, most artistic savants express themselves through realistic drawing and sculpture, and most rapid calculating savants have a fascination and facility with prime numbers.

Even so, savants vary markedly in their abilities. Savant skills fall along a continuum, ranging from "splinter skills" (such as memorization of license plates), to "talented" savants who have musical or artistic skills that exceed what is expected based on their handicap, to "prodigious" savants where the skill is so remarkable it would be impressive with or without the disability. To date, fewer than 100 prodigious savants have been documented. Interestingly, there is almost always no "dreaded trade-off" between the incredible skills of savants and their development of language, social skills, and daily living functioning.

Savant syndrome can be congenital or acquired. When congenital, the skill appears early in childhood, and when acquired, abilities appear to spring forth suddenly following stroke, brain injury, or dementia. Figure 11.2 shows a sampling of some of these remarkable individuals.

LESLIE LEMKE (LL) WAS BORN PREMATURELY, BLIND, AND WITH A FORM OF CEREBRAL PALSY THAT MANIFESTS ITSELF IN EXTREME STIFFNESS IN THE LOWER PART OF THE BODY. HIS MEASURED IQ WAS 58 AND AS A CHILD HE NEEDED HELP EATING, STANDING AND WALKING. FROM AN EARLY AGE HE WAS DRAWN TO MUSIC AND RHYTHM, BEATING OUT RHYTHMS ON HIS BEDSPRINGS. WHEN LL WAS 8, HIS FOSTER MOTHER BOUGHT HIM A PIANO. WHILE SHE WAS A NOVICE PIANO PLAYER, SHE WOULD PLACE LL'S HANDS OVER HER OWN HANDS AS SHE PLAYED SIMPLE TUNES. BY 9, LL WAS ABLE TO PLAY SIMPLE TUNES BY HIMSELF ON THE PIANO AS WELL AS OTHER INSTRUMENTS, INCLUDING THE BONGO DRUMS, CONCERTINA AND ACCORDION. HE NEVER HAD ANY FORMAL MUSIC LESSONS. ONE EVENING WHEN HE WAS 14, HE HEARD TCHAIKOVSKY'S PIANO CONCERT NO.1 ON THE TELEVISION. TO THE UTTER SHOCK OF HIS FOSTER PARENTS, LATER THAT EVENING HE PLAYED THE PIECE PERFECTLY ON THE PIANO. NOW HIS REPERTOIRE INCLUDES THOUSANDS OF PIECES, AND PROFESSIONAL MUSICIANS HAVE DESCRIBED LL AS INTUITIVELY KNOWING "THE RULES OF MUSIC." IN RECENT YEARS, HE HAS EVEN PROGRESSED FROM ROTE RECALL TO COMPLEX IMPROVISATIONS AND EVEN COMPOSITIONS. IN PUBLIC PERFORMANCES, HE CAN BE SEEN SINGING ALONG TO HIS MUSIC.

FLO AND KAY ARE AUTISTIC IDENTICAL TWINS. THEY ARE ALSO EXTRAORDINARY CALENDAR CALCULATORS. GIVE THEM ANY DATE PAST OR EVEN A THOUSAND YEARS IN THE FUTURE, AND THEY CAN TELL YOU THE DAY OF THE WEEK, HISTORICAL SIGNIFICANCE (IF ANY), AND WEATHER. THEY ALSO HAVE ENCYCLOPEDIC MEMORY FOR QUIZ SHOW QUESTIONS, MUSIC ALBUMS, AND ARTISTS AND RELEASE DATES OVER THE PAST FOUR DECADES, AS WELL AS PERFECT DAY-TO-DAY RECALL OF EPISODES IN THEIR OWN LIVES. NEITHER TWIN CAN EXPLAIN HOW THEY DO WHAT THEY DO, AND THEY NEVER CONSCIOUSLY SET OUT TO LEARN THE FORMULA FOR DOING CALENDAR CALCULATIONS. WHEN PEOPLE ASK THEM HOW THEY DO IT, THEY OFTEN RESPOND IN UNISON: "I'VE GOT THAT CHIP IN MY HEAD. THAT'S HOW I DO IT."

ALONZO CLEMENS IS COGNITIVELY IMPAIRED, AND HAS NEVER HAD ANY FORMAL TRAINING IN ART. AS A YOUNG CHILD HE SUFFERED A SEVERE HEAD INJURY, WHICH LEFT HIM WITH LIMITED VOCABULARY AND SPEECH. SOON AFTER THE ACCIDENT, WITHOUT ANY FORMAL TRAINING IN ART, HE DISPLAYED AN INTUITIVE UNDERSTANDING OF THE RULES OF ART, MOLDING ANIMALS HE SAW IN MAGAZINES OR AT THE ZOO OUT OF CRYSTALLINE CLAY. HIS REPLICATIONS WERE FLAWLESS. HE JUST "KNEW" HOW TO ARMATURE HIS BRONZE HORSE FIGURINES, A SKILL THAT TAKES SOME ARTISTS YEARS TO MASTER. IN 1986 HE HELD HIS WORLD PREMIERE OF 30 BRONZE SCULPTURES, WHICH SHOWCASED HIS LIFE-SIZED PIECE THREE FROLICKING FOULS. TODAY, AC'S SCULPTURES APPEAR IN ART GALLERIES RIGHT NEXT TO WORK BY ACCOMPLISHED SCULPTORS. AS DAROLD TREFFERT NOTES, "HIS WORKS ARE SPECTACULAR NOT BECAUSE THEY ARE DONE BY SOMEONE WITH A DISABILITY. THEY ARE SPECTACULAR IN THEIR OWN RIGHT."

JASON PADGETT WAS ATTACKED BY MUGGERS OUTSIDE A KARAOKE CLUB IN HIS EARLY 30S. AFTER THEY FINISHED KICKING HIM REPEATEDLY IN THE HEAD, THEY LEFT, LEAVING HIS MIND FOREVER CHANGED. PADGETT STARTED SEEING COMPLEX MATHEMATICAL FORMULAS LIKE THE PYTHAGOREAN THEOREM EVERYWHERE HE LOOKED. "EVERY SINGLE LITTLE CURVE, EVERY SINGLE SPIRAL, EVERY TREE IS PART OF THAT EQUATION," HE NOTED. HE ALSO BECAME FASCINATED WITH FRACTALS, BEAUTIFUL SHAPES IN WHICH EVERY SINGLE ELEMENT IS THE SAME AS THE WHOLE. BEFORE THE MUGGING, PADGETT HAD NO PARTICULAR INTEREST IN DRAWING, HAD NO ADVANCED MATH DEGREES AND WAS WORKING IN A FUTON STORE. AFTER THE MUGGING, HE CAN DRAW HIGHLY PRECISE FRACTALS WITH COMPLEX MATHEMATICAL FORMULAS EMBEDDED, AND HE SELLS HIS DRAWINGS FOR TOP DOLLAR. HE ALSO TEACHES OTHERS ABOUT THE BEAUTY OF MATH. SCIENTISTS WHO HAVE STUDIED HIS BRAIN HAVE FOUND THAT AREAS RELATING TO MATH AND MENTAL IMAGERY LIGHT UP ON COGNITIVE TASKS MORE THAN CONTROLS. PADGETT NOTES: "SOMETIMES I WOULD REALLY LIKE TO TURN IT OFF, AND IT WON'T. BUT THE GOOD FAR OUTWEIGH THE BAD. I WOULD NOT GIVE IT UP FOR ANYTHING."

FIGURE 11.2.

Sources: D. Treffert, "Savant Syndrome: A Compelling Case for Innate Talent," in *The Complexity of Greatness: Beyond Talent or Practice*, ed. S. B. Kaufman, 103–118 (New York: Oxford University Press, 2013); http://abcnews.go.com/blogs/health/2012/04/27/real-beautiful-mind-accidental-genius-draws-complex-math-formulas-photos/

How can we explain the extraordinary feats of savants? No one knows the whole story, but there are some clues. Bernard Rimland, who passed away in 2006, maintained the largest database in the world of people with autism (more than 34,000 cases).[61] He observed that the savant skills that were most frequently present were right-hemisphere skills, and their deficits were most strongly associated with left-hemisphere functions.

Treffert argues that we may all have a reservoir of inherited knowledge, but savants are able to access this knowledge through a process of rewiring, recruitment, and release.[62] According to Treffert's account, left-hemisphere damage or dysfunction causes recruitment of still-available intact cortical tissue elsewhere in the brain to compensate for the loss, and this rewiring releases dormant capacity within that still-intact cortical tissue. Although it's typically the case that left-hemisphere brain damage causes right-hemisphere brain recruitment, rewiring, and release, Treffert acknowledges this is not always the case.

Another prominent theory, proposed in the 1980s by Norman Geschwind and Albert Galaburda, offers an explanation as to why disorders involving the disruption of the left hemisphere of the brain (such as savantism, autism, dyslexia, delayed speech, stuttering, hyperactivity) occur so much more often in males than in females.[63] The left hemisphere typically completes its development later than the right hemisphere, so it is susceptible to prenatal influences for a longer period. Therefore, in the developing male fetus, circulating testosterone can slow the growth of the left hemisphere. This can cause compensation, in which the right hemisphere becomes bigger and more dominant in males.

This left-brain damage/right-brain compensation hypothesis is consistent with a number of recent studies. One thread of research involves elderly patients with frontotemporal dementia (FTD).[64] Bruce Miller and colleagues found that some of their patients with degeneration in very specific regions of the frontal and anterior temporal lobes on the left side of the brain suddenly expressed interest and skill in art and music as their dementia progressed. The paintings that the patients produced were generally realistic or surrealistic without symbolism or abstraction, and the patients approached their art in a compulsive way, repeating the same design many times. For some reason the colors purple, yellow, or blue were commonly repeated. Some of these patients described their experience as though their brain was "taken over" by a compulsive need to create.

Another fascinating thread comes from research on brain stimulation. Allan Snyder believes that savants have privileged access to lower level, less-processed information before it is packaged into concepts and meaningful labels.[65] He argues that due to a failure in conceptual inhibition, savants can tap into knowledge that exists in all of our brains but is typically outside of conscious awareness. For instance, when it comes to drawing, we aren't consciously aware of how our brain derives shape from shading, perspective from gradients of texture, size invariants from distance, and so on. But somehow artists and artistic savants can directly tap into this lower-level, less processed perceptual information before it becomes integrated into the holistic picture.

In recent years Snyder has been able to temporarily induce savant-like skills in normal people by using noninvasive brain stimulation. In his earlier work, he used low-frequency transcranial direct current stimulation (rTMS) to inhibit the left anterior temporal lobe while simultaneously increasing the excitability of the right anterior temporal lobe.[66] He was able to show a significant improvement among some of his participants in realistic drawing, proofreading, and the ability to accurately estimate a large number of objects. He has even found a reduction among some participants in susceptibility to false memories. Not all of Snyder's participants showed a marked improvement, however, and a study by Robyn Young and colleagues found that rTMS stimulation activated savant-like skills in only 5 out of 17 participants.[67]

I raised this point to Snyder, and he maintained his confidence that there are savant skills latent in all of us. He noted that there are a number of reasons not everyone shows the same improvement. One reason is individual differences—people who already lean toward a detail-oriented thinking style are "closer to the precipice than others."[68] Also, he told me that the effectiveness of brain stimulation techniques depends on the orientation of the sulci (grooves) of the person's brain and the amount of their neural conductivity (myelination). Snyder also noted that there are some technical issues and limitations with the procedure. He said stimulation is less effective in people with thick hair or skulls, and TMS has poor spatial resolution in general, which makes it difficult to target a specific location or neural network.

More recent work by Snyder and other researchers using transcranial direct current stimulation (tDCS) has shown a more powerful effect. Roi Cohen Kadosh and colleagues were able to show an improvement in numerical proficiency that lasted six months after tDCS stimulation, although in some cases the enhancement occurred at the expense of other cognitive functions.[69] Also, more recent research by Allan Snyder and Richard Chi has found powerful effects of tDCS on solving extremely difficult insight problems.[70] tDCS has also been applied to enhance other psychological functions, such as planning ability, and has been used to treat psychological disorders, such as depression and schizophrenia.[71]

Is tDCS ready for prime time? After all, the technique is portable, painless, inexpensive, safe, and feasible for home use. I think there is reason to be cautious before we start stocking Walmart with electric thinking caps. In addition to potential tradeoffs in ability, there are still major technical limitations, not to mention major ethical limitations if only some people can afford to zap targeted brain areas to enhance high-stakes test performance.

Nevertheless, Snyder believes that someday there might be a "thinking cap" that can temporarily reduce left-hemispheric dominance, allowing privileged access to literal details and a less prejudiced and more creative mind. As he told me, "My idealistic vision would be for the thinking cap to be accessible to any healthy adult, enabling them to see the world literally. . . . Maybe there'll be 'thinking cap bars,' like oxygen bars, in the future, where people can pop in to top up on inspiration—just kidding, but who knows?"[72]

Treffert believes savants are the best example of innate talent and represent 'nature' in its most basic form." To explain the emergence of savant skills, Treffert proposes the notion of "genetic memory," which he defines as the biological transfer of proclivities and knowledge that don't require additional instruction or learning. He argues that this knowledge is "factory-installed"[73] in all of us but remains dormant because we tend to use the same well-worn pathways and circuits that serve us well. He believes this inhibits the little Rain Man in all of us."

There are actually a number of elements to this theory. Let's put on Snyder's electric thinking cap for the moment and segment Treffert's concept of genetic memory. The first idea is that we have factory-installed "templates" that ease learning in a domain, the second notion is that we are born with full domain knowledge, and the third idea is that the major difference between savants and the rest of us is that they have more direct access to these templates and knowledge.

On the first part, Treffert is most surely correct. We aren't born blank slates. In recent years researchers have begun to map out the various domains of the human mind. An accumulating body of research suggests we have an innate facility to learn and reason about spatial relations, number, probability, logic, language, physical objects, living things, artifacts, music, aesthetics, and the beliefs and desires of other minds.[74]

According to Rochelle Gelman, our "core" domains operate by a number of specific principles. Critically, Gelman argues we don't start out with complete knowledge of a domain. Indeed, as we saw in Chapter 1, "innate" and "learning" are not opposed terms but are necessarily dependent. "Innate" mental structures are best thought of as an *innate learning mechanism*.[75]

Just as we have bodily structures, Gelman argues that we have various "mental structures" that direct our attention to domain knowledge. This process—called "structure mapping"—scans the environment for relevant data that fits our innate skeletal structure.[76] There was certainly enough time during the course of human evolution (and we're still evolving) for natural selection to capture the recurring patterns of different domains. It's highly likely that natural selection sculpted our genes to be exquisitely sensitive to learning domain-specific patterns that were important for the survival and reproduction of our ancestors.*

Core domains benefit humans greatly because they provide us with a leg-up on learning. This can easily be seen in young children all around the world, who learn core domains spontaneously and are highly motivated to learn them. A key element of Gelman's theory is that the relevant input has to be provided to the child, or else he won't assimilate the knowledge into the structures. But when the relevant inputs are provided, learning proceeds with relative ease and the knowledge that is learned is *implicit* (people can't express how they learned the knowledge).

There is support for this theory. Newborn babies all over the world get upset if you show them a face that doesn't have the right facial configuration, and they are incredibly accurate at distinguishing among facial expressions. In the first few years after birth, children spontaneously learn thousands of words, comprehend language before they can speak it, discover the grammatical rules of language without explicit instruction, and even go through a predictable pattern of grammatical errors. Infants show an innate understanding that physical objects can't pass through each other and know the basic principles of arithmetic, such as addition, subtraction, and ordering. Infants also have an amazing knack for telling whether an animated blob has intentions or is a nonliving object just floating about aimlessly. Learning in all these domains appears to be highly *domain specific*, constrained

---

*Although *which* domains were selected and whether they were *selected for* any specific adaptive purpose (or were by-products) is still hotly disputed among cognitive scientists, evolutionary psychologists, archeologists, and anthropologists.

by its own set of principles. For instance, 2-year-olds all around the world spontaneously care about the color of food, but they don't care much about the color of artifacts or countable entities.

Although we most certainly evolved numerous domains of mind dedicated to processing particular kinds of information, contemporary cognitive neuroscience shows that for most normal human brains, processing occurs broadly throughout the brain, with lots of interconnectivity among different brain regions.[77] Multiple brain components are constantly communicating with each other to facilitate solving problems that our ancestors faced during the bulk of our evolutionary history.

So Treffert is on firm ground when arguing that we have built-in mental structures. I'd also agree that we all have our own unique brain wiring that influences our interests in mastering a particular domain of human knowledge and even greatly facilitates such learning. What remains far more controversial, in my view, is Treffert's notion that genetic memory consists of built-in knowledge that doesn't require *any* learning or experience. To Treffert, the only way that it is possible for savants to "know" rules they never studied or learned is through the "biological transfer of knowledge."[78]

Allow me to suggest another way.

∾

Most, perhaps as much as 95 percent, of the learning that takes place in our day-to-day lives operates *implicitly*—no explicit instruction was available or necessary. Much of this learning is incredibly complex, considering that information in the environment includes so many multidimensional and interactive relations. Compared to conscious, deliberate thought, our implicit learning structures are much faster and more efficient. In their review of the literature on the implicit acquisition of knowledge, Paul Lewicki, Thomas Hill, and Maria Czyzewska argue that implicit learning *must* be considered intelligent, if "intelligence is understood as 'equipped to efficiently process complex information.'"[79]

In graduate school I first became fascinated with implicit learning when I came across evidence from Guido Gebauer—a doctoral student in my M. Phil advisor Nicholas Mackintosh's laboratory at the University of Cambridge—that there is a distinct separation between explicit and implicit learning. Gebauer and Mackintosh administered a variety of implicit learning tasks to 605 German pupils.[80] Crucially, they varied the instructions. In one condition, participants were instructed to explicitly discover the rule underlying the pattern. In another condition, participants weren't told anything about a rule; they were left to discover the rule all on their own. When participants received *explicit* instruction, the implicit learning tasks were significantly correlated with IQ. But when participants had to implicitly discover the rule, *there was no correlation with IQ*. I must admit, there are few other things in life that excited me as much as this finding.

But I wondered, What does it matter if some people are faster at implicitly soaking up the complex regularities of the environment? What does this relate to in the *real world*? At the time various researchers argued that there were no meaningful differences in implicit learning.[81] To these researchers, all of the important variation existed in explicit cognition. Researchers treated differences in the cognitive unconscious as "noise" to be experimentally controlled, not seriously investigated. For instance, in defining the functioning of the "autonomous mind" (consisting of cognitive processes that operate automatically and independently of working memory), Keith Stanovich has argued that "continuous individual differences in the autonomous mind are few. The individual differences that do exist largely reflect damage to cognitive modules that result in very discontinuous cognitive dysfunction such as autism or the agnosis and alexias."[82] I was skeptical.

For my doctoral dissertation I teamed up with an expert on implicit learning—Luis Jiménez from the Universidad de Santiago de Compostela in Spain—to help me construct a variety of implicit learning tasks that could capture important differences between individuals. I administered these tasks to a group of British high school students, along with measures of personality and traditional measures of cognitive ability. I found that nearly all of the implicit learning tasks were too easy for the students; there really weren't important individual differences on these tasks. Even though the students reported to me that they had no conscious awareness of learning, they were all able to implicitly learn the context of visual cues and the underlying grammar of a novel artificial language. I thought perhaps there really weren't any meaningful individual differences in implicit learning after all. That is, until I conducted an analysis of *probabilistic sequence learning*.

To measure sequence learning, I presented participants with a sequence of trials in which a stimulus appeared in one of four locations on the computer screen. Participants were instructed to press the corresponding key (z, x, n, m) as fast and accurately as possible (see Figure 11.3). *That's all they were told*. Unknown to the participants, the sequence followed a repeating sequence 85 percent of the time, intermixed with an alternative sequence 15 percent of the time. Arguably, this task is akin to real-world learning, where learning often happens in uncertain environments and patterns are

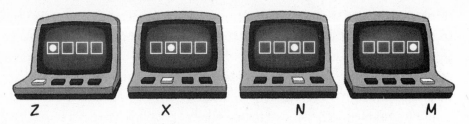

Z   X   N   M

FIGURE 11.3.

noisy and probabilistic instead of deterministic. The probabilistic nature of this task also makes it very difficult for the explicit system to figure out the pattern. Indeed, not one participant during interviews after the experiment said they consciously noticed the pattern. They were even quite shocked when I told them they were able to implicitly learn a complex probabilistic pattern!

I presented participants with 960 trials, more than enough time to learn the sequence. As a group, people gradually became faster and faster at learning the main sequence (the one that was 85 percent probable) throughout the course of the experiment. But I also found substantial individual differences in how fast people learned the sequence. Implicit learning ability wasn't significantly correlated with measures of explicit cognition: *g*, working memory, explicit associative learning, or a preference for engagement in intellectual, abstract material. Nevertheless, implicit learning *was* correlated with important outcomes.

Taking into account explicit cognition, implicit learning ability was independently associated with verbal analogical reasoning, processing speed, and performance on two foreign language exams (French and German). Implicit learning was also associated with various aspects of personality, including a preference for intuition, openness to perceptual and aesthetic experiences, and impulsivity. I also found a relationship between implicit learning and music creative achievement.[83] As you can imagine, I was very excited by these findings, which my colleagues and I published in 2010.[84]

Around the time I was conducting the study, I was approached by my friend and colleague Jamie Brown to collaborate on a study at the University of Cambridge on implicit learning in people with autism spectrum disorder.[85] Overcoming many of the prior limitations of earlier studies, we compared the performance of 26 children with high-functioning autism spectrum disorder to 26 typically developing children on four implicit learning tasks, each task designed to tap into a different domain of implicit learning. We even administered a measure of implicit social learning, which researchers assumed would show impairment in people with autism. On all of the tasks, we minimized reliance on explicit strategies. We also matched the two groups on IQ and administered a measure of explicit learning for comparison purposes. Finally, we administered a reliable index of real-world autistic symptomatology.

We found *no* difference in implicit learning ability between the autism spectrum disorder group and the typically developing control group. This wasn't a consequence of compensation by explicit learning ability or IQ: we found the usual difference in explicit learning. Finally, we found no relationship between implicit learning ability in the laboratory and real-world autism spectrum condition symptomatology. Our conclusion: whatever is causing the social, communicative, or motor impairments found in those with autism spectrum disorder, it is *not* a deficit in implicit learning.

Since our paper, other researchers have replicated this basic pattern of findings and have found intact implicit learning ability among people with ASD over longer periods of time.[86] These results are illuminating, and raise the question: Can intact implicit learning help explain the phenomenal feats of savants?

Perhaps savant skills are learned, just like any other skills. But the reason their skills appear to burst forth without any prior practice or explicit instruction is that their learning operated implicitly, facilitated by their unique brain wiring.

Consider the domain of calendar calculation. The calendar has many sequential regularities and redundancies that make it particularly attractive to savants.[87] While formulas exist online that anyone can use to become a calendar calculator, the underlying rules can be discovered with enough exposure to calendars. For instance, if instead of going to school dances and playing cops and robbers, you spent every waking second of your childhood obsessively studying calendars, your powerful implicit learning system would eventually discover the following regularities:

- There are always 7 days to a week.
- The 1st, 8th, 15th, 22nd, and 29th must always be the same day of the week.
- In any given year, particular pairs of months (such as April and July) always have the same starting day, regardless of leap year.

- The pair January and October and the triad February, March, and November have the same starting day only on non-leap years.
- Only in leap years do February and August have the same starting day. Same for January, April, and July.
- January 1st advances one day of the week each succeeding year, except leap years, when it advances two days.
- Because a day is added every 4 years, the calendar shifts 5 days every four years.
- Except for a few exceptions, the calendar repeats every 28 years.
- There is a 400-year cycle.[88]

Systematic studies on calendar-calculating savants—based on reaction time information and a look at systematic errors—suggests that calendar-calculating savants do indeed incorporate these redundancies into their strategy for making their calculations. As one researcher noted, "Something mysterious, though commonplace, is operating here—the mysterious human ability to form unconscious algorithms on the basis of examples."[89] Theoretically, all that is required to explain savant skills is an innate predisposition to find redundancies and sequential regularities fascinating and an intact implicit learning system that gradually extracts those regularities over many hours of experience.

Now consider the music domain, which also consists of highly structured sequential regularities. In recent years a number of studies have shown that, just as implicit learning plays an important role in acquiring the rules of language, various musical structures such as melody, harmony, timbre, and rhythm are implicitly acquired through mere exposure.[90] One study found that after being exposed to sequences of tones that conformed to a complex artificial grammar, participants later showed faster and more accurate processing for a new set of grammatical tones compared to un-grammatical tones, without any explicit awareness that they learned such information.[91]

Due to their language impairment, perhaps for savants their music *becomes* their language. Perhaps they are accessing the underlying patterns we all implicitly learn when we hear music or engage with language. Consider a telling study by Jonathan Sloboda and colleagues.[92] They studied a musical savant they referred to as NP who lived in a residential home for people with autism. From an early age, NP listened obsessively to music on the radio, and he showed an early propensity for mimicking speech and imitating sounds. A tape recording made between the ages of 5 and 8 shows that his musical skills were progressing at a fast rate.

At the time the researchers encountered NP he had a substantial repertoire of classical pieces and was able to learn a new sonata-length piece in three or four hearings. His verbal IQ was found to be 62 and his performance IQ was 60. His short-term memory was unexceptional: he could only remember 5 digits forward and 4 digits backward. Like other people on the autism spectrum, NP had an almost complete absence of speech, averted his eye gaze, and displayed obsessive behaviors. The researchers noted that NP would probably always live in an institutional setting.

The researchers played two unfamiliar piano recordings for NP. One piece was by Bartok and had a clear melody, whereas the other piece was atonal and consisted of whole tone scales. Compared to the Bartok, the atonal piece contained fewer notes, fewer voices, and an equally simple rhythmic and formal structure. The key difference was that it had no systematic tonal structure. After hearing each piece, NP was asked to play as much of the piece as he could. On another occasion the same pieces were given to a professional pianist roughly the same age and years of experience to memorize under the same conditions.

After about 12 minutes and hearing the piece no more than four times, NP played back the melodic piece almost perfectly. He also appeared to have perfect pitch, because he never needed to try out different positions before starting to play. NP was also able to play the melodic piece back perfectly 24 hours later, although his repeat performance had become "wooden" and "metronomic." The researchers observed that he retained the structural "husk" but discarded the expressive "flesh." In contrast, the professional pianist's performance was good only on the first eight bars, but she rapidly became overwhelmed with the rapid succession of notes. The researchers tested other professional pianists and found the same thing: none were able to perform even half as well as NP.

The atonal piece told a completely different story. By the third trial, the professional pianist could play the first 12 bars without error, whereas NP was still making errors on the third trial. NP (but not the professional pianist) declined to go any further and was visibly distressed that he couldn't memorize the atonal piece. The researchers analyzed NP's pattern of errors and concluded that they were "structure preserving." He seemed to be utilizing a framework that enabled him to rapidly encode material in terms of tonal structures and relations, but when the music went outside that framework he was unable to cope with the new information. Interestingly, they found that he was highly sensitive to structure in domains other than music. While his short-term memory for digits was below average, he was able to memorize conventionally ordered sentences.

They also noticed that NP was able to put appropriate chords under a melodic beginning, and then improvise a conventional conclusion—"the kind of elaboration that one might expect to find in a proficient improviser" (365). In contrast, the professional pianists' errors were more evenly distributed. The researchers conclude that a high IQ is not necessary for the development of high levels of musical memorization skill, and that when we look at the memory capacity of NP and Mozart, we are looking at the same phenomenon.

I wouldn't go *that* far—clearly Mozart's musical skills went well beyond the ability to memorize pieces and improvise within a particular structured framework. But these findings do highlight the notion that savants and prodigies aren't *superhuman*. Their phenomenal feats can be explained by the same powerful learning mechanisms that the rest of us use to make sense of our world. Of course, this shouldn't take any of the magic out of their truly magnificent performances. They significantly enrich our world. But let's not forget that these individuals have the same fundamental basic needs as the rest of us. They too, want to find a place in the world where they can engage their unique minds.

~

There are still so many mysteries left to solve. How do we explain the development of *acquired* savant syndrome? Do certain brain injuries allow privileged access to long-term memories and skills that were once learned implicitly but kept quiet by the tyranny of consciousness? Might injuries focus the mind on only the relevant details of a particular domain (in the way Jason Padgett saw math equations everywhere he looked), allowing the person to learn new skills very rapidly?

What distinguishes savantism from high-functioning autism? People with Asperger's syndrome tend to display right-hemisphere dysfunction.[93] Savants, on the other hand, are characterized by left-hemisphere dysfunction and right-hemisphere compensation. Does that difference in lateralization explain why most people with Asperger's do *not* show savant-like skills, even though they are able to build up a large expertise base in their specific area of interest? As mentioned earlier, people with Asperger's tend to do exceptionally well on perceptual tests of fluid reasoning, such as the Raven's progressive matrices test (see Chapter 10). Perhaps their enhanced ability to consciously detect nonverbal patterns is due to their spared working memory functions, fascination with order and structure, and enhanced perceptual abilities. These are all questions ripe for further research.

What distinguishes prodigies from savants? Their unifying theme appears to be an intense focus on detail, but what are their differentiating features? Ruthsatz and Urbach suggest that prodigies may have some sort of genetic "modifier" that prevents them from displaying the more severe deficits seen in most savants.[94] While I suspect there isn't a single genetic modifier that can possibly explain the breadth of their differences, and environmental factors are also essential, I do believe two key differences are (1) their off-the-charts working memory and (2) their intact language facility. Prodigies can consciously detect patterns and manipulate them in working memory, and are also capable of verbal inner chatter, so they are in a better position to devise complex strategies to reach even higher levels of performance.

Consider the "prodigious savant" Daniel Tammet, who, I believe, is better characterized as an extraordinary adult with Asperger's syndrome. He is too old to be a prodigy and doesn't show any severe disabilities that would warrant his being called a savant (he currently displays no marked island of genius). Tammet is very rare, however, in that he has so many characteristics all in one package, including savant-like skills, high-functioning autism, enhanced language functions, synesthesia, and high working memory, *and* he can reflect on all of this! A few years ago, Daniel was gracious enough to have an extensive two-day chat with me where he shared his unique way of seeing the world.[95]

In the first few years of his life Tammet had multiple epileptic seizures, which is typical among developing children on the autism spectrum. He told me that his earliest memory is falling down the stairs and seeing colors as he fell. As a child, he said, he displayed many stereotypical behaviors of autism spectrum disorder. This included repetitive behaviors, great difficulty socializing and making friends, and profound periods of social isolation and loneliness. He said he had difficulty understanding things most people take for granted, and repeatedly felt frustrated and confused as to why he was so different from others.

Daniel told me his best friends were numbers. As early as he can remember, he spontaneously saw numbers as shapes, colors, and textures. On the playground while all the other children were playing with each other, Daniel said he played with numbers in his head, visualizing the shapes and colors and seeing how they changed and interacted with each other. When all the kids sat on the carpet during story-time, he said, he sat there with his eyes shut and fingers in his ears while he continued visualizing a numerical landscape.

Today Daniel is in his thirties and can speak ten languages, including Estonian and Finnish. He told me he learned Spanish in a weekend and even *invented* his own language (Mänti). He can do calendar calculations as well as lightning mental calculations, including multiplying six-digit numbers in his head. "I'm able to dance with numbers, whereas the computers crunch them," he told me. He also said that when he does numerical calculations, the answer presents itself as a composite shape built from its constituent elements, and that the colors and shapes he sees are composed of smaller fragments of combinations of digits.

For instance, the shape for 6,943 is an emergent property of the shapes for 53 and 131. He says he sees 53 as round and lumpy, and 131 as taller. He told me he puts these two numbers side by side and the space in between takes the contours of the two shapes and creates a new shape. Many of the shapes he sees up to 10,000 are products of prime factors multiplied together, which considerably cut down on the total number of shapes possible. Daniel noted that both numbers and musical notes get constituted out of repetitions of smaller pieces. He said "the repetitions involved, and the coherence of it all together, makes it memorable and beautiful."

A few years ago, on March 14 (Pi day) Daniel recited the first 22,514 digits of the mathematical constant Pi during a public event for charity. It took him about five hours, and he didn't make a single mistake. During the event he said he simply took a mental walk in which he traversed a vast landscape of numbers in his mind and read them off one by one. In the three months leading up to the event, he spent every other day on average absorbing the numbers that he printed out. On off days he said he just let the numbers take shape in his mind. He said he saw a "vast symphony of numbers," as if the numbers were playing a song for him.

To be sure, the memorization process wasn't effortless. Daniel told me that he had to consciously and deliberately work out the most beautiful visualization for the numbers. During his practice sessions, he broke up the landscape in his mind into different chunks. For instance, he'd take 10 or 20 numbers at a time and break them up. How he grouped the numbers depended on images that spontaneously took place in his mind. If a group of numbers were particularly shiny as a four-digit segment, he said he would group them together. Or if 3 digits were dark in his mind, he'd keep that image. He said the process of memorizing the digits was organic and involved.

In the few years since Tammet's autobiographies have been released, he has noticed a huge change in his own life.[96] He told me he is more confident in his social interactions and travels more widely. He said he still has routines that give him feelings of security and control, but he observed that the ability to break out of them every so often when he travels the world allows him to grow and develop as a person.

In his book *Moonwalking with Einstein*, journalist Joshua Foer expresses skepticism that Daniel has any special talents and proposes that Daniel uses conventional memory techniques such as the method of loci (see Chapter 9) to memorize large streams of numbers.[97] In my view Foer makes a fundamental error by assuming that just because it's possible to do something a certain way, that's the *only* way to do it.

Consider a study conducted by John Wilding and Elizabeth Valentine.[98] They administered a variety of memory tests to all seven competitors at the 1991 First World Memory Championships in London, other people who claimed superior memory, and "control" people with no reported special memory ability. Their material included stories, faces, names for faces, word lists, telephone numbers, and snowflakes. Crucially, some of the tasks were more conducive than others to using well-learned mnemonic strategies.

They found differences in the patterns of performance between the "naturals" (those who did not report using mnemonic methods) and the "strategists" (those who reported they do rely heavily on traditional memory techniques). The strategists performed well on tasks that were conducive to mnemonic encoding, but they performed much worse on tasks that weren't as easily facilitated by such strategies. In contrast, the naturals performed above average across the board on all of the tasks, although they weren't quite as good as the strategists on tasks amenable to strategies. The researchers concluded that it is indeed possible to find people with superior memory who have not deliberately used memory techniques. These results are consistent with John Caroll's discovery of a broad "general memory and learning" factor of cognitive ability (see Chapter 10).

In my view, there is a sense in which Foer was correct but also a sense in which he might have been missing a bigger picture. Daniel clearly does use strategies to build upon the strengths of his unique brain wiring. But to deny that he has unique brain wiring is to deny his identity—*who he is*. Why should

Daniel's skill be any less remarkable if he used strategic maximization of his endowment? Isn't that the point of life? As you'll see in Chapter 13, I also firmly believe that's a crucial aspect of human intelligence.

What's more, Daniel's professed traits have been investigated and confirmed by scientists. Researchers have confirmed that Daniel has Asperger's syndrome.[99] His developmental history revealed 13 out of the 18 symptoms on their checklist. The researchers also found that his visual memory was exceptional, and he had an enhanced ability to quickly find a letter at the local level without being distracted by the bigger picture. His spatial memory and memory for faces were only average, however.

In his book *Embracing the Wide Sky*, Daniel reports that he took the WAIS IQ test and was struck by how "banal" the test items were, providing little opportunity for critical reasoning or creative thought.[100] He makes the insightful point that about 150 million people worldwide share the same IQ score. "Is human intelligence really so uniform that it can be summed up in just a handful of figures?"[101] Nevertheless, he scored 150, which is consistent with his exceptional verbal/conceptual abilities in addition to his enhanced visual/perceptual skills.

Multiple research teams have also confirmed that Daniel has synesthesia.[102] Synesthesia is a condition in which one sensory modality (such as sounds, numbers, or taste) spontaneously triggers another modality (such as color or texture). Synesthesia typically becomes evident before the age of 4. It is estimated that only 1 percent of the general population has synesthesia, and there is evidence that synesthesia is more common among art students.[103] Although there is emerging research that synesthesia can be trained,[104] neurological studies confirm atypical cross-wiring in people in whom the condition emerges spontaneously in childhood.[105] Every time Daniel has been tested, he has been almost perfectly consistent in his associations between numbers and colors, even when tested days later.

Daniel appears to have a unique form of synesthesia that may facilitate his remarkable memorization skills. One set of researchers found that Daniel's lateral prefrontal cortex was highly active when processing both structured and unstructured eight-digit number sequences, whereas control participants showed greater activation in the lateral prefrontal cortex only when the sequences were structured.[106] What's more, whereas Daniel reported that he didn't consciously recognize the difference between the sequences, and his memory for the numbers was equally good regardless of the sequence, control participants noticed that some sequences were structured and said they found those easier to memorize.

These findings suggest that Daniel's brain spontaneously recoded all the streams of numbers—structured and unstructured—into a holistic mental image whereas everyone else could only recode the structured types of trials, by using the mathematical patterns within the sequence to chunk them (see Chapter 10).* The researchers concluded that Daniel's exceptional numerical abilities stem from a combination of his distinct form of abstract/conceptual synesthesia, which facilitates mnemonic encodings, and the highly detailed cognitive style that arises from having Asperger's syndrome, which allows him to zoom in on contiguous sequences without being distracted by the holistic picture.

I believe cases like Daniel's, as well as the general phenomena of prodigies, savants, Asperger's, and every other kind of mind I discuss in this book, represent the amazing plasticity and possibility of the human brain. Every single brain on this planet *wants* to make meaning and will do so by any means (or unique cortical structure) necessary. Instead of treating talent as an "innate ability," with all the knowledge and skills fully present at birth, I think talent is more accurately defined as *a predisposition and passion to master the rules of a domain.*

By a lucky coincidence of factors, prodigies find their domains early. But once anyone, whatever the age, finds his or her talent (as I've defined the term), the learning process can proceed extremely rapidly.[107] Passion and inspiration can spark a drive that substantially accelerates the learning curve and also set off immense creativity (see Chapter 6).[108] We are all capable of extraordinary performance; the key is finding the mode of expression that allows you to create your own unique symphony.

---

*Another possibility is that Tammet was recruiting additional working memory processes associated with the lateral prefrontal cortex (see Chapter 10). The researchers consider this alternative explanation highly unlikely, considering that there was no difference in performance between Tammet and the control participants, and Tammet's memory capacity for digits was greater than that of controls.

Chapter 12

CREATIVITY

Fall 2003

I enter the clinical psychology classroom and sit at the back. I look around and don't recognize anyone, which means I'm probably the only cognitive psychology graduate student taking this class. I know absolutely nothing about clinical psychology. This should be interesting.

The professor, Jerome L. Singer, walks in and takes his spot at the front of the classroom. I watch him sort through some books. He looks confused for a moment, then a recognition comes across his face and he smiles. Immediately, I like him. I don't know why, but I feel a connection. Something about his quirkiness.

He welcomes the first-year graduate students and then proceeds to tell a thirty-minute story about how he met his wife during a chance encounter in the Liberty Music Shop on Madison Avenue in New York City. Both of them were listening to Bach, which led to a discussion about their shared interest in classical music. On their first date, he asked if he could borrow a book to read on the two-hour subway ride home. He chose *The Idiot* by Fyodor Dostoyevsky. His wife Dorothy figured that was a bad omen for a relationship. Nevertheless, they have been married for fifty-four years and have formed a lifetime collaboration on imagination, child development, and the impact of play and the media on creativity. Dr. Singer's story is so funny, at one point, I laugh hysterically. Perhaps *too* hysterically. The clinical psychology students look at me quizzically.

As the semester nears the end, we are asked to write a final paper that integrates various threads in the course. Dr. Singer asks to meet with each student privately to discuss our paper topic. Within the first few minutes of our meeting, I discover why I felt such an instant affinity.

"I'm thinking about writing my paper on ways we can integrate creativity into psychotherapy practice," I say. Dr. Singer's face lights up like a little child and he clasps his hands together. "That sounds very interesting! I was always such a daydreamer. I am still a huge daydreamer. Have you read my work on positive-constructive daydreaming?" he asks.

After our meeting, I rush to the library and devour all of his books on daydreaming. I find this research topic immensely exciting. "I love the idea that a wandering mind can be advantageous for creativity," I tell Dr. Singer during a meeting one day. This meeting wasn't mandatory. He liked my paper and wanted to discuss a possibility. "How would you like to work on a journal article with me?" he asks. "We can integrate Sternberg's three components of successful intelligence—analytical, creative, and practical—and come up with a new framework for psychotherapy?" he asks.

This time my face lights up like a firecracker. "Yes!!!" I respond giddily. I don't have any journal publications yet and don't even know how to write a scientific journal article, but *finally* I found a topic I feel good about.

∼

Once accused of being absentminded, the founder of American psychology, William James, quipped that he was really just present-minded to his own thoughts. William James didn't just live in his own head, but he also studied the phenomenon, coining the term "stream of thought" in 1890. In his famous textbook *Principles of Psychology*, he opened an early chapter with the following: "We now begin our study of the mind from within." He clearly saw the internal stream of consciousness as an important topic within psychology.

Heavily influenced by the writings of William James, Sigmund Freud, and Kurt Lewin, Jerome L. Singer began developing his research program on daydreaming and the stream of consciousness at Teachers College, Columbia University, in the 1950s.[1] The German-American psychologist Kurt Lewin argued for different "levels of reality"—shifts from responses directly evoked by "environmental forces" to possibilities and fantasy.[2] Lewin's ideas, the writings of William James, and Sigmund Freud's emphasis on clinical free association all encouraged Singer's belief that systematic experimentation was key to exploring "the mind within."

Singer and John Antrobus, his assistant and later close collaborator, began their study of "decoupled attention" by interviewing volunteer "normal" adults about their daydreams and the circumstances under which they drifted into daydreams. What immediately became clear was that daydreaming is a normal, widespread, human phenomenon that people are aware of consciously and can report reliably on questionnaires. Large numbers of people from different occupations, gender, and ethnicity reported considerable daydreaming in their daily lives. Additionally, those who reported they daydreamed more in their daily lives also showed similar patterns under systematic laboratory conditions.[3] Singer reported on these exciting findings in his path-breaking 1966 book, *Daydreaming*.[4]

To capture these ongoing mental processes in the laboratory, Singer and his colleagues used carefully controlled procedures based on signal detection research. Under the signal detection paradigm, participants are seated in a soundproof booth, and different tones are presented through headphones. The individual is requested to press different buttons depending on whether a high or low tone is presented. Correct signal detections are financially rewarded. Every fifteen seconds they are also asked to report whether they experienced what psychologist Leonard Giambra refers to as "task-unrelated images or thought" (TUITs).[5] Analysis of the content revealed that people's task-unrelated thoughts ranged widely, from fantasies about the experimenters to highly personal memories or daydreams.

Singer and his colleagues next used "thought sampling" methods. Participants were interrupted, either during the experiment or in their daily lives by a paging device, and had to immediately report what they were thinking and feeling at that moment. This methodology led to all sorts of interesting research and theory and confirmed that when at rest, people's minds wander to deeply personal thoughts about the future. Another early pioneer was Eric Klinger, whose research showed that most people's daydreams and night dreams reflect "current concerns," ranging from constant thoughts about incomplete tasks to unresolved desires, ranging from sexual and social strivings to altruistic or revenge urges and the entire panoply of human motivations.[6]

These early investigators also noticed that people differed in their styles of daydreaming. To capture these individual differences, Singer and his colleagues developed the Imaginal Processes Inventory (IPI).[7] Three main styles of daydreaming emerged from the scales: *positive-constructive daydreaming* (representing playful, wishful, and constructive imagery), *guilty-dysphoric daydreaming* (representing obsessive, anguished fantasies), and *poor attentional control* (representing the inability to concentrate on ongoing thought or external tasks).

Tang Zhiyan and Singer found that these three different styles of daydreaming were associated with different personality traits.[8] The positive-constructive daydreaming style was associated with openness to experience, reflecting curiosity, sensitivity, and exploration of ideas, feelings, and sensations. Poor attentional control was related to low levels of conscientiousness, and guilty-dysphoric daydreaming was positively related to neuroticism. Tang and Singer concluded: "The convergence of these models . . . suggests that these factorial structures are probably reflections of something fundamental about our brain and our physiological experience."

It turns out, they were right.

For years, cognitive neuroscientists treated inner chatter as noise, only serving the function of comparison with the mental activity of interest to the experimenter. But due to this "fortunate accident" of including the idle mind as a control condition, neuroscientists such as Nancy Andreasen, Marcus Raichle, Gordon Shulman, Jeffrey Binder, Debra Gusnard, and Randy Buckner began to ask what the brain actually *does* when not engaged in a goal-directed task.[9] This search led to a major paradigm shift in cognitive neuroscience, from a focus on task-based, goal-directed cognition to the more nebulous yet ubiquitous phenomenon of the wandering mind. As neuroscientist Kalina Christoff notes, "Such a paradigm shift may help us accept our drifting mind as a normal, even necessary, part of our mental existence—and may even enable us to try to take advantage of it in some creative, enjoyable way."[10]

Scientists have discovered a specific brain network, which they often refer to as "task negative," "resting," or "default," that is highly active during passive rest and when looking inward.[11] This network is not to be confused with the prefrontal parietal network that is crucial for fluid reasoning and executive function (see Chapter 10). That brain network is often referred to as the "task positive" or "executive attention" network, because it recruits brain regions associated with active mental engagement in the external world.

In contrast, the default network is heavily involved in the inner stream of consciousness. The default network consists of communication among a number of medial regions of the brain in both the parietal and frontal lobes, as well as inferior parts of the lateral parietal lobe and the medial part of the temporal lobe. It's the *entire coordination* of the default network that makes it so powerful, but understanding its various components is useful in understanding what emerges from their interaction.

Let's start with the areas in the prefrontal cortex. The *ventromedial prefrontal cortex* (vmPFC) is associated with the activation of social emotions and the modulation of the parasympathetic nervous system (which is responsible for our "rest-and-digest" activities, such as calming our heart rate). The *dorsomedial prefrontal cortex* (dmPFC) is associated with representations of the self, social and romantic evaluations, empathy, and the prediction of emotional outcomes.

Moving further toward the back of the brain, we arrive at the *anterior middle cingulate cortex* (ACC), which is highly connected to other regions in the cortex, including the somatosensory regions that contribute to our sensations. The ACC is also associated with goal monitoring, emotion, and empathy, physical and social pain, and, like the dmPFC, is also involved in the modulation of parasympathetic functions.

Moving even farther toward the back, we arrive at the posteromedial cortices (PMC), another extremely connected area of the cortex involved in construction of a subjective sense of self and highly active in tasks that involve social emotions, moral decision making, and recalling highly personal memories. Two important areas in this region are the precuneus and the posterior cingulate cortex (PCC).

Next we reach the inferior parietal lobe (IPL), which is associated with retrieving episodic memories and taking the perspective of others. Finally, we end our journey of the default network at the hippocampus, which is extremely important in forming and recalling our long-term memories. Figure 12.1 is a visual of the critical brain regions of the default network. Unsurprisingly, considering its many regions, the default network has been associated with a wide range of behaviors. To understand the unifying theme, let's first consider what kinds of tasks are *not* associated with this network. The default network is *not* heavily recruited when we reason about mechanical objects, retrieve factual information from long-term memory, consciously label an emotional facial expression, infer the knowledge state of another person, or emotionally react to another's skillful performance or physical injury.[12]

So what kind of information processing *is* the default network associated with? Brain activity in the default network has been associated with mind wandering, daydreaming, creative improvisation and evaluation, imagining the future, self-awareness, retrieval of deeply personal memories, reflective consideration of the meaning of events and experiences, simulating the perspective of another person, evaluating the implications of self and others' emotional reactions, moral reasoning, and reflective compassion.

Whew! What ties all of these mental processes together? According to Mary Helen Immordino-Yang, all of these behaviors involve the processing

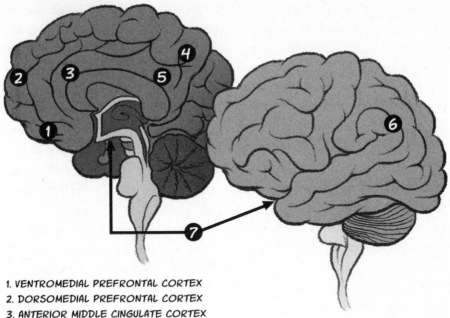

1. VENTROMEDIAL PREFRONTAL CORTEX
2. DORSOMEDIAL PREFRONTAL CORTEX
3. ANTERIOR MIDDLE CINGULATE CORTEX
4. PRECUNEUS
5. POSTERIOR CINGULATE CORTEX
6. INFERIOR PARIETAL LOBULE
7. HIPPOCAMPUS

FIGURE 12.1. THE DEFAULT NETWORK
Source: M. H. Immordino-Yang, J. A. Christodoulou, and V. Singh, "Rest Is Not Idleness: Implications of the Brain's Default Mode for Human Development and Education," *Perspectives on Psychological Science* 7 (2012): 352–364. Adapted with permission.

of "abstract information relevant to the psychological, affective, and subjective aspects of the self and other people, both in everyday contexts and for more complex moral, socioemotional, prospective, and retrospective functions. . . . This description is necessarily broad—after all, DM [default mode] activity could be said to underlie half of what the mind does."[13]

Because the default network is responsible for so much of our daily mental activity, it's hard to imagine that the undirected train of thought that arises from this network serves no adaptive purpose. In a 2011 review paper, Jonathan Schooler, Jonathan Smallwood, Kalina Christoff, and colleagues argue that mind wandering serves multiple adaptive functions, such as future planning, sorting out current concerns, cycling through different information streams, distributed learning (versus cramming), and creativity.[14] In the past few years alone the volume of research on the adaptive functions of spontaneous cognition has grown at a staggering pace.

Take compassion. Immordino-Yang's research team conducted one-on-one interviews with college-age participants, in which they told true stories, including one about a young boy growing up in China during an economic depression.[15] In the story, the boy's father died just after the boy was born, leaving his mother to work long hours as a laborer. They showed the participants a video clip in which the son, now grown, watches an interview where his now deceased mom describes how one winter she found a coin and used it to buy warm cakes for her hungry son, who offered her the last cake, despite his intense hunger. The mother declined, however, saying (falsely) that she had eaten already. The researchers asked the participants how this scenario made them feel. Immordino-Yang and colleagues found that the more participants reflectively paused during their response, the more cognitively abstract and complex their answers, and the greater their default network activity while feeling moral emotions, but not other emotions, in the fMRI scanner.

In a recent review, Immordino-Yang, Joanna Christodoulou, and Vanessa Singh point out the practical implications of this research, noting that imposing high attention demands on children may rob them of the chance for important reflection that can allow them to make personal meaning out of the material and reflect on the social and emotional implications of that knowledge.[16] They argue for a greater appreciation of "constructive reflection," a concept not that different from Singer's notion of positive-constructive daydreaming.

The notion of constructive reflection dovetails nicely with the work of Schooler and Smallwood who argue that mind wandering is a goal-driven process, even though it's not directed toward an external task.[17] They have found neural support for the notion that mind wandering accesses the same "global mental workspace" (in the words of consciousness researcher Bernard Baars)[18] as attention directed toward the external environment.

In their research with Christoff and other colleagues, they found that mind wandering recruited both executive attention *and* default network brain activity.[19] These findings are intriguing, considering that ordinarily the executive attention network and the default network work *in opposition* to each other: the more one network is engaged, the less the other network is engaged.[20] Mind wandering appears to be a unique mental state that allows these ordinarily antagonistic brain networks to work in harmony.

In a more recent paper, Smallwood makes a crucial distinction between two different—and equally as important—streams of consciousness. One stream involves *self-generated* mental content unrelated to the current environment, and the other stream involves *perceptually generated* content.[21] As Smallwood notes, attentional control can be applied to both streams of consciousness. This can make someone appear quite absentminded and "out of it," when they may just be deeply absorbed in a brilliant inner stream of consciousness!

Consider some recent studies supporting the adaptive value of constructive reflection. In one study, Benjamin Baird, Jonathan Smallwood, and Jonathan Schooler had participants engage in a boring, repetitive reaction time task conducive to mind wandering.[22] Participants were intermittently interrupted and asked to enter their thoughts in a textbox on the screen. The researchers found that a significant portion of the participants' mind-wandering episodes involved thoughts about the future. What's more, those who engaged in the greatest amount of thinking about the future showed the *highest* levels of working memory performance. This suggests that when we give people tasks that occupy their external attention, we may be preventing them from the chance to imagine their own personal future.

In another recent study, Jonathan Smallwood, Florence Ruby, and Tania Singer investigated the association between mind wandering and decisions that people make in daily life.[23] On each trial, participants were required to choose between a smaller but immediate monetary reward and a larger but later monetary reward. Participants also had to perform a simple reaction time task and a working memory task. The researchers found that greater mind wandering during the simple task was associated with a greater capacity to resist immediate temptation in favor of receiving a larger reward in the future. Importantly, when participants engaged in an attention-demanding task, mind wandering was not associated with better delay discounting. These results suggest that getting the chance to mind wander under undemanding circumstances allows you to make constructive, adaptive choices regarding the future. Other research supports the notion that the ability to mentally escape from the constraints of the present environment allows the management of personal goals in consciousness.[24]

In yet another recent study, Benjamin Baird, Jonathan Smallwood, and Jonathan Schooler had participants take a classic measure of divergent thinking that requires generating as many unusual uses as possible for a common object (such as a brick) in a limited amount of time. They assessed divergent thinking performance before and after an incubation period and found that participants who were given the same easy task used in the prior two experiments during an incubation period showed greater improvements in divergent thinking compared to those who engaged in a demanding task, had quiet rest, or had no break during the incubation period.[25] In fact, the individuals who were provided with the best conditions for mind wandering showed an improvement of 40 percent compared to their baseline level of divergent thinking performance!

These findings suggest that if we want to facilitate compassion, future planning, self-regulation, and divergent thinking, we should set up conditions that allow for mind wandering. Of course, too much *unwanted* mind wandering is not a good thing. Too much mind wandering in our daily lives can lead to unhappiness.[26] To be sure, it can be quite frustrating when you can't remain on task! Which is why working memory is so important for conducting our undirected train of thought. Michael Kane and colleagues have shown that people with higher levels of working memory are able to maintain on-task thoughts more in their daily lives, and the inability to maintain on-task thoughts is related to reduced reading comprehension.[27]

Fortunately we don't have to choose between working memory *or* spontaneous cognition. We can promote both. And in so doing, we are promoting real-world, practical creativity.

~

Creativity requires both novelty and usefulness. During the generative phase, it's important to generate a number of candidate ideas or solutions. This requires allowing anything to come into consciousness, no matter how seemingly irrelevant. Once a promising idea enters awareness, it's important to go through an exploratory phase where you examine the idea and painstakingly work out its implications. This requires deliberate thought and intense focus on an explicit goal.[28]

In recent years psychologists have investigated the various stages of the creative process—from that initial burst of inspiration to that last drop of paint on the canvas. While it's increasingly clear that fluid reasoning and executive functioning can be beneficial for creative cognition, some of those same mechanisms can also *inhibit* creativity at some stages in the creative process and for some forms of creative expression.[29] Children provide a great example. They are less immune to getting stuck in a single mode of thought, and their executive functions aren't fully developed.[30] An intriguing possibility is that their underdeveloped prefrontal cortex *enables* their creativity.[31]

To be sure, adults are undoubtedly better than children when it comes to actually implementing a divergent idea. Nevertheless, there is much to learn from children about creativity, especially during the idea generation stage. In a clever experiment, Darya Zabelina and Michael Robinson had college students imagine either that their classes had been canceled for the day or that they were their 7-year-old selves in the same situation.[32] Participants imagining themselves as children came up with more original responses on a test of divergent thinking, and the effect was particularly pronounced among introverted participants.

Creative problem solving involves finding a nonobvious solution, so working memory can also get in the way of allowing the conceptual restructuring necessary to arrive at an insightful solution. Ivan Ash and Jennifer Wiley administered two different types of insight problems. One type included many possible initial moves before the impasse, and another version had few moves available before the impasse.[33] Those with higher working memory scores tended to do better on tasks where many moves were initially available. There was no relationship, however, between working memory and problem solving on the version that isolated the restructuring component (few moves available before the impasse).

These results suggest that the restructuring stage of creative problem solving does not require controlled attention, whereas the initial search through the problem space does. A number of other studies suggest that deliberate thought plays a greater role in analytical problem solving than the restructuring stage of insightful problem solving.[34] People with high working memory have also been found to employ complex strategies when simpler, more direct approaches are more fruitful.[35]

Recent brain research has also increased our understanding of the cognitive mechanisms underlying different stages of the creative process. Consider insight, probably the most personally exciting stage of the creative process! To capture the insight process in the brain, John Kounios and Mark Beeman focused mainly on the Remote Associations Test (RAT). The RAT requires participants to find a word that connects three seemingly unrelated words (such as "fish," "mine," "rush").[36] This task requires conceptual restructuring, because the route to find the answer isn't immediately obvious but requires cycling between multiple possibilities. Although they found that the brain response associated with the Aha! moment consisted of the culmination of a series of neural events, they found distinct patterns of brain activity preceding problems solved with insight versus those solved analytically.

Before solving insight problems, there was greater neural activity over the temporal lobes of both cerebral hemispheres (around the ears) and over the medial frontal cortex. Before solving problems analytically, there was more neural activity measured over the posterior (visual) cortex. This suggests that during analytical problem solving the participants were preparing themselves to think analytically and focus outward. In contrast, it seems that when solving insight problems, people directed their attention *inward*, preparing themselves to detect unconscious solutions. In particular, the activations of both the right and left temporal lobes before insightful problem solving suggests that the brain areas associated with lexical and semantic information were being primed, and the medial frontal activity, which originated in the anterior cingulate, suggests that the brain was preparing itself to switch attention immediately to the most insightful stream of consciousness if a solution was detected.

As mentioned earlier, creativity doesn't just involve insight. A lot of work is involved before and after the cherished Aha! moment. To capture multiple stages of the creative process in the brain scanner, Melissa Ellamil and colleagues asked participants to design book cover illustrations while switching back and forth between the generative and exploratory stages of the creative process.[37] They used a special drawing tablet that was compatible with the fMRI and allowed for a more realistic creative environment. They found that creative generation and evaluation were associated with the recruitment of distinct neural processes. Compared to the exploratory stage, participants showed stronger activation in the medial temporal lobe (MTL) when they generated ideas. This makes sense, considering that MTL regions are associated with the spontaneous generation of thoughts and memories as well as enhanced associative processing.

In contrast, participants showed greater recruitment of the executive attention network when exploring and evaluating the possibilities compared to the generation stage. This also is unsurprising, considering that the evaluation of ideas requires focused, goal-directed attention. Intriguingly, participants also showed more activation in default network regions during creative evaluation compared to creative generation. Because the default network is related to the evaluation of internally generated affective information, the researchers suggest that the default network may help narrow down the options during creative evaluation by directing our attention to our "gut reactions."

The researchers also found greater activation in both the "salience" network and the lateral frontal pole during creative evaluation, compared to creative generation. The salience network consists of the anterior insular and dorsal anterior cingulate cortices. This network is constantly monitoring both external events and the internal stream of consciousness and flexibly passes the baton to either the executive control network or the default network, depending on the task requirements.[38] And as we saw in Chapter 10, the frontal pole (which is not part of the salience network) is particularly important for monitoring and integrating the outputs of multiple cognitive processes in consciousness.

This pattern of brain activations is consistent with a growing number of studies suggesting that people who perform well on tests of creativity have flexible attentional control: they can flexibly switch between convergent and divergent modes of thought depending on the stage of the creative process.[39] Liane Gabora has even argued that the "human revolution"* seen in the Middle-Upper Paleolithic era between 60,000 and 30,000 years ago was due, not to new brain structures per se, but to better use of the structures humans already had through the gradual emergence of the ability to switch between convergent and divergent modes of thought.[†,40] In recent computer simulations, Gabora and colleagues have shown that the ability to place things in context, and see things from different perspectives, can lead to more creative and appealing cultural products.[41]

---

*I put "human revolution" in quotes because recent archeological evidence has seriously challenged this story. Most of the claims for a revolution involve a "Eurocentric bias"—based on the European Paleolithic record and ignoring the African record. The truth is, most of the artifacts associated with the rapid transition to behavioral modernity found 40,000 and 50,000 years ago in Europe are also found in the African Middle Stone Age *tens of thousands of years earlier.* These include blades and microliths, bone tools, increased geographic range, specialized hunting, the use of aquatic resources, long-distance trade, art and decoration, the Berekhat Ram figurine from Israel, and an anthropomorphic figurine of quartzite from the Middle Acheulian site of Tan-tan in Morocco about 400,000 years ago. If Sally McBrearty and Alison Brooks are correct that modern human behaviors were gradually assembled starting as early as 250,000 to 300,000 years ago in Africa, this would mean that our cultural flourishing would have been more of a trickle than a burst, and would be consistent with Liane Gabora's idea that our cultural flourishing in Europe was the result of a gradual use of the mental structures that already existed. See S. McBrearty and A. S. Brooks, "The Revolution That Wasn't: A New Interpretation of the Origin of Modern Human Behavior," *Journal of Human Evolution* 39 (2000): 453–563. L. Gabora, "Mind," in *Handbook of Archeological Theories*, ed. H. D. G. Maschner and C. Chippindale, 283–296 (Walnut Creek, CA: Altamira Press, 2008); L. Gabora and S. B. Kaufman, "Evolutionary Approaches to Creativity," in *The Cambridge Handbook of Creativity*, ed. J. C. Kaufman and R. J. Sternberg, 279–300 (New York: Cambridge University Press, 2010).

†A similar idea can be found in the writings of Steven Mithen, who argues that the creativity of the modern mind resulted from the onset of "cognitive fluidity," the connecting of previously encapsulated brain modules. Note that this is a broader concept than "fluid intelligence" and is probably tied to the entire brain architecture for general intelligence and executive functioning (see Chapter 10). See S. Mithen, *The Prehistory of the Mind: The Cognitive Origins of Art and Science* (London: Thames and Hudson, 1996).

Ellamil and colleagues conclude that creative thinking recruits a "unique configuration" of brain regions not typically activated together during "regular" thought. As they note, creative minds across various fields—from the arts to the sciences—may share a "heightened ability to engage in contradictory modes of thought, including cognitive and affective, and deliberate and spontaneous processing."[42] This is certainly consistent with the results of interviews with creative people across a variety of domains.[43]

Other recent brain studies support the notion that creative minds tend to show a unique pattern of brain connections that allow them to simultaneously recruit seemingly contradictory brain structures. Hikaru Takeuchi and colleagues investigated the functional brain characteristics of participants while they engaged in a task involving the ability to constantly update the contents of working memory.[44] None of their subjects had a history of neurological or psychiatric illness, and all had intact working memory abilities. The researchers administered two different versions of the same working memory task during the fMRI scanning session, one version requiring much more concentration than the other.

Participants were asked to display their creativity in a number of ways: by generating unique ways of using typical objects, imagining desirable functions in ordinary objects, and imagining the consequences of "unimaginable things" happening. The researchers found that the more creative the participant, the more active the precuneus area of the default brain network while engaging in the more effortful working memory task. The precuneus is the area of the default network that typically displays the highest levels of activation during rest.

How is this conducive to creativity? According to the researchers, "An inability to suppress seemingly unnecessary cognitive activity may actually help creative subjects in associating two ideas represented in different networks."[45] In other words, the most creative individuals were those who had the working memory abilities to solve the effortful task but also were able to keep their minds open to a possible creative connection.

Recent studies on the neuroscience of creative improvisation also show unique patterns of brain activity during spontaneous creativity. Charles Limb and Allen Braun had professional jazz pianists improvise in the fMRI machine.[46] Compared to overlearned musical sequences, improvisation was consistently associated with deactivation of lateral regions of the prefrontal cortex and increased activation in key areas of the default network, including the anterior cingulate and medial prefrontal cortex, particularly in the frontal polar region.

Normally when someone gives us a task, the medial and lateral regions of the prefrontal cortex interact with each other to monitor the inner stream of consciousness and critically evaluate the response. The results of Limb and Braun suggest that jazz improvisation may represent a state of altered consciousness in which internally motivated spontaneous behaviors are allowed expression in the absence of critical self-evaluation. Without activation of the lateral prefrontal cortex, the spontaneous generation of ideas can bypass executive control and flow directly through the anterior cingulate pathway into the motor system to produce a creative response. According to the researchers, "deactivation [of the lateral prefrontal cortex] may have allowed a defocused, free-floating attention that permits spontaneous unplanned associations and sudden insights."[47]

The decreased activity in the lateral prefrontal cortex does not indicate that intense focus is not involved in creative improvisation. Deactivation of the lateral prefrontal cortex is more likely to reflect a reduction in critical self-evaluation of the current contents of consciousness. Indeed, Carsten De Dreu and colleagues found that working memory was associated with fluency of ideas and creative insight even after taking into account g.[48] They also found that semiprofessional cellists with greater working memory displayed *more* creative improvisations, and working memory predicted original ideation specifically because it allowed people to stay on task. Clearly both mental persistence *and* mental flexibility are key contributors to spontaneous creativity.[49] It's not very helpful if your mind wanders so much that you completely forget to improvise!

More recently, Charles Limb and other research teams have branched out to investigate different forms of musical improvisation, including rappers. In one study, Siyuan Liu and his colleagues investigated the neural pattern of activations among a sample of twelve professional freestyle rappers.[50] They compared improvised to rehearsed performance in the fMRI scanner. Their results were strikingly similar to what was found among the piano improvisers. Again they found stronger activations throughout the medial frontal regions (including the frontal pole) and stronger deactivations of the lateral prefrontal cortex during improvised performances compared to rehearsed performances.

The medial prefrontal activations were stronger in language areas in the left hemisphere during the improvised performances compared to the rehearsed performances, which makes sense considering that freestyle rap requires fast selection of new words and phrases that rhyme. The researchers also found that during improvisation the medial frontal regions were activated before the rappers consciously experienced the intention to act.

The researchers note this isn't inconsistent with the experience of many artists who describe the creative process as guided by an outside agency. To be sure, more research is needed that looks at a wider range of experimental control conditions, forms of creative expression, and stages of the creative process.[51] But the consistency of these findings from multiple studies does suggest that dissociation of activity in the medial and lateral prefrontal cortices is a defining characteristic of spontaneous musical creativity.

Looking at the whole network of brain activity in the medial prefrontal cortex, inferior frontal gyrus, medial premotor areas, and amygdala, the researchers suggest that spontaneous rap improvisation is associated with a brain network that integrates motivation, emotion, and motor function, and plays a role in multiple modes of sensory processing and the representation of subjective experience. They suggest that this brain network facilitates *flow*.

As we saw in Chapter 11, prodigies are often characterized by a state of flow. All of us, however, can enter a flow state when we're completely present and fully immersed in a task. When in flow, the creator and the universe become one, self-criticism evaporates, outside distractions recede from consciousness, and one's mind is fully open and attuned to the act of creating.[52] Because flow is so essential to creativity and well-being across many slices of life—from sports, to music, to physics, to religion, to spirituality, to sex—it's important that we learn more about the characteristics associated with flow so that we can all learn how to tap into this precious mental resource.

Recent research has found that proneness to flow in everyday life is not related to IQ scores but is related to engagement in daily activities, high self-esteem, a sense of fulfillment, life satisfaction, coping strategies, and reduced anxiety.[53] Intriguingly, flow has also been linked in recent years to mental illness. *How can this be?* If flow and creativity are such strong contributors to well-being and self-expression, why would flow be linked to mental and emotional instability?

Let's get to the bottom of this puzzle.

∽

> There is only one difference between a madman and me.
> I am not mad. —*Salvador Dali*

The romantic notion that mental illness and creativity are linked is so prominent in the popular mind that it is rarely challenged. Before we continue, let me nip this in the bud: *Mental illness is neither necessary nor sufficient for creativity*. The oft-cited studies by Kay Redfield Jamison, Nancy Andreasen, and Arnold Ludwig showing a link between mental illness and creativity have been criticized on the grounds that they involve small, highly specialized samples (such as eminent creators) with weak and inconsistent methodologies and a strong dependence on subjective and anecdotal accounts.[54]

To be sure, studies do show that eminent creators tend to have had harsh early life experiences (such as social rejection, parental loss, or physical disability) and have higher rates of mental and emotional instability compared to the general population.[55] However, this by no means suggests that debilitating mental illness is *necessary* for reaching eminence. There are plenty of eminent people without mental illness or harsh early life experiences, and multiple possibilities can explain the relationship between mental illness and eminence that does exist.

One possibility is that social rejection may *fuel* some eminent creators due to their extreme need for uniqueness.[56] Most people are driven both by the need to belong and the need for uniqueness and try to strike a balance between them.[57] For *some* people, the needs scale is tilted much heavier in one direction or the other. Recent research suggests this matters for creativity. In a recent series of studies, Sharon Kim and colleagues found that people who hold an independent self-concept showed increased imagination about otherworldly creatures and broader remote associations after explicitly being told that they were not selected to be in a group, compared to being told they would join the group after completing some tasks. The researchers found that this boost in creativity was specifically due to the mindset of feeling different from others.[58]

Rejection is not pleasant for anyone, even if it can fuel creativity, which is why it's important to investigate other environmental conditions that can stimulate the experience of rejection without actually making the person go through such a painful experience. Compelling new research suggests that *any* experience that violates how things are supposed to happen or forces someone to think like an outsider can enhance divergent thinking and cognitive flexibility.[59] This probably explains why periods of immigration often precede extraordinary periods of creative achievement: immigrants bring their own customs and ideas to a new environment, diversifying experiences for everyone.[60] This probably also explains why living abroad, multicultural experiences, and bilingualism are all related to the generation of ideas.[61]

When considering the link between creativity and mental illness, it's also important to recognize there are many different levels of creativity. James C.

Kaufman and Ronald Beghetto argue that we can display creativity in many different ways, from the creativity inherent in the learning process ("mini-c"), to everyday forms of creativity ("little-c") to professional-level expertise in any creative endeavor ("Pro-c"), to eminent creativity ("Big-C").[62] Engagement in everyday forms of creativity (mini-c and little-c) certainly do not require pain and suffering, and can in fact lead to profound joy, happiness, and contentment for *everyone*.[63]

What about professional-level creativity (Pro-c)? Simon Kyaga and colleagues recently looked at the relationship between mental illness and engagement in creative professions using Swedish total population registers.[64] Their sample included 65,589 patients with schizophrenia, 14,905 with schizoaffective disorder, 68,915 with bipolar disorder, and 438,372 with unipolar depression. They found that people holding creative professions had a *reduced* likelihood of being diagnosed with schizophrenia, schizoaffective disorder, unipolar depression, anxiety disorders, alcohol abuse, drug abuse, autism, ADHD, or of committing suicide.

There were two notable exceptions. First, bipolar disorder, in particular, was associated with creative occupations across the board. This is consistent with research showing that the personality trait hypomania—a key stage of the bipolar cycle— is a good predictor of the generation of ideas and self-rated creativity.[65] Hypomania typically consists of racing thoughts, distractibility, decreased sleep, high self-esteem, grandiose thoughts, increased goal-oriented behavior, and risk taking.[66] In other words, lots of skills that facilitate creativity, particularly artistic creativity.[67] Of course, the depressive stage of the bipolar cycle may also be conducive to creativity by narrowing the focus of attention and selecting the most practical ideas to pursue. This connection between the depressive phase of bipolar disorder and the evaluative phase of the creative process has received a lot less research attention. Clearly, the link between creative cognition and bipolar disorder requires a lot more research to more precisely reveal the cognitive mechanisms that both unite and distinguish between them.[68]

Kyaga and colleagues also found that writers were more likely to be diagnosed with unipolar depression, anxiety disorders, alcohol abuse, drug abuse, and to commit suicide. Again, this does *not* mean that you must have a mental illness to enter the writing professions. It does suggest, however, that there is something about writing that attracts people with cognitive and emotional instability.[69] There are various reasons why the rates of mental illness are so high in writing professions, including the possibility that constant self-reflective rumination inherent in the writing process may prolong or worsen existing mood disorders. Of course, writing can also be incredibly therapeutic for people suffering from mental illness, allowing the person to construct a coherent narrative to make sense of painful emotions and experiences.[70]

Finally, Kyaga and colleagues found that the patients' *first-degree relatives* were significantly overrepresented in creative professions. What to make of this? Could it be that the relatives inherited the aspects of the mental illness conducive to creativity while avoiding the aspects that are debilitating? Multiple studies support the notion that psychologically healthy biological relatives of people with schizophrenia have unusually creative jobs and hobbies and tend to show higher levels of schizotypal personality traits compared to the general population.[71]

Note that schizotypy is *not* schizophrenia. Schizotypy consists of a constellation of personality traits that are *evident in some degree in everyone.* Schizotypal traits can be broken down into two types. "Positive" schizotypy includes unusual perceptual experiences, thin mental boundaries between self and other, impulsive nonconformity, and magical beliefs. "Negative" schizotypal traits include cognitive disorganization and physical and social anhedonia (difficulty experiencing pleasure from social interactions and activities that are enjoyable for most people). People with schizotypy typically resemble schizophrenia patients much more along the positive schizotypal dimensions (such as unusual experiences) compared to the negative schizotypal dimensions (such as lack of affect and volition).[72]

Mark Batey and Adrian Furnham found that the unusual experiences and impulsive nonconformity dimensions of schizotypy, but not the cognitive disorganization dimension, were significantly related to self-ratings of creativity, "creative personality" (measured by a checklist of adjectives such as "confident," "individualistic," "insightful," "wide interests," "original," "reflective," "resourceful," "unconventional," and "sexy"), and everyday creative achievement among thirty-four activities ("written a short story," "produced your own website," "composed a piece of music," and so forth).[73]

Therefore, schizotypy is related to creative engagement. But with all this talk about schizotypy, you may be wondering: where does *autism* fit into the creativity puzzle? I believe understanding the similarities and differences between high-functioning autism and high-functioning schizophrenia has important implications for understanding how creativity manifests itself across domains. There is an emerging consensus that autism and schizophrenia have partially overlapping and partially diametric etiologies.[74] People with high-functioning autism and schizophrenia both report high levels of atypical social behaviors and "cognitive disorganization."[75] Interestingly, these groups also report a preference for details and patterns, but it's likely the survey items take on a different meaning for each population. People with Asperger's tend to be much more interested in consciously detecting patterns that exist in the environment, whereas people with schizotypy are much more likely to see patterns that aren't apparent in the environment due to contagion from their inner stream of consciousness.

This is consistent with their different brain wiring. Autism is associated with underactive default network activity and lower levels of spontaneous mentalizing (thinking about the minds of others), whereas schizophrenia is associated with *overactive* default network activity and a tendency to over-infer people's intentions.[76] It might not come as a surprise, then, that people with Asperger's tend to gravitate toward mathematics and the sciences where the conscious detection of patterns among noisy data is important, whereas people with schizotypy tend to gravitate toward poetry and art, where intuitive, emotional self-expression and the search for hidden meaning is important.[77] To be sure, math, art, and science all involve intuition and imagination in differing forms. If you ask mathematicians, they'll tell you they often draw heavily on their mathematical intuitions about the inherent patterns in the numbers, and it certainly takes a lot of imagination to formulate extraordinarily complex proofs.

Now that we've covered the link between mental illness and creativity, it's time to see where these pieces of the puzzle fit in with the flow experience.

Barnaby Nelson and David Rawlings found that positive schizotypy was associated with central features of the flow experience among a sample of 100 artists ranging from music, visual arts, theater, and literature.[78] In particular, positive schizotypy was associated with the following components of their "Experience of Creativity Questionnaire":

- Distinct Experience, "related to the creative process being a definite shift in nature or type of experience. This change in experience included such aspects as loss of self-awareness, a breakdown of boundaries, a sense of contact with a force beyond the individual self and a confidence and effortlessness about the artistic activity."
- Absorption, related to "the artist's feeling inspired and being deeply absorbed in the artistic activity."

- Power/Pleasure, "related to a sense of control, power and pleasure felt during the creative process."
- Anxiety, "related to a sense of anxiety and vulnerability associated with the creative process, particularly after completion of the process."

The first three of these aspects are central to the flow experience. These findings raise the question: What specific cognitive mechanisms account for the associations among schizotypy, flow, and the creative experience? The researchers argue that latent inhibition is of particular relevance. *Reduced* latent inhibition represents an inability to screen out from awareness stimuli that have previously been tagged as irrelevant.[79] A typical latent inhibition task involves two phases. During the first phase, participants are presented with a simple task (such as counting the number of times they hear a particular syllable). During this first phase, there is also the presence of a stimulus that is irrelevant to the goal of the task (such as white noise bursts). Then during a second phase, participants perform a seemingly independent task but now the irrelevant becomes relevant. For instance, participants may be asked to figure out what is causing a series of discs to appear on the screen, and the correct answer is the white noise that was a mere distraction in the first phase.

Prior research has shown an association between reduced latent inhibition and psychosis.[80] However, emeritus Professor David R. Hemsley at King's College, London, argues that while this loosening of expectations based on previous experience may cause a disruption in sense of self, this mental process may also confer *advantages* for creativity. The million dollar question is this: What distinguishes the person who, in the philosopher Søren Kierkegaard's phrase, "drowns in possibility" from the person who is able to use his or her reduced latent inhibition in a way that enables heightened levels of creativity?

Shelley Carson argues that working memory is a crucial factor that protects the individual with creative potential from falling over the edge into madness.[81] High executive functioning may protect the individual with reduced latent inhibition from getting overwhelmed by the influx of emotions and sensations they are experiencing and allow them to make good use of the broad range of novel input. Indeed, Carson and colleagues have found that the combination of high IQ *and* reduced latent inhibition is associated with creative achievement.[82] In my own research I've found that reduced latent inhibition is associated with a faith in intuition but *not* an analytical cognitive style.[83] Those with a greater faith in their intuition didn't just talk the talk: they actually made greater use of the seemingly "irrelevant" burst of white noise during the first phase of the experiment, reconsidering its relevance during the second phase, when it did in fact become relevant.

I found it fascinating to watch participants who just breezed through the Raven's test of fluid reasoning (which, as we saw in Chapter 10, relies heavily on the ability to consciously detect nonverbal patterns) become incredibly frustrated on the latent inhibition task because they couldn't figure out the answer to the seemingly simple task. Many of these individuals became so fixated on the syllables coming from their headphones that they simply didn't consider that the white noise burst could now be relevant. In contrast, I noticed that a very large proportion of the artists in my study were really good at the latent inhibition task, immediately spotting the seemingly irrelevant—but *correct*—connection. Indeed, when I did the formal analysis, I found that reduced latent inhibition was significantly associated with creative achievement in the arts, not the sciences.[84] In contrast, Raven's matrices test performance was significantly associated with creative achievement in the sciences, not in the arts.

Which raises a really intriguing idea: Instead of being an "inability" to screen out irrelevant information, maybe reduced latent inhibition involves an *ability*—to inhibit the conscious, "rational" mind.* Such inhibition has its advantages at times, especially during the generative stage of creative problem solving. This means, of course, that exerting our capacity for attentional control, working memory, and grit can also be conceptualized, at times, as an *inability* to permit the free flow of ideas, including those previously discarded, within the problem space.

Nelson and Rawlings suggest that reduced latent inhibition's "failure" to precategorize stimuli as irrelevant would "result in immediate experience not being shaped or determined by preceding events." What's more, "it is precisely this newness of appreciation, and the associated sense of exploration and discovery, that stimulates the deep immersion in the creative process, which itself may trigger a shift in quality of experience, generally in terms of an intensification or heightening of experience."[85]

---

*I should note that this idea was raised to me by my dear friend Rebecca McMillan in a flash of sudden insight after reading an earlier draft of this chapter.

In other words, the creative flow experience is intimately connected with *openness to experience*. But what exactly is openness to experience? Let's now immerse ourselves in this important domain of personality.

~

The openness to experience domain of human personality has been difficult for psychologists to describe. The problem is that it is such an all-encompassing domain, with linkages to art, aesthetic interests, unconventionality, emotional richness, imagination, creativity, IQ, perceived intelligence, and intellectual curiosity. The unifying force of the domain is a drive for cognitive exploration, but many different cognitive processes can be explored in humans.[86]

Recent research, at multiple levels of analysis (behavior, neuroscience, genetics), suggests that the complex problem solving and abstract reasoning aspects of the domain ("Intellect") can be separated from the fantasy, perceptual, aesthetic, and experiential aspects of the domain ("Openness").[87] Intellect appears to be a drive for the "truth," whereas Openness appears to be a drive for "beauty."[88] Nevertheless, both Intellect and Openness comprise lots of specific facets.

In a recent series of studies, Colin DeYoung, Rachael Grazioplene, and Jordan Peterson explored the vast terrain of the openness to experience domain.[89] Across two studies they administered a large battery of cognitive and personality tests, including measures of schizotypy, to well-educated middle-class Americans and Canadians. None of the participants were suffering from schizophrenia-spectrum disorders. The researchers measured *g* by averaging scores on tests of nonverbal, verbal, and spatial fluid reasoning.

They found that self-reported need for cognition was an excellent measure of Intellect. Here are some of the items on the scale:

> *I really enjoy a task that involves coming up with new solutions to problems.*
> *I tend to set goals that can be accomplished only by expending considerable mental effort.*
> *I think best when those around me are very intelligent.*
> *I prefer my life to be filled with puzzles that I must solve.*
> *I prefer complex to simple problems.*

In contrast, self-reported absorption was an excellent measure of Openness. Here are some of the items on the scale:[90]

I like to watch cloud shapes change in the sky.
Sometimes I feel as if my mind could envelope the whole world.
Sometimes I experience things as if they were doubly real.
Sometimes I am so immersed in nature or in art that I feel as if my whole
state of consciousness has somehow been temporarily changed.
Things that might seem meaningless to others make sense to me.

Interestingly, fantasy proneness was also a strong marker of Openness. This is consistent with other research by Eric Klinger and colleagues showing that fantasy proneness, a form of positive-constructive daydreaming, is not pathological but a normal varying trait in the general population.[91]

To get a better grasp on the full richness of the openness to experience domain, they arranged all of the test scores along a single dimension. This arrangement is called a *simplex*, and it describes, in a visual-spatial way, the strength of the relationships among the variables. Variables that are close together are more strongly related to each other than variables that are farther apart. As you can see in Figure 12.2, those who have high levels of traits in the Intellect end of the simplex (closer to the top) like *thinking* and live in a world of ideas, whereas those who have high levels of the traits in the Openness end of the simplex (closer to the bottom) prefer being heavily absorbed in flow and fantasy.* The most extreme form of Intellect is g, whereas the most extreme form of Openness is positive schizotypy. This makes sense considering that g is associated with the conscious search for patterns in the environment (see Chapter 10) and positive schizotypy involves seeing patterns that don't necessarily exist in the environment.

DeYoung and colleagues argue that when looking at normal human personality variation, "apophenia" is a desirable replacement for the term "positive schizotypy." For one thing, it's more descriptive of the actual phenomenon, and it also has more neutral connotations (schizotypy has connotations associated with schizophrenia). Apophenia is a general human propensity to see meaningful patterns when they don't really exist. Apophenia is a fundamental aspect of human nature. Examples include wearing good luck charms, seeing Jesus in toast, or mistaking random sounds for some-

---

*Note that it was an arbitrary decision made by the researchers to place Intellect at the top of the simplex, and Openness at the bottom. The simplex could be reversed (with Openness at the top and Intellect at the bottom) without any difference in the spacing among the variables.

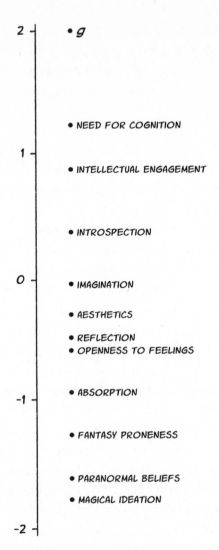

FIGURE 12.2. THE OPENNESS TO EXPERIENCE DOMAIN
Source: C. G. DeYoung, R. Grazioplene, and J. B. Peterson, "From Madness to Genius: The Openness/Intellect Trait Domain as a Paradoxical Simplex," *Journal of Research in Personality* 46 (2012): 63–78. Adapted with permission.

one calling your name. This can get more serious—compulsive gamblers, psychotic episodes in people with schizophrenia, and so on—but *we all lie somewhere on the apophenia spectrum.*

Psychologists have not done a very good job of measuring apophenia or figuring out where to place the trait in the structure of human personality. Along the way, psychologists tried renaming the positive traits of schizotypy with such wonderful labels as "Oddity,"[92] "Peculiarity,"[93] and

"Experiential Permeability."[94] The simplex results suggest that if more measures of apophenia are administered alongside other measures of openness to experience, apophenia does pop up as an important source of human personality variation that can be placed within the openness to experience domain. What's more, because they found only a weak negative association between *g* and apophenia, this leaves plenty of room for people who score high on both traits or on neither. After all, all of the tests that lie on the simplex are part of the same personality domain (openness to experience), even if some of the tests (such as for *g*) are miles away from other tests (such as for apophenia).

These results suggest that some forces cause Openness and Intellect to vary together, whereas other forces cause them to vary inversely. One system that is probably acting on the entire openness to experience domain is the dopaminergic system.[95] As we've seen, dopamine has mostly activating effects on behavior and cognition and contributes to approach behavior, sensitivity to rewards, and breadth of thinking (see Chapter 6). Dopamine has shown linkages to extraversion, positive affect, mental flexibility, and reduced latent inhibition.[96] Indeed, a recent study found that variations in two genes involved in the dopaminergic system were related to the overall openness to experience domain (although they found partial replication in two different samples of children and adults and the effects were small, which is to be expected considering that personality is determined by many interacting genes constantly interacting with the environment; see Chapter 1).[97] Another important biological substrate that supports many forms of cognitive exploration is the default network, which we've seen is associated with constructive reflection, positive constructive daydreaming, and the ability to imagine the future.[98] Therefore, while Intellect is more related to exploration of abstract information, and Openness is more related to exploration of perceptual/experiential information, there are common forces that play a role all across the openness to experience domain.

That's what brings them together. But what biological forces pull Openness *away* from Intellect? It is likely that Intellect, but not Openness, is heavily influenced by dopaminergic projections to the lateral prefrontal cortex, considering that dopamine is crucial for working memory and other cognitive functions of that brain region. In one fMRI study, Colin DeYoung and colleagues found that Intellect, but *not* Openness, was correlated with IQ, working memory, and brain activity typically related to working memory.[99]

In contrast, it is likely that Openness, but not Intellect, is more heavily influenced by dopaminergic projections to the striatum. As I mentioned earlier, my prior research found that Intellect was associated with working memory but not implicit learning, whereas Openness was associated with implicit learning but not working memory. DeYoung and colleagues point out that our normal human capacity for implicit learning can lead to *overinterpretation* of coincidence and sensory noise as meaningful patterns.[100] This may be what we see in people who score high in Openness. Prior research has shown that the tendency toward magical ideation (such as belief in telepathy) is positively related to the identification of meaningful patterns in noisy or random visual information.[101]

Dopamine's effect on the prefrontal cortex exhibits a U-shaped function: too much dopamine, or too little dopamine, and cognition is impaired.[102] Both Openness and Intellect are related to the dopaminergic system.[103] But there is some degree of antagonism between dopamine levels in the lateral prefrontal cortex (which is associated with working memory) and dopamine levels in the striatum (which is associated with implicit learning). Elevated levels of striatal dopamine are often associated with *reduced* dopamine in the lateral prefrontal cortex, and vice versa.[104] There is research showing that positive schizotypy is associated with elevated striatal dopamine levels.[105] And schizophrenia, schizotypy, and Openness are all related to reduced latent inhibition, which in turn is associated with increases in dopamine.[106]

Another possibility is that Openness and Intellect are associated in *opposite directions* with the integrity of white matter tracts. As we saw in Chapter 10, white matter consists of axons surrounded by fatty insulation called myelination and helps communicate between different regions of the brain. IQ and working memory are positively related to white matter integrity in tracts within the prefrontal and parietal cortices. In contrast, white matter tracts in the frontal lobes show *reduced* integrity in persons with schizophrenia as well as persons in the general population scoring high in positive schizotypy.[107] A recent study conducted on people with above-average IQ scores found that openness to experience and divergent thinking were related to *decreased* white matter integrity in the same areas seen in those with schizophrenia.[108] These findings suggest that even though reduced white matter integrity may be a sign of a cognitive "deficit," *some* reduction of white matter integrity in the frontal lobes can be conducive to flexible and creative cognition among nonclinical populations. DeYoung and colleagues suggest that white matter integrity in the frontal lobes may be a factor predisposing a person toward one end of the openness to experience simplex or the other.

Finally, lateralization of brain functions may be another factor that pulls Openness and Intellect in opposite directions. Although both hemispheres of the brain are constantly communicating with each other, at the gross level of analysis our left hemisphere specializes in functions relating to semantic and serial logical operations whereas the right hemisphere specializes in functions related to global pattern recognition, images, and spatial relations.[109] g is associated with the structure and function of many different brain regions in the frontal and parietal lobes, but more associations are typically found in the left hemisphere. In contrast, schizophrenia, apophenia, and divergent thinking are all typically associated with reduced left-hemisphere dominance for language.[110] Some psychologists argue that elevated levels of dopamine in the right hemisphere produce the magical thinking and loose associations associated with positive schizotypy.[111] DeYoung and colleagues suggest that a bias toward dominance of the left or right hemisphere may predispose people toward expressing traits at one end of the simplex or the other.

They also raise the intriguing idea that dreaming may be a dopaminergically driven cognitive exploration similar to Openness in waking life. Indeed, studies have found that sleep and dreaming inspire creative insight, and people who have creative insights tend to show brain activations more in the right hemisphere.[112] Therefore, it's likely that Openness is supported by dopamine surges to the right hemisphere, and this biological mechanism works hard day and night in the background to discover brilliant insights. Those with less of a boundary between sleeping and waking life may be at a distinct advantage in terms of coming up with insights. Edgar Allan Poe once wrote,

> Men have called me mad; but the question is not yet settled, whether madness is or is not the loftiest intelligence—whether much that is glorious—whether all that is profound—does not spring from disease of thought—from moods of mind exalted at the expense of the general intellect. They who dream by day are cognizant of many things which escape those who dream only by night. In their gray visions they obtain glimpses of eternity, and thrill, in waking, to find that they have been upon the verge of the great secret.[113]

Whatever combination of causal forces pull Openness and Intellect apart, one thing is clear: *both* can be important contributors to creativity and innovation, and both deserve appreciation and scientific investigation. While the relative balance of Openness and Intellect depends heavily on the domain (arts versus sciences, see below), too much of either is probably not conducive to practical creativity in any field of endeavor. With too strong a focus on the structure of reality, you miss out on hidden connections. But misidentify the structure of reality too frequently, and you're in danger of dipping too deep into madness. Therefore, a couple sprinkles of schizotypy combined with a reasonable amount of executive functioning and intellectual engagement is conducive to mental flexibility, innovation, and discovery.[114]

This may be why the genes for Openness remain in the human gene pool.[115] As DeYoung and his colleagues note, "[Intellect] may compensate for the overinclusive pattern recognition associated with apophenia, diminishing the attendant risk for schizophrenia. In fact, it may be precisely high Openness with insufficient [Intellect] that produces severe apophenia. It might even be that Intellect and Openness covary in part because Intellect has been selected by evolution to occur with high Openness, so as to avoid the maladaptive drift into severe apophenia."[116]

Research supports the view that there can be reproductive benefits to schizotypy. Daniel Nettle and Helen Clegg found that men and women scoring higher in apophenia tended to engage in higher levels of artistic creative activity, and artistic creative activity in turn predicted a higher number of sexual partners.[117] Similarly, Melanie Beaussart, James C. Kaufman, and I found among college-age males that schizotypy was significantly associated with engagement in creative activity across the performing arts, science, writing, and visual arts, and that a general tendency to engage in these creative activities in turn predicted total number of sexual partners in the past year.[118]

But people on the schizophrenia spectrum aren't the only ones who reap the benefits of high Openness. People with attention-deficit/hyperactivity disorder (ADHD) also tend to show increased mind wandering and a lack of default network suppression with increasing task difficulty.[119] At the same time, people with ADHD tend to score higher on tests of divergent thinking, creative style, and creative achievement.[120] Bonnie Cramond has noted the incredible similarities between the behavioral manifestations of ADHD and creativity.[121] Though teachers may find it frustrating to teach students who can't sit in their seats and pay attention to their prescribed goals, they should recognize that such "inattentive" children may just require a little executive functioning training to get on the path to creative greatness![122]

∼

These studies paint an important picture of how different kinds of minds process information and gravitate toward different forms of creative cognition. But how well can we predict actual real-world creative achievement, based on these psychological tests?

Let's first consider the openness to experience domain, since it's still fresh in our minds. Emily Nusbaum and Paul Silvia found among a sample of college students that Openness, but not Intellect, moderately predicted total creative achievement across ten domains in the arts and sciences.[123] In contrast, Intellect was not related to creative achievement but was correlated with fluid reasoning (Openness wasn't correlated with fluid reasoning).

This suggests that Openness is a stronger predictor of creative achievement across the board compared to Intellect. But what about *specific* forms of creative achievement? In a recent (and currently unpublished) study conducted on two large samples that included adults, my colleagues and I found that Openness was a stronger predictor of creative achievements in the arts, whereas Intellect was a stronger predictor of creative achievement in the sciences. In another study (which I conducted for my doctoral dissertation), I took a more finely grained look at openness to experience and its relationship to creative achievement. Among a sample of high school students, I found four partially independent factors of openness to experience:

1. Explicit cognitive ability (*g*, working memory)
2. Intellectual engagement (desire to engage in complex problem solving and abstract reasoning)
3. Affective engagement (desire to engage in the full range of emotions, including a preference for making decisions based on affect-laden intuitions)
4. Aesthetic engagement (desire to engage in holistic patterns, perceptual experiences, and fantasy)[124]

The four factors weren't completely independent of each other. Explicit cognitive ability, intellectual engagement, and aesthetic engagement were all positively correlated with each other, suggesting that there is a trend for people who score high on one of these factors to also be high on the others. Intriguingly, while affective engagement was positively correlated with aesthetic engagement, affective engagement was not correlated with explicit cognitive ability or intellectual engagement. What's more, affective engagement was highly correlated with compassion, whereas explicit cognitive ability and intellectual engagement were not correlated with compassion.

How were these four factors related to creative achievement? Explicit cognitive ability and intellectual engagement were significantly associated with creative achievement in the sciences (consisting of creative achievement in scientific discovery and inventions) but not in the arts (consisting of creative achievement in visual arts, music, dance, creative writing, humor, and theater and film). In fact, intellectual engagement was a *better* predictor of creative achievement in the sciences than was explicit cognitive ability. This is consistent with other research by Sophie von Stumm, Benedikt Hell, and Tomas Chamorro-Premzic, who found that a "hungry mind" (intellectual curiosity) predicted academic performance independently of traditional measures of intelligence.[125] My findings extend their important finding to creative achievement in the sciences. In contrast, I found that affective engagement and aesthetic engagement were significantly associated with creative achievement in the arts but not in the sciences. Compassion was very strongly related to both affective engagement and creative achievement in the arts—but not in the sciences.

Based on these findings, and the overall pattern of results I found during my doctoral studies, I proposed that the abstract reasoning and experiential aspects of the openness to experience domain are independently associated with different modes of information processing and each deserve appreciation and research attention on their own.[126] I was aware of a growing number of studies on modern dual-process theory, and felt the time was ripe to integrate the scientific study of intelligence with this important literature.

In recent years, dual-process theories have become increasingly required for explaining reasoning, rationality, decision making, creativity, and social behavior.[127] Although the precise specifications of the theories differ, there are some unifying themes. "Type 1" processes (as Jonathan St. B. T. Evans refers to them) include a grab bag of rapid, automatic cognitive processes, including intuition, implicit learning, latent inhibition, evolutionarily evolved domains of mind, regulation of emotions, and the firing of learned associations.[128] According to Keith Stanovich and Maggie Toplak, "the execution of Type 1 processes is mandatory when their triggering stimuli are encountered, and they are not dependent on input from high-level control systems."[129]

In contrast, Type 2 processes are slower and more cognitively controlled. A central feature of Type 2 processing is the ability to sustain decoupled representations—to keep real-world representations separate from cognitive representations. This facilitates hypothetical thinking, which, as we saw in Chapter 10, is associated with activity in the prefrontal parietal brain network. According to Stanovich and Toplak, Type 2 processes "enable one to distance oneself from representations of the world so that they can be reflected upon and potentially improved."[130] Type 2 processes typically correlate more strongly with fluid reasoning and working memory than Type 1 processes.

These distinctions are in line with one of the earliest and most prominent modern dual-process theories—Seymour Epstein's Cognitive-Experiential Self-Theory (CEST). According to Epstein, humans have two parallel but interacting modes of information processing.[131] The "rational" mode of thought (a Type 2 process) is analytic, logical, and abstract and requires justification via logic and evidence. In contrast, the "experiential" mode of thought (a Type 1 process) is holistic, affective, concrete, and experienced passively, and is self-evidently valid (experience alone is enough for belief). Importantly, Epstein believes that the two modes of thought are *complementary* to each other, with neither being universally better than the other.

In a recent study, Paul Norris and Seymour Epstein looked at a wide range of relationships between important outcomes and a preference for rational and experiential thinking.[132] Norris and Epstein found that rational thinking (which consisted of a preference for logical, abstract thought) and experiential thinking (which consisted of a preference for intuition, emotionality, and imagination) predicted different outcomes. A preference for experiential thinking, but not rational thought, was associated with objective performance measures of divergent thinking, aesthetic judgment, sense of humor, and intuition ability, as well as self-report measures of empathy and social popularity.[133] While a preference for rational thinking (but not experiential thinking) was associated with several measures of adjustment (e.g., meaning in life, self-acceptance), both thinking styles were positively associated with personal growth. What's more, people's reported preferences for their own rational and experiential thinking tended to agree with the observations of people who knew them well. The researchers argue that their findings support the validity of an adaptive unconscious mind associated with experiential thinking.

Taken together, this wealth of research suggests that cultivating the many different facets of the broad openness to experience domain may be conducive to becoming a polymath. As Epstein told me in a personal correspondence, "people who are high in both thinking styles [rational and experiential thinking] are Renaissance people. They have the brains of scientists and the sensibilities of poets. In other words, they have the positive features of both thinking styles and do not have their negative features because they are kept under control by the other thinking style." Looks like we have a lot we can learn from all kinds of minds for fostering creative achievement.

∼

What about divergent thinking? Throughout this chapter I have mentioned relationships with divergent thinking, but what exactly is divergent thinking and how well do such tests predict creative achievement? In the 1950s, J. P. Guilford argued that divergent thinking is an important aspect of creativity, involving idea production, fluency, flexibility, and originality. Guilford's theory led to the development of a number of tests of divergent thinking. In one large review consisting of data from 45,880 people, Kyung Hee Kim found a small but positive correlation between divergent thinking and IQ.[134] Convergent and divergent skills can also be investigated independently of each other even on the same IQ test, and both skills independently contribute to creativity.[135]

By far the most widely administered test of divergent thinking is the Torrance Tests of Creative Thinking (TTCT) developed by E. Paul Torrance in the late 1950s. Torrance was not pleased with America's obsession with IQ testing and convergent thinking, so he decided to come up with a test that measures the ability to come up with *new* ideas. The Torrance test includes both verbal and figural tests. In the first three verbal tests, you're presented with a picture and you have to ask as many questions as you can about the image, guess causes for how the image happened, and guess the consequences that will result. The other four verbal tests involve coming up with different ways a product can be improved, coming up with as many questions as possible about an object, and imagining what would happen if an impossible situation took place (for instance, "What would happen if people could become invisible at will?"). The three figural subtests involve making drawings that expand on pictures. A panel of scorers rate the responses on a variety of criteria, including fluency, elaboration, and originality.

The Torrance test has proved useful in a number of educational settings. For one thing, use of the Torrance tests is a helpful addition to gifted assessment.[136] Research shows that teachers are more likely to identify as gifted students who are achievers and teacher pleasers than students who are creative, because creative students are typically more unconventional. Torrance once estimated that if we identify gifted children only on the basis of IQ and achievement test scores, we are leaving out of consideration 70 percent of the top 20 percent of creative students. Considering divergent thinking as part of a giftedness assessment really isn't all that difficult for administrators. If they don't want to take the time to administer the full Torrance tests, even smaller steps can be taken. In a recent paper I teamed up with James C. Kaufman and Elizabeth Lichtenberger to recommend ways that IQ test administrators can find divergent thinking in the test taker by looking for creativity in the responses.[137]

Unfortunately, there's evidence that we aren't appreciating these skills in our students. Kim recently found that since 1990, Torrance test scores have significantly *decreased*, with the decline between kindergarten and third grade being the most significant.[138] This is also troublesome considering that ethnic differences on creativity tests are rare.[139] As James C. Kaufman points out, Torrance tests offer a fairer measure of cognitive ability and can reduce stereotype threat. Robert Sternberg has found that minority enrollment at college improves by adding to the admissions equation items like those on the Torrance tests.[140]

How well do the Torrance tests predict creative achievement? The strength of the prediction varies depending on the sample, testing conditions, and form of creative achievement, but on the whole the tests are somewhat predictive.[141] In one recent review based on 47,197 participants, Kim found a small but positive correlation between divergent thinking and creative achievement. She found a significantly higher relationship, however, between divergent thinking test scores and creative achievement than between IQ test scores and creative achievement in art, music, writing, science, leadership, and social skills.[142] The Torrance tests predicted creative achievement better than any other test of divergent thinking, and the relationship between divergent thinking and creative achievement was highest when measured eleven to fifteen years apart.

In the late 1950s Torrance conducted his own long-term study of creativity, providing one of the longest studies ever conducted on the relationship between creative abilities and achievement. His sample included every student attending two Minnesota elementary schools from 1958 to 1965. Students took the TTCT every year and also completed IQ and academic achievement tests. In 1999 Jonathan Plucker reanalyzed Torrance's data from 1958 to the present day and found that divergent thinking test scores explained about half of the differences in adult creative achievement.[143] What's more, TTCT scores explained more than three times the amount of variance in creative achievement compared to IQ scores.

A more recent analysis published in 2010 by Mark Runco and colleagues followed up Torrance's sample fifty years later.[144] By this point the Torrance tests scores no longer significantly predicted public creative achievement, but the tests did show a weak relationship with personal creative achievement (such as various hobbies). IQ wasn't correlated with any form of creative achievement (public or personal).* Tellingly, the best predictors *of them all* for both personal and public creative achievement were responses to the "Beyonder Checklist." Torrance created this checklist based on his observation of the qualities that distinguished the very highest creative achievers from all the rest. These characteristics include love of work, sense of mission, deep thinking, tolerance of mistakes, well-roundedness, and feeling comfortable as a minority of one. Runco and colleagues found that a composite of these characteristics endured the longest in contributing to both societally valued creativity as well as personal creativity fifty years later.

In 1983 Torrance noted how his experience and research with creative achievers made him increasingly aware of the particular importance of falling in love with your dream.[145] "One of the most powerful wellsprings of creative energy, outstanding accomplishment and self-fulfillment seems to be falling in love with something—your dream, your image of the future." This insight, along with his interviews with teachers, led him to come up with "The Manifesto for Children" (see Figure 12.3).

What about IQ? What if we lead with IQ—how far does that take us in predicting creative achievement? In the 1920s Catharine Cox scoured dictionaries in search of geniuses.[146] Basing her decision on length of entry, she came up with 301 men and women who had lived between 1450 and 1850 who could fairly be described as universally recognized geniuses. Based on their biographical information, she had multiple raters assign to each eminent person a child IQ and adult IQ score, and then she calculated the correlation between these estimated IQ scores and the level of eminence of each individual.

Some cases were no-brainers. For instance, John Stuart Mill learned Greek by the age of 3, finished writing a history of Rome by 6, was reading Plato by 7, and started studying mathematics, physics, and chemistry at 8. Cox—quite reasonably—assigned Mill an adolescent IQ of 190. But some other cases weren't quite so clear-cut. Take Wolfgang Amadeus Mozart. It's obvious he was a prodigy. By his fourth birthday he could play the clavier, by age 5 he began to compose keyboard pieces, and by age 6 his performing

---

*Although the researchers found that an interaction of IQ and divergent thinking was significantly related to public achievement but not to personal achievement.

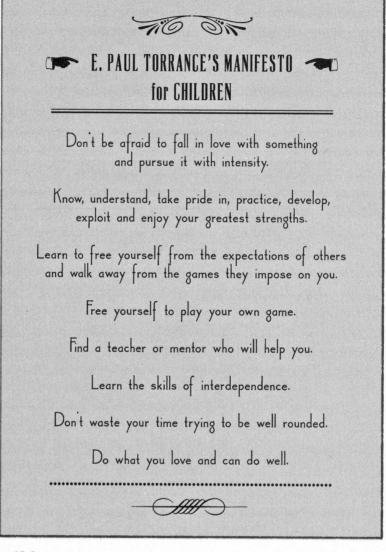

FIGURE 12.3.
Source: E. P. Torrance, *Manifesto for Children* (Athens, GA: Georgia Studies of Creative Behavior and Full Circle Counseling, Inc., 1983).

career had already started to take off. At 7 he published his first composition, and by 15 he had created sonatas, concerti, masses, symphonies, operettas, and an opera. Mozart's early music precocity isn't in doubt. But did he have a high IQ?

Cox thought so, assigning Mozart an adolescent IQ of 150. In reality, all of the evidence used to make this calculation was based on Mozart's music precocity. Although Cox notes that "Mozart mentions reading the *Arabian Nights* in Italian when he was 14," she also writes, "School standing and progress: no specific record." Musical genius is not the same thing as high IQ. There were other cases just as ambiguous. For instance, Jane Austen and George Eliot were both very talented writers, but there was simply no justification for assigning them a specific IQ score.[147]

Cox's premise was flawed. She assumed IQ was the most important variable in predicting creative greatness, so she saw IQ everywhere she looked. As the expression goes, "If all you have is a hammer, everything looks like a nail." Eventually Cox did consider other traits. She took a subset of 100 geniuses and had them rated on 67 personality traits. What she found astounded her: "High but not the highest intelligence, combined with the greatest degree of persistence, will achieve greater eminence than the highest degree of intelligence with somewhat less persistence."[148]

In 1921 Terman (who mentored Cox) began his own study on geniuses. He wanted to dispel the "early ripe, early rot myth" about high-IQ children that was popular at the time, and he also wanted to demonstrate the long-term predictive value of his IQ test. Terman took the opposite approach from Cox: so sure was he that IQ was the most important variable in predicting genius, he decided to *start* with high IQ and then just document their genius once they grew up.

Because Terman believed that potential had to be measured early in life, he had teachers nominate their brightest and youngest students. Teachers at the time most certainly had a bias toward identifying high-achieving, disciplined students. Many qualified students, such as highly creative but disruptive children, weren't even given the chance to take Terman's test. There was also most certainly a bias against high-achieving minority students. Indeed, out of a total of 168,000 children, Terman's sample only included 4 Japanese students, 1 black child, 1 Indian child, and 1 Mexican child.

Nominated students were given a group-administered IQ test. If they passed that hurdle, they then took an individually administered abbreviated version of the Stanford-Binet. If they passed *that*, then they had the pleasure of taking a full version of the Stanford-Binet. All children who scored 135 or above were then invited to join his study. Terman's final group of "Termites" (as they were affectionately called) averaged a whopping IQ of 151. Terman's results certainly looked promising. His high-IQ subjects at midlife were taller, healthier, physically better developed, and more socially adjusted compared to a group of kids with lower IQs. According to parental reports, the children were advanced in their intellectual development, speaking at about three and a half months, on average, earlier than the other kids. About half of the Termites were reading before they even started school, with some starting as young as 2. One 25-month-old was even reading at the level of a late first-grader. Reading times increased from one hour a day, on average, at the age of 7 to two hours a day at age 13.

The Termites also read a wider range of books than their peers, including nonfiction (science, biography, history), encyclopedias, and atlases. The parents reported that their children learned quickly, were intellectually curious, had good memories, and had a large vocabulary. Many Termites made collections, such as stamps. Teachers rated these children as having high willpower and a drive to achieve. In essence, these were good students.

To be sure, their accomplishments went beyond mere academics. In his thirty-five-year follow-up, Terman summarized the accomplishments of his elite group as follows: "Nearly 2000 scientific and technical papers and articles and some 60 books and monographs in the sciences, literature, arts, and humanities have been published. Patents granted amount to at least 230. Other writings include 33 novels, about 375 short stories, novelettes, and plays; 60 or more essays, critiques, and sketches; and 265 miscellaneous articles on a variety of subjects. The figures on publications do not include the hundreds of publications by journalists that classify as news stories, editorials, or newspaper columns, nor do they include the hundreds, if not thousands, of radio, television, or motion picture scripts."[149]

Though this list is undoubtedly impressive, sociologist Pitirim Sorokin showed that the accomplishments of the Termites could have been predicted on their socioeconomic status alone. These were mostly white, middle- to upper-middle-class children with opportunities and resources for success. It wasn't necessary for Terman to analyze their IQ scores—he could have stopped with SES and call it a day. But even more striking, the Termites did not come close in caliber to the true scientific elite of the very same nation and era.[150]

What's more, William Shockley was among the elementary school children tested by Terman's researchers in the 1920s. His IQ was not high enough for inclusion in the study. Nevertheless he went on to get a PhD from Harvard, joined Bell Telephone Laboratories, and helped devise the point-contact transistor in 1947 and the junction transistor in 1948. This latter accomplishment earned him the Nobel Prize in Physics in 1970. Terman also denied

Luis Alvarez, another Nobel Prize winner in physics. Not one of the Termites won a Nobel or Pulitzer.

Terman eventually had to come to terms with the fact that he had found no geniuses by selecting students based solely on their IQ scores. By the fifth edition of *Genetic Studies of Genius*, after thirty years of follow-up studies, he came to the following conclusion, which is strikingly similar to Cox's: "Notable achievement calls for more than a high order of intelligence. . . . Personality factors are extremely important determiners of achievement. . . . [particularly] persistence in the accomplishment of ends, integration toward goals, self-confidence, and freedom from inferiority feelings."[151]

A more recent series of studies, spearheaded by David Lubinski and Camilla Benbow, offers the modern-day version of Terman's studies.[152] They have been following up a selection of participants in the Study of Mathematically Precocious Youth (SMPY). Founded by Julian Stanley on September 1, 1971, at Johns Hopkins University (its current home is Vanderbilt University), SMPY was initially intended to help provide resources to children who demonstrate early mathematical precocity and to also conduct research on their development. Over the years the program has expanded to also include children with verbal precocity. Stanley preferred the term "precocious" over "talented" or "gifted." His guiding philosophy was "appropriate developmental placement."

Lubinski and Benbow have been tracking over 5,000 participants who were selected at age 12 or 13 for inclusion into the program when they were in seventh or eighth grade.[153] To qualify, these children first had to score in the top 3 percent on a standardized achievement test. If they passed that hurdle, they were administered the SAT. To qualify for the program, they were required to score in the top 3 percent on either the verbal or the math section. Unsurprisingly, the researchers found that the children's early SAT scores were predictive of academic achievement. Those who scored 500 or higher on either the math or the verbal section before age 13 (1 in 200, or the top 0.5 percent) learned an entire high school course load in three weeks during the summer program, and those who scored 700 or higher (1 in 10,000 or top 0.01 percent) learned the same amount at twice that rate.[154]

The participants were on average about 68 percent higher in socioeconomic status than the general population, and only 1 percent of the participants were African American or Latino. So we run into similar issues as in Terman's study. But taken at face value, the accomplishments of these children, based on thirty-five to forty years of research, are certainly impressive, and their accomplishments should certainly speak for themselves. In their twenty-year follow-up, 30 percent of the 12-year-olds with SAT scores above 500 on either the math or the verbal section had obtained doctorates. That portion shot up to 50 percent among those who scored 700 or above. Of the general population, only 1 percent obtain doctorates.

They also found that a 200-point difference on SAT scores at age 12 made a difference in terms of income, patents earned, and tenure-track academic positions at top U.S. universities thirty-five years later.[155] Some of the specific accomplishments were indeed remarkable. For instance, in one of their cohorts, 4 patented an invention, 1 person designed an image-correlation system for navigation for the Mars Landing Program, 2 received a Fulbright award, 1 person was named a Presidential Scholar for Creative Writing, 1 person made a solo violin debut at age 13 with the Cincinnati Symphony Orchestra, and 71 were inducted into Phi Beta Kappa. And though they weren't specifically included in the analyses, Lady Gaga and Mark Zuckerberg also participated in the SMPY program when they were young, and look at how they turned out.

The participants differed from one another quite a bit in their verbal and math strengths, interests, values, opportunities, and desire to work hard. Independently and collectively, these factors played a crucial role in predicting what fields they were drawn to across the sciences and humanities, and their ultimate level of success. As Lubinski and Benbow note, "these functions tell an important story about the intellectual character of intellectually talented populations and the environments they are motivated to seek out, avoid, and even create."[156]

But they don't stop there. Their ultimate conclusion from their studies is that "the profoundly gifted simply have greater capacity for accomplishment and creative contributions."[157] But is this conclusion really valid? Certainly their findings are important and show that talent (as I defined it in Chapter 11) and person–environment fit matters. But how can they conclude that these students have greater ultimate potential in life, considering that they took children who scored well on the SATs at age 12 and *left every other kind of mind behind*?

What's needed to see if their conclusion really holds is to open the gates to all students regardless of their SAT scores and see if they are equally capable of making contributions to society by harnessing their other characteristics. Remarkably, this actually has been done. The Posse Foundation, founded by Deborah Bial, began in 1989 because of one student who said he never would have dropped out of college if he'd had his posse with him.[158] This simple idea of sending an *entire team* of students together to college to support each other led to one of the most comprehensive college access and youth leadership development initiatives in the United States. Posse recruits seniors in high school and works with them throughout an eight-month precollegiate training program, supports them through all four years of college, and helps them find internships and jobs as they develop careers. To date, 4,245 students have earned close to $500 million in scholarships from Posse partner colleges and universities.

Posse does not screen for race or need, but the students reflect the diversity of the public high school in the cities in which they are recruited, so an overwhelming majority of the students belong to racial and ethnic groups that are sorely underrepresented at the selective colleges and universities they attend. Some of the participating schools are Bard College, Boston University, Bryn Mawr College, Bucknell University, Northwestern University, Oberlin College, Pomona College, Syracuse University, Union College, University of California, Berkeley, University of California, Los Angeles, University of Pennsylvania, University of Southern California, Vanderbilt University, and Wheaton College.

The Posse Scholarship is based entirely on merit. Those who earn the scholarship demonstrate exceptional leadership and academic potential and are expected to succeed in the classroom as well as help foster integrated diversity at their institutions. The Foundation has developed a unique strategy for identifying talent and potential to succeed in college that can be used as an alternative to (or along with) more traditional screening criteria such as the SAT. The selection strategy is not intended to become a replacement for tests such as the SAT but is meant to help admissions officers add to their set of criteria so they can identify talented students who typically fly under their radar.

The Dynamic Assessment Process (DAP) involves a three-month evaluation that allows The Posse Foundation to identify students with talent who might not show up through traditional admissions screening. The process begins with nominations that come from high schools and community-based organizations. Through large-group interviews, individual interviews, and small-group interviews for finalists, this dynamic process looks at various indicators such as leadership, communication, problem solving, and collaboration skills, allowing evaluators to observe students in a more holistic way.

The average SAT score of Posse alumni is 1053 (out of 1600), with 35.6 percent scoring under 1000, 30.5 percent scoring between 1000 and 1100, and 34 percent scoring above 1100. While these scores are typically much lower than the average SAT scores for the colleges and universities Posse Scholars attend, their success in college matches the success of the general student body at these institutions. Posse alumni have an average college GPA of 3.04 and perhaps more importantly are much more engaged in student life, with 79 percent becoming president, founder, or an officer of a student organization on campus. The diversity of accomplishments of Posse alumni is remarkable. Alumni include a college dean, surgeon, cardiologist, federal strategy and operations consultant, lieutenant in the U.S. Army, Gates Cambridge scholar, Fulbright scholar, school social worker, film director, senior vice president of a prestigious advertising agency, licensed clinical psychologist, business development associate, and multiple PhD candidates.

These results, along with the many others I've reviewed throughout this book, make it quite clear that people with *all different kinds of minds* are capable of accomplishing extraordinary things in their own way and in their own time. There's no need to pit people with different minds against each other. Why can't we value all kinds of minds without devaluing any? Surely we can value the talents of students identified by a single testing session while still giving less stellar and even poor performers multiple bites at the apple.

I find it striking that the *only* thread that runs through every single one of the long-term studies I just reviewed is the importance of drive, persistence, and love for the domain in distinguishing the highest creative achievers from everyone else. Why not keep our minds open to the possibility that people can discover their love and commitment to a domain at any point in their lives?

It's time to pull back all the labels, expectations, and preconceptions that have been in place over the past 100 years and finally *redefine intelligence*.

Chapter 13

REDEFINING INTELLIGENCE

Spring 2009—Friday Evening, 11 p.m.

I stare at the last sentence of my dissertation on the computer screen. After seven years of courses and research the deadline is a week away and I'm done. *I made it.* I should be ecstatic. I should go out and throw back a few beers with my friends and really celebrate my accomplishment. All the years of hard work, meticulous data collection, sophisticated statistical techniques, and logical argumentation have finally paid off. I will receive a PhD from Yale. Which was my goal all along, right? *Then why do I feel so unsatisfied?*

My best friend Elliot, who is working on his own dissertation in Philosophy, and who lives next door, knocks on my door. "Come in," I say. He walks in and sees me hunched over my laptop. "How's it going?" he asks. "I finished my dissertation," I say quietly. "Awesome man!" he says, smiling widely. "That's so great!" I know he's right. I should be just as excited as he is. "How's Descartes coming along?" I ask. "Good, I think I figured out what he actually meant by 'I think, therefore I am,'" he says giddily. "Nice! We should definitely celebrate this weekend," I proclaim.

Elliot goes back to his room and I return my attention to the computer screen. *What's the matter with me?* I slowly get up and plop myself on the bed lethargically. Before I know it, I am asleep.

Saturday Morning, Approximately 2 a.m.

As I dream, images of my life flash in my mind. I see myself on the bathroom floor in elementary school getting kicked. I see myself backstage at the Academy of Music, so proud of my grandfather. I see myself in middle school befriending the gifted kids. I see myself in high school practicing the cello with determination, and my time at Cambridge staring in awe at the architecture. Interposed on all of these images are data; lots and lots of data. A stream of numbers runs through my thoughts—correlation tables, structural equation models, and asterisks indicating which of the numbers are statistically significant. The images flash faster and faster. The numbers begin to crowd out the images. The images become more difficult to recognize. I start to panic. I feel like I'm drowning in numbers. I try to get back to the clear images, but I can't. I'm trapped. As my heart beats furiously, I am jolted awake.

Saturday Morning, 2:15 a.m.

Sweating profusely, but with a newfound energy, I jump back to my computer. I turn to the first chapter, which lists my study methodology in minute detail. I insert a chapter just before it. I call it "Chapter 1: Introduction." My head is swimming with research results. I see *engagement* as a major thread running through my research, and I see the multiple forms of engagement—intellectual engagement, affective engagement, aesthetic engagement, fantasy engagement, . . . —winding down an infinite road of human development. Then I see *ability* as another major thread, and I see the multiple forms of explicit cognition—fluid reasoning, working memory, . . . —and implicit cognition—implicit learning, latent inhibition, . . . —winding down the same infinite road in tandem with the engagement factors. Then my stream of consciousness flips to all of the other important research I've read about on passion, mindset, self-regulation, expertise, deliberate practice, domains of mind, and creativity.

As all of the research threads start to weave together in my mind, a bigger picture emerges. Suddenly it hits me: It's *all* human intelligence. *Every last thread.*

~

The aim of life is self-development. To realize one's nature perfectly—that is what each of us is here for. —*Oscar Wilde*

When I was 5 years old, my mother always told me that happiness was the key to life. When I went to school, they asked me what I wanted to be when I grew up. I wrote down "happy." They told me I didn't understand the assignment, and I told them they didn't understand life. —*John Lennon*

~

On December 13, 1994, a group of fifty-two experts in the scientific study of intelligence and allied fields provided the following unified definition of intelligence in the *Wall Street Journal*:[1]

> Intelligence is a very general mental capability that, among other things, involves the ability to reason, plan, solve problems, think abstractly, comprehend complex ideas, learn quickly and learn from experience. It is not merely book learning, a narrow academic skill, or test-taking smarts. Rather, it reflects a broader and deeper capability for comprehending our surroundings—"catching on," "making sense" of things, or "figuring out" what to do.

This is a reasonable definition of intelligence. It includes a description of behaviors relating to attention, perception, and learning that we would certainly want to include as key aspects of intellectual functioning. What's more, this definition captures how most people—*especially in Western cultures*[2]—conceptualize a "smart" person. When we talk about someone being "smarter" than someone else, we tend to invoke the notion of quick reasoning and problem solving. This conceptualization pervades Western media—from descriptions of presidential effectiveness to TV shows like *Jeopardy* and *The Big Bang Theory*.

But defining a term is one thing, measuring it is another. How can this definition be captured in the world? That is a much thornier issue. The framers of this definition argued that intelligence, as they defined it, can be measured, and IQ tests measure it well. Again, this is a reasonable statement. If you look at the characteristics of people who score high on IQ tests, they do tend to display the characteristics mentioned in this definition.

But if you consider the other ways people can display the characteristics in their definition, you realize how much more complex capturing intelligence is than merely administering an IQ test. Take reasoning. We can't conclude that a person who doesn't reason well in an IQ testing environment is *incapable* of displaying such skills. People reason much more competently when we relieve some of their working memory burden (see Chapter 10). We live in an age where we can easily unload much of the contents of our mind to an electronic device, leaving our working memory freer to manipulate symbols and solve personally relevant problems.

Throughout this book we've seen that when we give people the chance to develop their cognitive skills in a broader environment and over a longer time span than a testing situation, they are capable of quite complex reasoning all across the IQ bell curve. In Chapter 8 we saw that students who participated in Project Bright IDEA showed a meaningful increase in a wide range of skills relating to novel and complex reasoning (see Chapter 8). When people with lower SAT scores are given a chance to capitalize on other characteristics, they meet or surpass the college academic performance of those selected with higher SAT scores (see Chapter 12). Prodigies, savants, and people with learning disabilities achieve extraordinary mental feats, despite, and even sometimes *because of,* their lower IQ scores (see Chapters 3 and 11). We've also seen that IQ test performance is not related to the social or clerical/conventional clusters of traits (see Chapter 9), or to creative achievement in a wide range of arts domains (see Chapter 12).

What about the ability to learn quickly from experience? Again, there are multiple ways someone can manifest these skills. I've shown that the implicit learning system is capable of learning extraordinarily complex associations often better than explicit cognition (see Chapter 11). Additionally, once we are inspired and motivated to learn something (see Chapter 6), or we acquire a large database of domain-specific expertise (see Chapter 9), our reasoning can become quite sophisticated and learning of new content within the domain can proceed quite rapidly.

Why aren't all of those mental routes considered forms of intelligence? Intelligence researchers count abstract reasoning, general cultural knowledge, and knowledge of arcane vocabulary words as intelligence, but many forms of reasoning, problem solving, and knowledge personally relevant to our lives don't count? *Why not?*

～

Another claim of the *Wall Street Journal* definition is that intelligence, as measured by IQ tests, is a "very general mental capability." Here we immediately run into thorny territory again. Since IQ test scores are best thought of as the summary of a range of cognitive mechanisms, their statement surely reifies IQ (see Chapter 10). For the sake of advancing our discussion, however, let's assume what they mean is that the cognitive skills that are most strongly related to g^* (e.g., fluid reasoning, working memory, abstract

---

*Technically defined as the first factor derived from a factor analysis of a diverse battery of cognitive tests, representing a diverse sample of the general population, explaining the largest

relational complexity) are highly general because they facilitate the speed and efficiency of learning novel and complex information. This much is empirically true (see Chapter 10).

But there's another sense in which I think they may mean "general." The framers of the *Wall Street Journal* definition point out that "IQ is related, probably more so than any other single measurable human trait, to many important educational, occupational, economic, and social outcomes."[3] This is statistically true. *g* is part of a large "nexus" of positively correlated societal outcomes.[4] *g* correlates positively with family income, socioeconomic status, school and occupational performance, military training assignments, law-abiding-ness, healthful habits, illness, and morality. In contrast, *g* is negatively correlated with welfare, psychopathology, crime, inattentiveness, boredom, delinquency, and poverty. The correlations exist. What remains far more ambiguous, in my view, is the *interpretation* of these correlations.

Tellingly, all of these outcomes are also correlated with one another, forming a large interconnected web of positively related variables. For instance, income is not only positively correlated with IQ, but is also positively correlated with amount of schooling, parental income, and parental status—all of which are individually also positively correlated with IQ. This makes it extremely difficult to disentangle all these variables from each other to figure out what's causing what.

To be sure, IQ tests don't simply measure family background. IQ and SAT scores are still correlated with important academic and societal outcomes even after taking into account socioeconomic status.[5] But let's not forget: IQ test performance is also an *outcome*—a person's score on a brief test measured at one moment in time. As convenient as it would be for a person's IQ score to measure something completely divorced from any learning, experience, and background, that's not how IQ tests work, and that's certainly not how the world works. Any single person's IQ test performance is itself a measure of many things in addition to their intellectual functioning across a range of cognition, including the person's current levels of socioeconomic status, motivation, level of anxiety, self-belief, prior education, experience, opportunity, language, and many other things that are strongly connected to the very outcomes they are trying to predict.

---

source of variance in the dataset (typically about 50 percent of the variance). See I. J. Deary, "Human Intelligence Differences: A Recent History," *Trends in Cognitive Sciences* 5 (2001): 127–130.

The truth is, many factors operate together to produce a broad positive manifold of "desirable" social outcomes (e.g., high IQ, life expectancy, health, occupational success, etc.).* The path from IQ to academic achievement to occupational achievement to high achievement is far from direct. As we've seen throughout this book, the rich get richer and the poor get poorer. Small differences multiply over the years to create large differences.

Ten-year-olds with good fluid reasoning skills and high executive functioning are a pleasure to teach, and they receive more challenging materials. They are *expected* to go to a good university. The positive expectations and increased intellectual enrichment only increase their chances of graduating from high school and getting into a prestigious university, which in turn will increase their chances of obtaining a "prestigious" job. Meanwhile, the child who early on finds school difficult, unrewarding, and perhaps even boring, is fed a less enriched curriculum, which exerts downward pressure on both expectations and achievement. As a result, the child is likely to get poorer and poorer grades, and leave school at the first opportunity.

But we must not forget that *we* are the ones who choose how schools should be structured, and what counts as a "good grade." These are subjective decisions. What's more, *we* are the ones who created a societal structure that establishes academic qualification as the mighty gatekeeper in life, and decided that the essential skills for attaining this qualification are those that are most highly correlated with g.†

Many other definitions of intelligence have been proposed over the years. Figure 13.1 lists some of the most prominent definitions from over the past 150 years. Definitions of intelligence have certainly been all over the place! Nevertheless, there are some recurring themes. One major theme is *adaptation to the environment*. This was the stated definition of both Binet and Wechsler—two foundational figures in the history of IQ testing (see Chapter 2). Yet they gave children no opportunity to decide what environment they'd like to

---

*Importantly, and often underappreciated, if you get a large enough number of participants and variables, then even the slightest positive correlation between one variable and the next will be statistically significant without necessarily being practically significant.
†In fact, it's quite likely that the cognitive skills that comprise g are positively correlated with each other in large part because we chose them to represent the foundation of education. In other words, we laid the groundwork for them to be positively correlated as they are mutually developed in school (see Chapter 10).

HERBERT SPENCER: "INSTINCT, REASON, PERCEPTION, CONCEPTION, MEMORY, IMAGINATION, FEELING, WILL, ETC... HOWEVER WIDELY CONTRASTED THEY MAY SEEM, THESE VARIOUS FORMS OF INTELLIGENCE CANNOT BE ANYTHING ELSE THAN EITHER PARTICULAR MODES IN WHICH THE ADJUSTMENT OF INNER TO OUTER RELATIONS IS ACHIEVED; OR PARTICULAR PARTS OF THE PROCESS OF ADJUSTMENT."

ALFRED BINET AND THEODORE SIMON: "INTELLIGENCE SERVES IN THE DISCOVERY OF TRUTH. BUT THE CONCEPTION IS STILL TOO NARROW; AND WE RETURN TO OUR FAVORITE THEORY; THE INTELLIGENCE MARKS ITSELF BY THE BEST POSSIBLE ADAPTATION OF THE INDIVIDUAL TO HIS ENVIRONMENT."

ALFRED BINET: "THE TENDENCY TO TAKE AND MAINTAIN A DEFINITE DIRECTION; THE CAPACITY TO MAKE ADAPTATIONS FOR THE PURPOSE OF ATTAINING A DESIRED END; AND THE POWER OF AUTO-CRITICISM."

WILLIAM STERN: "INTELLIGENCE IS A GENERAL CAPACITY OF AN INDIVIDUAL CONSCIOUSLY TO ADJUST TO NEW REQUIREMENTS: IT IS GENERAL MENTAL ADAPTABILITY TO NEW PROBLEMS AND CONDITIONS OF LIFE."

LEWIS TERMAN: "THE ESSENTIAL DIFFERENCE, THEREFORE, IS IN THE CAPACITY TO FORM CONCEPTS TO RELATE IN DIVERSE WAYS, AND TO GRASP THEIR SIGNIFICANCE: AN INDIVIDUAL IS INTELLIGENT IN PROPORTION AS HE IS ABLE TO CARRY ON ABSTRACT THINKING."

E.G. BORING: "INTELLIGENCE AS A MEASUREABLE CAPACITY MUST AT THE START BE DEFINED AS THE CAPACITY TO DO WELL IN AN INTELLIGENCE TEST. INTELLIGENCE IS WHAT THE TESTS TEST."

DAVID WECHSLER: "INTELLIGENCE IS THE AGGREGATE OR GLOBAL CAPACITY OF THE INDIVIDUAL TO ACT PURPOSELY, TO THINK RATIONALLY AND TO DEAL EFFECTIVELY WITH HIS ENVIRONMENT."

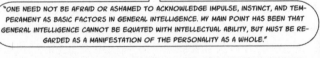

"ONE NEED NOT BE AFRAID OR ASHAMED TO ACKNOWLEDGE IMPULSE, INSTINCT, AND TEMPERAMENT AS BASIC FACTORS IN GENERAL INTELLIGENCE. MY MAIN POINT HAS BEEN THAT GENERAL INTELLIGENCE CANNOT BE EQUATED WITH INTELLECTUAL ABILITY, BUT MUST BE REGARDED AS A MANIFESTATION OF THE PERSONALITY AS A WHOLE."

ANNE ANASTASI: "INTELLIGENCE IS NOT AN ENTITY WITHIN THE ORGANISM BUT A QUALITY OF BEHAVIOR. INTELLIGENT BEHAVIOR IS ESSENTIALLY ADAPTIVE, INSOFAR AS IT REPRESENTS EFFECTIVE WAYS OF MEETING THE DEMANDS OF A CHANGING ENVIRONMENT."

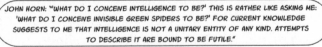

JOHN HORN: "'WHAT DO I CONCEIVE INTELLIGENCE TO BE?' THIS IS RATHER LIKE ASKING ME: 'WHAT DO I CONCEIVE INVISIBLE GREEN SPIDERS TO BE?' FOR CURRENT KNOWLEDGE SUGGESTS TO ME THAT INTELLIGENCE IS NOT A UNITARY ENTITY OF ANY KIND. ATTEMPTS TO DESCRIBE IT ARE BOUND TO BE FUTILE."

SANDRA SCARR: "TO BE AN EFFECTIVE, INTELLIGENT HUMAN BEING REQUIRES A BROADER FORM OF PERSONAL ADAPTATION AND LIFE STRATEGY, ONE THAT HAS BEEN DESCRIBED IN 'INVULNERABLE' CHILDREN AND ADULTS: THEY ARE COPERS, MOVERS, AND SHAPERS OF THEIR OWN ENVIRONMENTS."

ROBERT STERNBERG: "THE ABILITY TO ACHIEVE SUCCESS IN LIFE ACCORDING TO ONE'S PERSONAL STANDARDS WITHIN ONE'S SOCIOCULTURAL CONTEXT."

HOWARD GARDNER: "A BIOPSYCHOLOGICAL POTENTIAL TO PROCESS INFORMATION THAT CAN BE ACTIVATED IN A CULTURAL SETTING TO SOLVE PROBLEMS OR CREATE PRODUCTS THAT ARE OF VALUE IN A CULTURE."

FIGURE 13.1. DEFINITIONS OF INTELLIGENCE

Source: J. D. Wasserman, "A History of Intelligence Assessment: The Unfinished Tapestry," in *Contemporary Intellectual Assessment: Theories, Tests, and Issues,* ed. D. P. Flanagan and P. L. Harrison, 3rd ed., 3–55 (New York: Guilford, 2012).

adapt to—children were confined to the IQ testing environment. Even my former advisor Robert Sternberg, who emphasizes the importance of combining his three forms of intelligence—analytical, creative, and practical—to "adapt to, shape, and select environments,"[6] has measured his three forms of intelligence among college applicants within a single testing environment.

Let me be clear: I do see great value in expanding our measures of intelligence for K–12 accommodations and college admissions. Sternberg's tests have shown an improvement in reducing ethnic and racial disparities and have given more people a chance to attain educational qualifications (see Chapter 12). But regardless of what labels psychologists decide to put on their tests—IQ, SAT, GRE— if a battery of tests places a heavy burden on working memory, those with lower levels of working memory won't get the chance to fully express themselves. It's very difficult—if not impossible—to design a test that is administered in a short time span and requires novel problem-solving that doesn't place considerable demands on working memory (see Chapter 10).

What's more, an extended period of engagement in a particular domain can greatly facilitate creativity and new insights. Indeed, in many cases an extended period of expertise acquisition is *necessary* (see Chapter 9). Therefore, novel, decontextualized tests of divergent thinking miss out on the kind of creativity that operates on a deep knowledge base acquired over many years of engagement with a domain.

Also, what if a person has a different kind of creativity than the divergent thinking necessary to do well on the test? Say, someone with Asperger's who may have difficulty imagining the possibilities on the artificial, decontextualized items of the test, but solely by being *who he or she is*, is inherently creative due to his or her unique perspective on the world (see Chapter 11)?

Many of these criticisms also apply to Howard Gardner's theory of "multiple intelligences." Gardner emphasizes that intelligence creates something valued within a particular culture, and then promotes the eight intelligences he deems valuable: logical-mathematical, spatial, linguistic, bodily-kinesthetic, musical, interpersonal, intrapersonal, and naturalistic. But do we really want to tie our definition of intelligence to a single person's interpretation of the skills and products that are considered societally valuable? What if the individual manifests an entirely new kind of intelligence that has never been seen or formally described before—shouldn't that count as intelligence? At the very least, shouldn't we keep our minds open to that possibility?

Also, there are many skills I don't see on Gardner's list, such as artistic intelligence, intuitive intelligence, compassionate intelligence, spiritual intelligence, cultural intelligence,[7] ecological intelligence,[8] executive intelligence[9]— even *mating intelligence*.[10] Why don't any of them count? It can't be because they don't satisfy all of Gardner's criteria (isolation of brain function, clear developmental trajectory, evolutionary history, support from the experimental and psychometric literatures, etc.). Some of his own proposed intelligences don't satisfy all of his criteria. For instance, one of Gardner's criteria is support from the psychometric literature. But the psychometric evidence suggests that many of his intelligences, particularly his logical-mathematical, spatial, and linguistic intelligences, are highly correlated with each other (see Chapter 10).

To be sure, Gardner argues that's just the point (see Chapter 10). That we shouldn't try to directly test his intelligences; we should just observe them in children as they unfold naturally, and offer instruction that best suits each of his eight intelligences. At first blush, this sounds like a very admirable and sensible goal. For one, this approach allows us to minimize the working memory and fluid reasoning demands of a brief standardized test, and lets the individual choose how the individual typically expresses his or her unique intelligence.

But if we look deeper, problems emerge. For one, the multiple intelligences approach fosters a fixed mindset. Telling people that "It's OK if you're not good at <insert intelligence here>, you can still be good at <insert a different intelligence here>" causes people to give up on cultivating key skills that can be developed, to some large extent, in *everyone* (see Chapter 7). By promoting a multiple intelligences mindset, we are actually limiting people with self-fulfilling prophecies, despite the best of intentions.

Also, what if none of Gardner's intelligences are readily observable in a child in the school environment? Is that child unintelligent across the board? What do you do then? Even when children do appear to prefer learning in a particular way, there is no compelling evidence that tailoring an academic curriculum to each child's preferred mode of learning (visual, auditory, kinesthetic) will increase learning outcomes.[11]

This doesn't mean that we shouldn't appreciate numerous personal characteristics such as passions, background knowledge, life experiences, personality, grit, and so on. Understanding these differences and applying that information in the classroom is *immensely* important. But simply asking students how they learn best and then delivering the same standard, decon-textualized curriculum in their preferred mode of instruction is not the magic bullet. In fact, an emphasis on "multiple intelligences" and "learning styles" can get in the way of us appreciating the student characteristics that truly affect learning.[12]

Which leads us to another major theme across our smorgasbord of definitions of intelligence: the inclusion of *multiple personal characteristics*, such as motivation and drive, in addition to the intellectual skills required to do well on IQ tests. The earliest IQ test makers themselves recognized the importance of multiple personal characteristics for intellectual functioning in addition to the intellectual skills measured on their tests.* Binet acknowl-edged the importance of motivation ("desired ends") and persistence ("main-tain a definite direction").

But here's the thing: how much can you really expect to measure these skills when (a) the test constructor, not the test taker, set the goals of the test and chooses the answers, (b) the test is only a couple of hours long (if that), and (c) the test problems are far removed from anything most of the test takers are actually motivated to pursue? Binet was aware of these problems, but his best solution was to instruct examiners to "encourage in order that everyone may do his best."[13]

David Wechsler also warned against equating general intelligence with intellectual ability. In one address, Wechsler concluded that "one need not be afraid or ashamed to acknowledge impulse, instinct and temperament as basic factors in general intelligence . . . My main point has been that general intelligence cannot be equated with intellectual ability, but must be regarded as a manifestation of the personality as a whole."[14]

But like Binet, Wechsler hoped that a lack of motivation could be improved through encouragement. The test manual for the revised edition of the Wechsler Intelligence Scale for Children (WISC-R) states: "If the child says that he or she cannot perform a task or cannot answer a question, encourage

---

*The spirit of this notion isn't new. Philosophers have long recognized that three general functions—cognition, affect, and volition—are all important aspects of the human mind. This tripartite division was especially prominent in the period between Gottfried Leibniz and Immanuel Kant. Kant wrote, "There are three absolutely irreducible faculties of the mind, namely, knowledge, feeling, and desire." But even Plato distinguished between the rational, appetitive, and spirited souls in *The Republic*. See E. R. Hilgard, "The Trilogy of Mind: Cognition, Affection, and Conation," *Journal of the History of the Behavioral Sciences* 16 (1980): 107–117; R. E. Allen, *Plato: The Republic* (New Haven, CT: Yale University Press, 2006).

the child by saying, 'Just try it' or 'I think you can do it. Try again.'"[15] As if this would make all children suddenly passionate about solving abstract puzzles.

A key aspect of the intelligent testing approach, pioneered by Alan Kaufman, is inferring the child's personality during the testing session by carefully watching his or her pattern of responding to the IQ test questions (see Chapter 2). While I have a deep respect for the intelligent testing approach, it still operates under the assumption that the personality children display in the testing environment is their typical personality, representative across multiple environments.[16] Furthermore, it assumes that it is also the *best* manifestation of their personality.

Annemarie Roeper presented an alternative technique for measuring intelligence: a qualitative interview that doesn't involve solving IQ test items but involves providing a safe environment for children to express themselves (see Chapter 5). I also have immense respect for this approach and think Roeper's technique is both compassionate and can assist the psychologist in ascertaining a child's typical personality. But such an unstructured approach is prone to subtle self-fulfilling prophecies, despite the best of intentions. Children who are deemed "gifted" are brought to the psychologist, and the psychologist is on high alert for "gifted characteristics," such as passion, intensity, compassion, humor, and the like (see Chapter 5). But as we've seen all throughout this book, when we look closely enough at people across a broad range of environments in which they are engaged and feel comfortable expressing themselves fully, we see these characteristics in people all across the IQ spectrum.

The educational psychologist Richard Snow also made a call to take into account personal characteristics, but he held a very different perspective than his colleagues. Instead of starting with measuring a child's "potential" through static ability tests, Snow argued we should conceptualize potential as *degree of readiness* to perform in a particular situation or domain.[17] He believed in multiple paths to the same outcome. Snow was much more interested in helping students figure out the best way to develop their expertise, given all the characteristics they personally bring to the table. He started with the *endpoint*—math achievement, physics achievement, music achievement, and so on—and looked at the combination of characteristics and forms of expertise required to succeed in that particular domain. Then he looked at the various paths and demands ("affordances"), and the opportunities a person has to develop their expertise in that domain.

In his 1980 paper titled "Intelligence for the Year 2001," Snow wrote: "It is not unreasonable to hypothesize that both conative and affective aspects of persons and situations influence the details of cognitive processing. . . . A theoretical account of intelligent behavior in the real world requires a synthesis of cognition, conation and affect. We have not really begun to envision this synthesis."[18] Well, 2001 came and went without much of a hint of this synthesis.

∾

For too long, there has been a mismatch between theory and practice. *Theoretically*, the two main threads running through definitions of intelligence have been (a) adaptation to the environment, and (b) the cognitive, affective, and volitional characteristics that enable that adaptation. *Practically*, IQ tests measure an important but limited slice of intellectual functioning in a very limited testing environment. Why such a disconnect?

If you recall, intelligence tests were born out of necessity (see Chapter 2). Binet was given the task of inventing a test that would distinguish fast learners from slow learners in a school environment. From the very first test of intelligence, we've been operating in an individual differences paradigm, and have been stuck in that paradigm ever since. Attempts to go beyond IQ seem to just add on more individual difference variables, and slap the label "intelligence" on them. This creates more tests, and more ways to compare one person to another on whatever tests of intelligence the psychologist has created. But here's the thing: *there's no objective reason why society still needs to operate in this paradigm.*

While standardized tests can certainly be useful for scientifically investigating the mind and brain, and can greatly inform educational interventions, there's no reason why educators or anyone else for that matter needs to compare the intelligence of one person to another based on a single dimension of human variation. Truth is, *g*—the largest source of cognitive variation ever discovered in humans—is merely a description of patterns of variation found between people; it doesn't actually exist within any individual (see Chapter 10).

Developmental psychologists are devoloping exciting new techniques to study variation *within* the person (see Chapter 1).[19] Instead of selecting a few fixed time points and range of cognitive skills, and aggregating the results across subjects, the new person-specific paradigm focuses on a *single person*, selects a range of time points, and considers the trajectory of a dynamic system of cognitive, emotional, and personality processes as they unfold over time. The results from the traditional individual differences paradigm—where we compare people to each other—do not apply at the person-specific level.[20]

I believe this has major implications for our understanding of human intelligence. For over 100 years, the field of intelligence has mostly concerned itself with intellectual functions that show the largest variation between humans, while less attention has been given to functions that display minimal difference between people. But I believe shifting our level of analysis to the person presents enormous opportunities. It allows us to more clearly see, and appreciate, the richness of human intelligence. As Steven Pinker notes, "Humans everywhere on the planet see, talk, and think about objects and people in the same basic way. The difference between Einstein and a high school dropout is trivial compared to the difference between the high school dropout and the best robot in existence, or between the high school dropout and a chimpanzee."[21]

Once we look at how individuals actually attain their personal goals in the real world, many more aspects of human intelligence become visible than when we focused only on the characteristics that most strongly differentiate people. Virtually every human being on this planet has the same basic needs for competence, autonomy, relatedness, belonging, and uniqueness, even if we differ in the balance of those needs (see Chapters 6 and 12). We all have the capacity to cultivate a growth mindset (see Chapter 7), learn how to practice deliberately (see Chapter 10), or flex our self-regulation muscles (see Chapter 8). We've all been endowed with powerful "structure mapping" attentional mechanisms that allow us to soak up fundamental knowledge about spatial relations, numbers, probability, logic, language, physical objects, living things, artifacts, music, aesthetics, and the beliefs and desires of other minds, even if we differ in what captivates our attention (see Chapter 11). Virtually everyone draws on a robust implicit learning system to soak up the probabilistic rule structure of the world (see Chapter 11) and can use powerful long-term working memory mechanisms to acquire a deep, rich expertise base in *some* domain of human knowledge (see Chapter 9).

Some researchers might emphasize that these capabilities are evolutionarily older than fluid reasoning or working memory.[22] But keep in mind that our complex minds didn't appear overnight. For most of our human evolution, new structures were gradually built on top of older structures.[23] The complexity of the human brain is the result of millions of years of trial-and-error in a variety of different environments. Minds that were adaptive for survival and reproduction in particular niches were maintained. Drafts that weren't adaptive were gradually put into the waste bin. You can think of our minds as a layer cake. Each layer is important, and has contributed significantly to who we are as a species, and what we are capable of.[24] Just because a mechanism of the mind is evolutionarily older does not make it any less important for adaptive functioning.

It is my belief that it's time for a new definition of human intelligence that takes all of these aspects of the human mind into account. One that emphasizes the value of an individual's personal journey. That extends the time course of intelligence from a two-hour testing session of decontextualized problem solving to a lifetime of deeply meaningful engagement. That arms students with the mindsets and strategies they need to realize their personal goals, without limiting or pre-judging their chances of success at any stage in the process. That shifts the focus from doing everything right to a lifelong learning process where bumps and detours are par for the course. From a fixed mindset to a growth mindset. From product to process.

*Enter the Theory of Personal Intelligence.**

~

At long last, Objective and Subjective Scott can speak together with a single voice. I no longer have to feel the inner struggle between objective, statistical generalizations and subjective developmental experiences. My new definition of human intelligence, which I call the Theory of Personal Intelligence, is consistent with the intent of prior definitions of intelligence, remains empirically defensible, and affords the greatest number of people the opportunity to flourish. According to the Theory of Personal Intelligence,

> *Intelligence is the dynamic interplay of engagement and abilities in pursuit of personal goals.*

Note that the focus of analysis is the *person*. All that exists for that individual is a series of *intelligent behaviors* that unfold across his or her life. At no point is there a comparison between that person's behaviors and the

---

*The theory of personal intelligence presented here is not to be confused with what John Mayer, A. T. Panter, and David Caruso define as "the ability to reason about personality and its processes, as applied to oneself and others." See J. D. Mayer, A. T. Panter, and D. R. Caruso, "Does Personal Intelligence Exist? Evidence from a New Ability-Based Measure," *Journal of Personality Assessment* 94 (2012): 124–140, at 124.

behaviors of others, because that person's intelligence is not measured or judged relative to the behaviors of others.

Any behavior that narrows the distance between the starting state and the goal state of a person's personal goal counts as an intelligent behavior. This approach adopts the traditional general problem solving paradigm (see Chapter 9), but extends the problem solving from a single decontextualized task (e.g., Tower of Hanoi) to a lifetime of problem solving in pursuit of a personal goal.

What kind of intelligent behaviors are possible? *Any behavior you want.* You're only limited by your own imagination. This is where the importance of devising strategies and acquiring knowledge comes into play (see Chapter 9). Under this theory, the formulation of multiple strategies to overcome obstacles and reduce the discrepancy between the starting state and the goal state is an incredibly important manifestation of human intelligence (see Chapter 9).

My definition of an "intelligent behavior" is in line with Steven Pinker's definition of intelligence. Informed by the latest research in cognitive science and evolutionary psychology, Steven Pinker argued that intelligence is "the ability to attain goals in the face of obstacles by means of decisions based on rational (truth-obeying) rules."[25] It's also in line with Keith Stanovich's notion of rationality. According to Stanovich, "to think rationality means adopting appropriate goals, taking the appropriate action given one's goals and beliefs, and holding beliefs that are commensurate with available evidence."[26]

The Theory of Personal Intelligence has four central tenets that have important implications for education and society. The first tenet is that *the self is a core aspect of human intelligence.* The self includes all of the personal characteristics that an individual has integrated into his or her identity. I think a consideration of the self, and the individual's need to express that self, is *essential* if we are to truly understand the person's goals, and the intelligent behaviors he or she is displaying. Of course, the self is constantly evolving throughout the lifetime, and our self at one stage in life can differ radically from our self at another stage.[27]

Another key tenet is that *engagement and ability are inseparable throughout human development, dynamically feeding off each other as we engage in the world.*[28] Our interests and passions direct our attention to key aspects of a stimulus, and cause us to ignore other aspects. Importantly, our continual engagement builds up the expertise base that allows us to reach higher and higher heights of performance (see Chapter 9). Crucially, each individual can mix and match his or her own unique package of personal characteristics to attain the same outcome or even forge a new path. Throughout this book, I've provided evidence that there are *many paths to greatness*.

The third main tenet of the theory is that *both controlled and spontaneous cognitive processes can be adaptive for acquiring a personal goal*. This is an important departure from how intelligence has traditionally been conceptualized. This is due in large part to the original purpose of intelligence testing: to develop a test that predicts the ability to learn from *explicit* instruction. But once we take into account personal goals in addition to the goals of others (e.g., teachers, parents, IQ test administrators), we see the adaptive value of a wider range of spontaneous cognitive processes such as daydreaming, pretend play, spontaneous creative generation, implicit learning, and intuition (see Chapters 11 and 12).

This is also a departure from traditional notions of "rationality," which emphasize the rationality of controlled cognition. For instance, Stanovich argues that a critical function of the "reflective mind" is to "override" spontaneous cognitive processes (the "autonomous mind") because such processing is often "quick and dirty."[29] Stanovich's list of "irrational" cognitive processes include superstitious thinking, belief in the paranormal, faith in intuition, belief in "special" expertise, and overoptimistic theories of one's own introspective powers.[30]

The Theory of Personal Intelligence offers a different perspective. Rather than categorizing some cognitive processes as more intelligent or rational than others across environments, the emphasis is on *flexible cognition*. While it's often important for controlled cognitive processes to inhibit the automatic firing of well-learned patterns that might impede intelligent behaviors, sometimes it's *equally intelligent* for spontaneous cognitive processes to express themselves.

Sometimes being overly optimistic is highly rational, by allowing us to ignore our inner critic (and the criticism of others) and take bold action that gets us closer to our goal. As we saw in Chapter 12, positive schizotypal characteristics, such as faith in intuition, superstitious thinking, and unrealistic flights of fancy are not always irrational, even by Stanovich's definition of rationality; they are often conducive to reaching one's goals. We saw that faith in intuition is associated with a reduced latent inhibition, which in turn, is associated with higher levels of creative achievement. Many spontaneous processes in the openness to experience domain make strong contributions to creative achievement, especially in the arts. To the extent that these cognitive processes are employed at the right time, and move the person closer to realizing his or her personal goal, they are *very* intelligent and rational.

The fourth major tenet of my theory is that *there are no "ten-year rules" or "creativity thresholds,"* in which a person *must* attain a certain amount of knowledge, or score above an arbitrary level on a standardized test (e.g., IQ, SAT) to reach his or her personal goals. We must take into account an individual's personal goals, as that determines what sort of personal characteristics will have to be developed to reduce the discrepancy between the starting and goal state.

This is not to say that at the *individual differences* level of analysis we are all equally intelligent, even by my definition. To be sure, some personal characteristics are more conducive to publicly recognized success in certain fields than others. For instance, if you want to become a great scientist, your odds are greater if you have higher levels of a particular constellation of personal characteristics, such as intellectual curiosity, mental flexibility, tolerance for other's beliefs and values, self-discipline, patience, drive, and ambition. However, statistical predictions only tell us what a person is *likely* to achieve in the future, not whether they are *capable* of achieving the outcome.

Potential is a constantly moving target. The more we engage in something, the more potential grows. The latest research on the dynamic, nonlinear, and probabilistic nature of human development suggests that it's best to conceptualize potential as *readiness for engagement* (see Chapter 1). This is also consistent with the many cases, reviewed throughout this book, of people who start out with seemingly insurmountable odds and eventually exceed all expectations. Through the course of long-term engagement in a domain these individuals literally changed their odds, and hence their actual potential.

Also, there are certainly some characteristics that are more important to cultivate across the board than others. No matter where a person starts out or how lofty his or her goal, we should arm all young people with a very general set of skills that will serve them well in life, enabling them to realize the *many* goals they will adopt throughout their life span.

Characteristics such as critical thinking, working memory, mental flexibility, deliberate practice, communication and social skills, public speaking skills, compassion, emotional self-regulation, self-regulated learning strategies, growth mindset, and divergent thinking are essential for *everyone*.[31] Importantly, virtually everyone can develop these characteristics to a very useful degree.

My point is that when we apply arbitrary thresholds without taking personal goals into account, we limit possibility. No matter what the dream—whether it's dancing *The Nutcracker*, ending poverty, promoting world peace, creating modern art, dropping freestyle rhymes, or even coming up with a new theory of string theory—there are no clear-cut IQ thresholds or prescribed years of engagement in a domain required for a person to realize his or her personal goal. We can enhance the chances of personal success for both prodigies and late bloomers, and for every other kind of bloomer in between.

The deep implication here is that there should be no external pressure to realize a goal at a particular rate. The comparison isn't with others; it's with your former and future selves. If we rid ourselves of the notion that any of us ever reach a state labeled "failure," then there's no problem whatsoever in encouraging people to engage with a domain. If anything, there's an abundance of evidence suggesting we *should* encourage all people with a love for a specific domain to engage in what they love.

Throughout this book, I've tried to illustrate the incredible transformation people can undergo when they are allowed to engage in a domain that is aligned with their self-identity. In some cases, such as people with Asperger's, when engaging in their area of special interest their "disabled" characteristics completely evaporate (see Chapter 11). In Chapter 12 we also saw that a love for the domain was the single best predictor of lifelong creative achievement—both societal and personal—long after the effects of IQ and divergent thinking faded away.

It's a myth that geniuses consistently produce great work.[32] The output of most creators, including those we label "genius," tends to be highly uneven.[33] The key for expertise is consistency, but the key for greatness is *quantity*.[34] According to the "equal-odds rule," quality is a linear function of quantity: the more you create (regardless of the quality), the greater your chances of producing a masterpiece.[35]

This suggests we should encourage children to dream the impossible, to think beyond the standard expectations, to dare to be *unrealistic*. Such encouragement promotes the importance of perseverance and questioning the established order. What's more, this instills in all people a mindset of lifelong learning and growth.

While some may consider the world I've described beyond our reach, I can already see glimpses of it today. Throughout this book, I've highlighted the many progressive educators who are promoting learning goals, emotional self-regulation, self-regulated learning strategies, self-expression, self-pacing, context, deliberate practice, grit, passion, persistence, and play. All of these fundamentally human characteristics are part of human intelligence, because they contributed to the adaptation of our species. Without them, we wouldn't be here today to be able to use them to adapt to our personal goals within our own lives.

In the rest of this chapter, I'll spotlight some cutting-edge approaches to personal learning that I think are particularly in line with the Theory of Personal Intelligence. I hope this sampling of approaches inspires more people to take the insights of these extraordinary educators and infuse them into education. With enough people taking action, we really can realize an entirely new society.

∼

Of all the school transformation initiatives I've seen, perhaps none has excited me more than The Future Project, founded by two recent Yale grads—Andrew Mangino and Kanya Balakrishna. Tired of what they felt was a stale debate over the future of school, they embarked with a team of dozens on a simple mission: to design the "Future School," an inside-out approach to transforming education.

The Future Project model aims to combine Apple elegance and Disney magic with breakthrough research on what inspires, engages, and unleashes young people to attain their fullest possibility. The team dispatches Dream Directors—part human catalysts, social imagineers, and education entrepreneurs (think your high school guidance counselor, principal, and favorite teacher all in one)—into high schools, including some of the most troubled in the nation.

These Dream Directors are responsible for engineering a large-scale cultural shift within the school until the school is overflowing with a sense of possibility generated by the students themselves. But the Dream Directors don't stop there. They go into the surrounding community and enroll volunteers from the community as "Future Coaches" and pair them one-on-one with students in all four grade levels who become "Future Fellows." That's when the magic begins.

Over the course of the school year, Future Fellows are challenged to design and build their own "Future Projects"—dream-inspired initiatives that turn student passions into tangible, actionable projects. All of this, though, amounts to a massive schoolwide and community transformation, as every Fellow recruits anywhere from five to twenty peers to join his or her team until at least 80 percent of the school is involved in a Future Project. All together, this culminates in a massive transformation of both the school and surrounding community. Students come to see that education can be more than an apathetic march from Kindergarten to High School and that school can be a place where radical possibility is unleashed to help them realize their dreams.

The application to become a Future Fellow is a telling example of how The Future Project's approach represents a radical departure from the way schools traditionally assess young people. Rather than asking students to list their grades or test scores, they ask students to talk about their passions, dreams, and most audacious goals.

After meeting with their Dream Director, who individually assesses their grit and desire to engage in a personally meaningful project, they are challenged to:

- Upload a motivational video to YouTube.
- Post one dream on a social networking profile starting with the prompt "I have a dream, that someday . . ."
- Make an inspirational music playlist of exactly eight songs.
- Make a list of 5 *Things I Wish Adults Knew About Teenagers*.
- Make a list of 5 *Life Lessons for Teenagers*.
- Fill out "Dream Cards" that include the dreams of classmates and hand them to the Dream Director.

All dreams are welcome. To take some examples from the first year: Terrance dreamed of creating a dance troupe for students with special needs. Despite struggling in high school and being classified as a "special needs" student, he went on to create the troupe he had envisioned. Tatyana dreamed of sharing her love for African drumming with other teens, and she created a project to do so with the local Boys & Girls Club and consequently became a teacher. Devan dreamed of being the next Shakespeare and wrote an extraordinary play before he turned 18.

Here are some examples of first-year projects: Mariely founded "Perfectly Made," an online campaign that promotes self-acceptance and the importance of valuing yourself. Amanda and Dana created a fashion show to raise money for leukemia research. Keyla wouldn't stand for her high school failing anymore, so she created "Restart Day" and recruited dozens of her peers to help fight for their school to stay open. Juan fused his passions for boxing, poetry, and New Haven Academy to inspire his peers to build a workshop to end youth violence. Team Swagg produced a documentary that chronicles the effects of bullying and released it through a multimedia campaign.

The results from the The Future Project's first year are immensely promising. The year-end enrollment was five times the principal's expectations, with an overall retention rate of 86 percent. Seven out of ten Fellows said The Future Project changed the culture of their school. Eight out of ten Fellows accomplished something they didn't think was possible. Nine out of ten Fellows became more excited to learn at school, viewed themselves as leaders, and experienced an increase in confidence. But perhaps most importantly, *ten out of ten Fellows* were more hopeful about their futures, and the peers of Future Fellows say the experience of going to school began to transform in unexpected ways.

The Future Project is a potent demonstration of what can happen when students actually *want* to be in school. While the past two decades of school reform have focused on performance above all, The Future Project focuses first and foremost on possibility—and lets performance follow.

The core elements of The Future Project—projects, coaches, engagement with the community, risk of failure, recognition of success, and public exhibition—are also the key ingredients of the emerging field of educational design. The field's objective is to determine how design thinking and design methodologies can empower teachers, students, and communities. Various schools have adopted design methodologies to create spaces that promote passion, play, and collaboration through project-based learning and inquiry-based learning.

Examples of such schools and programs include High Tech High Charter School in San Diego, California; Prototype Design Camp; The Blue School in New York City; Blue Valley Center for Advanced Professional Studies in Overland Park, Kansas; The School at Columbia University; The Nueva School in Hillsborough, California; and Real Charter School & Studio H in Oakland, California. One of the leaders in the educational design movement is The Third Teacher+, a start-up consultancy group within Cannon Design.[36] Based on Reggio Emilia's notion that there are three teachers of children (adults, peers, and their environment), the goal of the diverse team (which includes architects, educators, anthropologists, and organizational strategists) is to use design principles and space to transform teaching and learning, increase student engagement, and empower students, teachers, and communities.

~

"Education tends to be about becoming an expert," notes Beau Lotto, director of the Lottolab Studio at University College London. "If a bus is coming at you, you don't want to be creative; you want to be an efficient expert. We treat life like a bus is always coming at us."[37]

While Lotto sees a role for expertise, he believes we should teach children many different strategies, including the ability to flexibly switch between them depending on the context. Recently Lotto created a safe space for uncertainty by moving his lab into a science museum. There he and his colleagues created a six-day program called "I, scientist." Lotto believes all of us are already scientists because we all learn through trial and error. He sees science as a way of *being*—a state of play where a person moves between various mental states, and where learning is its own reward. To facilitate this spirit, the program is intentionally left unstructured.

Still, Lotto believes it's crucial to establish trust with the students and make sure you are speaking their language, showing them how the program can help them, and why they should care about science. "Uncertainty is a very scary, dangerous place," Lotto told me. Once students feel comfortable, they engage in observation and start asking questions. Lotto believes the best questions are the ones that lead to more questions. "The good questions, when answered, create more uncertainty because it leads to understanding instead of information."

If they are asking why a bee acts a certain way, they are encouraged to ask—Why do *I* act that way? The students are also encouraged to ask *What if*? and come up with ways to test their questions. Lotto believes that without realizing it, the students are engaging in the scientific method. But Lotto doesn't say they are running "experiments." Instead, he believes they are creating *games*—the combination of a state of play with rules. After designing and playing these games, the final phase in their framework is *sharing*, where students produce a report of their findings.

One group of 8- to 10-year-olds has already published their findings on bumblebees in the prestigious journal *Biology Letters*.[38] As Lotto reported to the crowd at TEDGlobal 2012, "this was the first ever peer-reviewed scientific article published in a top journal reporting a truly unique finding, in which all 25 authors are 8-year-olds—or younger."

In his latest project, Lotto hopes to radically change the experience of school by making play, uncertainty, tolerance for ambiguity, and failure not only OK, but *enjoyable*. Lotto wants to create a truly ambiguous environment where all boundaries are blurred: People don't know whether they're walking into a lab, a nightclub, or a theater. He wants to then set up these spaces in different cities and create a buzz around them. "Imagine science is the top entertainment venue," he told me, his voice bubbling with excitement.

$\sim$

Imagine being 6 or 7 years old again, learning about addition and subtraction for the first time. How wonderful would it be, while taking a quiz, to be able to rub a genie's bottle and choose from a number of on-the-spot metaphors for mathematical concepts, like what a fraction really means? Or picture this: Rather than working through equations in daunting rows on a sheet of paper, your task is to play a game on a tablet computer in which you share a dinner table with aliens. There's a bowl of apples in the center of the table. Suddenly the apple bowl zooms in, focusing your attention on the task at hand, which is to divide the apples equally. The aliens have a strong sense of justice and will let you know if you don't give them their fair share. If you answer correctly, you earn stars, which you can redeem for all sorts of goodies (new games, onscreen props, and so on).

These examples may seem charming and even silly—and they're meant to be. They're also designed to engage students in learning by harnessing online, interactive media to hone their math skills in entertaining ways. But they're not just playful games. The two described above are real software applications developed by Shimon Schocken, a professor of computer science at Israel's IDC Herzliya, an educator with wise eyes and a deep, authoritative voice.

His apps track students' progress and deliver results to teachers and parents as an alternative to grades. The genie and alien programs represent a growing wave of educational materials using the same technologies that students from kindergarten through graduate school associate with *fun*—there's none of the usual boredom or competitive pressure that typically characterize kids' relationship with required schooling.

The new wave of educational tools include fresh ways of deploying phone and tablet apps, online games and videos, and social networking. The goal is to create effective learning tools, new methods of grading, and virtual classrooms of unprecedented sizes—even numbering in the tens of thousands online. While these goals have certainly been attempted before, the latest crop of mass-market, interactive learning tools are also intended for mass-market, global consumption. And enjoyment. "We should try to bring back the joy of learning because you want to learn, not because someone is going to give you a grade at the end of the semester," Schocken told me.

As he noted in his TEDGlobal 2012 talk, Schocken believes that the traditional grading system is "degrading"—and he'd rather talk about a more positive approach to teaching that he calls "upgrading." This means rejecting the traditional focus on correct answers. Instead, Schocken thinks we should encourage mistakes. In his app-based learning environments, if you give the wrong answer, nothing horrible happens. "We never say 'incorrect,' 'wrong,' and so on. Instead, when students give answers that aren't the right ones, we use a non-verbal and neutral visual gesture, like vibrating the image a little," Schocken told me. This implies something like "nice try, keep trying, I'm waiting patiently, take your time." After two wrong answers are entered in a row, the program gives a tip leading to the correct answer.

Schocken's quest is to shake up education by creating new tools and, more important, a new attitude toward learning.

～

Skeptics may argue that the resources, technical skills, and university networks required to participate in the current education revolution are available only to well-connected computer science professors such as Schocken. But initiatives are attempting to include teachers of all levels around the world to participate. One such example is TED-Ed, the new educational arm of TED.

In March 2012, Logan Smalley and his team at TED-Ed put out a call for anyone anywhere to nominate top-notch educators and animators around the world to help package existing TEDTalks as classroom material—to be experienced online and outside the classroom.

The goal was to fashion dynamic, informative, and entertaining lessons, all under ten minutes. To their delight, the TED-Ed team received thousands of nominations. In March they started posting a series of these crafted lessons on their YouTube channel.

But by the end of April, they had to figure out what to do with all of the lessons they were accumulating. In a world of interactivity, it wasn't enough to just aggregate them. "Simply watching them is not the same as teaching," says the fresh-faced Smalley, who favors T-shirts and plaid button-downs and jeans and looks like a gentle teacher-type—or education grad student. "It's a step. We want to get into higher order thinking skills."[39] To take learning to a deeper level, they created a framework that allows students and teachers to personalize the content.

On April 25, 2012, they launched the TED-Ed website. With the single click of the "Flip This Lesson" button, educators (and really anybody—you don't need a teaching role to do it) can transform any TED-Ed video into his or her very own teaching lesson. Once the video is "flipped," teachers can add in their own "quick quiz" of multiple-choice questions, a "Think" section for short answers, and a "Dig Deeper" section with resources for more in-depth learning about the topic. The new lesson gets its own unique URL and can easily be shared on social networking sites. The educator who created the video can also easily measure the lesson's effect, tracking which students watched the video, what answers they got right and wrong, the quality of short-answer responses, and whether the students engaged in the Dig Deeper materials. According to Smalley, this makes "every visitor to the TED-Ed website a potential student and a potential teacher."

In only the first few months since they launched, the site gathered over 5,000 "flips." One video about biological sex determination created by science teacher Aaron Reedy went viral. A few days after he published the lesson, he tweeted, "7 years as a teacher: I explain sex determination to 1000 students. 3 days with @TED_ED: I have explained it to 13000!" This tweet was written back in late April of 2012. As of December, his video has 870,123 views on YouTube. As Smalley notes, "take economies of scale and apply it and you're in a pretty exciting space."

While these examples of the new frontiers of education certainly seem fresh and exciting, they actually reflect an idea that's been circulated among educators long before tablets or YouTube or even the Web existed. Way back in 1984, psychologist Benjamin Bloom reported some shocking study results: Students who engaged in individualized tutoring with a teacher scored 98 percent better than the average performance of students in the traditional classroom.[40] This led Bloom to propose his famous "2 Sigma Problem": How can we accomplish the same results using methods other than peer tutoring, which are "too costly for most societies to bear on a large scale"? If Bloom were alive today, he'd surely be astonished—and encouraged—by the mass-market, low-cost and, perhaps most strikingly, engaging possibilities that Schocken, Smalley, and their colleagues are developing. He'd have to consider changing the name "Problem" to "Solution."

∾

All journeys must end, and I'm afraid our journey ends here. Thanks for taking the trip with me. While we've climbed *this* peak, there are so many more to climb. Many puzzles of human intelligence are left unresolved, and the Theory of Personal Intelligence requires much more fleshing out and testing. I look forward to the many discussions, debates, and collaborations to come. But at the very least, I hope I succeeded in showing you that the full landscape of human intelligence really is so much more beautiful, exciting, and hopeful than any single perspective can possibly reveal.

EPILOGUE

EPILOGUE

April 23, 2012

"Hi, I'm here to see the principal," I say to the secretary. She looks at me curiously. I think she is assessing whether I am one of the middle school students. "I'll get her," she says skeptically, while she motions for me to sit down. I feel like I'm 13 years old again.

As I take a seat, I try to picture the principal in my mind. All I have is the faintest memory of that special day, all those years ago, when she took me aside and asked me what I was doing in the resource room. In a flash, she came into my life but left it forever changed. As I researched this book, I decided I wanted to track her down and thank her for giving me the courage to believe in myself.

So I contacted the gifted education teacher from high school who was so kind to let me into her classroom unofficially, and we narrowed down who it must have been. After trying a few leads, *I found her*. She replied to my email almost immediately, recalling exactly who I was. She told me she is now a principal at a local middle school and welcomed a reunion. So here I am, about to meet my angel.

"Scott?" I break out of my trance. I look up and recognize her immediately. You don't forget people who touch your life, no matter how short your time with them. Suddenly all the memories and emotions come flooding back. The feelings of inferiority, self-doubt, and anxiety, and then self-belief and determination. Many thanks to this one person, who saw something in me that one day no one else took the time to see, causing me to question my place in this world.

I jump up and give her a great big hug. She introduces me to the school psychologist, whom she invited to join us. I think I am older than him. What an incredibly crazy world we live in. Here I am, above the system. *Finally,* no more IQ tests, no more standardized achievement tests, no more any other irrelevant tests that only serve to get in the way of realizing my dreams.

I shake the school psychologist's hand, and we head to the special education classroom. Although this time I'm not the student. I can't wait to tell the kids how the world truly works, about the need to be your own self-advocate in life, and to believe in yourself regardless of other people's expectations. Not everyone will be lucky enough to have a teacher who takes him or her aside, but that doesn't mean we can't inspire everyone to take themselves aside.

As I approach the special education classroom, I feel like I've seen the light. I've seen that all possibilities are within reach if we allow children to dream and take their dreams seriously.

Because you never, ever know. Dreams do come true.

The Cattell-Horn-Carroll (CHC) Model of Intelligence v2.2:

A visual tour and summary

Dr. Joel Schneider

Dr. Kevin McGrew

CHC model v2.2 – Part 1 (Schneider & McGrew, 2012)

General

General Intelligence (*g*)

Broad

Narrow

Processing Speed (Gs)
- Perceptual speed (P)
- Rate of test-taking (R9)
- Number facility (N)
- Reading speed/fluency (RS)
- Writing speed/fluency (WS)

General Speed +

Auditory Processing (Ga)
- Phonetic coding (PC)
- Speech sound discrimination (US)
- Resistance to auditory stimulus distortion (UR)
- Memory for sound patterns (UM)
- Maintaining & judging rhythm (U8)
- Musical discrim. & judgment (U1 U9)
- Absolute pitch (UP)
- Sound localization (UL)

Visual Processing (Gv)
- Visualization (Vz)
- Speeded rotation (SR)
- Closure speed (CS)
- Flexibility of closure (CF)
- Visual memory (MV)
- Spatial scanning (SS)
- Serial perceptual integration (PI)
- Length estimation (LE)
- Perceptual illusions (IL)
- Perceptual alternations (PN)
- Imagery (IM)

Sensory-Motor Domain
Specific Abilities (**Sensory**) +

Long-Term Storage & Retrieval (Glr)
- Associative memory (MA) *
- Meaningful memory (MM) *
- Free-recall memory (M6) *
- Ideational fluency (FI) **
- Associational fluency (FA) **
- Expressional fluency (FE) **
- Sens. to probs. /altern. Sol. fluency (SP) **
- Originality /creativity (FO) **
- Naming facility (NA) **
- Word Fluency (FW) **
- Figural Fluency (FF) **
- Figural flexibility (FX) **

Memory
* Learning Efficiency
** Retrieval Fluency

Short-Term Memory (Gsm)
- Memory span (MS)
- Working memory capacity (MW)

Fluid Reasoning (Gf)
- Induction (I)
- General sequential reasoning (RG)
- Quantitative reasoning (RQ)

Domain-Independent General Capacities +

Comp - Knowledge (Gc)
- General verbal information (KO)
- Language development (LD)
- Lexical knowledge (VL)
- Listening ability (LS)
- Communication ability (CM)
- Grammatical sensitivity (MY)

Reading & Writing (Grw)
- Reading decoding (RD)
- Reading comprehension (RC)
- Reading speed (RS)
- Spelling ability (SG)
- English usage (EU)
- Writing ability (WA)
- Writing speed (WS)

Quantitative Knowledge (Gq)
- Mathematical knowledge (KM)
- Mathematical achievement (A3)

Acquired Knowledge +

Functional groupings

Conceptual groupings

+ = additional CHC abilities in groupings in Part 2 of model

© Institute for Applied Psychometrics (IAP) 01-03-13

CHC model v2.2 – Part 2 (Schneider & McGrew, 2012)

General

General Intelligence (*g*)

Broad

| Domain Specific Know. (Gkn) | Reaction & Decision Speed (Gt) | Psychomotor Speed (Gps) | Olfactory Abilities (Go) | Tactile Abilities (Gh) | Kinesthetic Abilities (Gk) | Psychomotor Abilities (Gp) |

Narrow

Domain Specific Know. (Gkn): ?

Reaction & Decision Speed (Gt):
- Simple reaction time (R1)
- Choice reaction time (R2)
- Semantic processing speed (R4)
- Mental comparison speed (R7)
- Inspection time (IT)

Psychomotor Speed (Gps):
- Speed of limb movement (R3)
- Writing speed (fluency) WS
- Speed of articulation (PT)
- Movement time (MT)

Olfactory Abilities (Go):
- Olfactory memory (OM)

Tactile Abilities (Gh): ?

Kinesthetic Abilities (Gk): ?

Psychomotor Abilities (Gp):
- Static strength (P3)
- Multilimb coordination (P6)
- Finger dexterity (P2)
- Manual dexterity (P1)
- Arm-hand steadiness (P7)
- Control precision (P8)
- Aiming (A1)
- Gross body equilibrium (P4)

Acquired Knowledge +

General Speed +

Sensory-Motor Domain Specific Abilities +

Motor

Functional groupings

Conceptual groupings

+ = additional CHC abilities in groupings in Part I of model

© Institute for Applied Psychometrics (IAP) 01-03-13

Cattell-Horn-Carroll (CHC) Theory of Cognitive Abilities Definitions (CHC v2.2)

Joel Schneider & Kevin McGrew

(01-13-03; v2.2)

The following table of CHC definitions is abstracted from a lengthy narrative description of contemporary CHC theory in:

Schneider, W. J., & McGrew, K. (2012). The Cattell-Horn-Carroll model of intelligence. In, D. Flanagan & P. Harrison (Eds.), *Contemporary Intellectual Assessment: Theories, Tests, and Issues (3rd ed.)* (p. 99-144). New York: Guilford.

The current table presents only the "bare bones" definitional information from the above mentioned book chapter. Readers are encouraged to consult the Schneider and McGrew (2012) chapter for details.

CHC v2.2 differs from prior **CHC v1.0** organized tables of definitions for a number of reasons. First, we conducted a detailed review of the original writings of the primary architects of CHC theory to ascertain places where CHC v1.0 may have erred (all contemporary CHC v1.0 published tables can be traced to the second authors first CHC table in the first edition of *Contemporary Intellectual Assessment*—McGrew, 1997). Second, we reviewed contemporary intelligence research to answer unanswered issues regarding various components of CHC v1.0. Third, we attempted to define each of the constructs in CHC theory in terms that clinicians will find useful. Fourth, in the chapter, we provide guidance as to which constructs are more central to the theory or have more validity data available. Fifth, also in the chapter (but not included in this summary table) we alert readers to existing controversies and raise some questions of our own. Finally, we propose a number of additions, deletions, and rearrangements in the list of CHC theory abilities.

As stated in the conclusion of our chapter:

The end goal, however, has always been for CHC theory to undergo continual upgrades so it would evolve toward an ever-more accurate summary of human cognitive diversity. With that end in mind, we have attempted to simplify the model where it needed simplification. We have also elaborated upon aspects of the model that needed elaboration. We hope our research- and reasoning-based conclusions and hypotheses will make CHC theory more accurate, more understandable to practitioners, and ultimately more helpful to people who undergo psychoeducational assessment. We hope many readers, especially long-time CHC users and researchers, are placed into a state of thoughtful disequilibrium regarding their understanding of the prevailing CHC model. Even if such users are unconvinced by our arguments, if the schemas of CHC users are broadened and refined by considering the ideas we have presented, our chapter will have been a success. The original source theorists of CHC theory would not idly stand by and let the current consensus CHC calcify and suffer from hardening of the CHC categories. We believe Cattell, Horn, and Carroll, and all the psychometric giants upon whose shoulders they stood, would smile on our efforts, and would then promptly engage us, and others, in spirited debates and empirical- and theory-based discourse.

I.   **Domain-Independent General Capacities**

Fluid Reasoning (Gf): *The deliberate but flexible control of attention to solve novel "on the spot" problems that cannot be performed by relying exclusively on previously learned habits, schemas, and scripts.* Fluid reasoning is a multi-dimensional construct but its parts are unified in their purpose: solving unfamiliar problems. Fluid reasoning is most evident in abstract reasoning that depends less on prior learning. However, it is also present in day-to-day problem solving. Fluid reasoning is typically employed in concert with background knowledge and automatized responses. That is, fluid reasoning is employed, even if for the briefest of moments, whenever current habits, scripts, and schemas are insufficient to meet the demands of a new situation. Fluid reasoning is also evident in inferential reasoning, concept formation, classification of unfamiliar stimuli, generalization of old solutions to new problems and contexts, hypothesis generation and confirmation, identification of relevant similarities, differences, and relationship among diverse objects and ideas, the perception of relevant consequences of newly acquired knowledge, and extrapolation of reasonable estimates in ambiguous situations.

1. **Induction (I).** The ability to observe a phenomenon and discover the underlying principles or rules that determine its behavior.
2. **General Sequential Reasoning (RG).** The ability to reason logically using known premises and principles. This ability is also known as deductive reasoning or rule application.
3. **Quantitative Reasoning (RQ):** The ability to reason, either with induction or deduction, with numbers, mathematical relations, and operators.

Memory

Short-Term Memory (Gsm): *The ability to encode, maintain, and manipulate information in one's immediate awareness.* Gsm refers to individual differences in both the capacity (size) of primary memory and to the efficiency of attentional control mechanisms that manipulate information within primary memory.
1. **Memory Span (MS).** The ability to encode information, maintain it in primary memory, and immediately reproduce the information in the same sequence in which it was represented.
2. **Working Memory Capacity (WM).**[1] The ability to direct the focus of attention to perform relatively simple manipulations, combinations, and transformations of information within *primary* memory while avoiding distracting stimuli and engaging in strategic/controlled searches for information in *secondary* memory.

Long-Term Storage & Retrieval (Glr): *The ability to store, consolidate, and retrieve information over periods of time measured in minutes, hours, days, and years.* Short-term memory has to do with information that has been encoded seconds ago and must be retrieved while it is being actively maintained in primary memory. Short-term memory tests often involve information that is stored in long-term memory. What distinguishes Gsm from Glr tests is that there is a continuous attempt to maintain awareness of that information. A Glr test involves information that has been put out of immediate awareness long enough for the contents of primary memory to be displaced completely. In Glr tests, continuous maintenance of information in primary memory is difficult, if not impossible.

 Glr-Learning Efficiency: All tasks of learning efficiency must present more information than can be retained in Gsm

1. **Associative Memory (MA).** The ability to remember previously unrelated information as having been paired.
2. **Meaningful Memory (MM).** The ability to remember narratives and other forms of semantically related information.
3. **Free Recall Memory (M6).** The ability to recall lists in any order.

---

[1] This factor was previously named *working memory*. However, as explained in McGrew (2005), this term does not refer to an individual difference variable but instead to a set of interrelated cognitive structures. *Working memory capacity* is an individual difference variable that is a property of the working memory system as a whole.

Glr-Retrieval Fluency: The rate and fluency at which individuals can access information stored in long-term memory.

(Fluency factors that involve the production of ideas)

1. **Ideational Fluency (FI)**. Ability to rapidly produce a series of ideas, words, or phrases related to a specific condition or object. Quantity, not quality or response originality, is emphasized.
2. **Associational Fluency (FA)**. Ability to rapidly produce a series of original or useful ideas related to a particular concept. In contrast to Ideational Fluency (FI), quality rather quantity of production is emphasized.
3. **Expressional Fluency (FE)**. Ability to rapidly think of different ways of expressing an idea.
4. **Sensitivity to Problems/Alterative Solution Fluency (SP)**. Ability to rapidly think of a number of alternative solutions to a particular practical problem.
5. **Originality/Creativity (FO)**. Ability to rapidly produce original, clever, and insightful responses (expressions, interpretations) to a given topic, situation, or task.

(Fluency abilities that involve the recall of words)

6. **Naming Facility (NA)**. Ability to rapidly call objects by their names. In contemporary reading research, this ability is called rapid automatic naming (RAN) or speed of lexical access.
7. **Word Fluency (FW)**. Ability to rapidly produce words that share a non-semantic feature.

(Fluency abilities related to figures)

8. **Figural Fluency (FF)**. Ability to rapidly draw or sketch as many things (or elaborations) as possible when presented with a nonmeaningful visual stimulus (e.g., set of unique visual elements). Quantity is emphasized over quality.
9. **Figural Flexibility (FX)**. Ability to rapidly draw different solutions to figural problems.

General Speed

Processing Speed (Gs): *The ability to perform simple repetitive cognitive tasks quickly and fluently*. This ability is of secondary importance (compared to Gf and Gc) when predicting performance during the learning phase of skill acquisition. However, it becomes an important predictor of skilled performance once people know how to do a task. That is, once people know how to perform a task, they still differ in the speed and fluency with which they perform. For example, two people may be equally accurate in their addition skills but one recalls math facts with ease and the other has to think about the answer for an extra half-second and sometimes counts on his or her fingers.

1. **Perceptual Speed (P)**. Speed at which visual stimuli can be compared for similarity or difference. Much like Induction is at the core of Gf, Perceptual Speed is at the core of Gs. Recent research (Ackerman, Beier, & Boyle, 2002; Ackerman & Cianciolo, 2000; see McGrew, 2005) suggests that Perceptual Speed may be an intermediate stratum ability (between narrow and broad) defined by four narrow subabilities: (1) Pattern Recognition (Ppr)—the ability to quickly recognize simple visual patterns; (2) Scanning (Ps)—the ability to scan, compare, and look up visual stimuli; (3) Memory (Pm)—the ability to perform visual perceptual speed tasks that place significant demands on immediate Gsm, and (d) Complex (Pc)—the ability to perform visual pattern recognition tasks that impose additional cognitive demands, such as spatial visualization, estimating and interpolating, and heightened memory span loads.
2. **Rate-of-Test-Taking (R9)**. Speed and fluency with which simple cognitive tests are completed. Through the lens of CHC theory, the definition of this factor has narrowed to simple tests that do not require visual comparison (so as not to overlap with Perceptual Speed) or mental arithmetic (so as not to overlap with Number Facility). The next three factors are related to the ability to perform basic academic skills rapidly.
3. **Number Facility (N)**. Speed at which basic arithmetic operations are performed accurately. Although this factor includes recall of math facts, Number Facility includes speeded performance of any simple calculation (e.g., subtracting 3 from a column of 2-digit numbers). Number Facility does not involve understanding or organizing mathematical problems and is not a major component of mathematical/quantitative reasoning or higher mathematical skills.
4. **Reading Speed (fluency) (RS)**. Rate of reading text with full comprehension. Also listed under Grw.
5. **Writing Speed (fluency) (WS):** Rate at which words or sentences can be generated or copied. Also listed under Grw and Gps.

Reaction and Decision Speed (Gt): *The speed of making very simple decisions or judgments when items are presented one at a time.* The primary use of Gt measures has been in research settings. Researchers are interested in Gt as it may provide some insight into the nature of *g* and some very basic properties of the brain (e.g., neural efficiency). One of the interesting aspects of Gt is that not only is faster reaction time in these very simple tasks associated with complex reasoning but so is greater consistency of reaction time (less variability).

1. **Simple Reaction Time (R1).** Reaction time to the onset of a single stimulus (visual or auditory). R1 frequently is divided into the phases of decision time (DT; the time to decide to make a response and the finger leaves a home button) and movement time (MT; the time to move finger from the home button to another button where the response is physically made and recorded).
2. **Choice Reaction Time (R2).** Reaction time when a very simple choice must be made. For example, examinees see two buttons and must hit the one that lights up.
3. **Semantic Processing Speed (R4).** Reaction time when a decision requires some very simple encoding and mental manipulation of the stimulus content.
4. **Mental Comparison Speed (R7).** Reaction time where stimuli must be compared for a particular characteristic or attribute.
5. **Inspection Time (IT).** The speed at which differences in stimuli can be perceived.

Psychomotor Speed (Gps): *The speed and fluidity with which physical body movements can be made.* In skill acquistion, Gps is the ability that determines performance differences after a comparable population (e.g., manual laborers in the same factory) has practiced a simple skill for a very long time.

1. **Speed of Limb Movement (R3).** The speed of arm and leg movement. This speed is measured after the movement is initiated. Accuracy is not important.
2. **Writing Speed (fluency) (WS).** The speed at which written words can be copied. Also listed under Grw and Gps.
3. **Speed of Articulation (PT).** Ability to rapidly perform successive articulations with the speech musculature.
4. **Movement Time (MT).** Recent research suggests that MT may be an intermediate stratum ability (between narrow and broad strata) that represents the second phase of reaction time as measured by various elementary cognitive tasks (ECTs). The time taken to physically move a body part (e.g., a finger) to make the required response is movement time (MT). MT may also measure the speed of finger, limb, or multilimb movements or vocal articulation (*diadochokinesis*; Greek for "successive movements") and is also listed under Gt.

I.   Acquired Knowledge Systems

Comprehension-Knowledge (Gc): *Depth and breadth of knowledge and skills that are valued by one's culture.* Every culture values certain skills and knowledge over others. Gc reflects the degree to which a person has learned practically useful knowledge and mastered valued skills. Thus, by definition it is impossible to measure Gc independent of culture. Gc is theoretically broader than what is measured by any existing cognitive battery.

1. **General Verbal Information (K0).** Breadth and depth of knowledge that one's culture deems essential, practical, or otherwise worthwhile for everyone to know.
2. **Language Development (LD).** General understanding of spoken language at the level of words, idioms, and sentences. In the same way that Induction is at the core of Gf, Language Development is at the core of Gc. Although listed as a distinct narrow ability in Carroll's model, his description of his analyses make it clear that he meant Language Development as an intermediate category between Gc and more specific language-related abilities such as Lexical Knowledge, Grammatical Sensitivity, and Listening Ability. Language development appears to be a label for all language abilities working together in concert.
3. **Lexical Knowledge (VL).** Knowledge of the definitions of words and the concepts that underlie them. Whereas Language Development is more about understanding words in context, Lexical Knowledge is more about understanding the definitions of words in isolation.
4. **Listening Ability (LS).** Ability to understand speech. Tests of listening ability typically have simple vocabulary but increasingly complex syntax or increasingly long speech samples to listen to.
5. **Communication Ability (CM).** Ability to use speech to communicate one's thoughts clearly. This ability is comparable to Listening Ability except that it is productive (expressive) rather than receptive.

6. **Grammatical Sensitivity (MY).** Awareness of the formal rules of grammar and morphology of words in speech. This factor is distinguished from English Usage in that it is manifest in oral language instead of written language and that it measures more the awareness of grammar rules rather than correct usage.

Domain-Specific Knowledge (Gkn): *Depth, breadth, and mastery of specialized knowledge (knowledge not all members of a society are expected to have).* Specialized knowledge is typically acquired via one's career, hobby, or other passionate interest (e.g., religion, sports).

1. **Foreign Language Proficiency (KL).** Similar to Language Development but in another language. This ability is distinguished from Foreign Language Aptitude in that it represents achieved proficiency instead of potential proficiency. Presumably, most people with high Foreign Language Proficiency have high Foreign Language Aptitude but not all people with high Foreign Language Aptitude have yet developed proficiency in any foreign languages. This ability was previously classified as an aspect of Gc. However, since Gkn was added to CHC, it is clear that specialized knowledge of a particular language should be reclassified. Although Knowledge of English as a Second Language was previously listed as a separate ability in Gkn, it now seems clear that it is a special case of the more general ability of Foreign Language Proficiency. Note that this factor is unusual because it is not a single factor. There is a different Foreign Language Proficiency factor for every language.
2. **Knowledge of Signing (KF).** Knowledge of finger-spelling and signing (e.g., American Sign Language).
3. **Skill in Lip-Reading (LP).** Competence in the ability to understand communication from others by watching the movement of their mouths and expressions.
4. **Geography Achievement (A5).** Range of geography knowledge (e.g., capitals of countries).
5. **General Science Information (K1).** Range of scientific knowledge (e.g., biology, physics, engineering, mechanics, electronics).
6. **Mechanical Knowledge (MK).** Knowledge about the function, terminology, and operation of ordinary tools, machines, and equipment. There are many tests of mechanical knowledge and reasoning used for the purpose of personnel selection (e.g., ASVAB, Wiesen Test of Mechanical Aptitude).
7. **Knowledge of Behavioral Content (BC).** Knowledge or sensitivity to nonverbal human communication/interaction systems (e.g., facial expressions and gestures). The field of emotional intelligence (EI) research is very large but it is not yet clear which EI constructs should be included in CHC theory. CHC theory is about abilities rather than personality and thus the constructs within it are measured by tests in which there are correct answers (or speeded performance).

Reading and Writing (Grw): *Depth and breadth of knowledge and skills related to written language.* People with high Grw read with little effort and write with little difficulty. When Grw is sufficiently high, reading and writing become perfect windows for viewing a person's language development. Whatever difficulties they have understanding text or communicating clearly, it is most likely a function of Gc or Gkn. For people with low Grw, however, high language skills may not be evident in reading and writing performance. Although reading and writing are clearly distinct activities, the underlying sources of individual differences in reading and writing skills do not differentiate between the two activities cleanly. It appears that the ability that is common across all reading skills also unites all writing skills.

1. **Reading Decoding (RD).** Ability to identify words from text. Typically this ability is assessed by oral reading tests with words arranged in ascending order of difficulty. Tests can consist of phonetically regular words (words that are spelled how they sound such as bathtub or hanger), phonetically irregular words (words that do not sound how they are spelled such as sugar or colonel), or phonetically regular pseudowords (fake words that conform to regular spelling rules such as gobbish or choggy).
2. **Reading Comprehension (RC).** Ability to understand written discourse. Reading comprehension is measured in a variety of ways..
3. **Reading Speed (RS).** Rate at which a person can read connected discourse with full comprehension. Reading Speed is classified as a mixed measure of Gs (Broad cognitive Speed) and Grw in a hierarchical speed model.
4. **Spelling Ability (SG).** Ability to spell words. This factor is typically measured with traditional written spelling tests. However, just as with Reading Decoding, it can also be measured via spelling tests consisting of phonetically regular nonsense words (e.g., "grodding"). It is worth noting that Carroll (1993) considered this factor to be weakly defined and in need of additional research.
5. **English Usage (EU).** Knowledge of the mechanics of writing (e.g., capitalization, punctuation, and word usage).
6. **Writing Ability (WA).** Ability to use text to communicate ideas clearly.
7. **Writing Speed (WS).** Ability to copy or generate text quickly. Writing Speed tasks are considered to measure both Grw and Gps (Broad Psycho-Motor Speed) as per a hierarchical speed hierarchy.

© Institute for Applied Psychometrics (IAP), 01-03-13

Quantitative Knowledge (Gq): *Depth and breadth of knowledge related to mathematics.* Gq is distinct from Quantitative Reasoning (a facet of Gf) in the same way that Gc is distinct from the non-quantitative aspects of Gf. It consists of acquired knowledge about mathematics such as knowledge of mathematical symbols (e.g., $\int$, π, Σ, ∞, $\neq$, $\leq$, $+$, $-$, $\times$, $\div$, $\sqrt{}$, and many others), operations (e.g., addition/subtraction, multiplication/division, exponentiation/n^{th} rooting, factorials, negation, and many others), computational procedures (e.g., long division, reducing fractions, quadratic formula, and many others), and other math-related skills (e.g., using a calculator, math software, and other math aids).

1. **Mathematical Knowledge (KM).** Range of general knowledge about mathematics. Not the performance of mathematical operations or the solving of math problems. This factor is about "what" rather than "how" knowledge (e.g., What does π mean? What is the Pythagorean theorem?).
2. **Mathematical Achievement (A3).** Measured (tested) mathematics achievement.

II.   Sensory/Motor-Linked Abilities

Sensory

Visual Processing (Gv): *The ability to make use of simulated mental imagery (often in conjunction with currently perceived images) to solve problems.* Once the eyes have transmitted visual information, the visual system of the brain automatically performs a large number of low-level computations (e.g., edge detection, light/dark perception, color-differentiation, motion-detection, and so forth). The results of these low-level computations are used by various higher-order processors to infer more complex aspects of the visual image (e.g., object recognition, constructing models of spatial configuration, motion prediction, and so forth).

1. **Visualization (Vz).** The ability to perceive complex patterns and mentally simulate how they might look when transformed (e.g., rotated, changed in size, partially obscured, and so forth). In the same way that Induction is central to Gf and Language Development is central to Gc, this is the core ability of Gv.
2. **Speeded Rotation (Spatial Relations; SR).** The ability to solve problems quickly using mental rotation of simple images. This ability is similar to visualization because it involves rotating mental images but it is distinct because it has more to do with the *speed* at which mental rotation tasks can be completed. Speeded Rotation tasks typically involve fairly simple images.
3. **Closure Speed (CS).** Ability to quickly identify a familiar meaningful visual object from incomplete (e.g., vague, partially obscured, disconnected) visual stimuli, without knowing in advance what the object is. This ability is sometimes called Gestalt Perception because it requires people to "fill in" unseen or missing parts of an image to visualize a single percept.
4. **Flexibility of Closure (CF).** Ability to identify a visual figure or pattern embedded in a complex distracting or disguised visual pattern or array, when knowing in advance what the pattern is.
5. **Visual Memory (MV).** Ability to remember complex images over short periods of time (less than 30 seconds). The tasks that define this factor involve being shown complex images and then identifying them soon after the stimulus is removed.
6. **Spatial Scanning (SS).** Ability to visualize a path out of a maze or a field with many obstacles. This factor is defined by performance on paper and pencil maze tasks. It is not clear whether this ability is related to complex large-scale real-world navigation skills.
7. **Serial Perceptual Integration (PI).** Ability to recognize an object after only parts of it are shown in rapid succession.
8. **Length Estimation (LE).** The ability to visually estimate the length of objects.
9. **Perceptual Illusions (IL).** The ability to not be fooled by visual illusions.
10. **Perceptual Alternations (PN).** Consistency in the rate of alternating between different visual perceptions.
11. **Imagery (IM).** Ability to mentally imagine very vivid images. Small scale brain imaging studies have suggested that visual spatial imagery may not be a single faculty, rather, visualizing spatial location and mentally transforming locating rely on distinct neural networks. This research suggests a transformational process versus memory for location substructure. An objective versus spatial imagery dichotomy has also been suggested as well as the possibility of quality and speed of imagery abilities.

Auditory Processing (Ga):. *The ability to detect and process meaningful nonverbal information in sound.* This definition may cause confusion because we do not have a well developed vocabulary for talking about sound unless we are talking about speech sounds or music. Ga encompasses both of these domains but also much more. There are two common misperceptions about Ga. First, although Ga depends on sensory input, it is not sensory input itself. Ga is what the brain does with sensory information from the ear, sometimes long after a sound has been heard. The second extremely common misconception is that Ga is oral language comprehension. It is true that one aspect of Ga (parsing speech sounds or Phonetic Coding) is related to oral language comprehension but this is simply a precursor to comprehension, not comprehension itself.

1. **Phonetic Coding (PC).** Ability to hear phonemes distinctly. This ability is also referred to as phonological processing and phonological awareness. People with poor phonetic coding have difficulty hearing the internal structure of sound in words.
2. **Speech Sound Discrimination (US).** Ability to detect and discriminate differences in speech sounds (other than phonemes) under conditions of little or no distraction or distortion. Poor speech sound discrimination can produce difficulty in the ability to distinguish variations in tone, timbre, and pitch in speech.
3. **Resistance to Auditory Stimulus Distortion (UR).** Ability to hear words correctly even under conditions of distortion or loud background noise.
4. **Memory for Sound Patterns (UM).** Ability to retain (on a short-term basis) auditory events such as tones, tonal patterns, and voices.
5. **Maintaining and Judging Rhythm (U8).** Ability to recognize and maintain a musical beat. This may be an aspect of Memory for Sound Patterns as short-term memory is clearly involved. However, it is likely that there is something distinct about rhythm that warrants a distinction.
6. **Musical Discrimination and Judgment (U1 U9).** Ability to discriminate and judge tonal patterns in music with respect to melodic, harmonic, and expressive aspects (phrasing, tempo, harmonic complexity, intensity variations).
7. **Absolute Pitch (UP).** Ability to perfectly identify the pitch of tones. As a historical tidbit, John Carroll had perfect pitch.
8. **Sound Localization (UL).** Ability to localize heard sounds in space.

Olfactory Abilities (Go): *The ability to detect and process meaningful information in odors.* Go refers not to sensitivity of the olfactory system but to the cognition one does with whatever information the nose is able to send. The Go domain is likely to contain many more narrow abilities than currently listed in the CHC model as a cursory skim of Go-related research reveals reference to such abilities as olfactory memory, episodic odor memory, olfactory sensitivity, odor specific abilities, odor identification and detection, odor naming, olfactory imagery, to name but a few.

1. *Olfactory Memory (OM).* Ability to recognize previously encountered distinctive odors. OM is involved in the oft-noted experience of smelling a distinctive smell and being flooded with vivid memories of the last time that odor was encountered. Memory for distinctive odors has a much flatter forgetting curve than many other kinds of memory.

Tactile Abilities (Gh): *The ability to detect and process meaningful information in haptic (touch) sensations.* Gh refers not to sensitivity of touch but to the cognition one does with tactile sensations. Because this ability is not yet well defined and understood, it is hard to describe it authoritatively. The domain may include such abilities as tactile visualization (object identification via palpation), tactile localization (i.e., where has one been touched), tactile memory (i.e., remembering where one has been touched), texture knowledge (naming surfaces and fabrics by touch), and many others. There are no well-supported narrow cognitive ability factors within Gh yet. *Tactile Sensitivity* (TS), a sensory acuity ability, refers to the ability to make fine discriminations in haptic sensations (e.g., if two caliper points are placed on the skin simultaneously, we perceive them as a single point if they are close together. Some people are able to make finer discriminations than others).

Motor

Kinesthetic Abilities (Gk): *The ability to detect and process meaningful information in proprioceptive sensations.* Proprioception refers to the ability to detect limb position and movement via *proprioreceptors* (sensory organs in muscles and ligaments that detect stretching). Gk refers not to the sensitivity of proprioception but to the cognition one does with proprioceptive sensations. There are no well-supported narrow cognitive ability factors within Gk yet. *Kinesthetic Sensitivity* (KS), a sensory acuity ability, refers to the ability to make fine discriminations in proprioceptive sensations (e.g., whether and how much a limb has been moved).

Psychomotor Abilities (Gp): *The ability to perform physical body motor movements (e.g., movement of fingers, hands, legs) with precision, coordination, or strength.*

1. **Static Strength (P3).** The ability to exert muscular force to move (push, lift, pull) a relatively heavy or immobile object.
2. **Multilimb Coordination (P6).** The ability to make quick specific or discrete motor movements of the arms or legs.
3. **Finger Dexterity (P2).** The ability to make precisely coordinated movements of the fingers (with or without the manipulation of objects).
4. **Manual Dexterity (P1).** Ability to make precisely coordinated movements of a hand or a hand and the attached arm.
5. **Arm-Hand Steadiness (P7).** The ability to precisely and skillfully coordinate arm–hand positioning in space.
6. **Control Precision (P8).** The ability to exert precise control over muscle movements, typically in response to environmental feedback (e.g., changes in speed or position of object being manipulated).
7. **Aiming (AI).** The ability to precisely and fluently execute a sequence of eye–hand coordination movements for positioning purposes.
8. **Gross Body Equilibrium (P4).** The ability to maintain the body in an upright position in space or regain balance after balance has been disturbed.

NOTES

Prologue

1. D. Coyle, *The Talent Code: Greatness Isn't Born, It's Grown, Here's How* (New York: Bantam, 2009); G. Colvin, *Talent Is Overrated* (New York: Portfolio Trade, 2010); M. Gladwell, *Outliers: The Story of Success* (New York: Back Bay Books, 2008); D. Shenk, *The Genius in All of Us: New Insights into Genetics, Talent and IQ* (New York: Anchor Books, 2011); M. Syed, *Bounce: Mozart, Federer, Picasso, Beckham, and the Science of Success* (New York: Harper, 2010); P. Tough, *How Children Succeed: Grit, Curiosity, and the Hidden Power of Character* (New York: Houghton Mifflin Harcourt, 2012); R. Greene, *Mastery* (New York: Viking, 2012); P. Bronson and A. Merryman, *Top Dog: The Science of Winning and Losing* (New York: Twelve, 2013).

Chapter 1

1. S. B. Kaufman, ed., *The Complexity of Greatness: Beyond Talent or Practice* (New York: Oxford University Press, 2013).

2. I. Kant, *The Critique of Judgement*, in *Great Books of the Western World*, ed. R.M. Hutchins, 2:459–613 (Chicago: Encyclopaedia Britannica, 1952). (Originally published 1790.)

3. J. Reynolds, *Discourses on Art* (New York: Collier, 1966), 37. (Originally published 1769–1790.)

4. F. Galton, *Hereditary Genius* (London: Macmillan, 1869).

5. F. Galton, *Memories of My Life* (London: Methuen, 1908), at 205.

6. F. Galton, *English Men of Science: Their Nature and Nurture* (London: Macmillan, 1874).

7. A. de Candolle, *Histoire des sciences et des savants depuis deux siècles* (Geneva: Georg, 1873).

8. T. J. Bouchard Jr., D. T. Lykken, M. McGue, N. L. Segal, and A. Tellegen, "Sources of Human Psychological Differences: The Minnesota Study of Twins Reared Apart," *Science* 250 (1990): 223–228.

9. W. Johnson, E. Turkheimer, I. I. Gottesman, and T. J. Bouchard Jr., "Beyond Heritability: Twin Studies in Behavioral Research," *Current Directions in Psychological Science* 18 (2009): 217–220.

10. S. Pinker, *The Blank Slate: The Modern Denial of Human Nature* (New York: Penguin Books, 2003).

11. D. Moore, *The Dependent Gene: The Fallacy of Nature vs. Nurture* (New York: Henry Holt, 2003); D. S. Moore, "A Very Little Bit of Knowledge: Re-Evaluating the Meaning of the

Heritability of IQ," *Human Development* 49 (2006): 347–353; S. B. Kaufman, "Straight Talk About Twin Studies, Genes, and Parenting: What Makes Us Who We Are," *Beautiful Minds* (blog), *Psychology Today,* October 24, 2008, http://www.psychologytoday.com/blog/beautiful -minds/200810/straight-talk-about-twin-studies-genes-and-parenting-what-makes-us -who-w.

12. L. T. Rose and K. Ellison, *Square Peg: My Story and What It Means for Raising Innovators, Visionaries, and Out-of-the-Box Thinkers* (New York: Hyperion, 2013); L. T. Rose and K. W. Fischer, "Intelligence in Childhood," in *The Cambridge Handbook of Intelligence,* ed. R. J. Sternberg and S. B. Kaufman, 130–143 (New York: Cambridge University Press, 2011); P. C. M. Molenaar and C. G. Campbell, "The New Person-Specific Paradigm in Psychology," *Current Directions in Psychological Science* 18 (2009): 112–117.

13. P. C. M. Molenaar, D. J. A. Smit, D. I. Boomsma, and J. R. Nesselroade, "Estimation of Subject-Specific Heritabilities from Intra-individual Variation: iFACE," *Twin Research and Human Genetics* 15 (2012): 393–400.

14. P. C. M. Molenaar, H. M. Huizenga, and J. R. Nesselroade, "The Relationship Between the Structure of Interindividual and Intraindividual Variability: A Theoretical and Empirical Vindication of Developmental Systems Theory," in *Understanding Human Development: Dialogues with Life-Span Psychology,* ed. U. M. Staudinger and U. Lindenberger (Dordrecht, the Netherlands: Kluwer, 2003); E. L. Hamaker, J. R. Nesselroade, and P. C. M. Molenaar, "The Integrated Trait-State Model," *Journal of Research in Personality* 41 (2007): 295–315.

15. C. A. Prescott, R. C. Johnson, and J. J. McArdle, "Genetic Contributions to Television Viewing," *Psychological Science* 2 (1991): 430–431.

16. R. Plomin, J. C. DeFries, V. S. Knopik, and J. M. Neiderhiser, *Behavioral Genetics,* vol. 6 (New York: Worth, 2012); C. M. A. Haworth et al., "The Heritability of General Cognitive Ability Increases Linearly from Childhood to Young Adulthood," *Molecular Psychiatry* 15 (2010): 1112–1120.

17. J. R. Harris, *The Nurture Assumption: Why Children Turn Out the Way They Do,* rev. ed. (New York: Free Press, 2009).

18. E. M. Tucker-Drob, M. Rhemtulla, K. P. Harden, E. Turkheimer, and D. Fask, "Emergence of a Gene x Socioeconomic Status Interaction on Infant Mental Ability between 10 Months and 2 Years," *Psychological Science* 22 (2011): 125–133.

19. Johnson et al., "Beyond Heritability," at 218.

20. R. Plomin and J. Crabbe, "DNA," *Psychological Bulletin* 126 (2000): 806–828, at 806.

21. K. Silventoinen et al., "Heritability of Adult Body Height: A Comparative Study of Twin Cohorts in Eight Countries," *Twin Research and Human Genetics* 6 (2003): 399–408.

22. D. F. Gudbjartsson, D. F. Walters, H. S. Thorleifsson, et al., "Many Sequence Variants Affecting Diversity of Adult Human Height," *Nature Genetics* 40 (2008): 609–615; G. Lettre, A. U. Jackson, C. Gieger, et al., "Identification of Ten Loci Associated with Height Highlights New Biological Pathways in Human Growth," *Nature Genetics* 5 (2008): 584–591; M. N. Weedon, H. Lango, C. M. Lindgren, et al., "Genome-Wide Association Analysis Identifies 20 Loci That Influence Adult Height," *Nature Genetics* 40 (2008): 575–583.

23. G. Davies et al., "Genome-Wide Association Studies Establish That Human Intelligence Is Highly Heritable and Polygenic," *Molecular Psychiatry* 16 (2011): 996–1005.

24. C. F. Chabris et al., "Most Reported Genetic Associations with General Intelligence Are Probably False Positives," *Psychological Science* 23 (2011): 1314–1323.

25. Although there are a few exceptions, such as Huntington's disease.

26. E. Turkheimer, "Genome Wide Association Studies of Behavior Are Social Science," *Philosophy of Behavioral Biology* 282 (2012): 43–64, at 62.

27. W. Johnson, "Greatness as a Manifestation of Experience-Producing Drives," in *The Complexity of Greatness: Beyond Talent or Practice*, ed. S. B. Kaufman, 3–16 (New York: Oxford University Press, 2013).

28. Moore, *The Dependent Gene*.

29. Johnson, *Greatness as a Manifestation*.

30. M. Ridley, *Nature via Nurture: Genes, Experience, and What Makes Us Human* (New York: Harper, 2003).

31. C. H. Waddington, "Canalization of Development and the Inheritance of Acquired Characters," *Nature* 150 (1942): 563–565; J. L. Hartman, B. Garvik, and L. Hartwell, "Principles for the Buffering of Genetic Variation," *Science* 291 (2001): 1001–1004.

32. G. Marcus, *The Birth of the Mind: How a Tiny Number of Genes Creates the Complexities of Human Thought* (New York: Basic Books, 2004), at 169.

33. E. Turkheimer and I. I. Gottesman, "Individual Differences and the Canalization of Human Behavior," *Developmental Psychology* 27 (1991): 18–22.

34. G. Gibson and I. Dworkin, "Uncovering Cryptic Genetic Variation," *Nature Reviews Genetics* 5 (2004): 681–690; C. D. Schlichting, "Hidden Reaction Norms, Cryptic Genetic Variation, and Evolvability," *Annals of the New York Academy of Sciences* 1133 (2008): 187–203; W. Johnson, "Developmental Genetics and Psychopathology: Some New Feathers for a Fine Old Hat," *Development and Psychopathology* 24 (2012): 1165–1177.

35. S. J. Ceci, S. M. Barnett, and T. Kanaya, "Developing Childhood Proclivities into Adult Competencies: The Overlooked Multiplier Effect," in *The Psychology of Abilities, Competences, and Expertise*, ed. R. J. Sternberg and E. L. Grigorenko, 70–92 (New York: Cambridge University Press, 2008).

36. R. K. Merton, "The Matthew Effect in Science," *Science* 159 (1968): 56–63.

37. U. Bronfenbrenner and S. Ceci, "Nature-Nurture Reconceptualized in Developmental Perspective: A Bioecological Model," *Psychological Review* 101 (1994): 568–586; J. Gleick, *Chaos: Making a New Science* (New York: Viking Penguin, 1987); S. Ceci, *On Intelligence . . . More or Less: A Biological Treatise on Intellectual Development*, 2nd ed. (Cambridge, MA: Harvard University Press, 1996).

38. J. Belsky and K. M. Beaver, "Cumulative-Genetic Plasticity, Parenting and Adolescent Self-Regulation," *Journal of Child Psychology and Psychiatry* 52 (2011): 619–626; R. G. Grazioplene, C. G. DeYoung, F. A. Rogosch, and D. Cicchetti, "A Novel Differential Susceptibility Gene: CHRNA4 and Moderation of the Effect of Maltreatment on Child Personality," *Journal of Child Psychology and Psychiatry* (2012), doi:10.1111/jcpp.12031.

39. B. J. Ellis and W. T. Boyce, "Biological Sensitivity to Context: I. An Evolutionary-Developmental Theory of the Origins and Functions of Stress Reactivity," *Development and Psychopathology* 17 (2005): 271–301; B. J. Ellis, M. J. Essex, and W. Thomas Boyce, "Biological Sensitivity to Context: II. Empirical Explorations of an Evolutionary-Developmental Theory," *Development and Psychopathology* 17 (2005): 303–328.

40. D. Dobbs, "The Science of Success," *The Atlantic*, December 2009; J. Belsky and M. Pluess, "The Nature (and Nurture?) of Plasticity in Early Human Development," *Perspectives on Psychological Science* 4 (2009): 345–351; S. Cain, *Quiet: The Power of Introverts in a World That Can't Stop Talking* (New York: Broadway, 2012).

41. J. Belsky, M. J. Bakermans-Kranenburg, and M. H. van IJzendoorn, "For Better and for Worse: Differential Susceptibility to Environmental Influences," *Current Directions in Psychological Science* 6 (2007): 300–304; E. N. Aron, A. Aron, and J. Jagiellowicz, "Sensory Processing Sensitivity: A Review in the Light of the Evolution of Biological Responsivity," *Personality and Social Psychology Review* 16 (2012): 262–282.

42. R. C. Hill and F. P. Stafford, "The Allocation of Time to Preschool Children and Educational Opportunity," *Journal of Human Resources* 9 (1974): 323–341; D. T. Willingham, "Ask the Cognitive Scientist: Why Does Family Wealth Affect Learning?," *American Educator*

36 (2012): 33–39; J. Protzko, J. Aronson, and C. Blair, "How to Make a Young Child Smarter: Evidence from the Database of Raising Intelligence," *Perspectives on Psychological Science* 8 (2013): 25–40.

43. K. E. Stanovich, "Matthew Effects in Reading: Some Consequences of Individual Differences in the Acquisition of Literacy," *Reading Research Quarterly* 21 (1986): 360–406.

44. B. Hart and T. R. Risley, *Meaningful Differences in the Everyday Experience of Young American Children* (Baltimore: Paul H. Brookes, 1995).

45. R. H. Bradley, L. Whiteside, B. Caldwell, et al., "Maternal IQ, the Home Environment, and Child IQ in Low Birthweight, Premature Children," *International Journal of Behavioral Development* 16 (1993): 61–74; M. Phillips, J. Brooks-Gunn, G. J. Duncan, P. K. Klebanov, and J. Crane, "Family Background, Parenting Practices, and the Black–White Test Score Gap," in *The Black–White Test Score Gap,* ed. C. Jencks and M. Phillips, 102–145 (Washington, DC: Brookings Institution Press, 1998).

46. C. Locurto, "The Malleability of IQ as Judged from Adoption Studies," *Intelligence* 14 (1990): 275–292; M. Duyme, A. Dumaret, and S. Tomkiewicz, "How Can We Boost IQs of 'Dull' Children? A Late Adoption Study," *Proceedings of the National Academy of Sciences, USA* 96 (1999): 8790–8794; M. H. van IJzendoorn, F. Juffer, and C. W. K. Poelhuis, "Adoption and Cognitive Development: A Meta-Analytic Comparison of Adopted and Non-adopted Children's IQ and School Performance," *Psychological Bulletin* 131 (2005): 301–316. Although the adopted children do not do as well as the biological siblings in those families; see Nancy L. Segal's work on virtual twins in her *Someone Else's Twin: The True Story of Babies Switched at Birth* (New York: Prometheus Books, 2011).

47. B. A. Shaywitz, T. R. Holford, J. M. Holahan, et al., "A Matthew Effect for IQ but Not for Reading: Results from a Longitudinal Study," *Reading Research Quarterly* 30 (1995): 894–906.

48. H. J. Walberg and S.-L. Tsai, "Matthew Effects in Education," *American Educational Research Journal* 20 (1983): 359–373.

49. S. Scarr and K. McCartney, "How People Make Their Own Environments: A Theory of Genotype → Environment Effects," *Child Development* 54 (1983): 424–435.

50. K. J. Hayes, "Genes, Drives, and Intellect," *Psychological Reports* 10 (1962): 299–342; T. J. Bouchard Jr., "Experience Producing Drive Theory: How Genes Drive Experience and Shape Personality," *Acta Paediatrica Supplement* 422 (1997): 60–64.

51. W. Johnson, "Extending and Testing Tom Bouchard's Experience Producing Drive Theory—Revised," *Personality and Individual Differences, Special Issue,* 49 (2010): 296–301; Johnson, "Greatness as a Manifestation of Experience-Producing Drives," in *The Complexity of Greatness: Beyond Talent or Practice,* ed. S. B. Kaufman (New York: Oxford University Press, 2013).

52. Kant, *The Critique of Judgement.*

53. D. K. Simonton, *Scientific Genius: A Psychology of Science* (New York: Cambridge University Press, 1988).

54. For a list of some of this generation's highest IQ test scores (although some of the listed scores are estimated), see the *Huffington Post* article, "Smartest People in the World: The 10 Smartest People Alive Today," September 27, 2012.

55. Kaufman, *The Complexity of Greatness;* D. K. Simonton, *Greatness: Who Makes History and Why* (New York: The Guilford Press, 1994); D. K. Simonton, "Exceptional Creativity and Chance: Creative Thought as a Stochastic Combinatorical Process," in *Beyond Knowledge: Extracognitive Aspects of Developing High Ability,* ed. L. V. Shavinina and M. Ferrari, 39–72 (Mahwah, NJ: Lawrence Erlbaum Associates, 2004); G. J. Feist and F. X. Barron, "Predicting Creativity from Early to Late Adulthood: Intellect, Potential, and Personality," *Journal of Research in Personality* 37 (2003): 62–88; G. J. Feist, "How Development and

Personality Influence Scientific Thought, Interest, and Achievement," *Review of General Psychology* 10 (2006): 163–182; G. Feist, "Scientific Talent: Nature Shaped by Nurture," in *The Complexity of Greatness: Beyond Talent or Practice*, ed. S. B. Kaufman (New York: Oxford University Press, 2013); D. K. Simonton, "Scientific Talent, Training, and Performance: Intellect, Personality, and Genetic Endowment," *Review of General Psychology* 12 (2008): 28–46.

56. D. K. Simonton, "Talent and Its Development: An Emergenic and Epigenetic Model," *Psychological Review* 106 (1999): 435–457.

57. G. Marcus, *Guitar Zero: The New Musician and the Science of Learning* (New York: Penguin, 2012).

58. Ibid., at 103.

Chapter 2

1. Quoted in T. Wolf, *Alfred Binet* (Chicago: University of Chicago Press, 1973).

2. R. S. Siegler, "The Other Alfred Binet," *Developmental Psychology* 28 (1992): 179–190.

3. R. B. Cairns, "The Emergence of Developmental Psychology," in *Handbook of Child Psychology: History, Theory, and Methods*, ed. W. Kessen, 41–102 (New York: Wiley, 1983), at 47.

4. Quoted in Wolf, *Alfred Binet*, at 23.

5. Ibid., at 36.

6. Siegler, "The Other Alfred Binet," at 186.

7. A. Binet and V. Henri, "Le développement de la mémoire visuelle chez les enfants," *Revue Générale des Sciences Pures et Appliquées* 5 (1894): 162–169, at 167. Translated by J. Carson, *The Measure of Merit: Talents, Intelligence, and Inequality in the French and American Republics, 1750–1940* (Princeton: Princeton University Press, 2007), at 132.

8. A. Binet and V. Henri, "La psychologie individuelle," *L'Année Psychologique* 2 (1895): 411–465, translated by S. E Sharp as "Individual Psychology: A Study in Psychological Method," *American Journal of Psychology* 10 (1899): 329–391, at 14.

9. T. Wolf, *Alfred Binet*.

10. A. Binet, *L'étude expérimentale de l'intelligence* (Paris: Schleicher Frères, 1903).

11. A. Binet, "The Perception of Lengths and Numbers in Some Small Children," *Revue Philosophique* 30 (1890): 68–81, translated by T. Wolf as "Intuition and Experiment: Alfred Binet's First Efforts in Child Psychology," *Journal of the History of the Behavioral Sciences* 2 (1966): 233–239, at 235.

12. A. Binet and T. Simon, "New Methods for the Diagnosis of the Intellectual Level of Subnormals," in *The Development of Intelligence in Children*, ed. H. H. Goddard, trans. E. S. Kite (Nashville, TN: Williams Printing Co., 1916/1980), at 42–43. (Originally published 1905.)

13. Ibid.

14. Ibid., at 37.

15. A. Binet and T. Simon, *The Development of Intelligence in Children*.

16. J. S. Mill, *A System of Logic Ratiocinative and Inductive, Being a Connected View of the Principles of Evidence and the Methods of Scientific Investigation*, 2 vols., 9th ed. (London: Longmans, Green, Reader and Dyer, 1875), at 432.

17. Binet and Simon, *The Development of Intelligence in Children*.

18. Siegler, "The Other Alfred Binet."

19. A. Binet and T. Simon, "New Investigations upon the Measure of the Intellectual Level among School Children," in *The Development of Intelligence in Children*, 274–329. (Originally published 1911.)

20. Wolf, *Alfred Binet*.

21. A. S. Kaufman, *IQ Testing 101* (New York: Springer, 2011).

22. Binet and Simon, "New Methods," at 10.

23. J. Carson, *The Measure of Merit.*

24. A. Binet, *Modern Ideas about Children,* trans. S. Heisler (Menlo Park, CA: Suzanne Heisler, 1975), at 105–107. (Originally published 1909.)

25. H. H. Goddard, editor's introduction, in Goddard, *Development of Intelligence in Children,* 5–8.

26. H. H. Goddard, *Human Efficiency and Levels of Intelligence* (Princeton, NJ: Princeton University Press, 1920), at 1; L. Zenderland, *Measuring Minds: Henry Herbert Goddard and the Origins of American Intelligence Testing* (New York: Cambridge University Press, 1998).

27. D. J. Kevles, *In the Name of Eugenics: Genetics and the Uses of Human Heredity* (New York: Knopf, 1985).

28. L. M. Terman, *The Measurement of Intelligence* (Boston: Houghton Mifflin, 1916), at 6–7.

29. L. Terman, *Genetic Studies of Genius,* vol. 1: *Mental and Physical Traits of a Thousand Gifted Children* (Stanford: Stanford University Press, 1925), at 2–3.

30. Terman, *Measurement of Intelligence.*

31. W. Stern, *Die psychologische Methoden der Intelligenzprufung* (Leipzig: Barth, 1912).

32. L. M. Terman and M. A. Merrill, *Measuring Intelligence* (Boston: Houghton Mifflin, 1937).

33. Ibid., at 80.

34. L. M. Terman, "An Autobiography," in *A History of Psychology in Autobiography,* vol. 2, ed. C. Murchison (Worcester, MA: Clark University Press, 1932).

35. D. Wechsler, *Measurement of Adult Intelligence* (Baltimore: Williams and Wilkins, 1939).

36. Terman and Merrill, *Measuring Intelligence.*

37. Kaufman, *IQ Testing 101.*

38. R. L. Thorndike, E. P. Hagen, and J. M. Sattler, *Stanford-Binet Intelligence Scale,* 4th ed. (Chicago: Riverside, 1986).

39. A. S. Kaufman, *Intelligent Testing with the WISC-R* (New York: Wiley, 1979).

40. Ibid., at 161–162.

41. G. Roid, *Stanford-Binet Intelligence Scales,* 5th ed. (Itasca, IL: Riverside, 2003); D. Wechsler, *Wechsler Intelligence Scale for Children—Fourth Edition (WISC-IV)* (San Antonio: Psychological Corporation, 2003); Wechsler, *Wechsler Adult Intelligence Scale—Fourth Edition (WAIS-IV)* (San Antonio: Psychological Corporation, 2008).

42. Kaufman, *IQ Testing 101.*

43. T. Z. Keith, "Questioning the K-ABC: What Does It Measure?," *School Psychology Review* 14 (1985): 9–20.

44. K. S. McGrew, "The Cattell-Horn-Carroll Theory of Cognitive Abilities: Past, Present, and Future," in *Contemporary Intellectual Assessment: Theories, Tests, and Issues,* ed. D. P. Flanagan and P. L. Harrison, 2nd ed., 136–181 (New York: Guilford Press, 2005), at 144, 149.

45. K. S. McGrew, "Analysis of the Major Intelligence Batteries According to a Proposed Comprehensive *Gf-Gc* Framework," in *Contemporary Intellectual Assessment: Theories, Tests, and Issues,* ed. D. P. Flanagan, J. L. Genshaft, and P. L. Harrison, 151–179 (New York: Guilford Press, 1997); K. S. McGrew, "The Cattell-Horn-Carroll Model of Intelligence," in *Contemporary Intellectual Assessment: Theories, Tests, and Issues,* ed. D. P. Flanagan and P. L. Harrison, 3rd ed., 99–144 (New York: Guilford Press, 2012).

46. D. Flanagan, & K. McGrew, "A Cross-Battery Approach to Assessing and Interpreting Cognitive Abilities. Narrowing the Gap Between Practice and Science," in *Contemporary Intellectual Assessment,* 314–325; D. P. Flanagan, S. O. Ortiz, and V. C. Alfonso, *Essentials of Cross-Battery Assessment,* 2nd ed. (Hoboken, NJ: Wiley, 2007).

47. G. Roid, *Stanford-Binet Intelligence Scales,* 5th ed. (Itasca, IL: Riverside, 2003); A. S. Kaufman, E. O. Lichtenberger, E. Fletcher-Janzen, and N. L. Kaufman, *Essentials of KABC-II Assessment* (Hoboken, NJ: Wiley, 2005); R. W. Woodcock, K. S. McGrew, and N. Mather, *Woodcock-Johnson III* (Itasca, IL: Riverside, 2001); C. D. Elliot, *Differential Ability Scales— Second Edition (DAS II)* (San Antonio, TX: The Psychological Corporation, 2007).

48. I used the following reference as a guide to the CHC mappings: T. Z. Keith and M. R. Reynolds, "Using Confirmatory Factor Analysis to Aid in Understanding the Constructs Measured by Intelligence Tests," in *Contemporary Intellectual Assessment*, 3rd ed.

49. K. S. McGrew and B. J. Wendling, "Cattell-Horn-Carroll Cognitive-Achievement Relations: What We Have Learned from the Past 20 Years of Research, *Psychology in the Schools* 47 (2010): 651–675.

Chapter 3

1. J. Kerr, "School Hygiene in Its Mental, Moral and Physical Aspects," *Journal of the Royal Statistical Society* 60 (1897): 613–680; C. Schmitt, "Extreme Retardation in Arithmetic," *Elementary School Journal* 21 (1921): 529–547.

2. W. P. Morgan, "A Case of Congenital Wordblindness," *British Medical Journal* 2 (1896), at 1378.

3. S. Orton, "Specific Reading Disability—Strephosymbolia," *Journal of the American Medical Association* 90 (1928): 1095–1099.

4. A. A. Strauss and H. Werner, "Comparative Psychopathology of the Brain-Injured Child and the Traumatic Brain-Injured Adult," *American Journal of Psychiatry* 99 (1943): 835–838.

5. A. A. Strauss and L. E. Lehtinen, *Psychopathology and Education of the Brain-Injured Child,* vol. 2: *Progress in Theory and Clinic* (New York: Grune and Stratton, 1947).

6. J. E. Peters, J. J. Davis, C. M. Goolsby, and S. D. Clements, *Physician's Handbook: Screening for MBD* (New York: CIBA Medical Horizons, 1973).

7. D. D. Hammill and N. R. Bartel, *Teaching Children with Learning and Behavior Problems,* 2nd ed. (Boston: Houghton-Mifflin, 1978).

8. M. J. Shepherd, "History Lessons," in *Specific Learning Disabilities and Difficulties in Children and Adolescents: Psychological Assessment and Evaluation,* ed. A. S. Kaufman and N. L. Kaufman, 3–28 (Cambridge: Cambridge University Press, 2001).

9. S. A. Kirk, "Behavioral Diagnosis and Remediation of Learning Disabilities," *Proceedings of the Annual Meeting of the Conference on Exploration into the Problems of the Perceptually Handicapped Child* (Chicago) 1 (1963): 3–7.

10. U.S. Office of Education, *First Annual Report of the National Advisory Committee on Handicapped Children* (Washington, DC: Author, 1968).

11. A. S. Kaufman, *IQ Testing 101* (New York: Springer, 2009).

12. S. A. Cohen, "Dyspedagogia as a Cause of Reading Retardation: Definition and Treatment," in *Learning Disorders,* ed. B. Bateman (Seattle: Special Child Press, 1971), 4:269–291.

13. M. Rutter and W. Yule, "The Concept of Specific Reading Retardation," *Journal of Child Psychology and Psychiatry* 16 (1975): 181–197.

14. I. J. Deary, L. J. Whalley, H. Lemmon, J. R. Crawford, and J. M. Starr, "The Stability of Individual Differences in Mental Ability from Childhood to Old Age: Follow-up of the 1932 Scottish Mental Survey," *Intelligence* 28 (2000): 49–55; I. J. Deary, M. C. Whiteman, J. M. Starr, L. J. Whalley, and H. C. Fox, "The Impact of Childhood Intelligence on Later Life: Following Up the Scottish Mental Surveys of 1932 and 1947," *Journal of Personality and Social Psychology* 86 (2004): 130–147; J. F. Fagan, C. R. Holland, and K. Wheeler, "The Prediction, from Infancy, of Adult IQ and Achievement," *Intelligence* 35 (2007): 225–231; S. A. Rose,

J. F. Feldman, and J. J. Jankowski, "Information Processing in Toddlers: Continuity from Infancy and Persistence of Preterm Deficits," *Intelligence* 37 (2009): 311–320.

15. E. Ramos, V. Alfonso, and S. M. B. Schermerhorn, "Graduate Students' Administered Scoring Errors on the Woodcock-Johnson III Tests of Cognitive Abilities," *Psychology in the Schools* 46 (2009): 651–657.

16. K. S. McGrew, *IAP AP101 Brief #10: Understanding IQ Score Differences: Examiner Errors* (2011), http://www.iqscorner.com/2011/09/iap-ap101-brief-10-understanding-iq.html.

17. Kaufman, *IQ Testing 101*, at 141.

18. K. S. McGrew, "Understanding Global IQ Test Correlations," *Applied Psychometrics 101: IQ Test Score Difference Series #1* (2009), http://www.iapsych.com/iapap101/iapap101_1 .pdf.

19. S. J. Ceci, "How Much Does Schooling Influence Intelligence and Its Cognitive Components? A Reassessment of the Evidence," *Developmental Psychology* 27 (1991): 703–722.

20. P. Shaw et al., "Intellectual Ability and Cortical Development in Children and Adolescents," *Nature* 440 (2006): 676–679; S. Ramsden et al., "Verbal and Non-Verbal Intelligence Changes in the Teenage Brain," *Nature* 479 (2011): 113–116.

21. A. L. Duckworth, P. D. Quinn, D. R. Lynam, et al., "Role of Test Motivation in Intelligence Testing," *PNAS* 19 (2011): 7716–7720.

22. J. A. Naglieri and B. T. Bornstein, "Intelligence and Achievement: Just How Correlated Are They?," *Journal of Psychoeducational Assessment* 21 (2003): 244–260.

23. M. C. Wang, G. D. Haertel, and H. J. Walberg, "Toward a Knowledge Base for School Learning," *Review of Educational Research* 63 (1993): 249–295.

24. A. L. Duckworth, P. D. Quinn, and E. Tsukayama, "What No Child Leaves Behind: The Roles of IQ and Self-Control in Predicting Standardized Achievement Test Scores and Report Card Grades," *Journal of Educational Psychology* 104 (2012): 439–451.

25. K. S. McGrew, *Expectations for Students with Cognitive Disabilities: Is the Cup Half Empty or Half Full? Can the Cup Flow Over?* Synthesis Report 54 (Minneapolis: University of Minnesota, National Center on Educational Outcomes, 2004).

26. C. Burt, *The Backward Child* (London: University of London Press, 1937), at 477.

27. R. Sternberg and E. Grigorenko, *Our Labeled Children: What Every Parent and Teacher Needs to Know about Learning Disabilities* (Reading, MA: Perseus Books, 1999).

28. P. A. Zirkel and L. B. Thomas, "State Laws for RTI: An Updated Snapshot," *Teaching Exceptional Children* 42, no. 3 (2010): 56–63.

29. J. M. Fletcher, D. J. Francis, S. E. Shaywitz, et al., "Intelligent Testing and the Discrepancy Model for Children with Learning Disabilities," *Learning Disabilities Research and Practice* 13 (1998): 186–203.

30. S. E. Shaywitz, J. M. Fletcher, J. M. Holahan, et al., "Persistence of Dyslexia: The Connecticut Longitudinal Study at Adolescence," *Pediatrics* 104 (1999): 1351–1359.

31. J.M. Fletcher, G. R. Lyon, L. S. Fuchs, and M. A. Barnes, *Learning Disabilities: From Identification to Intervention* (New York: Guilford Press, 2007); K. K. Stuebing, A. E. Barth, et al., "IQ Is *Not* Strongly Related to Response to Reading Instruction: A Meta-Analytic Interpretation," *Exceptional Children* 76 (2009): 31–51; F. R. Vellutino, D. M. Scanlon, and G. R. Lyon, "Differentiating between Difficult to Remediate and Readily Remediated Poor Readers: More Evidence against the IQ Achievement Discrepancy Definition of Reading Disability," *Journal of Learning Disabilities* 33 (2000): 223–238.

32. U.S. Department of Education, *Individuals with Disabilities Education Improvement Act*, 20 U.S.C. § 1400 (Washington, DC: Author, 2004).

33. Kaufman, *IQ Testing 101*, at 275.

34. K. S. McGrew and B. J. Wendling, "Cattell-Horn-Carroll Cognitive-Achievement Relations: What We Have Learned from the Past 20 Years of Research," *Psychology in the Schools* 47 (2010): 651–675, at 670.

35. D. P. Flanagan, V. C. Alfonso, J. T. Mascolo, and M. Sotelo-Dynega, "Use of Ability Tests in the Identification of Specific Learning Disabilities within the Context of an Operational Definition," in *Contemporary Intellectual Assessment*, ed. D. P. Flanagan and P. L. Harrison, 3rd ed. (New York: Guilford Press, 2012).

36. N. Mather and L. E. Jaffe, *Woodcock-Johnson III: Reports, Recommendations, and Strategies* (New York: Wiley, 2002).

37. D. P. Flanagan, C. A. Fiorello, and S. O. Ortiz, "Enhancing Practice Through Application of Cattell-Horn-Carroll Theory and Research: A 'Third Method' Approach to Specific Learning Disability Identification," *Psychology in the Schools* 47 (2010): 739–760.

38. K. A. Kavale, "Identifying Specific Learning Disability: Is Responsiveness to Intervention the Answer?," *Journal of Learning Disabilities* 38 (2005): 553–562.

39. D. P. Flanagan, S. O. Ortiz, and V. C. Alfonso, "The Pattern of Strengths and Weaknesses Analyzer (PSW-A v1.0)," in *Essentials of Cross-Battery Assessment*, 3rd ed., ed. D. P. Flanagan, S. O. Ortiz, and V. C. Alfonso (Hoboken, NJ: Wiley, 2013).

40. H. Blume, "Neurodiversity," *The Atlantic*, September 1998.

41. T. Armstrong, *Neurodiversity: Discovering the Extraordinary Gifts of Autism, ADHD, Dyslexia, and Other Brain Differences* (Cambridge, MA: Da Capo Lifelong Books, 2010).

42. B. L. Eide and F. F. Eide, *The Dyslexic Advantage: Unlocking the Hidden Potential of the Dyslexic Brain* (New York: Plume, 2012).

43. C. von Karolyi, E. Winner, W. Gray, and G. F. Sherman, "Dyslexia Linked to Talent: Global Visual-Spatial Ability," *Brain and Language* 85 (2003): 427–431.

44. M. L. Lorusso, A. Facoetti, S. Pesenti, et al., "Wider Recognition in Peripheral Vision Common to Different Subtypes of Dyslexia," *Vision Research* 44 (2004): 2413–2424.

45. G. Geiger and J. Y. Lettvin, "Developmental Dyslexia: A Different Perceptual Strategy and How to Learn a New Strategy for Reading," *Saggi Neuropsicologia Infantile—Psicopedagogia Reabilitazione* 26 (2000): 73–89.

46. G. Geiger, C. Cattaneo, R. Galli, et al., "Wide and Diffuse Perceptual Modes Characterize Dyslexics in Vision and Audition," *Perception* 37 (2008): 1745–1764.

47. M. H. Schneps, J. R. Brockmole, G. Sonnert, and M. Pomplun, "History of Reading Struggles Linked to Enhanced Learning in Low Spatial Frequency Scenes," *PLoS ONE* 7 (2012): e35724.

48. A. Murphy Paul, "The Upside of Dyslexia," *New York Times*, February 4, 2012, http://www.nytimes.com/2012/02/05/opinion/sunday/the-upside-of-dyslexia.html.

49. J. Logan, "Dyslexic Entrepreneurs: The Incidence; Their Coping Strategies and Their Business Skills," *Dyslexia* 15 (2009): 328–346.

50. Ibid., at 344.

51. U. Wolff and I. Lunderberg, "The Prevalence of Dyslexia among Art Students," *Dyslexia* 8 (2002): 34–42.

52. Nicola Brunswick, *Living with Dyslexia* (New York: Rosen Publishing Group, 2011), at 60.

53. S. B. Kaufman, "Introducing Conversations on Creativity (Starting with Writer Piers Anthony)," *Beautiful Minds* (blog), *Psychology Today*, Novemer 3, 2008, http://www.psychologytoday.com/blog/beautiful-minds/200811/introducing-conversations-creativity-starting-writer-piers-anthony.

Chapter 4

1. L. M. Terman, "The Physical and Mental Traits of Gifted Children," in *Report of the Society's Committee on the Education of Gifted Children*, ed. G. M. Whipple, 157–167 (Bloomington, IL: Public School Publishing, 1924).

2. L. M. Terman, "The Intelligence Quotient of Francis Galton in Childhood," *American Journal of Psychology* 28 (1917): 209–215.

3. Ibid., at 210.

4. Ibid., at 214.

5. L. M. Terman, *The Measurement of Intelligence* (Boston: Houghton Mifflin, 1916), at 14.

6. S. Scarr, "Culture-Fair and Culture-Free Tests," in *Encyclopedia of Human Intelligence*, ed. Robert J. Sternberg, 322–328 (New York: Macmillan, 1994).

7. M. G. P. Hessels and J. H. M. Hamers, "A Learning Potential Test for Ethnic Minorities," in *Learning Potential Assessment: Theoretical, Methodological and Practical Issues*, ed. J. H. M. Hamers, K. Sijtsma, and A. J. J. M. Ruijssenaars, 285–311 (Amsterdam: Swets and Zeitlinger, 1993); D. F. Lohman, "Identifying Academically Gifted Children in a Linguistically and Culturally Diverse Society" (invited presentation at the Eighth Biennial Henry B. & Jocelyn Wallace National Research Symposium on Talent Development, University of Iowa, Iowa City, 2006).

8. D. F. Lohman and J. L. Gambrell, "Using Nonverbal Tests to Help Identify Academically Talented Children," *Journal of Psychoeducational Assessment* 30 (2012): 25–44.

9. D. F. Lohman, "The Role of Nonverbal Ability Tests in Identifying Academically Gifted Students: An Aptitude Perspective," *Gifted Child Quarterly* 49 (2005): 111–138.

10. Lohman and Gambrell, "Using Nonverbal Tests to Help Identify Academically Talented Children," at 30. Also see R. L. Rhodes, S. H. Ochoa, and S. O. Ortiz, *Assessing Culturally and Linguistically Diverse Students: A Practical Guide* (New York: Guilford Press, 2005).

11. D. A. Bors and F. Vigneau, "The Effect of Practice on Raven's Advanced Progressive Matrices," *Learning and Individual Differences* 13 (2001): 291–312; L. G. Weiss, D. H. Saklofske, A. Prifitera, and J. A. Holdnack, *Wechsler Intelligence Scale for Children-4 Advanced Clinical Interpretation* (San Diego, CA: Academic Press, 2006); D. F. Lohman, K. Korb, and J. Lakin, "Identifying Academically Gifted English Language Learners Using Nonverbal Tests: A Comparison of the Raven, NNAT, and CogAT," *Gifted Child Quarterly* 52 (2008): 275–296.

12. J. M. Sattler, *Assessment of Children: Cognitive Foundations* (La Mesa, CA: Jerome M. Sattler, 2008); D. F. Lohman, "The Role of Nonverbal Ability Tests in Identifying Academically Gifted Students: An Aptitude Perspective," *Gifted Child Quarterly* 49 (2005): 111–138.

13. J. A. Naglieri, *Naglieri Nonverbal Ability Test*, 2nd ed. (Upper Saddle River, NJ: Pearson, 2008).

14. C. A. Carman and D. K. Taylor, "Socioeconomic Status Effects on Using the Naglieri Nonverbal Ability Test (NNAT) to Identify the Gifted/Talented," *Gifted Child Quarterly* 54 (2010): 75–84.

15. D. F. Lohman and K. A. Korb, "Gifted Today but Not Tomorrow? Longitudinal Changes in Ability and Achievement during Elementary School," *Journal for the Education of the Gifted* 29 (2006): 451–484, at 452.

16. Ibid., at 478.

17. S. B. Kaufman and R. J. Sternberg, "Giftedness in the Euro-American Culture," in *Conceptions of Giftedness: Socio-cultural Perspectives*, ed. S. N. Phillipson and M. McCann, 377–413 (Mahwah, NJ: Lawrence Erlbaum, 2007); S. B. Kaufman and R. J. Sternberg, "Conceptions of Giftedness," in *Handbook of Giftedness in Children: Psycho-educational Theory, Research, and Best Practices*, ed. S. Pfeiffer, 71–92 (New York: Plenum, 2008).

18. J. L. French, ed., *Educating the Gifted* (New York: Henry Holt, 1959).

19. A. J. Tannenbaum, "A History of Giftedness in School and Society," in *International Handbook of Giftedness and Talent*, ed. K. A. Heller, F. J. Monks, R. J. Sternberg, and R. F. Subotnik, 23–55 (Oxford: Elsevier Press, 2000).

20. S. P. Marland, *Education of the Gifted and Talented: Report to the Congress of the United States by the U.S. Commissioner of Education* (Washington, DC: Department of Health, Education, and Welfare, 1972).

21. L. B. Abeel, C. M. Callahan, and S. L. Hunsaker, *The Use of Published Instruments in the Identification of Gifted Students* (Washington, DC: National Association of Gifted Children, 1994).

22. J. S. Renzulli, "What Makes Giftedness? Reexamining a Definition," *Phi Delta Kappan* 60 (1978): 180–184. For a more recent and expanded version of Renzulli's model, see J. S. Renzulli and S. D'Souza, "Intelligences Outside the Normal Curve: Co-cognitive Factors that Contribute to the Creation of Social Capital and Leadership Skills in Young People," in *Critical Issues and Practices in Gifted Education: What the Research Says*, 2nd ed., ed. J. A. Plucker and C. M. Callahan (Waco, TX: Prufrock Press).

23. Renzulli, "What Makes Giftedness? Reexamining a Definition," at 181.

24. J. S. Renzulli, "The Three-Ring Definition of Giftedness: A Developmental Model for Promoting Creative Productivity," in *Conceptions of Giftedness*, 2nd ed., ed. R. J. Sternberg and J. E. Davidson, 246–280 (New York: Cambridge University Press, 2005), at 256.

25. Renzulli, "What Makes Giftedness? Reexamining a Definition," at 5.

26. H. Gardner, *Frames of Mind: The Theory of Multiple Intelligences* (New York: Basic Books, 1983). For Gardner's more recent discussions of his theory, see H. Gardner, *Creating Minds: An Anatomy of Creativity Seen Through the Lives of Freud, Einstein, Picasso, Stravinsky, Eliot, Graham, and Ghandi* (New York: Basic Books, 1993); H. Gardner, *Intelligence Reframed: Multiple Intelligences for the 21st Century* (New York: Basic Books, 2000); H. Gardner, *Multiple Intelligences: New Horizons in Theory and Practice* (New York: Basic Books, 2006); K. Davis, J. Christodoulou, S. Seider, and H. Gardner, "The Theory of Multiple Intelligences," in *The Cambridge Handbook of Intelligence*, ed. R. J. Sternberg and S. B. Kaufman, 485–503 (New York: Cambridge University Press, 2011).

27. R. J. Sternberg, *Beyond IQ: A Triarchic Theory of Human Intelligence* (New York: Cambridge University Press, 1984).

28. R. J. Sternberg, *Successful Intelligence: How Practical and Creative Intelligence Determine Success in Life* (New York: Plume, 1997); R. J. Sternberg, "The Theory of Successful Intelligence," in *Cambridge Handbook of Intelligence*, 504–527.

29. R. J. Sternberg, *Wisdom, Intelligence, and Creativity Synthesized* (New York: Cambridge University Press, 2007); Sternberg, "The WICS Model of Giftedness," in Sternberg and Davidson, *Conceptions of Giftedness*.

30. D. J. Treffinger and J. F. Feldhusen, "Talent Recognition and Development: Successor to Gifted Education," *Journal for the Education of the Gifted* 19 (1996): 181–193; J. A. Plucker, *Intelligence 101* (New York: Springer, 2013).

31. R. F. Subotnik, P. Olszewski-Kubilius, and F. C. Worrell, "Rethinking Giftedness and Gifted Education: A Proposed Direction Forward Based on Psychological Science," *Psychological Science* 12 (2011): 3–54, at 29.

32. Ibid., at 30.

33. Ibid., at 40.

34. J.H. Borland, "Gifted Education without Gifted Children," in Sternberg and Davidson, *Conceptions of Giftedness*, 1–19.

35. U.S. Department of Education, *National Excellence: A Case for Developing America's Talent* (Washington, DC: Author, 1993).

36. In a recent edition of the journal *Gifted Child Quarterly*, eight commentators responded to the mega-model of talent development. A range of opinions were presented both for and against Subotnik and colleagues' proposed direction forward. See the special issue of *Gifted Child Quarterly* 56, no. 4 (October 2012), edited by Jonathan A. Plucker.

37. S. I. Pfeiffer, *Serving the Gifted: Evidence-Based Clinical and Psychoeducational Practice* (New York: Routledge, 2012), at 147.

38. L. K. Silverman, "The Moral Sensitivity of Gifted Children and the Evolution of Society," *Roeper Review* 17 (2010): 110–116, at 115.

Chapter 5

1. L. S. Hollingworth, *Leta Stetter Hollingworth* (Lincoln: University of Nebraska Press, 1943).

2. Ibid., at 44.

3. L. Stetter, "Lone Pine," *Roeper Review* 12 (1990): 142.

4. L. S. Hollingworth, *Leta Stetter Hollingworth*, at 63.

5. L. S. Hollingworth, *The Psychology of the Adolescent* (New York: Appleton, 1928).

6. L. S. Hollingworth, *Prairie Years* (New York: Columbia University Press, 1940).

7. L. S. Hollingworth, *Children above 180 IQ Stanford-Binet: Origin and Development* (Yonkers-on-Hudson, NY: World Book, 1942), at 253.

8. Ibid., at 280.

9. Ibid.

10. Ibid., at 299.

11. C. R. Harris, "The Fruits of Early Intervention: The Hollingworth Group Today," *Advanced Development* 4 (1992): 91–104; W. L. White, "The Perceived Effects of an Early Enrichment Experience: A Forty Year Follow-Up Study of the Speyer School Experiment for Gifted Students" (PhD diss., University of Connecticut, Storrs, 1984).

12. B. A. Kerr, "Leta Hollingworth's Legacy to Counseling and Guidance," *Roeper Review* 12 (1990): 178–181, at 178.

13. A. Roeper, *The "I" of the Beholder: A Guided Journey to the Essence of a Child* (Scottsdale, AZ: Great Potential Press, 2007).

14. A. Roeper, *Annemarie Roeper: Selected Writings and Speeches* (Minneapolis: Free Spirit, 1995), 142.

15. A. Roeper, *The "I" of the Beholder*, at 101.

16. Ibid., at 102.

17. Ibid., at 106.

18. Ibid., at 104–105.

19. Ibid., at 109.

20. Ibid., at 108–109.

21. K. Dabrowski, *Positive Disintegration* (Boston: Little, Brown, 1964); S. Mendaglio and W. Tillier, "Dabrowski's Theory of Positive Disintegration and Giftedness: Overexcitability Research Findings," *Journal for the Education of the Gifted* 30 (2006): 68–87; S. Daniel and M. M. Piechowski, *Living with Intensity: Understanding the Sensitivity, Excitability, and the Emotional Development of Gifted Children, Adolescents, and Adults* (Scottsdale, AZ: Great Potential Press Inc., 2008); L. Silverman, *Giftedness 101* (New York: Springer, 2012).

22. M. M. Piechowski, "Developmental Potential," in *New Voices in Counseling the Gifted*, ed. N. Colangelo and R. T. Zaffrann, 25–57 (Dubuque, IA: Kendall Hunt, 1979).

23. Mendaglio and Tillier, "Dabrowski's Theory."

24. L. Wirthwein and D. H. Rost, "Focusing on Overexcitabilities: Studies with Intellectually Gifted and Academically Talented Adults," *Personality and Individual Differences* 51 (2011): 337–342.

25. S. Tolan, "Hollingworth, Dabrowski, Gandhi, Columbus, and Some Others: The History of the Columbus Group," in *Off the Charts: Asynchrony and the Gifted Child*, ed. C. S. Nevile, M. M. Piechowski, and S. S. Tolan (Unionville, NY: Royal Fireworks Press, 2012).

26. Columbus Group, unpublished transcript of the meeting of the Columbius Group, Columbus, Ohio, July 1991.

27. M. J. Morelock, "Giftedness: The View from Within," *Understanding Our Gifted* 4 (1992): 11–15.

28. J. S. Peterson and K. E. Ray, "Bullying and the Gifted: Victims, Perpetrators, Prevalence, and Effects," *Gifted Child Quarterly* 50 (2006): 148–168.

29. M.-C. McClain and S. Pfeiffer, "Identification of Gifted Students in the United States Today: A Look at State Definitions, Policies, and Practices," *Journal of Applied School Psychology* 28 (2011): 59–88.

30. C. J. Maker, "Identification of Gifted Minority Students: A National Problem, Needed Changes and a Promising Solution," *Gifted Child Quarterly* 40 (1996): 41–50.

Chapter 6

1. D. I. Cordova and M. R. Lepper, "Intrinsic Motivation and the Process of Learning: Beneficial Effects of Contextualization, Personalization, and Choice," *Journal of Educational Psychology* 88 (1996): 715–730.

2. E. A. Linnenbrink and P. R. Pintrich, "Motivation as an Enabler for Academic Success," *School Psychology Review* 31 (2002): 313–327, at 313.

3. F. H. Previc, *The Dopaminergic Mind in Human Evolution and History* (New York: Cambridge University Press, 2011).

4. For more on the complex role of dopamine on motivation, see J. D. Salamone and M. Correa, "The Mysterious Motivational Functions of Mesolimbic Dopamine," *Neuron* 76 (2012): 470–485; E. S. Bromberg-Martin, M. Matsumoto, and O. Hikosaka, "Dopamine in Motivational Control: Rewarding, Aversive, and Alerting," *Neuron* 68 (2010): 815–834. K. C. Berridge, "The Debate over Dopamine's Role in Reward: The Case for Incentive Salience," *Psychopharmacology* 191 (2007): 391–431; K. C. Berridge, "From Prediction Error to Incentive Salience: Mesolimbic Computation of Reward Motivation," *European Journal of Neuroscience* 35 (2012): 1124–1143.

5. M. T. Treadwell et al., "Dopaminergic Mechanisms of Individual Differences in Human Effort-Based Decision-Making," *Journal of Neuroscience* 32 (2012): 6170–6176.

6. J. Dewey, *Interest and Effort in Education* (Boston: Houghton Mifflin, 1913); J. S. Bruner, *Toward a Theory of Instruction* (Cambridge, MA: Harvard University Press, 1966); D. Perkins, *Smart Schools: From Training Memories to Educating Minds* (New York: Free Press, 1992).

7. Study described in S. J. Ceci, *On Intelligence . . . More or Less: A Bio-ecological Treatise on Intellectual Development* (Englewood Cliffs, NJ: Prentice Hall, 1996); S. J. Ceci, "Cast in Six Ponds and You'll Reel In Something: Looking Back on 25 Years of Research," *American Psychologist* 58 (2003): 855–864.

8. Ceci, "Cast in Six Ponds," at 857.

9. S. J. Ceci and A. Roazzi, "The Effects of Context on Cognition: Postcards from Brazil," in *Mind in Context: Interactionist Perspectives on Human Intelligence,* ed. R. J. Sternberg and R. K. Wagner, 74–101 (Cambridge: Cambridge University Press, 1994). For a discussion of the role of context in assessing giftedness, see J. Plucker and S. A. Barab, "The Importance of Contexts in Theories of Giftedness: Learning to Embrace the Messy Joys of Subjectivity," in *Conceptions of Giftedness,* 2nd ed., ed. R. J. Sternberg and J. A. Davidson, 201–216 (New York: Cambridge University Press, 2005).

10. Ceci and Roazzi, "The Effects of Context," at 98.

11. R. M. Ryan and E. L. Deci, "Self-Determination Theory and the Facilitation of Intrinsic Motivation, Social Development, and Well-Being," *American Psychologist* 55 (2000): 68–78.

12. M. Vansteenkiste, J. Simons, W. Lens, E. L. Deci, and K. M. Sheldon, "Motivating Learning, Performance, and Persistence: The Synergistic Effects of Intrinsic Goal Contents

and Autonomy-Supportive Contexts," *Journal of Personality and Social Psychology* 87 (2004): 246–260.

13. Cordova and Lepper, "Intrinsic Motivation and the Process of Learning."

14. T. M. Thrash and A. J. Elliot, "Inspiration as a Psychological Construct," *Journal of Personality and Social Psychology* 84 (2003): 871–889; T. M. Thrash and A. J. Elliot, "Inspiration: Core Characteristics, Component Processes, Antecedents, and Function," *Journal of Personality and Social Psychology* 87 (2004): 957–973.

15. Thrash and Elliot, "Inspiration as a Psychological Construct," at 887.

16. Ibid.

17. M. Milyavskaya, I. Ianakieva, E. Foxen-Craft, A. Colantuoni, and R. Koestner, "Inspired to Get There: The Effects of Trait and Goal Inspiration on Goal Progress," *Personality and Individual Differences* 52 (2012): 56–60.

18. Ibid., at 59.

19. T. M. Thrash and A. J. Elliot, "Inspiration: Core Characteristics, Component Processes, Antecedents, and Function"; T. M. Thrash, A. J. Elliot, L. A. Maruskin, and S. E. Cassidy, "Inspiration and the Promotion of Well-Being: Tests of Causality and Mediation," *Journal of Personality and Social Psychology* 98 (2010): 488–506.

20. T. M. Thrash, L. A. Maruskin, S. E. Cassidy, and J. Fryer, "Mediating between the Muse and the Masses: Inspiration and the Actualization of Creative Ideas," *Journal of Personality and Social Psychology* 98 (2010): 469–487.

21. J.-A. Rony, *Les passions* [The passions] (Paris: Presses Universitaires de France, 1990); E. Hatfield and G. W. Walster, *A New Look at Love* (Reading, MA: Addison Wesley, 1978).

22. R. J. Vallerand, "On the Psychology of Passion: In Search of What Makes People's Lives Most Worth Living," *Canadian Psychology* 49 (2008): 1–13.

23. R. J. Vallerand, C. M. Blanchard, et al., "Les passions de l'âme: On Obsessive and Harmonious Passion," *Journal of Personality and Social Psychology* 85 (2003): 756–767, at 757.

24. Ibid.

25. E. H. Erikson, *Identity: Youth and Crisis* (New York: Norton, 1968).

26. Vallerand, Blanchard et al., "Les Passions de L'âme: On Obsessive and Harmonious Passion."

27. For a review, see B. Frederickson, *Positivity: Groundbreaking Research Reveals How to Embrace the Hidden Strength of Positive Emotions, Overcome Negativity, and Thrive* (New York: Crown Archetype, 2009).

28. J. A. Fredricks, C. Alfeld, and J. Eccles, "Developing and Fostering Passion in Academic and Nonacademic Domains," *Gifted Child Quarterly* 54 (2010): 18–30.

Chapter 7

1. C. S. Dweck and E. S. Elliot, "Achievement Motivation," in *Handbook of Child Psychology*, ed. P. Mussen and E. M. Hetherington, 643–692 (New York: Wiley, 1983).

2. C. S. Dweck, *Self-Theories: Their Role in Motivation, Personality, and Development* (New York: Psychology Press, 1999).

3. A. J. Elliot and J. M. Harackiewicz, "Approach and Avoidance Achievement Goals and Intrinsic Motivation: A Mediational Analysis," *Journal of Personality and Social Psychology* 70 (1996): 461–475; A. J. Elliot and M. A. Church, "A Hierarchical Model of Approach and Avoidance Achievement Motivation," *Journal of Personality and Social Psychology* 72 (1997): 218–232.

4. D. C. McClelland, "Measuring Motivation in Phantasy: The Achievement Motive," in *Groups, Leadership, and Men*, ed. H. Guetzkow, 191–205 (Pittsburgh, PA: Carnegie Press,

1951), at 202; also see J. W. Atkinson, "Motivational Determinants of Risk Taking Behavior," *Psychological Review* 64 (1957): 359–372.

5. A. J. Elliot and J. M. Harackiewicz, "Approach and Avoidance Achievement Goals and Intrinsic Motivation: A Mediational Analysis"; A. J. Elliot and M. A. Church, "A Hierarchical Model of Approach and Avoidance Achievement Motivation."

6. L. J. Rawsthorn and A. J. Elliot, "Achievement Goals and Intrinsic Motivation: A Meta-Analytic Review," *Personality and Social Psychology Review* 3 (1999): 326–344.

7. M. K. Rothbart, S. A. Ahadi, and D. E. Evans, "Temperament and Personality: Origins and Outcomes," *Journal of Personality and Social Psychology* 78 (2000): 122–135; A. J. Elliot and T. M. Thrash, "Approach and Avoidance Temperament as Basic Dimensions of Personality," *Journal of Personality* 78 (2010): 865–906.

8. J. A. Gray, "A Critique of Eysenck's Theory of Personality," in *A Model for Personality*, ed. H. J. Eysenck, 246–276 (New York: Springer, 1981).

9. D. E. Evans and M. K. Rothbart, "Developing a Model for Adult Temperament," *Journal of Research in Personality* 41 (2007): 868–888.

10. N. McNaughton and J. A. Gray, "Anxiolytic Action on the Behavioural Inhibition System Implies Multiple Types of Arousal Contribute to Anxiety," *Journal of Affective Disorders* 61 (2000): 161–176.

11. A. J. Elliot and T. M. Thrash, "Approach-Avoidance Motivation in Personality: Approach and Avoidance Temperaments and Goals," *Journal of Personality and Social Psychology* 82 (2002): 804–818.

12. S. Epstein, "The Stability of Behavior: I. On Predicting Most of the People Much of the Time," *Journal of Personality and Social Psychology* 37 (1979): 1097–1126; S. Epstein, "The Stability of Behavior: II. Implications for Psychological Research," *American Psychologist* 35 (1980): 790–806; W. Fleeson, "Toward a Structure- and Process-Integrated View of Personality: Traits as Density Distributions of States," *Journal of Personality and Social Psychology* 80 (2001): 1011–1027; W. Fleeson, "Moving Personality Beyond the Person-Situation Debate: The Challenge and the Opportunity of Within-Person Variability," *Current Directions in Psychological Science* 13 (2004): 83–87; W. Fleeson and P. Gallagher, "The Implications of Big Five Standing for the Distribution of Trait Manifestation in Behavior: Fifteen Experience-Sampling Studies and a Meta-Analysis," *Journal of Personality and Social Psychology* 97 (2009): 1097–1114.

13. S. D. Gosling and O. P. John, "Personality Dimensions in Nonhuman Animals: A Cross-Species Review," *Current Directions in Psychological Science* 8 (1999): 69–75; A. Weiss, M. Inoue-Murayama, J. E. King, M. J. Adams, and T. Matsuzawa, "All Too Human? Chimpanzee and Orang-utan Personalities Are Not Anthropomorphic Projections," *Animal Behaviour* 83 (2012): 1355–1365.

14. C. Ames, "Achievement Goals and the Classroom Motivational Climate," in *Student Perceptions in the Classroom*, ed. D. H. Schunk and J. L. Meece, 327–348 (Hillsdale, NJ: Erlbaum, 1992); Ames, "Classroom: Goals, Structures, and Student Motivation," *Journal of Educational Psychology* 84 (1992): 261–271.

15. P. A. O'Keefe, A. Ben-Eliyahu, and L. Linnenbrink-Garcia, "Shaping Achievement Goal Orientations in a Mastery-Structured Environment and Concomitant Changes in Related Contingencies of Self-Worth," *Motivation and Emotion* (forthcoming), doi: 10.1007/s11031-012-9293-6.

16. C. S. Dweck and E. L. Leggett, "A Social-Cognitive Approach to Motivation and Personality," *Psychological Review* 95 (1988): 256–273.

17. J. A. Mangels, B. Butterfield, J. Lamb, C. Good, and C. S. Dweck, "Why Do Beliefs About Intelligence Influence Learning Success? A Social Cognitive Neuroscience Model," *Social Cognitive and Affective Neuroscience* 1 (2006): 75–86.

18. Y. Hong, C. Chiu, C. S. Dweck, D. M. Lin, and W. Wan, "Implicit Theories, Attributions, and Coping: A Meaning System Approach," *Journal of Personality and Social Psychology* 77 (1999): 588–599.

19. L. S. Blackwell, K. H. Trzesniewski, and C. S. Dweck, "Implicit Theories of Intelligence Predict Achievement Across an Adolescent Transition: A Longitudinal Study and an Intervention," *Child Development* 78 (2007): 246–263.

20. J. Aronson and E. E. Jones, "Inferring Abilities After Influencing Performance," *Journal of Experimental Social Psychology* 28 (1992): 277–299.

21. C. M. Mueller and C. S. Dweck, "Praise for Intelligence Can Undermine Children's Motivation and Performance," *Journal of Personality and Social Psychology* 75 (1998): 33–52.

22. A. Rattan, C. Good, and C. S. Dweck, "'It's OK—Not Everyone Can Be Good at Math': Instructors with an Entity Theory Comfort (and Demotivate) Students," *Journal of Experimental Social Psychology* 48 (2012): 731–737.

23. Ibid., at 736.

24. Dweck, *Self-Theories*, at 122.

25. L. Olson, "Enveloping Expectations," *Education Week (Quality Counts)* 23 (2004): 8–21.

26. N. B. Hertzog, "Impact of Gifted Programs from the Students' Perspectives," *Gifted Child Quarterly* 47 (2003): 131–143.

27. R. K. Merton, "The Self-Fulfilling Prophecy," *Antioch Review* 8 (1948): 193–210.

28. R. Rosenthal and L. F. Jacobson, "Teachers' Expectancies: Determinants of Pupils' IQ Gains," *Psychological Reports* 1 (1966): 115–118.

29. See L. Jussim and K. D. Harber, "Teacher Expectations and Self-Fulfilling Prophecies: Knowns and Unknowns, Resolved and Unresolved Controversies," *Personal and Social Psychology Review* 9 (2005): 131–155.

30. E. Babad, "Pygmalion: 25 Years After Interpersonal Expectations in the Classroom," in *Interpersonal Expectations: Theory, Research, and Applications—Studies in Emotion and Social Interaction*, ed. P. D. Blanck, 125–153 (Cambridge: Cambridge University Press, 1993); H. H. Spitz, "Beleaguered Pygmalion: A History of the Controversy over Claims That Teacher Expectancy Raises Intelligence," *Intelligence* 27 (1999): 199–234; J. P. Allen, R. C. Pianta, A. Gregory, A. Y. Mikami, and J. Lun, "An Interaction-Based Approach to Enhancing Secondary School Instruction and Student Achievement," *Science* 333 (2011): 1034–1037; B. K. Hamre et al., "A Course on Effective Teacher-Child Interactions: Effects on Teacher Beliefs, Knowledge, and Observed Practice," *American Educational Research Journal* 49 (2012): 88–123; L. J. Jussim, S. Madon, C. Chatman, et al., "Teacher Expectations and Student Achievement: Self-Fulfilling Prophecies, Biases, and Accuracy," in *Applications of Heuristics and Biases to Social Issues*, ed. L. Heath et al., 303–334 (New York: Plenum Press, 1994).

31. K. Cotton, "Expectations and Student Outcomes" (January 2001), http://www.nwerel.org/scpd/sirs/4/cu7.html.

32. J. P. Van Oudenhoven and F. Siero, "Evaluative Feedback as a Determinant of the Pygmalion Effect," *Psychological Reports* 57 (1985): 755–761.

33. K. T. Kishida, D. Yang, et al., "Implicit Signals in Small Group Settings and Their Impact on the Expression of Cognitive Capacity and Associated Brain Responses," *Philosophical Transactions of the Royal Society B* 367 (2012): 704–716.

34. Jussim, Madon, et al., "Teacher Expectations."

35. G. J. Meyer et al., "Psychological Testing and Psychological Assessment: A Review of Evidence and Issues," *American Psychologist* 56 (2001): 128–165.

36. S. B. Kaufman and K. McGrew, "The Need to Believe in the Ability of Disability," *Beautiful Minds* (blog), *Psychology Today,* January 30, 2012, http://www.psychologytoday.com/blog/beautiful-minds/201201/the-need-believe-in-the-ability-disability.

37. K. S. McGrew, D. R. Johnson, A. Cosio, and J. Evans, "Increasing the Chance of No Child Being Left Behind: Beyond Cognitive and Achievement Abilities," Office of Special

Education Programs, Paper (2004). For more on bridging the gap between psychological theory/research and practice, see http://themindhub.com/research-reports.

38. B. M. Byrne, "Validating the Measurement and Structure of Self-Concept: Snapshots of Past, Present, and Future Research," *American Psychologist* 57 (2002): 897–909; H. W. Marsh, D. Chessor, R. Craven, and L. Roche, "The Effects of Gifted and Talented Programs on Academic Self-Concept: The Big Fish Strikes Again," *American Educational Research Journal* 32 (1995): 285–319.

39. M. C. Makel, S.-Y. Lee, P. Olszewki-Kubilius, and M. Putallaz, "Changing the Pond, Not the Fish: Following High-Ability Students Across Different Educational Environments," *Journal of Educational Psychology* 104 (2012): 778–792.

40. C. M. Steele and J. Aronson, "Stereotype Threat and the Intellectual Test Performance of African Americans," *Journal of Personality and Social Psychology* 69 (1995): 797–811.

41. J. Aronson and M. S. McGlone, "Stereotype and Social Identity," in *The Handbook of Prejudice, Stereotyping, and Discrimination*, ed. T. Nelson, 153–178 (New York: Psychology Press, 2009); J. Aronson and T. Dee, "Stereotype Threat in the Real World," in *Stereotype Threat: Theory, Process, and Application*, ed. M. Inzlicht and T. Schmader, 264–279 (New York: Oxford University Press, 2011); J. Aronson and L. Juarez, "Growth Mindsets in the Laboratory and the Real World," in *Malleable Minds: Translating Insights from Psychology and Neuroscience to Gifted Education*, ed. R. F. Subotnik, A. Robinson, C. M. Callahan, and E. J. Grubbins, 19–36 (Storrs, CT: University of Connecticut Press, 2012).

42. N. J. Mackintosh, *IQ and Human Intelligence*, 2nd ed. (Oxford: Oxford University Press, 2011), at 344.

43. J. F. Fagan, D. Drotar, et al., "The Fagan Test of Infant Intelligence: Cross-Cultural and Racial Comparisons," *Journal of Developmental and Behavioral Pediatrics* 12 (1991): 168; Fagan, "A Theory of Intelligence as Processing: Implications for Society," *Psychology, Public Policy, and Law* 6 (2000): 168–179; Fagan, "Intelligence in Infancy," in *The Cambridge Handbook of Intelligence*, ed. R. J. Sternberg and S. B. Kaufman (New York: Cambridge University Press, 2011).

44. Fagan, "Intelligence in Infancy," at 137.

45. W. T. Dickens and J. R. Flynn, "Black Americans Reduce the Racial IQ Gap," *Psychological Science* 17 (2006): 913–920.

46. H.-H. D. Nguyen and A. M. Ryan, "Does Stereotype Threat Affect Test Performance of Minorities and Women? A Meta-analysis of Experimental Evidence," *Journal of Applied Psychology* 93 (2008): 1314–1334.

47. Ibid., at 1329.

48. K. Danaher and C. S. Crandall, "Stereotype Threat in Applied Settings Reexamined," *Journal of Applied Social Psychology* 38 (2008): 1639–1655.

49. C. M. Steele and J. Aronson, "Stereotype Threat and the Intellectual Test Performance of African Americans," at 809.

50. T. Schmader and S. L. Beilock, "Mechanisms: An Integration of Processes That Underlie Stereotype Threat," in *Stereotype Threat: Theory, Process, and Application*, ed. T. Schmader and M. Inzlicht (New York: Oxford University Press, 2012).

51. A. C. Krendl, J. A. Richeson, W. M. Kelley, and T. F. Heatherton, "The Negative Consequences of Threat: An fMRI Investigation of the Neural Mechanisms Underlying Women's Underperformance in Math," *Psychological Science* 19 (2008): 168–175.

52. M. Wraga, M. Helt, E. Jacobs, and K. Sullivan, "Neural Basis of Stereotype-Induced Shifts in Women's Mental Rotation Performance," *Social Cognition and Affective Neuroscience* 2 (2007): 12–19.

53. C. Forbes, T. Schmader, and J. J. B. Allen, "The Role of Devaluing and Discounting in Performance Monitoring: A Neurophysiological Study of Minorities Under Threat," *Social Cognitive Affective Neuroscience* 3 (2008): 253–261.

54. T. Schmader and M. Johns, "Converging Evidence That Stereotype Threat Reduces Working Memory Capacity," *Journal of Personality and Social Psychology* 85 (2003): 440–452.

55. C. M. Steele, S. J. Spencer, and J. Aronson, "Contending with Images of One's Group: The Psychology of Stereotype and Social Identity Threat," in *Advances in Experimental Social Psychology*, ed. M. Zanna (San Diego: Academic Press, 2002).

56. M. Cadinu, A. Maass, A. Rosabianca, and J. Kiesner, "Why Do Women Underperform Under Stereotype Threat? Evidence for the Role of Negative Thinking," *Psychological Science* 16 (2005): 572–578.

57. M. J. Johns, M. Inzlicht, and T. Schmader, "Stereotype Threat and Executive Resource Depletion: Examining the Influence of Emotion Regulation," *Journal of Experimental Psychology: General* 137 (2008): 691–705.

58. S. L. Beilock, W. A. Jellison, R. J. Rydell, A. R. McConnell, and T. H. Carr, "On the Causal Mechanisms of Stereotype Threat: Can Skills That Don't Rely Heavily on Working Memory Still Be Threatened?," *Personality and Social Psychology Bulletin* 32 (2006): 1059–1071.

59. S. Beilock, *Choke: What the Secrets of the Brain Reveal About Getting It Right When You Have To* (New York: Free Press, 2010).

60. C. E. Forbes and T. Schmader, "Retraining Implicit Attitudes and Stereotypes to Distinguish Motivation from Performance in a Stereotype Threatening Domain," *Journal of Personality and Social Psychology* 99 (2010): 740–754.

61. C. Good, A. Rattan, and C. S. Dweck, "Why Do Women Opt Out? Sense of Belonging and Women's Representation in Mathematics," *Journal of Personality and Social Psychology* 102 (2012): 700–717; G. M. Walton and G. L. Cohen, "A Question of Belonging: Race, Social Fit, and Achievement," *Journal of Personality and Social Psychology* 92 (2007): 82–96; Schmader and Beilock, "Mechanisms: An Integration of Processes That Underlie Stereotype Threat."

62. J. Aronson, C. B. Fried, and C. Good, "Reducing the Effects of Stereotype Threat on African American College Students by Shaping Theories of Intelligence," *Journal of Experimental Social Psychology* 38 (2002): 113–125; C. Good, J. Aronson, and M. Inzlicht, "Improving Adolescents' Standardized Test Performance: An Intervention to Reduce the Effects of Stereotype Threat," *Journal of Applied Developmental Psychology* 24 (2003): 645–662.

63. A. Mattarella-Micke, A. Mateo, et al., "Choke or Thrive? The Relation between Salivary Cortisol and Math Performance Depends on Individual Differences in Working Memory and Math-Anxiety," *Emotion* 11 (2011): 1000–1005.

64. T. Schmader, C. E. Forbes, S. Zhang, and W. B. Mendes, "A Meta-cognitive Perspective on Cognitive Deficits Experienced in Intellectually Threatening Environments," *Personality and Social Psychology Bulletin* 35 (2009): 584–596.

65. J. P. Jamieson, W. B. Mendes, E. Blackstock, and T. Schmader, "Turning the Knots in Your Stomach into Bows: Reappraising Arousal Improves Performance on the GRE," *Journal of Experimental Social Psychology* 46 (2010): 208–212.

66. M. Johns, T. Schmader, and A. Martens, "Knowing Is Half the Battle: Teaching Stereotype Threat as a Means of Improving Women's Math Performance," *Psychological Science* 16 (2005): 175–179.

67. E. A. Maloney, and S. L. Beilock, "From Onset to Inoculation," *Trends in Cognitive Sciences* 16 (2012): 404–406.

68. I. M. Lyons and S. L. Beilock, "Mathematics Anxiety: Separating the Math from the Anxiety," *Cerebral Cortex* 22 (2011): 2102–2110.

69. G. Ramirez and S. L. Beilock, "Writing about Testing Worries Boosts Exam Performance in the Classroom," *Science* 331 (2011): 211–213.

Chapter 8

1. W. Mischel, "Processes in Delay of Gratification," in *Advances in Experimental Social Psychology*, ed. L. Berkowitz, 7:249–292 (New York: Academic Press, 1974); W. Mischel, Y. Shoda, and P. K. Peake, "The Nature of Adolescent Competencies Predicted by Preschool Delay of Gratification," *Journal of Personality and Social Psychology* 54 (1988): 687–696.

2. Y. Shoda, W. Mischel, and P. K. Peake, "Predicting Adolescent Cognitive and Self-Regulatory Competencies from Preschool Delay of Gratification: Identifying Diagnostic Conditions," *Developmental Psychology* 26 (1990): 978–986.

3. Mischel, "Processes in Delay"; Mischel, Shoda, and Peake, "Nature of Adolescent Competencies."

4. W. Mischel et al., "'Willpower' over the Life Span: Decomposing Self-Regulation," *SCAN* 6 (2011): 252–256.

5. N. A. Shamosh and J. R. Gray, "Delay Discounting and Intelligence: A Meta-analysis," *Intelligence* 36 (2008): 289–305.

6. A. L. Duckworth and M. E. P. Seligman, "Self-Discipline Outdoes IQ in Predicting Academic Performance of Adolescents," *Psychological Science* 16 (2005): 939–944.

7. C. Blair and A. Diamond, "Biological Processes in Prevention and Intervention: The Promotion of Self-Regulation as a Means of Preventing School Failure," *Development and Psychopathology* 20 (2008): 899–911.

8. C. C. Raver and J. K. Knitzer, *Ready to Enter: What Research Tells Policy Makers About Strategies to Promote Social and Emotional School Readiness Among Three- and Four-Year-Old Children* (New York: National Center for Children in Poverty, 2002).

9. T. O'Shaughnessy, K. L. Lane, F. M. Gresham, and M. Beebe-Frankenberger, "Children Placed at Risk for Learning and Behavioral Difficulties: Implementing a School-Wide System of Early Identification and Prevention," *Remedial and Special Education* 24 (2003): 27–35; A. Diamond, "How I Came Full Circle from the Social End of Psychology, to Neuroscience, and Back Again, in an Effort to Understand the Development of Cognitive Control," in *Malleable Minds: Translating Insights from Psychology and Neuroscience to Gifted Education*, ed. R. F. Subotnik, A. Robinson, C. M. Callahan, and E. J. Grubbins, 55–84 (Storrs, CT: University of Connecticut Press, 2012).

10. C. Blair and R. P. Razza, "Relating Effortful Control, Executive Function, and False Belief Understanding to Emerging Math and Literacy Ability in Kindergarten," *Child Development* 78 (2007): 647–663.

11. T. E. Moffitt et al., "A Gradient of Childhood Self-Control Predicts Health, Wealth, and Public Safety," *PNAS* 108 (2011): 2693–2698.

12. Ibid., at 2696.

13. Ibid., at 2694.

14. E. Bodrova and D. J. Leong, *Tools of the Mind: The Vygotskian Approach to Early Childhood Education*, 2nd ed. (New York: Merrill / Prentice Hall, 2007).

15. A. Diamond, W. S. Barnett, J. Thomas, and S. Munro, "Preschool Program Improves Cognitive Control," *Science* 318 (2007): 1387–1388; also see W. S. Barnett, K. Jung, et al., "Educational Effects of the Tools of the Mind Curriculum: A Randomized Trial," *Early Childhood Research Quarterly* 23 (2008): 299–313.

16. A. Lillard and N. Else-Quest, "The Early Years: Evaluating Montessori Education," *Science* 313 (2006): 1893–1894.

17. A. Diamond, "Activities and Programs That Improve Children's Executive Functions," *Current Directions in Psychological Science* 22 (2012): 1–7.

18. C. A. Kusche and M. T. Greenberg, *The PATHS Curriculum* (Seattle: Developmental Research and Programs, 1994); N. R. Riggs, M. Greenberg, et al., "The Mediational Role of

Neurocognition in the Behavioral Outcomes of a Social-Emotional Prevention Program in Elementary School Students: Effects of the PATHS Curriculum," *Prevention Science* 7 (2006): 91–102.

19. C. C. Raver, S. M. Jones, et al., "Improving Preschool Classroom Processes: Preliminary Findings from a Randomized Trial Implemented in Head Start Settings," *Early Childhood Research Quarterly 23* (2008): 10–26; C. C. Raver, S. M. Jones, et al., "CSRP's Impact on Low-Income Preschoolers' Pre-academic Skills: Self-Regulation as a Mediating Mechanism," *Child Development 82* (2011): 362–378.

20. K. L. Bierman et al., "Promoting Academic and Social-Emotional School Readiness: The Head Start REDI Program," *Child Development* 79 (2008): 1802–1817.

21. J. M. Jenkins and J. W. Astington, "Theory of Mind and Social Behavior: Casual Models Tested in a Longitudinal Study," *Merrill-Palmer Quarterly* 46 (2000): 203–220; A. M. Leslie, "Pretense and Representation: The Origins of 'Theory of Mind,'" *Psychological Review* 94 (1987): 412–426; D. G. Singer and J. L. Singer, *The House of Make Believe: Children's Play and the Developing Imagination* (Cambridge, MA: Harvard University Press, 1990); D. G. Singer and J. L. Singer, *Imagination and Play in the Electronic Age* (Cambridge, MA: Harvard University Press, 2005).

22. S. W. Russ, *Play in Child Development and Psychotherapy* (Mahwah, NJ: Earlbaum, 2004).

23. J. F. Jent, L. N. Niec, and S. E. Baker, "Play and Interpersonal Processes," in *Play in Clinical Practice: Evidence-Based Approaches*, ed. S. W. Russ and L. N. Niec (New York: Guilford Press, 2011).

24. L. E. Berk, T. D. Mann, and A. T. Ogan, "Make-Believe Play: Wellspring for Development of Self-Regulation," in *Play = Learning: How Play Motivates and Enhances Children's Cognitive and Social-Emotional Growth*, ed. D. Singer, R. M. Golinkoff, and K. Hirsh-Pasek (New York: Oxford University Press, 2006); K. Hirsh-Pasek, R. M. Golinkoff, L. E. Berk, and D. G. Singer, *A Mandate for Playful Learning in Preschool: Presenting the Evidence* (New York: Oxford University Press, 2009).

25. F. P. Hughes, *Children, Play, and Development*, 3rd ed. (Needham Heights, MA: Allyn and Bacon, 1999); P. Gray, *Free to Learn: Why Unleashing the Instinct to Play Will Make Our Children Happier, More Self-Reliant, and Better Students for Life* (New York: Basic Books, 2013).

26. S. Russ and J. Fiorelli, "Developmental Approaches to Creativity," in *The Cambridge Handbook of Creativity*, ed. J. C. Kaufman and R. J. Sternberg, 233–249 (New York: Cambridge University Press, 2010).

27. M. Root-Bernstein, "The Creation of Imaginary Worlds," in *The Oxford Handbook of the Development of Imagination*, ed. M. Taylor (Oxford: Oxford University Press, 2012).

28. D. Shmukler, "Mother-Child Interaction and Its Relationship to the Predisposition of Imaginative Play," *Genetic Psychology Monographs* 104 (1981): 215–235; Singer and Singer, *Imagination and Play*.

29. G. S. Ashiabi, "Play in the Preschool Classroom: Its Socioemotional Significance and the Teacher's Role in Play," *Early Childhood Education Journal* 35 (2007): 199–207; J. L. Singer and M. A. Lythcott, "Fostering School Achievement and Creativity Through Sociodramatic Play in the Classroom," in *Children's Play: The Roots of Reading*, ed. E. F. Zigler, D. G. Singer, and S. J. Bishop-Joseph, 77–93 (Washington, DC: Zero to Three Press, 2004).

30. H. P. Ginsburg, "Mathematical Play and Playful Mathematics: A Guide for Early Education," in Singer et al., *Play = Learning*, 145–68.

31. D. G. Singer, J. L. Singer, S. L. Plaskon, and A. E. Schweder, "The Role of Play in the Preschool Curriculum," in *All Work and No Play: How Educational Reforms Are Harming Our Preschoolers*, ed. S. Olfman, 43–70 (Westport, CT: Praeger, 2003).

32. K. M. Kapp, *The Gamification of Learning and Instruction: Game-Based Methods and Strategies for Training and Education* (New York: Pfeiffer, 2012).

33. C. Thorn, *The S & M Feminist: Best of Clarisse Thorn*, CreateSpace, http://www.createspace.com.

34. D. Ruiz-Aranda et al., "Short- and Midterm Effects of Emotional Intelligence Training on Adolescent Mental Health," *Journal of Adolescent Health* 51 (2012): 462–467.

35. M. A. Brackett, S. E. Rivers, M. R. Reyes, and P. Salovey, "Enhancing Academic Performance and Social and Emotional Competence with the RULER Feeling Words Curriculum," *Learning and Individual Differences* 22 (2010): 218–224.

36. C. G. Grande, "Delinquency: The Learning Disabled Student's Reaction to Academic School Failure," *Adolescence* 23 (1988): 209–218; T. W. Farmer and J. H. Hollowell, "Social Networks in Mainstream Classrooms: Social Affiliations and Behavioral Characteristics of Students with Emotional and Behavioral Disorders," *Journal of Emotional and Behavioral Disorders* 2 (1994): 143–155, 163.

37. W. N. Bender, C. B. Rosenkrans, and M. K. Crane, "Stress, Depression, and Suicide Among Students with Learning Disabilities: Assessing the Risk," *Learning Disability Quarterly* 22 (1999): 143–156; W. N. Bender and M. E. Wall, "Social–Emotional Development of Students with Learning Disabilities," *Learning Disability Quarterly* 17 (1994): 323–341.

38. C.-M. Kam, M. T. Greenberg, and C. A. Kusche, "Sustained Effects of the PATHS Curriculum on the Social and Psychological Adjustment of Children in Special Education," *Journal of Emotional and Behavioral Disorders* 12 (2004): 66–78.

39. Exceptional Children Division, North Carolina Department of Public Instruction and the American Association for Gifted Children at Duke University. Javits Education Program funded by the U.S. Department of Education, 2004–2010.

40. A. L. Costa and B. Kallick, *Discovering and Exploring Habits of Mind, Book 1* (Alexandria, VA: Association for Supervision & Curriculum Development, 2000), back cover.

41. A. Diamond and K. Lee, "Interventions Shown to Aid Executive Function Development in Children 4 to 12 Years Old," *Science* 333 (2011): 959–964; R. E. Nisbett, *Intelligence and How to Get It* (New York: W. W. Norton, 2010).

42. A. Diamond, "The Evidence Base for Improving School Outcomes by Addressing the Whole Child and by Addressing Skills and Attitudes, Not Just Content," *Early Education and Development* 21 (2010): 780–793.

43. R. Chetty, J. N. Friedman, N. Hilger, E. Saez, et al., *How Does Your Kindergarten Classroom Affect Your Earnings? Evidence from Project Star* (Cambridge, MA: National Bureau of Economic Research, 2010).

44. David Leonhardt, "The Case for $320,000 Kindergarten Teachers," *New York Times*, July 27, 2010, http://www.nytimes.com/2010/07/28/business/economy/28leonhardt.html.

45. D. S. Yeager and G. M. Walton, "Social-Psychological Interventions in Education: They're Not Magic," *Review of Educational Research* 81 (2011): 267–301; J. Protzko, J. Aronson, and C. Blair, "How to Make a Young Child Smarter: Evidence from the Database of Raising Intelligence," *Perspectives on Psychological Science* 8 (2013): 25–40.

Chapter 9

1. A. Newell and H. A. Simon, *Human Problem Solving* (Englewood Cliffs, NJ: Prentice-Hall, 1972).

2. A. Newell, J. C. Shaw, and H. A. Simon, "Report on a General Problem-Solving Program," in *Proceedings of the International Conference on Information Processing*, 256–264 (Paris: UNESCO, 1959).

3. G. Miller, "The Magical Number Seven, Plus or Minus Two: Some Limits on Our Capacity for Processing Information," *Psychological Review* 17 (1956): 748–762.

4. N. Cowan, "The Magical Number 4 in Short-Term Memory: A Reconsideration of Mental Storage Capacity," *Behavioral and Brain Sciences* 24 (2000): 87–185.

5. A. de Groot, *Thought and Choice in Chess* (1946; The Hague: Mouton, 1978).

6. W. G. Chase and H. A. Simon, "The Mind's Eye in Chess," in *Visual Information Processing*, ed. W. G. Chase, 215–281 (New York: Academic Press, 1973); Chase and Simon, "Perception in Chess," *Cognitive Psychology* 4 (1973): 55–81.

7. H. A. Simon and W. G. Chase, "Skill in Chess," *American Scientist* 61 (1973): 394–403.

8. Ibid., at 402.

9. F. Gobet and N. Charness, "Expertise in Chess," in *The Cambridge Handbook of Expertise and Expert Performance*, ed. K. A. Ericsson et al., 523–538 (New York: Cambridge University Press, 2006).

10. P. R. Martin and S. W. Fernberger, "Improvement in Memory Span," *American Journal of Psychology* 41 (1929): 91–94.

11. B. O'Neil, "Walking in Steve Faloon's Footsteps," *Pittsburgh Post-Gazette*, April 25, 2007.

12. Ibid.

13. K. A. Ericsson, W. G. Chase, and S. Faloon, "Acquisition of a Memory Skill," *Science* 208 (1980): 1181–1182; K. A. Ericsson, "Memory Skill," *Canadian Journal of Psychology* 39 (1985): 188–231.

14. K. A. Ericsson and W. G. Chase, "Exceptional Memory," *American Scientist* 70 (1982): 607–615, at 609.

15. J. Foer, *Moonwalking with Einstein: The Art and Science of Remembering Everything* (New York: Penguin Books, 2012).

16. E. A. Maguire, E. R. Valentine, J. M. Wilding, and N. Kapur, "Routes to Remembering: The Brains behind Superior Memory," *Nature Neuroscience* 6 (2002): 90–95.

17. M. Takahashi, H. Shimizu, S. Saito, and H. Tomoyori, "One Percent Ability and Ninety-Nine Percent Perspiration: A Study of a Japanese Memorist," *Journal of Experimental Psychology: Learning, Memory, and Cognition* 32, no. 5 (2006): 1195–1200.

18. "William G. Chase, 43; Tested Memory as Skill," *New York Times*, December 18, 1983, http://www.nytimes.com/1983/12/18/obituaries/william-g-chase-43-tested-memory -as-skill.html.

19. K. A. Ericsson and J. Smith, *Toward a General Theory of Expertise: Prospects and Limits* (New York: Cambridge University Press, 1991).

20. J. Bedard and T. H. Chi, "Expertise," *Current Directions in Psychological Science* 1 (1992): 178–183; Ericsson et al., *Cambridge Handbook of Expertise and Expert Performance*.

21. K. A. Ericsson and E. Kintsch, "Long-Term Working Memory," *Psychological Review* 102 (1995): 211–245.

22. S. J. Ceci and J. K. Liker, "A Day at the Races: A Study of IQ, Expertise, and Cognitive Complexity," *Journal of Experimental Psychology: General* 115 (1986): 255–266. For a critique, see D. K. Detterman and K. M. Spry, "Is It Smart to Place the Horses? Comment on 'A Day at the Races: A Study of IQ, Expertise, and Cognitive Complexity,'" *Journal of Experimental Psychology: General* 117 (1988): 91–95; C. H. Walker, "Relative Importance of Domain Knowledge and Overall Aptitude on Acquisition of Domain-Related Information," *Cognition and Instruction* 4 (1987): 25–52.

23. S. J. Ceci and A. Roazzi, "The Effects of Context on Cognition: Postcards from Brazil," in *Mind in Context: Interactionist Perspectives on Human Intelligence*, ed. R. J. Sternberg and R. K. Wagner (Cambridge: Cambridge University Press, 1994).

24. H. L. Bennett, "Remembering Drink Orders: The Memory Skills of Cocktail Waitresses," *Human Learning: Journal of Practical Research and Applications* 2 (1983): 157–170; J. Lave, M. Murtaugh, and O. de la Roche, "The Dialectic of Arithmetic in Grocery Shopping," in *Everyday Cognition: Its Development in Social Context*, ed. B. Rogoff and J. Lave (Cambridge, MA: Harvard University Press, 1984).

25. G. Klein, *Sources of Power: How People Make Decisions* (Cambridge: Cambridge University Press, 1999).

26. V. F. Reyna, "How People Make Decisions That Involve Risk: A Dual-Process Approach," *Current Directions in Psychological Science* 13 (2004): 60–66.

27. T. D. Wilson and J. W. Schooler, "Thinking Too Much: Introspection Can Reduce the Quality of Preferences and Decisions," *Journal of Personality and Social Psychology* 60 (1991): 181–192.

28. S. Martin, *Born Standing Up: A Comic's Life* (New York: Scribner, 2008), at 139.

29. R. M. Dawes, *House of Cards: Psychology and Psychotherapy Built on Myth* (New York: Free Press, 1994); C. F. Camerer and E. J. Johnson, "The Process-Performance Paradox in Expert Judgment: How Can the Experts Know So Much and Predict So Badly?," in *Towards a General Theory of Expertise: Prospects and Limits*, ed. K. A. Ericsson and J. Smith, 195–217 (Cambridge: Cambridge University Press, 1991); D. Valentin, M. Pichon, V. de Boishebert, and H. Abdi, "What's in a Wine Name? When and Why Do Wine Experts Perform Better Than Novices?," *Abstracts of the Psychonomic Society* 5 (2000): 36. For more on the hazards of too much expertise, see P. A. Frensch and R. J. Sternberg, "Expertise and Intelligent Thinking: When Is it Worse to Know Better?," in *Advances in the Psychology of Human Intelligence*, Vol. 5., ed. R. J. Sternberg, 157–188 (Hillsdale, NJ: Lawrence Erlbaum Associates, 1989); D. K. Simonton, "Creative Development as Acquired Expertise: Theoretical Issues and an Empirical Test," *Developmental Review* 20 (2000): 283–318; D. K. Simonton, "Expertise, Competence, and Creative Ability: The Perplexing Com-plexities," in *The Psychology of Abilities, Competencies, and Expertise*, ed. R. J. Sternberg and E. L. Grigorenko, 213–239 (New York: Cambridge University Press, 2003).

30. C. F. Chabris and D. Simons, *The Invisible Gorilla: How Our Intuitions Deceive Us* (New York: Crown Archetype, 2010).

31. C. F. Chabris and E. S. Hearst, "Visualization, Pattern Recognition, and Forward Search: Effects of Playing Speed and Sight of the Position on Grandmaster Chess Errors," *Cognitive Science* 27 (2003): 637–648.

32. Chabris and Simons, *The Invisible Gorilla*, at 235.

33. K. A. Ericsson, R. T. Krampe, and C. Tesch-Römer, "The Role of Deliberate Practice in the Acquisition of Expert Performance," *Psychological Review* 100 (1993): 363–406.

34. Ibid., at 367.

35. J. R. Hayes, *The Complete Problem Solver* (Hillsdale, NJ: Erlbaum, 1981).

36. Ibid., at 366.

37. W. L. Bryan and N. Harter, "Studies in the Physiology and Psychology of the Telegraphic Language," *Psychological Review* 4 (1897): 27–53.

38. Ibid., at 358.

39. Ibid., at 361.

40. Ericsson, Krampe, and Tesch-Römer, "The Role of Deliberate Practice," at 399.

41. Ibid., at 400.

42. A. L. Duckworth, C. Peterson, M. D. Matthews, and D. R. Kelly, "Grit: Perseverance and Passion for Long-Term Goals," *Personality and Individual Differences* 92 (2007): 1087–1101.

43. B. S. Bloom, *Developing Talent in Young People* (New York: Ballantine Books, 1985).

44. Ibid., at 533.

45. D. C. McClelland, *The Achieving Society* (Oxford: Van Nostrand, 1961).

46. A. L. Duckworth et al., "Deliberate Practice Spells Success: Why Grittier Competitors Triumph at the National Spelling Bee," *Social Psychological and Personality Science* 2 (2011): 174–181.

47. A. L. Duckworth and P. D. Quinn, "Development and Validation of the Short Grit Scale (Grit-S)," *Journal of Personality Assessment* 91 (2009): 166–174.

48. A. Bandura, *Principles of Behavior Modification* (New York: Holt, Rinehart and Winston, 1969).

49. B. J. Zimmerman and M. M. Pons, "Development of a Structured Interview for Assessing Student Use of Self-Regulated Learning Strategies," *American Educational Research Journal* 23 (1986): 614–628.

50. B. J. Zimmerman, "Investigating Self-Regulation and Motivation: Historical Background, Methodological Developments, and Future Prospects," *American Educational Research Journal* 45 (2008): 166–183; K. Nandagopal and K. A. Ericsson, "Enhancing Students' Performance in Traditional Education: Implications from the Expert Performance Approach and Deliberate Practice," in *APA Educational Psychology Handbook,* vol 1: *Theories, Constructs, and Critical Issues*, ed. K. R. Harris, S. Graham, S. Urdan, G. M. Sinatra, and J. Sweller, 257–293 (Washington, DC: American Psychological Association, 2012).

51. K. Nandagopal and K. A. Ericsson, "An Expert Performance Approach to the Study of Individual Differences in Self-Regulated Learning Activities in Upper-Level College Students," *Learning and Individual Differences* 22 (2012): 597–609.

52. Ibid., at 600.

53. K. Murayama, R. Pekrun, S. Lichtenfeld, and R. vom Hofe, "Predicting Long-Term Growth in Students' Mathematics Achievement: The Unique Contributions of Motivation and Cognitive Strategies," *Child Development* (2012), doi:10.1111/cdev.12036.

54. C. R. Snyder et al., "The Will and the Ways: Development and Validation of an Individual-Differences Measure of Hope," *Journal of Personality and Social Psychology* 60 (1991): 570–585.

55. G. Oettingen and P. M. Gollwitzer (2001), "Goal Setting and Goal Striving," in *Intraindividual Processes,* vol. 1 of the *Blackwell Handbook in Social Psychology*, ed. P. Sheeran, T. L. Webb, and P. M. Gollwitzer, 329–347 (Oxford: Blackwell, 2005); P. Sheeran, T. L. Webb, P. M., Gollwitzer, "The Interplay between Goal Intentions and Implementation Intentions," *Personality and Social Psychology Bulletin* 31 (2005): 87–98.

56. A. L. Duckworth, H. Grant, B. Loew, G. Oettingen, and P. M. Gollwitzer, "Self-regulation Strategies Improve Self-discipline in Adolescents: Benefits of Mental Contrasting and Implementation Intentions," *Educational Psychology* 31 (2011): 17–26.

57. C. R. Snyder, H. S. Shorey, et al., "Hope and Academic Success in College," *Journal of Educational Psychology* 94 (2002): 820–826.

58. Ibid.

59. L. A. Curry et al., "Role of Hope in Academic and Sport Achievement," *Journal of Personality and Social Psychology* 73 (1997): 1257–1267.

60. L. Day et al., "Hope Uniquely Predicts Objective Academic Achievement Above Intelligence, Personality, and Previous Academic Achievement," *Journal of Research in Personality* 44 (2010): 550–553.

61. R. Görres, "Situational Hope Facilitates Creative Problem-Solving" (bachelor's thesis, University College Utrecht, The Netherlands, June 2011).

62. P. R. Magaletta and J. M. Oliver, "The Hope Construct, Will, and Ways: Their Relations with Self-Efficacy, Optimism, and General Well-Being," *Journal of Clinical Psychology* 55 (1999): 539–551.

63. K. L. Rand, A. D. Martin, and A. M. Shea, "Hope, but Not Optimism, Predicts Academic Performance of Law Students Beyond Previous Academic Achievement," *Journal of Research in Personality* 45 (2011): 683–686.

64. J. L. Burnette, E. J. O'Boyle, et al., "Mind-Sets Matter: A Meta-Analytic Review of Implicit Theories and Self-Regulation," *Psychological Bulletin* (2012). doi: 10.1037/a0029531.

65. C. S. Carver and M. F. Scheier, *On the Self-Regulation of Behavior* (New York: Cambridge University Press, 1998).

66. R. J. Vallerand, S,-J. Salvy, et al., "On the Role of Passion in Performance," *Journal of Personality* 75 (2007): 505–534.

67. A. Bonneville-Roussy, G. L. Lavigne, and R. J. Vallerand, "When Passion Leads to Excellence: The Case of Musicians," *Psychology of Music* 39 (2011): 123–138; R. J. Vallerand et al., "Passion and Performance Attainment in Sport," *Psychology of Sport and Exercise* 3 (2008): 373–392.

68. D. K. Simonton, "Expertise, Competence, and Creative Ability: The Perplexing Complexities," in *The Psychology of Abilities, Competencies, and Expertise*, ed. R. J. Sternberg and E. L. Grigorenko, 213–239 (New York: Cambridge University Press).

69. Hayes, *The Complete Problem Solver*, at 296.

70. D. K. Simonton, "Emergence and Realization of Genius: The Lives and Works of 120 Classical Composers," *Journal of Personality and Social Psychology* 61 (1991): 829–840.

71. D. K. Simonton, "Career Landmarks in Science: Individual Differences and Interdisciplinary Contrasts," *Developmental Psychology* 27 (1991): 119–130.

72. J. C. Kaufman and C. A. Gentile, "The Will, the Wit, the Judgement: The Importance of an Early Start in Productive and Successful Creative Writing," *High Ability Studies* 13 (2002): 115–123.

73. S. B. Kaufman and J. C. Kaufman, "Ten Years to Expertise, Many More to Greatness: An Investigation of Modern Writers," *Journal of Creative Behavior* 41 (2007): 114–124.

74. S. B. Kaufman, "Commentary on the Deliberate Practice View: Investigating the Role of Domain General Mechanisms in the Acquisition of Domain Specific Expertise," *High Ability Studies* 18 (2008): 71–73.

75. P. L. Ackerman and E. D. Heggestad, "Intelligence, Personality, and Interests: Evidence for Overlapping Traits," *Psychological Bulletin* 121 (1997): 219–245.

76. P. L. Ackerman, "Domain-Specific Knowledge as the 'Dark Matter' of Adult Intelligence: Gf/Gc, Personality and Interest Correlates," *Journal of Gerontology, Series B* 55 (2000): P69–P84.

77. A. S. Kaufman and J. L. Horn, "Age Changes on Tests of Fluid and Crystallized Intelligence for Women and Men on the Kaufman Adolescent and Adult Intelligence Test (KAIT) at Ages 17–94 Years," *Archives of Clinical Neuropsychology* 11 (1996): 97–121; A. S. Kaufman, C. K. Johnson, and X. Liu, "A CHC Theory-Based Analysis of Age Differences on Cognitive Abilities and Academic Skills at Ages 22 to 90 Years," *Journal of Psychoeducational Assessment* 26 (2008): 350–381.

78. P. B. Baltes and R. Kliegl, "Further Testing of Limits of Cognitive Plasticity: Negative Age Differences in a Mnemonic Skill Are Robust," *Developmental Psychology* 28 (1992): 121–125.

79. P. L. Ackerman, "A Theory of Adult Intellectual Development: Process, Personality, Interests, and Knowledge," *Intelligence* 22 (1996): 227–257. P. Ackerman and M. E. Beir, "Trait Complexes, Cognitive Investment, and Domain Knowledge," in The Psychology of Abilities, Competencies, and Expertise, ed. R. J. Sternberg and E. L. Grigorensco, 1–30 (New York: Cambridge University Press, 2003).

80. Ackerman, "Domain-Specific Knowledge as the 'Dark Matter,'" at 83.

Chapter 10

1. C. Spearman, "General Intelligence, Objectively Determined and Measured," *American Journal of Psychology* 15 (1904): 201–293.

2. S. J. Gould, *The Mismeasure of Man*, 2nd ed. (London: Penguin Books, 1997).

3. Interestingly, these early battles over *g* mirror modern-day arguments over how best to conceptualize human intelligence. For an informative online resource on the scientific study of human intelligence, including key historical influences, see http://www.intelltheory.com.

4. L. L. Thurstone, *Primary Mental Abilities* (Chicago: University of Chicago Press, 1938).

5. L. L. Thurstone and T. G. Thurstone, *Factorial Studies of Intelligence* (Chicago: University of Chicago Press, 1941).

6. J.-E. Gustafsson, "Hierarchical Models of Individual Differences in Cognitive Abilities," in *Advances in the Psychology of Human Intelligence*, vol. 4, ed. R. J. Sternberg (Hillsdale, NH: Erlbaum, 1988).

7. J. L. Horn and R. B. Cattell, "Refinement and Test of the Theory of Fluid and Crystallized General Intelligences," *Journal of Educational Psychology* 57 (1966): 253–270.

8. J. L. Horn and J. Noll, "Human Cognitive Capabilities: Gf-Gc Theory," in *Contemporary Intellectual Assessment: Theories, Tests, and Issues*, ed. D. P. Flanagan, J. L. Genshaft, and P. L. Harrison, 53–91 (New York: Cambridge University Press, 1997).

9. J. B. Carroll, *Human Cognitive Abilities* (Cambridge: Cambridge University Press, 1993).

10. J. L. Horn, "A Basis for Research on Age Differences in Cognitive Abilities," in *Human Cognitive Abilities in Theory and Practice*, ed. J. J. McArdle and R. W. Woodcock, 57–92 (Mahwah, NJ: Erlbaum, 1998), at 58.

11. J. T. Major, W. Johnson, and I. J Deary, "Comparing Models of Intelligence in Project TALENT: The VPR Model Fits Better than the CHC and Extended Gf-Gc Models," *Intelligence* 40 (2012): 543–559; J.-E. Gustafsson, "Measuring and Understanding G: Experimental and Correlational Approaches," in *Learning and Individual Differences: Process, Trait, and Content Determinants*, ed. P. L. Ackerman et al., 275–289 (Washington, DC: American Psychological Association, 1999).

12. I. J. Deary, S. Strand, P. Smith, and C. Fernandes, "Intelligence and Educational Achievement," *Intelligence* 35 (2007): 13–21.

13. W. Johnson, T. J. Bouchard Jr., et al., "Just One *g*: Consistent Results from Three Test Batteries," *Intelligence* 32 (2004): 95–107.

14. T. R. Coyle and D. R. Pillow, "SAT and ACT Predict College GPA After Removing *g*," *Intelligence* 36 (2008): 719–729; E. Hunt, *Human Intelligence* (New York: Cambridge University Press, 2010).

15. S. B. Kaufman, M. R. Reynolds, et al., "Are Cognitive *g* and Academic Achievement *g* One and the Same *g*? An Exploration on the Woodcock-Johnson and Kaufman Tests. *Intelligence* 40 (2012): 123–138.

16. S. B. Kaufman, C. G. DeYoung, D. L. Reis, and J. R. Gray, "General Intelligence Predicts Reasoning Ability Even for Evolutionary Familiar Content," *Intelligence* 39 (2011): 311–322.

17. B. A. Visser, M. C. Ashton, and P. A. Vernon, "Beyond *g*: Putting Multiple Intelligences Theory to the Test," *Intelligence* 34 (2006): 487–502.

18. H. G. Gardner, "On Failing to Grasp the Core of MI Theory: A Response to Visser et al.," *Intelligence* 34 (2006): 503–505, at 503.

19. Ibid., at 503–504.

20. A. T. Cianciolo, E. L. Grigorenko, et al., "Practical Intelligence and Tacit Knowledge: Advancements in the Measurement of Developing Expertise," *Learning and Individual Differences* 16 (2006): 235–253; S. A. Kornilov, M. Tan, et al., "Gifted Identification with Aurora: Widening the Spotlight," *Journal of Psychoeducational Assessment* 30 (2012): 117–133.

21. M. J. Schulte, M. J. Ree, and T. R. Carretta, "Emotional Intelligence: Not Much More than *g* and Personality," *Personality and Individual Differences* 37 (2004): 1059–1068.

22. J. D. Mayer, P. Salovey, D. R. Caruso, and L. Cherkasskiy, "Emotional Intelligence," in *The Cambridge Handbook of Intelligence*, ed. R. J. Sternberg and S. B. Kaufman, 528–549 (New York: Cambridge University Press, 2011); R. J. Sternberg, "The Theory of Successful Intelligence," in *Cambridge Handbook of Intelligence*, 504–527.

23. C. F. Chabris, "Cognitive and Neurobiological Mechanisms of the Law of General Intelligence," in *Integrating the Mind: Domain General Versus Domain Specific Processes in Higher Cognition*, ed. M. J. Roberts, 449–491 (New York: Psychology Press, 2007).

24. D. Wechsler, *The Measurement and Appraisal of Adult Intelligence*, 4th ed. (Baltimore: Williams and Wilkins, 1958), at 64.

25. G. H. Thomson, "A Hierarchy Without a General Factor," *British Journal of Psychology* 8 (1916): 271–281.

26. D. J. Bartholomew, I. J. Deary, and M. Lawn, "A New Lease of Life for Thomson's Bonds Model of Intelligence," *Psychological Review* 116 (2009): 567–579.

27. R. E. Snow and D. F. Lohman, "Implications of Cognitive Psychology for Educational Measurement," in *Educational Measurement*, ed. R. Linn, 3rd ed., 263–332 (New York: American Council on Education/Macmillan, 1989).

28. T. Nettelbeck, "Basic Processes of Intelligence," in *Cambridge Handbook of Intelligence*, 371–393; A. C. Neubauer and A. Fink, "Basic Information Processing and the Psychophysiology of Intelligence," in *Cognition & Intelligence: Identifying the Mechanisms of the Mind*, ed. R. J. Sternberg and J. E. Pretz, 68–87 (New York: Cambridge University Press, 2005); I. J. Deary, *Looking Down on Human Intelligence: From Psychometrics to the Brain* (New York: Oxford University Press, 2000). For the view of processing speed as a central component of *g*, see A. R. Jensen, *Clocking the Mind: Mental Chronometry and Individual Differences* (Oxford, UK: Elsevier, 2006).

29. W. Johnson and T. J. Bouchard Jr., "The Structure of Human Intelligence: It Is Verbal, Perceptual, and Image Rotation (VPR), not Fluid and Crystallized," *Intelligence* 33 (2005): 393–416; W. Johnson and T. J. Bouchard Jr., "Constructive Replication of the Visual-Perceptual-Image Rotation Model in Thurstone's (1941) Battery of 60 Tests of Mental Ability," *Intelligence* 33 (2005): 417–430; W. Johnson, J. Te Nijenhuis, and T. J. Bouchard Jr., "Replication of the Hierarchical Visual-Perceptual-Image Rotation Model in de Wolff and Buiten's (1963) Battery of 46 Tests of Mental Ability," *Intelligence* 35 (2007): 69–81; W. Johnson, T. J. Bouchard Jr., M. McGue, N. L. Segal, A. Tellegen, M. Keyes, and I. I. Gottesman, "Genetic and Environmental Influences on the Verbal-Perceptual-Image Rotation (VPR) Model of the Structure of Mental Abilities in the Minnesota Study of Twins Reared Apart," *Intelligence* 35 (2007): 542–562; W. Johnson and T. J. Bouchard Jr., "Sex Differences in Mental Abilities: *g* Masks the Dimensions on Which They Lie," *Intelligence* 35 (2007): 23–39; Major, Johnson, and Deary, "Comparing Models of Intelligence in Project TALENT."

30. Johnson et al., "Genetic and Environmental Influences"; N. J. Mackintosh, *IQ and Human Intelligence*, 2nd ed. (New York: Cambridge University Press, 2011); C. G. DeYoung, "Intelligence and Personality," in *Cambridge Handbook of Intelligence*.

31. P. A. Carpenter, M. A. Just, and P. Shell, "What One Intelligence Test Measures: A Theoretical Account of the Processing in the Raven Progressive Matrices Test," *Psychological Review* 97 (1990): 404–431; D. F. Lohman, "Fluid Intelligence, Inductive Reasoning, and Working Memory: Where the Theory of Multiple Intelligences Falls Short," in *Talent Development IV: Proceedings from the 1998 Henry B. and Jocelyn Wallace National Research Symposium on Talent Development*, ed. N. Colangeloa and S. Assouline, 219–228 (Scottsdale, AZ: Gifted Psychology Press, 2001).

32. N. Cowan, "What Are the Differences Between Long-Term, Short-Term, and Working Memory?," *Progress in Brain Research* 169 (2008): 323–338.

33. M. Daneman and P. A. Carpenter, "Individual Differences in Working Memory and Reading," *Journal of Verbal Learning and Verbal Behavior* 19 (1980): 450–466.

34. M. Proust, *In Search of Lost Time*, vol. 2: *The Guermantes Way*, Everyman's Library Edition (New York: Random House, 2001), at 471; example borrowed from Mackintosh, *IQ and Human Intelligence*, at 127.

35. A. R. A. Conway, N. Cowan, et al., "A Latent Variable Analysis of Working Memory Capacity, Short-Term Memory Capacity, Processing Speed, and General Fluid Intelligence," *Intelligence* 30 (2002): 163–183.

36. M. J. Kane, D. Z. Hambrick, and A. R. A. Conway, "Working Memory Capacity and Fluid Intelligence Are Strongly Related Constructs: Comments on Ackerman, Beier, and Boyle (2005)," *Psychological Bulletin* 131 (2005): 66–71; A. Conway, C. Jarrold, M. Kane, and A. Miyake, eds., *Variation in Working Memory* (New York: Oxford University Press, 2007); A. R. A Conway, S. J. Getz, B. Macnamara, and P. M. J. Engel de Abreu, "Working Memory and Intelligence," in *Cambridge Handbook of Intelligence*, 394–418; A. R. A. Conway and K. Kovacs, "Individual Differences in Intelligence and Working Memory: A Review of Latent Variable Models," in *The Psychology of Learning and Motivation*, vol. 58, ed. B. H. Ross, 233–270 (New York: Academic Press, 2013).

37. J. Duncan et al., "A Neural Basis for General Intelligence," *Science* 289 (2000): 457–460.

38. M. J. Kane, "Full Frontal Fluidity? Looking in on the Neuroimaging of Reasoning and Intelligence," in *Handbook of Understanding and Measuring Intelligence*, ed. O. Wilhelm and R. W. Engle (New York: Sage, 2005); V. Prabhakaran, B. Rypma, and D. E. Gabrieli, "Neural Substrates of Mathematical Reasoning: A Functional Magnetic Resonance Imaging Study of Neocortical Activation during Performance of the Necessary Arithmetic Operations," *Neuropsychology* 15 (2001): 115–127; V. Prabhakaran, K. Narayanan, Z. Zhao, and J. D. Gabriele, "Integration of Diverse Information in Working Memory Within the Frontal Lobe," *Nature Neuroscience* 3 (2000): 85–90; A. K. Barbey, R. Colom, and J. Grafman, "Dorsolateral Prefrontal Contributions to Human Intelligence," *Neuropsychologia* (in press); D. E. Nee, J. W. Brown, M. K. Askren, M. G. Berman, E. Demiralp, A. Krawitz, and J. Jonides, "A Meta-Analysis of Executive Components of Working Memory," *Cerebral Cortex* (2012), doi:10.1093/cercor/bhs007.

39. J. R. Gray, C. F. Chabris, and T. S. Braver, "Neural Mechanisms of General Fluid Intelligence," *Nature Neuroscience* 6 (2003): 316–322.

40. R. E. Jung and R. J. Haier, "The Parieto-Frontal Integration Theory (P-FIT) of Intelligence: Converging Neuroimaging Evidence," *Behavioral and Brain Sciences* 30 (2007): 135–154.

41. S. Norgate and K. Richardson, "On Images from Correlations," *Behavioral and Brain Science* 30 (2007): 162–163.

42. R. Colom, "Intelligence? What Intelligence?," *Behavioral and Brain Sciences* 30 (2007): 155–156; R. E. Nisbett, J. Aronson, et al., "Intelligence: New Findings and Theoretical Developments," *American Psychologist* 67 (2012): 130–159.

43. R. J. Haier, "Biological Basis of Intelligence," in *Cambridge Handbook of Intelligence*, 351–370.

44. A. Woolgar et al., "Fluid Intelligence Loss Linked to Restricted Regions of Damage Within Frontal and Parietal Cortex," *PNAS* 107 (2010): 14899–14902; J. Gläscher et al., "Distributed Neural Systems for General Intelligence Revealed by Lesion Mapping," *PNAS* 107 (2010): 4705–4709; A. K. Barbey et al., "An Integrative Architecture for General Intelligence and Executive Function Revealed by Lesion Mapping," *Brain* 135 (2012): 1154–1164; Barbey, Colom, and Grafman, "Dorsolateral Prefrontal Contributions."

45. A. K. Barbey et al., "An Integrative Architecture for General Intelligence and Executive Function Revealed by Lesion Mapping."

46. K. Semendeferi, E. Armstrong, et al., "Prefrontal Cortex in Humans and Apes: A Comparative Study of Area 10," *American Journal of Physical Anthropology* 114 (2001): 224–241; D. C. Van Essen and D. L. Dierker, "Surface-Based and Probabilistic Atlases of Primate Cerebral Cortex," *Neuron* 56 (2007): 209–225.

47. D. Falk, F. E. Lepore, and A. Noe, "The Cerebral Cortex of Albert Einstein: A Description and Preliminary Analysis of Unpublished Photographs," *Brain* (2012), doi:10.1093/brain/aws295.

48. P. W. Burgess, I. Dumontheil, and S. J. Gilbert, "The Gateway Hypothesis of Rostral Prefrontal Cortex (Area 10) Function," *Trends in Cognitive Sciences* 11 (2007): 290–298, at 290.

49. Woolgar et al., "Fluid Intelligence Loss"; Gläscher et al., "Distributed Neural Systems"; N. Ramnani and A. M. Owen, "Anterior Prefrontal Cortex: Insights into Function from Anatomy and Neuroimaging," *Nature Reviews Neuroscience* 5 (2004): 184–194; M. Buda, A. Fornito, Z. M. Bergstrom, and J. S. Simons, "A Specific Brain Structural Basis for Individual Differences in Reality Monitoring," *Journal of Neuroscience* 31 (2011): 14308–14313; S. M. Fleming and R. J. Dolan, "The Neural Basis of Metacognitive Ability," *Philosophical Transactions of the Royal Society: B* 367 (2012): 1338–1349; A. E. Green, J. A. Fugelsang, D. J. M. Kraemer, N. A. Shamosh, and K. N. Dunbar, "Frontopolar Cortex Mediates Abstract Integration in Analogy," *Brain Research* 1096 (2006): 125–137; A. E. Greene, D. J. M. Kraemer, J. A. Fugelsang, J. R. Gray, and K. N. Dunbar, "Neural Correlates of Creativity in Analogical Reasoning," *Journal of Experimental Psychology* 38 (2012): 264–272; M. Ellamil, C. Dobson, M. Beeman, and K. Christoff, "Evaluative and Generative Modes of Thought during the Creative Process," *NeuroImage* 59 (2012): 1783–1794; J. K. Kroger, F. W. Sabb, C. L. Fales, S. Y. Bookheimer, M. S. Cohen, and K. J. Holyoak, "Recruitment of Anterior Dorsolateral Prefrontal Cortex in Human Reasoning: A Parametric Study of Relational Complexity," *Cerebral Cortex* 12 (2002): 477–485; A. Hampshire, R. Thompson, J. Duncan, and A. M. Owen, "Lateral Prefrontal Cortex Subregions Make Dissociable Contributions During Fluid Reasoning," *Cerebral Cortex* 21 (2011): 1–10; J. D. Greene, L. E. Engell, A. D. Darley, and J. M. Cohen, "The Neural Bases of Cognitive Conflict and Control in Moral Judgment," *Neuron* 44 (2004): 389–400.

50. S. M. Fleming, J. Huijgen, and R. J. Dolan, "Prefrontal Contributions to Metacognition in Perceptual Decision Making," *Journal of Neuroscience* 32 (2012); L. Stankov, L. Jihyun, W. Luo, and D. J. Hogan, "Confidence: A Better Predictor of Academic Achievement Than Self-Efficacy, Self-Concept and Anxiety?," *Learning and Individual Differences* 22 (2012): 747–758.

51. K. Christoff and J. D. E. Gabriele, "The Frontopolar Cortex and Human Cognition: Evidence for a Rostrocaudal Hierarchical Organization Within the Human Prefrontal Cortex," *Psychobiology* 28 (2000): 168–186; Burgess, Dumontheil, and Gilbert, "Gateway Hypothesis"; Ramnani and Owen, "Anterior Prefrontal Cortex"; C. Kim, N. F. Johnson, S. E. Cilles, and B. T. Gold, "Common and Distinct Mechanisms of Cognitive Flexibility in Prefrontal Cortex," *Journal of Neuroscience* 31 (2011): 4771–4779; Ellamil et al., "Evaluative and Generative Modes of Thoughts."

52. Barbey et al., "An Integrative Architecture," at 1160.

53. J. Gläscher et al., "Lesion Mapping of Cognitive Control and Value-Based Decision Making in the Prefrontal Cortex," *PNAS* 109 (2012): 14681–14686; C. Blair and A. Diamond, "Biological Processes in Prevention and Intervention: The Promotion of Self-Regulation as a Means of Preventing School Failure," *Development and Psychopathology* 20 (2012): 899–911; F. Krueger et al., "The Neural Bases of Key Competencies of Emotional Intelligence," *PNAS* 106 (2009): 22486–22491; A. K. Barbey, R. Colom, and J. Grafman, "Distributed Neural System for Emotional Intelligence Revealed by Lesion Mapping," *Social Cognitive and Affective Neuroscience* (2012), doi:10.1093/scan/nss124; A. K. Barbey, F. Krueger, and J. Grafman, "An

Evolutionary Adaptive Neural Architecture for Social Reasoning," *Trends in Neurosciences* 32 (2009): 603–610.

54. A. Miyake, N. P. Friedman, M. J. Emerson, A. H. Witzki, A. Howerter, and T. D. Wager, "The Unity and Diversity of Executive Functions and Their Contributions to Complex 'Frontal Lobe' Tasks: A Latent Variable Analysis," *Cognitive Psychology* 41 (2000): 49–100; A. Miyake and N. P. Friedman, "The Nature and Organization of Individual Differences in Executive Functions: Four General Conclusions," *Current Directions in Psychological Science* 21 (2012): 8–14; N. P. Friedman, A. Miyake, et al., "Individual Differences in Executive Functions Are Almost Entirely Genetic in Origin," *Journal of Experimental Psychology: General* 137 (2008): 201–225.

55. N. P. Friedman, A. Miyake, J. L. Robinson, and J. K. Hewitt, "Developmental Trajectories in Toddlers' Self-Restraint Predict Individual Differences in Executive Functions 14 Years Later: A Behavioral Genetic Analysis," *Developmental Psychology* 47 (2011): 1410–1430.

56. N. P. Friedman, A. Miyake, et al., "Not All Executive Functions Are Related to Intelligence," *Psychological Science* 17 (2006): 172–179.

57. D. Bor, *The Ravenous Brain: How the New Science of Consciousness Explains Our Insatiable Search for Meaning* (New York: Basic Books, 2012).

58. D. Bor and A. K. Seth, "Consciousness and the Prefrontal Parietal Network: Insights from Attention, Working Memory, and Chunking," *Frontiers in Psychology* 3 (2012): 1–14; Prabhakaran, Narayanan, Zhao, and Gabriele, "Integration of Diverse"; V. Prabhakaran et al., "Capacity-Speed Relationships in Prefrontal Cortex," *PLoS ONE* 6 (2011): e277504; D. Bor, C. N. Cumming, E. Scott, and A. M Owen, "Prefrontal Cortical Involvement in Verbal Encoding Strategies," *European Journal of Neuroscience* 19 (2004): 3365–3370; D. Bor and A. M. Owen, "A Common Prefrontal- Parietal Network for Mnemonic and Mathematical Recoding Strategies Within Working Memory," *Cerebral Cortex* 17 (2007): 778–786.

59. Bor and Owen, "A Common Prefrontal-Parietal Network."

60. Bor, *The Ravenous Brain*, at 180–181.

61. S. B. Kaufman, C. G. DeYoung, J. R. Gray, J. Brown, and N. Mackintosh, "Associative Learning Predicts Intelligence Above and Beyond Working Memory and Processing Speed," *Intelligence* 37 (2009): 374–382.

62. K. Nandagopal, R. Roring, K. A. Ericsson, and J. Taylor, "Strategies May Mediate Heritable Aspects of Memory Performance: A Twin Study," *Cognitive Behavioral Neuroscience* 23 (2010): 224–230.

63. R. J. Haier, B. Siegel, C. Tang, L. Abel, and M. S. Buchsbaum, "Intelligence and Changes in Regional Cerebral Glucose Metabolic-Rate following Learning," *Intelligence* 16 (1992): 415–426.

64. Mackintosh, *IQ and Human Intelligence*.

65. E. D. Reichle, P. A. Carpenter, and M. A. Just, "The Neural Bases of Strategy and Skill in Sentence-Picture Verification," *Cognitive Psychology* 40 (2000): 261–295.

66. R. J. Haier, R. Colom, et al., "Gray Matter and Intelligence Factors: Is There a Neurog?," *Intelligence* 37 (2009): 136–144.

67. R. A. Kievit et al., "Intelligence and the Brain: A Model-Based Approach," *Cognitive Neuroscience* 3 (2012): 89–97.

68. Also see R. Colom, R. J. Haier, et al., "Gray Matter Correlates of Fluid, Crystallized, and Spatial Intelligence: Testing the P-FIT Model," *Intelligence* 37 (2009): 124–135.

69. D. J. Bartholomew, *Measuring Intelligence: Facts and Fallacies* (Cambridge: Cambridge University Press, 2004); C.D. Rabaglia, G. F. Marcus, and S. P. Lane, "What Can Individual Differences Tell Us About the Specialization of Function?," *Cognitive Neuropsychology* 28 (2011): 288–303; A. Hampshire, R. R. Highfield, B. L. Parkin, and A. M. Owen, "Fractionating Human Intelligence," *Neuron* 76 (2012): 1225–1237.

70. H. L. J. van der Maas et al., "A Dynamical Model of General Intelligence: The Positive Manifold of Intelligence by Mutualism," *Psychological Review* 113 (2006): 842–861.

71. P. Shaw et al., "Intellectual Ability and Cortical Development in Children and Adolescents," *Nature* 440 (2006): 676–679.

72. P. M. Thompson, T. D. Cannon, et al., "Genetic Influences on Brain Structure," *Nature Neuroscience* 4 (2001): 1253–1258; M.-C. Chiang et al., "Genetics of Brain Fiber Architecture and Intellectual Performance," *Journal of Neuroscience* 29 (2009): 2212–2224.

73. R. J. Zatorre, R. D. Fields, and H. Johansen-Berg, "Plasticity in Gray and White: Neuroimaging Changes in Brain Structure During Learning," *Nature Neuroscience* 4 (2012): 528–536.

74. B. Draganski et al., "Neuroplasticity: Changes in Grey Matter Induced by Training," *Nature* 427 (2004): 311–312.

75. E. A. Maguire et al., "Navigation-Related Structural Change in the Hippocampi of Taxi Drivers," *Proceedings of the National Academy of Sciences: USA* 97 (2000): 4398–4403; N. A. Farb, Z. V. Segal, and A. K. Anderson, "Mindfulness Meditation Training Alters Cortical Representations of Interoceptive Attention," *Social Cognitive and Affective Neuroscience* (forthcoming, 2013), doi: 10.1093/scan/nss066.

76. P. Bermudez, A. C. Evans, J. P. Lerch, and R. J. Zatorre, "Neuro-Anatomical Correlates of Musicianship as Revealed by Cortical Thickness and Voxel-Based Morphometry," *Cerebral Cortex* 19 (2009): 1583–1596; P. Schneider et al., "Morphology of Heschl's Gyrus Reflects Enhanced Activation in the Auditory Cortex of Musicians," *Nature Neuroscience* 5 (2002): 688–694.

77. T. Elbert, C. Pantev, C. Wienbruch, B. Rockstroh, and E. Taub, "Increased Cortical Representation of the Fingers of the Left Hand in String Players," *Science* 270 (1995): 305–307.

78. S. L. Bengtsson et al., "Extensive Piano Practicing Has Regionally Specific Effects on White Matter Development," *Nature Neuroscience* 8 (2005): 1148–1150.

79. K. L. Hyde, J. Lerch, et al., "Musical Training Shapes Structural Brain Development," *Journal of Neuroscience* 29 (2009): 3019–3025.

80. H. Takeuchi et al., "Training of Working Memory Impacts Structural Connectivity," *Journal of Neuroscience* 30 (2010): 3297–3303.

81. A. P. Mackey, K. Whitaker, and S. A. Bunge, "Experience-Dependent Plasticity in White Matter Microstructure: Reasoning Training Alters Structural Connectivity," *Frontiers in Neuroanatomy* 6 (2012): 32.

82. S. Bergman Nutley, S. Söderqvist, et al., "Gains in Fluid Intelligence After Training Non-Verbal Reasoning in 4-Year-Old Children: A Controlled, Randomized Study," *Developmental Science* 14 (2011): 591–601; J. Holmes, S. E. Gathercole, et al., "Working Memory Deficits Can Be Overcome: Impacts of Training and Medication on Working Memory in Children with ADHD," *Applied Cognitive Psychology* 24 (2010): 827–836; T. Klingberg, E. Fernell, et al., "Computerized Training of Working Memory in Children with ADHD: A Randomized, Controlled Trial," *Journal of American Academy of Child & Adolescent Psychiatry* 44 (2005): 177–186; L. B. Thorell, S. Lindqvist, N. Bergman, G. Bohlin, and T. Klingberg, "Training and Transfer Effects of Executive Functions in Preschool Children," *Developmental Science* 12 (2009): 106–113; T. Klingberg, "Training and Plasticity of Working Memory," *Trends in Cognitive Science* 14 (2010): 317–324; A. P. Mackey, S. S. Hill, S. I. Stone, and S. A. Bunge, "Differential Effects of Reasoning and Speed Training in Children," *Developmental Science* 14 (2011): 582–590; A. Morrison and J. Chein, "Does Working Memory Training Work? The Promise and Challenges of Enhancing Cognition by Training Working Memory," *Psychonomic Bulletin & Review* 18 (2011): 46–60; M. Melby-Lervåg and C. Hulme, "Is Working Memory Training Effective? A Meta-Analytic Review," *Developmental Psychology* 49 (2013): 270–291.

83. S. M. Jaeggi, M. Buschkuehl, J. Jonides, and W. J. Perrig, "Improving Fluid Intelligence with Training on Working Memory," *Proceedings of the National Academy of Sciences*

105 (2008): 6829–6833; S. M. Jaeggi, B. Studer-Luethi, M. Buschkuehl, Y-F Su, J. Jonides, and W.J. Perrig, "The Relationship Between n-back Performance and Matrix Reasoning—Implications for Training and Transfer," *Intelligence* 38 (2010): 625–635; S. M. Jaeggi, M. Buschkuehl, J. Jonides, and P. Shah, "Short- and Long-Term Benefits of Cognitive Training," *PNAS* 108 (2011): 10081–10086; T. S. Redick et al., "No Evidence of Intelligence Improvement After Working Memory Training: A Randomized, Placebo-Controlled Study," *Journal of Experimental Psychology: General* (forthcoming, 2013), doi:10.1037/a0029082; S. R. Rudenbeck, D. Bor, J. Ormond, X. O'Reilly, and A. C. H. Lee, "A Potential Spatial Working Memory Training Task to Improve Both Episodic Memory and Fluid Intelligence," *PLoS ONE* 7 (2012): e50431; O. Vartanian, M-E. Jobidon, F. Bouak, A. Nakashima, I. Smith, Q. Lam, and B. Cheung, "Working Memory Training Is Associated with Lower Prefrontal Cortex Activation in a Divergent Thinking Task," *Neuroscience* (2013), doi:http://dx.doi.org/10.1016/j.neuroscience.2012.12.060; Melby-Lervåg and Hulme, "Is Working Memory Training Effective?"

84. J. te Nijenhuis, A. E. M. van Vianen, and H. van der Flier, "Score Gains on *g*-Loaded Tests: No *g*," *Intelligence* 35 (2007): 283–300.

85. A. Diamond, "Activities and Programs That Improve Children's Executive Functions," *Psychological Science* 21 (2012): 335–341.

86. S. Soderqvist, S. B. Nutley, et al., "Dopamine, Working Memory, and Training Induced Plasticity: Implications for Developmental Research," *Developmental Psychology* 48 (2012): 836–843; also see F. McNab, A. Varrone, L. Farde, A. Jucaite, P. Bystritsky, H. Forssberg, and T. Klingberg, "Changes in Cortical Dopamine D1 Receptor Binding Associated with Cognitive Training," *Science* 323 (2009): 800–802.

87. B. Studer-Luethi, S. M. Jaeggi, M. Buschkuehl, and W. J. Perrig, "Influence of Neuroticism and Conscientiousness on Working Memory Training Outcome," *Personality and Individual Differences* 53 (2012): 44–49.

88. Diamond, "Activities and Programs."

89. P. N. Johnson-Laird, "Mental Models and Reasoning," in *The Nature of Reasoning*, ed. J. P. Leighton and R. J. Sternberg, 169–204 (New York: Cambridge University Press, 2004).

90. P. N. Johnson-Laird and M. Steadman, "The Psychology of Syllogisms," *Cognitive Psychology* 10 (1978): 64–99.

91. Ibid., at 77.

92. R. S. Nickerson, "Teaching Reasoning," in Leighton and Sternberg, *The Nature of Reasoning*, 410–442.

93. P. Fleming, L. J. Ball, T. C. Ormerod, and A. F. Collins, "Analogue Versus Propositional Representation in Congenitally Blind Individuals," *Psychonomic Bulletin & Review* 13 (2006): 1049–1055; M. Knauff and E. May, "Mental Imagery, Reasoning, and Blindness," *Quarterly Journal of Experimental Psychology* 59 (2006): 161–177.

94. K. J. Gilhooly, R. H. Logie, N. E. Wetherick, and V. Wynn, "Working Memory and Strategies in Syllogistic Reasoning Tasks," *Memory and Cognition* 21 (1993): 115–124.

95. J. L. Plass, R. Moreno, and R. Brunken, *Cognitive Load Theory* (New York: Cambridge University Press, 2010); T. van Gog, F. Paas, and J. Sweller, "Cognitive Load Theory: Advances in Research on Worked Examples, Animations, and Cognitive Load Measurement," *Educational Psychology Review* 22 (2010): 375–378.

96. D. Z. Hambrick, "I.Q. Points for Sale, Cheap," *New York Times*, May 5, 2012, http://www.nytimes.com/2012/05/06/opinion/sunday/iq-points-for-sale-cheap.html.

97. F. A. Campbell, C. T. Ramey, E. Pungello, J. Sparling, and S. Miller-Johnson, "Early Childhood Education: Young Adult Outcomes from the Abecedarian Project," *Applied Developmental Science* 6 (2002): 42–57; H. L. Garber, *The Milwaukee Project: Preventing Mental Retardation in Children at Risk* (Washington, DC: American Association on Mental Retardation, 1988).

98. M. J. A. Howe, *IQ in Question: The Truth About Intelligence* (New York: Sage, 1997), at 56.

99. R. J. Sternberg, "Intelligence as Developing Expertise," *Contemporary Educational Psychology* 24 (1999): 359–375; D. F. Lohman, "Beliefs About Differences Between Ability and Accomplishment: From Folk Theories to Cognitive Science," *Roeper Review* 29 (2006): 1–13.

100. Diamond, "Activities and Programs."

101. J. R. Flynn, *What Is Intelligence? Beyond the Flynn Effect* (New York: Cambridge University Press, 2006); J. R. Flynn, *Are We Getting Smarter? Rising IQ in the Twenty-First Century* (New York: Cambridge University Press, 2012).

102. Flynn, *What Is Intelligence?*

103. Ibid., at 28.

104. M. C. Fox and A. L. Mitchum, "A Knowledge-Based Theory of Rising Scores on 'Culture-Free' Tests," *Journal of Experimental Psychology: General* (2012), doi:10.1037/a0030155.

105. R. Schulz and C. Curnow, "Peak Performance and Age Among Superathletes: Track and Field, Swimming, Baseball, Tennis, and Golf," *Journal of Gerontology: Psychological Sciences* 43 (1988): 113–120; K. A. Ericsson, R. W. Roring, and K. Nandagopal, "Giftedness and Evidence for Reproducibly Superior Performance: An Account Based on the Expert Performance Framework," *High Ability Studies* 18 (2007): 3–56.

106. J. Starkes and K. A. Ericsson, *Expert Performance in Sport: Recent Advances in Research on Sport Expertise* (Champaign, IL: Human Kinetics, 2003).

107. M. J. Karvonen and M. Niemi, "Factor Analysis of Performance in Track and Field Events," *European Journal of Applied Physiology and Occupational Physiology* 15 (1953): 127–133; S. Le, J. Josse, and F. Husson, "FactorMineR: An R Package for Multivariate Analysis," *Journal of Statistical Software* 25 (2008): 1–18.

108. W. T. Dickens and J. R. Flynn, "Heritability Estimates Versus Large Environmental Effects: The IQ Paradox Resolved," *Psychological Review* 108 (2001): 346–369.

109. S. Johnson, *Everything Bad Is Good for You: How Today's Popular Culture Is Actually Making Us Smarter* (New York: Riverhead Trade, 2006); D. F. Marks, "IQ Variations Across Time, Race, and Nationality: An Artifact of Differences in Literacy Skills," *Psychological Reports* 106 (2010): 643–664.

110. C. Spearman, "Some Issues in the Theory of 'g' (Including the Law of Diminishing Returns)," *Nature* 116 (1925): 436–439.

111. D. K. Detterman, "Correlations of Mental Tests with Each Other and with Cognitive Variables Are Highest for Low IQ Groups," *Intelligence* 13 (1989): 349–359; M. R. Reynolds and T. Z. Keith, "Spearman's Law of Diminishing Returns in Hierarchical Models of Intelligence for Children and Adolescents," *Intelligence* 35 (2007): 267–281; E. M. Tucker-Drob, "Differentiation of Cognitive Abilities Across the Life Span," *Developmental Psychology* 45 (2009): 1097–1118.

112. D. Goleman, *Emotional Intelligence* (New York: Bantam Books, 1995), at 37.

Chapter 11

1. THNKR, "Prodigies" series on YouTube, http://www.youtube.com/playlist?list=PLB1860C67A2998C0B.

2. E. Winner, *Gifted Children: Myths and Realities* (New York: Basic Books, 1997).

3. M. J. Morelock, "The Profoundly Gifted Child in Family Context" (PhD diss., Tufts University, Medford, MA, 1995).

4. D. H. Feldman and L. T. Goldsmith, *Nature's Gambit: Child Prodigies and the Development of Human Potential* (New York: Teachers College Press, 1991).

5. Also see D. H. Feldman, "The Development of Creativity," in *International Handbook of Giftedness and Talent*, ed. R. J. Sternberg and R. F. Subotnik, 271–282 (Oxford: Elsevier Science, 2000).

6. D. H. Feldman, "Prodigies and Their Domains" (paper presented at the European Council for High Ability, Munster, Germany, September 13, 2012).

7. J. Ruthsatz and J. B. Urbach, "Child Prodigy: A Novel Cognitive Profile Places Elevated General Intelligence, Exceptional Working Memory and Attention to Detail at the Root of Prodigiousness," *Intelligence* 40 (2012): 419–426.

8. D. J. Feldman and M. J. Morelock, "Prodigies and Savants," in *The Cambridge Handbook of Intelligence*, ed. R. J. Sternberg and S. B. Kaufman, 210–234 (New York: Cambridge University Press, 2011).

9. J. A. Achter, C. P. Benbow, and D. Lubinski, "Rethinking Multipotentiality Among the Intellectually Gifted: A Critical Review and Recommendations," *Gifted Child Quarterly* 41 (1997): 5–15; D. F. Lohman, J. Gambrell, and J. Lakin, "The Commonality of Extreme Discrepancies in the Ability Profiles of Academically Gifted Students," *Psychology Science Quarterly* 50 (2008): 269–282; Winner, *Gifted Children*.

10. D. Z. Hambrick and E. J. Meinz, "Limits on the Predictive Power of Domain-Specific Experience and Knowledge in Skilled Performance," *Current Directions in Psychological Science* 20 (2011): 275–279; E. J. Meinz and D. Z. Hambrick, "Deliberate Practice Is Necessary but Not Sufficient to Explain Individual Differences in Piano Sight-Reading Skill," *Psychological Science* 21 (2010): 914–919.

11. "What Is Autism," Autism Speaks, http://www.autismspeaks.org/what-autism.

12. T. Attwood, *Asperger's Syndrome: A Guide for Parents and Professionals* (London: Jessica-Kingsley, 1998); R. Hobson and A. Lee, "Hello and Goodbye: A Study of Social Engagement in Autism," *Journal of Autism and Developmental Disorders* 28 (1998): 117–127, at 70.

13. S. Baron-Cohen and S. Wheelwright, "The Friendship Questionnaire: An Investigation of Adults with Asperger Syndrome or High-Functioning Autism, and Normal Sex Differences," *Journal of Autism and Developmental Disorders* 33 (2003): 509–517; A. M. Scheeren et al., "Can You Tell Me Something About Yourself?," *Autism* 14 (2010): 457–473, at 72.

14. W. Hudenko et al., "Laughter Differs in Children with Autism: An Acoustic Analysis of Laughs Produced by Children With and Without the Disorder," *Journal of Autism and Developmental Disorders* 39 (2009): 1392–1400.

15. C. Chevallier, G. Kohls, V. Troiani, E. S. Brodkin, and R. T. Schultz, "The Social Motivation Theory of Autism," *Trends in Cognitive Sciences* 16 (2012): 231–239; S. Baron-Cohen, *Mindblindness: An Essay on Autism and Theory of Mind* (Cambridge, MA: MIT Press, 1995).

16. H. Asperger, "Die autistischen Psychopathen im Kindesalter," in *Autism and Asperger Syndrome*, ed. and trans. U. Frith, 37–92 (1944; New York: Cambridge University Press, 1991).

17. I. Dziobek et al., "Dissociation of Cognitive and Emotional Empathy in Adults with Asperger Syndrome Using the Multifaceted Empathy Test (MET)," *Journal of Autism and Developmental Disorders* 38 (2008): 464–473.

18. F. Castelli, "Understanding Emotions from Standardized Facial Expressions in Autism and Normal Development," *Autism* 9 (2005): 428–449; F. Happe, "An Advanced Test of Theory of Mind: Understanding of Story Characters' Thoughts and Feelings by Able Autistic, Mentally Handicapped and Normal Children and Adults," *Journal of Autism and Developmental Disorders* 2 (1994): 129–154.

19. J. Birch, *Congratulations! It's Asperger's Syndrome* (London: Jessica-Kingsley, 2003); R. Jones, A. Zahl, and J. Huws, "First-Hand Accounts of Emotional Experiences in Autism: A Qualitative Analysis," *Disability and Society* 16 (2001): 393–401; C. Sainsbury, *Martian in the Playground* (London: Book Factory, 2000).

20. J. Miller, *Women from Another Planet? Our Lives in the Universe of Autism* (Milan: Dancing Mind Books, 2003).

21. A. H. Rutgers et al., "Autism and Attachment: A Meta-Analytic Review," *Journal of Child Psychology and Psychiatry* 45 (2004): 1123–1134.

22. M. D. Del Giudice et al., "The Evolution of Autistic-Like and Schizotypal Traits: A Sexual Selection Hypothesis," *Frontiers in Psychology* 1 (2010): 1–18.

23. K. O'Connor and I. Kirk, "Brief Report: Atypical Social Cognition and Social Behaviours in Autism Spectrum Disorder: A Different Way of Processing Rather Than an Impairment," *Journal of Autism and Developmental Disorders* 38 (2008): 1989–1997.

24. K. Plaisted, J. Swettenham, and L. Rees, "Children with Autism Show Local Precedence in a Divided Attention Task and Global Precedence in a Selective Attention Task," *Journal of Child Psychology and Psychiatry* 40 (1999): 733–742; U. Frith, *Autism: Explaining the Enigma* (Oxford: Blackwell, 1989); F. Happe and U. Frith, "The Weak Coherence Account: Detail-Focused Cognitive Style in Autism Spectrum Disorders," *Journal of Autism and Developmental Disorders* 28 (2006): 1–21.

25. E. Courchesne and K. Pierce, "Why the Frontal Cortex in Autism Might Be Talking Only to Itself: Local Over-Connectivity but Long-Distance Disconnection," *Current Opinion in Neurobiology* 15 (2005): 225–230; C. Frith, "What Do Imaging Studies Tell Us About the Neural Basis of Autism?," in *Autism: Neural Basis and Treatment Possibilities*, ed. G. Bock and J. Goode, 149–176 (Chichester, UK: John Wiley, 2003); J. M. Peters, M. Taquet, C. Vega, S. S. Jeste, I. S. Fernandez, J. Tan, C. A. Nelson III, M. Sahin, and S. K. Warfield, "Brain Functional Networks in Syndromic and Non-Syndromic Autism: A Graph Theoretical Study of EEG Connectivity," *BMC Medicine* 11:54 (2013), doi:10.1186/1741-7015-11-54.

26. N. Rinehart, J. Bradshaw, S. Moss, A. Brereton, and B. Tonge, "A Deficit in Shifting Attention Present in High-Functioning Autism but Not Asperger's Disorder," *Autism* 5, no. 1 (2001): 67–80.

27. D. M. Riby and P. J .B. Hancock, "Viewing It Differently: Social Scene Perception in Williams Syndrome and Autism," *Neuropsychologia* 46 (2008): 2855–2860; A. Klin et al., "Visual Fixation Patterns During Viewing of Naturalistic Social Situations as Predictors of Social Competence in Individuals with Autism," *Archives of General Psychiatry* 59 (2002): 809–816.

28. K. Pierce et al., "Preference for Geometric Patterns Early in Life as a Risk Factor for Autism," *Archives of General Psychiatry* 68 (2011): 101–109; H. M. Wellman et al., "Infant Social Attention Predicts Preschool Social Cognition," *Developmental Science* 7 (2004): 283–288.

29. Chevallier et al., "Social Motivation Theory of Autism."

30. O'Connor and Kirk, "Brief Report: Atypical Social Cognition."

31. M. A. Winter-Messiers et al., "How Far Can Brian Ride the Daylight 4449 Express? A Strength-Based Model of Asperger Syndrome Based on Special Interest Areas," *Focus on Autism and Other Development Disabilities* 22 (2007): 67–79; T. Grandin and S. Barron, *The Unwritten Rules of Social Relationships: Decoding Social Mysteries Through the Unique Perspectives of Autism* (Arlington, TX: Future Horizons, 2005); L. Soraya, *Living Independently on the Autism Spectrum: What You Need to Know to Move into a Place of Your Own, Succeed at Work, Start a Relationship, Stay Safe, and Enjoy Life as an Adult on the Autism Spectrum* (Avon, MA: Adams Media, 2013).

32. Attwood, *Asperger Syndrome*; Birch, *Congratulations! It's Asperger's Syndrome*; Miller, *Women from Another Planet?*; Sainsbury, *Martian in the Playground*; O'Connor and Kirk, "Brief Report: Atypical Social Cognition."

33. O'Connor and Kirk, "Brief Report: Atypical Social Cognition."

34. T. Grandin, *Thinking in Pictures and Other Reports from My Life with Autism* (New York: Vintage Books, 1995); O'Connor and Kirk, "Brief Report: Atypical Social Cognition";

Birch, *Congratulations! It's Asperger's Syndrome*; Miller, *Women from Another Planet?*; Sainsbury, *Martian in the Playground*; J. Endow, *Learning the Hidden Curriculum: The Odyssey of One Autistic Adult* (Overland, Park, KS: Autism Asperger Publishing Company, 2012); Soraya, *Living Independently on the Autism Spectrum.*

35. Chevallier et al., "Social Motivation Theory of Autism."

36. Grandin and Barron, *The Unwritten Rules of Social Relationships*; also see Endow, *Learning the Hidden Curriculum*; Soraya, *Living Independently on the Autism Spectrum.*

37. J. A. Bartz et al., "Social Effects of Oxytocin in Humans: Context and Person Matter," *Trends in Cognitive Sciences* 15 (2011): 301–309; M. E. Modi and L. J. Young, "The Oxytocin System in Drug Discovery for Autism: Animal Models and Novel Therapeutic Strategies," *Hormones and Behavior* 61 (2012): 340–350.

38. C. Chevallier et al., "Social Motivation Theory of Autism," at 235.

39. M. A. Winter-Messiers et al., "How Far Can Brian Ride."

40. L. Mottron, M. Dawson, I. Soulieres, B. Hubert, and J. Burack, "Enhanced Perceptual Functioning in Autism: An Update and Eight Principles of Autistic Perception," *Journal of Autism and Developmental Disorders* 36, no. 1 (2006): 27–43.

41. M. Dawson, I. Soulieres, M. A. Grensbacher, and L. Mottron, "The Level and Nature of Autistic Intelligence," *Psychological Science* 18 (2007): 657–662; A. Shah and U. Frith, "Why Do Autistic Individuals Show Superior Performance on the Block Design Task?," *Journal of Child Psychology: Psychiatry* 34 (1993): 1351–1364.

42. T. Jolliffe and S. Baron-Cohen, "Are People with Autism and Asperger's Syndrome Faster Than Normal on the Embedded Figures Test?," *Journal of Child Psychology and Psychiatry* 38 (1997): 527–534.

43. A. M. Remington, J. G. Swettenham, and N. Lavie, "Lightening the Load: Perceptual Load Impairs Visual Detection in Typical Adults but Not in Autism," *Journal of Abnormal Psychology* 121 (2012): 544–551.

44. Attwood, *Asperger Syndrome*, at 127.

45. U. Frith, ed., *Autism and Asperger Syndrome* (New York: Cambridge University Press, 1991), 239.

46. M. A. Winter-Messiers, "From Tarantulas to Toilet Brushes: Understanding the Special Interest Areas of Children and Youth with Asperger Syndrome," *Remedial and Special Education* 28 (2007): 140–152.

47. Ibid., at 141–142.

48. Winter-Messiers et al., "How Far Can Brian Ride," at 70.

49. Winter-Messiers, "From Tarantulas to Toilet Brushes," at 147.

50. Winter-Messiers et al., "How Far Can Brian Ride," at 72.

51. Winter-Messiers, "From Tarantulas to Toilet Brushes," at 149.

52. Winter-Messiers et al., "How Far Can Brian Ride," at 78.

53. Asperger, "Die autistischen Psychopathen," at 88.

54. T. Grandin and K. Duffy, *Developing Talents: Careers for Individuals with Asperger Syndrome and High-Functioning Autism* (Shawnee Mission, KS: Autism Asperger, 2004), vii; also see Soraya, *Living Independently on the Autism Spectrum.*

55. S. B. Kaufman, "Conversations on Creativity with Allan Snyder," *Beautiful Minds* (blog), *Psychology Today*, January 13, 2010, http://www.psychologytoday.com/blog/beautiful-minds/201001/conversations-creativity-allan-snyder.

56. B. Weber, "Kim Peek, Inspiration for 'Rain Man,' Dies at 58," *New York Times*, December 26, 2009, http://www.nytimes.com/2009/12/27/us/27peek.html.

57. Ibid.

58. J. Wilding, "Memory Expertise or Experts' Memory?," in *The Complexity of Greatness: Beyond Talent and Practice*, ed. S. B. Kaufman, 293–308 (New York: Oxford University Press, 2013).

59. D. M. Aram and J. M. Healy, "Hyperlexia: A Review of Extraordinary Word Recognition," in *The Exceptional Brain: Neuropsychology of Talent and Special Abilities*, ed. L. K. Obler and D. Fein, 70–102 (New York: Guilford Press, 1988).

60. D. Treffert, "Savant Syndrome: A Compelling Case for Innate Talent," in *The Complexity of Greatness: Beyond Talent and Practice*, ed. S. B. Kaufman, 103–118 (New York: Oxford University Press, 2013).

61. D. A. Treffert and G. L. Wallace, "Islands of Genius," *Scientific American Mind*, January 2004, 14–23.

62. D. A. Treffert, *Islands of Genius: The Bountiful Mind of the Autistic, Acquired, and Sudden Savant* (London: Jessica Kingsley, 2010).

63. N. Geschwind and A. M. Galaburda, *Cerebral Lateralization: Biological Mechanisms, Associations and Pathology* (Cambridge, MA: MIT Press, 1987).

64. B. L. Miller, J. L. Cummings, et al., "Emergence of Artistic Talent in Frontotemporal Dementia," *Neurology* 51 (1998): 978–981; B. L. Miller, K. Boone, et al., "Functional Correlates of Musical and Visual Ability in Fronto Temporal Dementia," *British Journal of Psychiatry* 176 (2000): 458–463; B. Miller and C. E. Hou, "Portraits of Artists: Emergence of Visual Creativity in Dementia," *Neurological Review* 61 (2004): 842–844.

65. A. Snyder, "Explaining and Inducing Savant Skills: Privileged Access to Lower Level, Less-Processed Information," *Philosophical Transactions of the Royal Society: B* 364 (2009): 1399–1405.

66. Ibid.

67. R. L. Young, M. C. Ridding, and T. L. Morrell, "Switching Skills On by Turning Off Part of the Brain," *Neurocase* 10 (2004): 215–222.

68. Kaufman, "Conversations on Creativity with Allan Snyder."

69. R. C. Kadosh, S. Soskic, T. Luculano, R. Kanai, and V. Walsh, "Modulating Neuronal Activity Produces Specific and Long-Lasting Changes in Numerical Competence," *Current Biology* 20 (2010): 2016–2020; T. Iuculano and R. C. Kadosh, "The Mental Cost of Cognitive Enhancement," *The Journal of Neuroscience* 33 (2013): 4482–4486.

70. R. P. Chi and A. W. Snyder, "Facilitate Insight by Non-Invasive Brain Stimulation," *PLoS ONE* 6 (2011): e16655; Chi and Snyder, "Brain Stimulation Enables the Solution of an Inherently Difficult Problem," *Neuroscience Letters* 515 (2012): 121–124.

71. R. C. Kadosh, N. Levy, J. O'Shea, N. Shea, and J. Savulescu, "The Neuroethics of Non-Invasive Brain Stimulation," *Current Biology* 22 (2012): R108–R111; R. E. Hoffman, K. Wu, B. Pittman, J. D. Cahill, K. A. Hawkins, T. Fernandez, and J. Hannestad, "Transcranial Magnetic Stimulation of Wenicke's and Right Homologous Sites to Curtail 'Voices': A Randomized Trial," *Biological Psychiatry* (2013), doi:10.1016/j.biopsych.2013.01.016.

72. Kaufman, "Conversations on Creativity with Allan Snyder."

73. Treffert, "Savant Syndrome," at 113, 107, 108.

74. R. Gelman, "Innate Learning and Beyond," in *Of Minds and Language*, ed. M. Piatelli-Palmirini, J. Uriagereka, and P. Salaburu, 223–238 (New York: Oxford University Press, 2009); R. Gelman and J. Lucariello, "Role of Learning in Cognitive Development," in *Stevens' Handbook of Experimental Psychology*, ed. H. Pashler and C. R. Gallistel, 3rd ed., 3:395–443 (New York: Wiley, 2002); L. A. Hirschfeld and S. A. Gelman, *Mapping the Mind: Domain Specificity in Cognition and Culture* (New York: Cambridge University Press, 1994); G. J. Feist, *The Psychology of Science and the Origins of the Scientific Mind* (New Haven, CT: Yale University Press, 2006); S. Pinker, *How the Mind Works* (New York: W. W. Norton, 1999); M. Anderson, *Intelligence and Development: A Cognitive Theory* (New York: Wiley, 1992); M. Anderson, "Marrying Intelligence and Cognition: A Developmental Review," in *Cognition & Intelligence: Identifying the Mechanisms of the Mind*, ed. R. J. Sternberg and J. E. Pretz, 268–288 (Cambridge, UK: Cambridge University Press, 2004); Z. Ivcevic and J. D. Mayer, "Mapping Dimensions of Creativity in the Life-Space," *Creativity Research*

Journal 21 (2009): 152–165; J. C. Kaufman, "Counting the Muses: Development of the Kaufman Domains of Creativity Scale (K-DOCS)," *Psychology of Aesthetics, Creativity, and the Arts* 6 (2012): 298–308.

75. Gelman and Lucariello, "Role of Learning"; Pinker, *How the Mind Works.*

76. Gelman and Lucariello, "Role of Learning," at 400.

77. J. J. Bolhuis, G. R. Brown, R. C. Richardson, and K. N. Laland, "Darwin in Mind: Opportunities for Evolutionary Psychology," *PLoS Biology* 9 (2011): e1001109.

78. Treffert, "Savant Syndrome."

79. P. Lewicki, T. Hill, and M. Czyzewska, "Nonconscious Acquisition of Information," *American Psychologist* 47 (1992): 796–801, at 801.

80. G. F. Gebauer and N. J. Mackintosh, "Psychometric Intelligence Dissociates Implicit and Explicit Learning," *Journal of Experimental Psychology: Learning, Memory, and Cognition* 33 (2007): 34–54.

81. A. S. Reber, *Implicit Learning and Tacit Knowledge: An Essay on the Cognitive Unconscious* (New York: Oxford University Press, 1993); A. S. Reber, F. F. Walkenfeld, and R. Hernstadt, "Implicit and Explicit Learning: Individual Differences and IQ," *Journal of Experimental Psychology: Learning, Memory, and Cognition* 17 (1991): 888–896; K. E. Stanovich, "Distinguishing the Reflective, Algorithmic, and Autonomous Minds: Is It Time for a Tri-Process Theory?," in *In Two Minds: Dual Processes and Beyond*, ed. J. S. B. T. Evans and K. Frankish, 55–88 (Oxford: Oxford University Press, 2009).

82. Stanovich, "Distinguishing the Reflective, Algorithmic, and Autonomous Minds," at 59.

83. S. B. Kaufman, "Beyond General Intelligence: The Dual-Process Theory of Human Intelligence" (PhD diss., Yale University, New Haven, CT, 2009).

84. S. B. Kaufman, C. G. DeYoung, J. R. Gray, L. Jiménez, J. Brown, and N. Mackintosh, "Implicit Learning as an Ability," *Cognition* 116 (2010): 321–340.

85. J. Brown, B. Aczel, L. Jiménez, S. B. Kaufman, and K. P. Grant, "Implicit Learning in Autism Spectrum Conditions," *Quarterly Journal of Experimental Psychology* 1 (2010): 1–24.

86. D. Nemeth et al., "Learning in Autism: Implicitly Superb," *PLoS ONE* 5 (2010): 1–7.

87. G. L. Wallace, "Neuropsychological Studies of Savant Skills: Can They Inform the Neuroscience of Giftedness?," *Roeper Review* 30 (2008): 229–246; H. H. Spitz, "Calendar Calculating Idiots Savants and the Smart Unconscious," *New Ideas in Psychology* 13 (1995): 167–182.

88. Spitz, "Calendar Calculating."

89. S. B. Smith, *The Great Mental Calculators: The Psychology, Methods, and Lives of Calculating Prodigies, Past and Present* (New York: Columbia University Press, 1983), 30.

90. M. Rohrmeier and P. Rebuschat, "Implicit Learning and Acquisition of Music," *Topics in Cognitive Science* 4 (2012): 525–553; M. Ettlinger, E. H. Margulis, and P. C. M. Wong, "Implicit Memory in Music and Language," *Frontiers in Psychology* 2 (2011), doi:10.3389/fpsyg.2011.00211.

91. B. Tillmann and B. Poulin-Charronnat, "Auditory Expectations for Newly Acquired Structures," *Quarterly Journal of Experimental Psychology* 63 (2010): 1646–1664.

92. J. A. Sloboda, B. Hermelin, and N. O'Connor, "An Exceptional Musical Memory," *Music Perception* 3 (1985): 155–170.

93. J. R. McKelvey, R. Lambert, L. Mottron, and M. I. Shevell, "Right-Hemisphere Dysfunction in Asperger's Syndrome," *Journal of Child Neurology* 10 (1995): 310–314.

94. Ruthsatz and Urbach, "Child Prodigy."

95. S. B. Kaufman, "Conversations on Creativity with Daniel Tammet," *Beautiful Minds* (blog), *Psychology Today*, January 2, 2010, http://www.psychologytoday.com/blog/beautiful-minds/201001/conversations-creativity-daniel-tammet.

96. D. Tammet, *Born on a Blue Day: Inside the Extraordinary Mind of an Autistic Savant* (New York: Free Press, 2007); D. Tammet, *Embracing the Wide Sky: A Tour Across the Horizons of the Mind* (New York: Free Press, 2009).

97. J. Foer, *Moonwalking with Einstein: The Art and Science of Remembering Everything* (New York: Penguin Books, 2012).

98. J. M. Wilding and E. R. Valentine, *Superior Memory* (Hove, East Sussex: Psychology Press, 1997).

99. S. Baron-Cohen, D. Bor, et al., "Savant Memory in a Man with Colour Form-Number Synaesthesia and Asperger Syndrome," *Journal of Consciousness Studies* 14 (2007): 9–10.

100. D. Tammet, *Embracing the Wide Sky.*

101. Ibid., at 47.

102. D. Bor, J. Billington, and S. Baron-Cohen, "Savant Memory for Digits in a Case of Synaesthesia and Asperger Syndrome Is Related to Hyperactivity in the Lateral Prefrontal Cortex," *Neurocase* 13 (2007): 311–319; S. Azoulai, E. Hubbard, and V. S. Ramachandran, "Does Synesthesia Contribute to Mathematical Savant Skills?," *Journal of Cognitive Neuroscience, Supplement* 69 (2005): 69.

103. N. Rothen and B. Meier, "Higher Prevalence of Synaesthesia in Art Students," *Perception* 39 (2010): 718–720.

104. N. Rothen, A. Andrea-Laura, and B. Meier, "Training Synaesthesia," *Perception* 40 (2011): 1248–1250; O. Colizoli, M. Jaap, and R. R. Murre, "Pseudo-Synesthesia through Reading Books with Colored Letters," *PlOS ONE* 7, no. 6 (2012): e39799; N. Witthoft and J. Winawer, "Learning, Memory, and Synesthesia," *Psychological Science* (2013), doi:10.1177 /0956797612452573.

105. R. E. Cytowic, D. M. Eagleman, and D. Nabokov, *Wednesday Is Indigo Blue: Discovering the Brain of Synesthesia* (Boston: MIT Press, 2011).

106. D. Bor, J. Billington, and S. Baron-Cohen, "Savant Memory for Digits in a Case of Synaesthesia and Asperger Syndrome Is Related to Hyperactivity in the Lateral Prefrontal Cortex," *Neurocase, 13* (2007): 311–319.

107. S. B. Kaufman, "Confessions of a Late Bloomer," *Psychology Today,* November 1, 2008, 71–79.

108. K. Robinson and L. Aronica, *The Element: How Finding Your Passion Changes Everything* (New York: Penguin Books, 2009).

Chapter 12

1. S. B. Kaufman and J. L. Singer, "The Origins of Positive-Constructive Daydreaming," *Scientific American* (guest blog), December 22, 2011, http://blogs.scientificamerican.com/ guest-blog/2011/12/22/the-origins-of-positive-constructive-daydreaming/.

2. K. Lewin, *A Dynamic Theory of Personality: Selected Papers* (New York: McGraw-Hill, 1935).

3. J. S. Antrobus, R. Coleman, and J. L. Singer, "Signal-Detection Performance by Subjects Differing in Predisposition to Daydreaming," *Journal of Consulting Psychology* 31 (1967): 487–491.

4. J. L. Singer, *Daydreaming: An Introduction to the Experimental Study of Inner Experience* (New York: Random House, 1966).

5. L. M. Giambra, "A Laboratory Method for Investigating Influences on Switching Attention to Task-Unrelated Imagery and Thought," *Consciousness and Cognition* 4 (1995): 1–21.

6. E. Klinger and W. M. Cox, "Motivation and the Theory of Current Concerns," in *Handbook of Motivational Counseling: Concepts, Approaches, and Assessment*, ed. W. M. Cox and E. Klinger, 3–27 (New York: Wiley, 2004).

7. J. L. Singer, "Daydreaming and the Stream of Thought," *American Scientist* 62 (1974): 417–425.

8. T. Zhiyan and J. L. Singer, "Daydreaming Styles, Emotionality and the Big Five Personality Dimensions," *Imagination, Cognition and Personality* 16 (1997): 399–414.

9. R. L. Buckner, "The Serendipitous Discovery of the Brain's Default Network," *Neuro-Image* 62 (2012): 1137–1145.

10. K. Christoff, "Undirected Thought: Neural Determinants and Correlates," *Brain Research* 1428 (2012): at 57–58.

11. R. L. Buckner, J. R. Andrews-Hanna, and D. L. Schacter, "The Brain's Default Network: Anatomy, Function, and Relevance to Disease," *Annals of the New York Academy of Sciences* 1124 (2008): 1–38.

12. M. H. Immordino-Yang, J. A. Christodoulou, and V. Singh, "Rest Is Not Idleness: Implications of the Brain's Default Mode for Human Development and Education," *Perspectives on Psychological Science* 7 (2012): 352–364; A. I. Jack, A. Dawson, et al., "fMRI Reveals Reciprocal Inhibition Between Social and Physical Cognitive Domains," *NeuroImage* 66 (2013): 385–401.

13. Immordino-Yang, Christodoulou, and Singh, "Rest Is Not Idleness," at 356.

14. J. W. Schooler, J. Smallwood, et al., "Meta-Awareness, Perceptual Decoupling and the Wandering Mind," *Trends in Cognitive Sciences* 15 (2011): 319–326.

15. Immordino-Yang, et al., "Rest Is Not Idleness"; M. H. Immordino-Yang, A. McColl, H. Damasion, and A. Damasio, "Neural Correlates of Admiration and Compassion," *Proceedings of the National Academy of Sciences* 106 (2009): 8021–8026; M. H. Immordino-Yang, "Me, Myself and You: Neuropsychological Relations Between Social Emotions, Self Awareness, and Morality," *Emotion Review* 3 (2011): 313–315. Further research found that spontaneous descriptions of personal memories during the interview was related to default network connectivity of hubs involved in memory retrieval and self/social processing at rest. See X. Yang, J. Bossman, B. Schiffhauer, M. Jordan, and M. H. Immordino-Yang, "Intrinsic Default Mode Network Connectivity Predicts Spontaneous Verbal Descriptions of Autobiographical Memories During Social Processing," *Frontiers in Psychology* 3 (2013), doi:10.3389/fpsyg.2012.00592.

16. Ibid.; also see J. Bruner, *Acts of Meaning: Four Lectures on Mind and Culture* (Cambridge, MA: Harvard College, 1990).

17. J. Smallwood and J. W. Schooler, "The Restless Mind," *Psychological Bulletin* 132 (2006): 946–958.

18. B. J. Baars, *In the Theatre of Consciousness: The Workspace of the Mind* (New York: Oxford University Press, 2001).

19. K. Christoff, A. M. Gordon, J. Smallwood, R. Smith, and J. W. Schooler, "Experience Sampling During fMRI Reveals Default Network and Executive System Contributions to Mind Wandering," *PNAS* 106 (2009): 8719–8724.

20. M. D. Fox, A. Z. Snyder, et al., "The Human Brain Is Intrinsically Organized into Dynamic, Anticorrelated Functional Networks," *PNAS* 27 (2005): 9673–9678.

21. J. Smallwood, "Distinguishing How from Why the Mind Wanders: Process-Occurrence Framework for Self-Generated Mental Activity," *Psychological Bulletin* (in press).

22. B. Baird, J. Smallwood, and J. W. Schooler, "Back to the Future: Autobiographical Planning and the Functionality of Mind-Wandering," *Consciousness and Cognition* 20 (2011): 1604–1611.

23. J. Smallwood, F. J. M. Ruby, and T. Singer, "Letting Go of the Present: Mind-Wandering Is Associated with Reduced Delay Discounting," *Consciousness and Cognition* 22 (2013): 1–7.

24. D. B. Levinson, J. Smallwood, and R. J. Davidson, "The Persistence of Thought: Evidence for a Role of Working Memory in the Maintenance of Task-Unrelated Thinking," *Psychological Science* 23 (2012): 375–380.

25. B. Baird, J. Smallwood, et al., "Inspired by Distraction: Mind Wandering Facilitates Creative Incubation," *Psychological Science* (2012), doi:10.1177/0956797612446024.

26. M. A. Killingsworth and D. T. Gilbert, "A Wandering Mind Is an Unhappy Mind," *Science* 330 (2010): 932.

27. J. C. McVay and M. J. Kane, "Why Does Working Memory Capacity Predict Variation in Reading Comprehension? On the Influence of Mind Wandering and Executive Attention," *Journal of Experimental Psychology: General* 141 (2011): 302–320.

28. J. C. Kaufman, *Creativity 101* (New York: Springer, 2009); R. K. Sawyer, *Explaining Creativity: The Science of Human Innovation,* 2nd ed. (New York: Oxford University Press, 2012); T. B. Ward and Y. Kolomyts, "Cognition and Creativity," in *The Cambridge Handbook of Creativity,* ed. J. C. Kaufman and R. J. Sternberg, 93–112 (New York: Cambridge University Press, 2010); R. A. Finke, T. B. Ward, and S. M. Smith, *Creative Cognition: Theory, Research, and Applications* (Cambridge, MA: MIT Press, 1992); M. Batey and A. Furnham, "Creativity, Intelligence, and Personality: A Critical Review of the Scattered Literature," *Genetic, Social, and General Psychology Monographs* 132 (2006): 355–429.

29. K. J. Gilhooly, E. Fioratou, S. H. Anthony, and V. Wynn, "Divergent Thinking: Strategies and Executive Involvement in Generating Novel Uses for Familiar Objects," *British Journal of Psychology* 98 (2007): 611–625; K. J. Gilhooly and E. Fioratou, "Executive Functions in Insight Versus Non-Insight Problem Solving: An Individual Differences Approach," *Thinking & Reasoning* 15 (2009): 355– 376; E. C. Nusbaum and P. J. Silvia, "Are Intelligence and Creativity Really So Different? Fluid Intelligence, Executive Processes, and Strategy Use in Divergent Thinking," *Intelligence* 39 (2011): 36–45; R. E. Beaty and P. J. Silvia, "Why Do Ideas Get More Creative Across Time? An Executive Interpretation of the Serial Order Effect in Divergent Thinking," *Psychology of Aesthetics, Creativity, and the Arts* 6 (2012): 309–319; R. E. Beaty and P. J. Silvia, "Metaphorically Speaking: Cognitive Abilities and the Production of Figurative Language," *Memory & Cognition* 41 (2013): 255–267; C. G. DeYoung, J. L. Flanders, and J. B. Peterson, "Cognitive Abilities Involved in Insight Problems: An Individual Differences Model," *Creativity Research Journal* 20 (2008): 278–290; J. Wiley and A. F. Jarosz, "Working Memory Capacity, Attentional Focus, and Problem Solving," *Current Directions in Psychological Science* 21 (2012): 258–262; J. Wiley and A.F. Jarosz, "How Working Memory Capacity Affects Problem Solving," in *The Psychology of Learning and Motivation,* vol. 56, ed. B. H. Ross, 185–228 (New York: Academic Press, 2012); W.-L. Lin and Y.-W. Lien, "The Different Role of Working Memory in Open-Ended Versus Closed-Ended Creative Problem Solving: A Dual-Process Theory Account," *Creativity Research Journal* 25 (2013): 85–96.

30. T. P. German and M.A. Defeyter, "Immunity to Functional Fixedness in Young Children," *Psychonomic Bulletin & Review* 7 (2000): 707–712.

31. S. L. Thompson-Schill, M. Ramscar, and E. G. Chrysikou, "Cognition Without Control: When a Little Frontal Lobe Goes a Long Way," *Current Directions in Psychological Science* 18 (2009): 259–263.

32. D. L. Zabelina and M. D. Robinson, "Child's Play: Facilitating the Originality of Creative Output by a Priming Manipulation," *Psychology of Aesthetics, Creativity, and the Arts* 4 (2010): 57–65; C. Martindale, "Biological Bases of Creativity," in *Handbook of Creativity,* ed. R. J. Sternberg, 137–152 (New York: Cambridge University Press, 1999).

33. I. K. Ash and J. Wiley, "The Nature of Restructuring in Insight: An Individual-Differences Approach," *Psychonomic Bulletin & Review* 13 (2006): 66–73.

34. J. I. Fleck, "Working Memory Demands in Insight Versus Analytic Problem Solving," *European Journal of Cognitive Psychology* 20 (2008): 139–176; K. J. Gilhooly and P. Murphy, "Differentiating Insight from Non-Insight Problems," *Thinking and Reasoning* 11 (2005): 279–302; Gilhooly and Fioratou, "Executive Functions in Insight"; A. Lavric, S. Forstmeier,

and G. Rippon, "Differences in Working Memory Involvement in Analytical and Creative Tasks: An ERP Study," *Neuroreport* 11 (2000): 1613–1618.

35. M. S. DeCaro and S. L. Beilock, "The Benefits and Perils of Attentional Control," in *Effortless Attention: A New Perspective in the Cognitive Science of Attention and Action*, ed. M. Csikszentmihalyi and B. Bruya, 51–73 (Cambridge, MA: MIT Press, 2010).

36. J. Kounios and M. Beeman, "The Aha! Moment: The Cognitive Neuroscience of Insight," *Current Directions in Psychological Science* 18 (2009): 210–216.

37. M. Ellamil, C. Dobson, M. Beeman, and K. Christoff, "Evaluative and Generative Modes of Thought During the Creative Process," *Neuroimage* 59 (2012): 1783–1794.

38. S. L. Bressler and V. Menon, "Large-Scale Brain Networks in Cognition: Emerging Methods and Principles," *Trends in Cognitive Sciences* 14 (2010): 277–290; L. Q. Uddin, K. S. Supekar, S. Ryali, and V. Menon, "Dynamic Reconfiguration of Structural and Functional Connectivity Across Core Neurocognitive Brain Networks with Development," *Journal of Neuroscience* 31 (2011): 18578–18589.

39. A. S. Bristol and I. V. Viskontas, "Dynamic Processes Within Associative Memory Stores: Piecing Together the Neural Basis of Creative Cognition," in *Creativity and Reason in Cognitive Development*, ed. J. C. Kaufman and J. Baer, 60–80 (New York: Cambridge University Press, 2006); D. L. Zabelina and M. D. Robinson, "Creativity as Flexible Cognitive Control," *Psychology of Aesthetics, Creativity, and the Arts* 4 (2010): 136–143; O. Vartanian, "Variable Attention Facilitates Creative Problem Solving," *Psychology of Aesthetics, Creativity, and the Arts* 3 (2009): 57–59; L. Gabora, "The Beer Can Theory of Creativity," in *Creative Evolutionary Systems*, ed. P. Bentley and D. Corne 147–161 (San Francisco: Morgan Kauffman, 2000); L. Gabora, "Revenge of the 'Neurds': Characterizing Creative Thought in Terms of the Structure and Dynamics of Human Memory," *Creativity Research Journal* 22 (2010): 1–13; Nusbaum and Silvia, "Are Intelligence and Creativity Really So Different?," 36–45; S. Jaarsveld, P. Srivastava, M. Welter, and T. Lachmann, "Are Attentional Blink and Creative Reasoning Related Through General Cognitive Flexibility?," ECVP Abstract Supplement, *Perception* 40, (2011): 22.

40. L. Gabora, "Contextual Focus: A Cognitive Explanation for the Cultural Transition of the Middle/Upper Paleolithic," in *Proceedings of the 25th Annual Meeting of the Cognitive Science Society*, ed. R. Alterman and D. Hirsch 432–437 (Boston: Erlbaum, 2003); L. Gabora, "Mind," in *Handbook of Archeological Theories*, ed. H. D. G. Maschner and C. Chippindate, 283–296 (Walnut Creek, CA: Altamira Press, 2008); L. Gabora and S. B. Kaufman, "Evolutionary Approaches to Creativity," in *The Cambridge Handbook of Creativity*, 279–300.

41. L. Gabora and M. Saberi, "How Did Human Creativity Arise? An Agent-Based Model of the Origin of Cumulative Open-Ended Cultural Evolution," *Proceedings of the ACM Conference on Cognition & Creativity*, 299–306, November 3–6, 2011, Atlanta; L. Gabora and S. DiPaola, "How Did Humans Become So Creative?," *Proceedings of the International Conference on Computational Creativity*, 203–210, May 31–June 1, 2012, Dublin; L. Gabora and K. Kitto, "Concept Combination and the Origins of Complex Cognition," in *Origins of Mind*, ed. E. Swan, 361–382 (Berlin: Springer, 2012).

42. Ellamil, Dobson, Beeman, and Christoff, "Evaluative and Generative," at 1792.

43. M. Csikszentmihalyi, *Creativity: The Work and Lives of 91 Eminent People* (New York: HarperCollins, 1996); M. Csikszentmihalyi, *Creativity: Flow and the Psychology of Discovery and Invention* (New York: Harper Perennial, 1997); S. B. Kaufman, "After the Show: The Many Faces of the Performer," *Huff Post Healthy* (blog), March 6, 2011, http://www.huffingtonpost.com/scott-barry-kaufman/creative-people_b_829563.html.

44. H. Takeuchi et al., "Failing to Deactivate: The Association Between Brain Activity During a Working Memory Task and Creativity," *NeuroImage* 55 (2011): 681–687.

45. Ibid., at 685.

46. C. J. Limb and A. R. Braun, "Neural Substrates of Spontaneous Musical Performance: An fMRI Study of Jazz Improvisation," *PLoS One* 3 (2012): e1679.

47. Ibid., at 4.

48. C. K. W. De Dreu, B. A. Nijstad, M. Baas, I. Wolsink, and M. Roskes, "Working Memory Benefits Creative Insight, Musical Improvisation, and Original Ideation Through Maintained Task-Focused Attention," *Personality and Social Psychology Bulletin* 38 (2012): 656–669.

49. B. A. Nijstad, C. K. W. De Dreu, E. F. Rietzschel, and B. Matthijs, "The Dual Pathway to Creativity Model: Creative Ideation as a Function of Flexibility and Persistence," *European Review of Social Psychology* 21: 34–77.

50. S. Liu et al., "Neural Correlates of Lyrical Improvisation: An fMRI Study of Freestyle Rap," *Scientific Reports* 2 (2012), doi:10.1038/srep00834.

51. A. Dietrich and R. Kanso, "A Review of EEG, ERP, and Neuroimaging Studies of Creativity and Insight," *Psychological Bulletin* 136 (2010): 822–848.

52. M. Csikszentmihalyi, *Creativity: Flow and the Psychology of Discovery and Invention* (New York: Harper, 1997).

53. K. Asakawa, "Flow Experience, Culture, and Well-Being: How Do Autotelic Japanese College Students Feel, Behave, and Think in Their Daily Lives?," *Journal of Happiness Studies* 11 (2010): 205–223; F. Ullen et al., "Proneness for Psychological Flow in Everyday Life: Associations with Personality and Intelligence," *Personality and Individual Differences* 52 (2012): 167–172.

54. J. Schlesinger, "Creative Mythconceptions: A Closer Look at the Evidence for the 'Mad Genius' Hypothesis," *Psychology of Aesthetics, Creativity, and the Arts* 3 (2009): 62–72; P. Silvia and J. C. Kaufman, "Creativity and Mental Illness," in *The Cambridge Handbook of Creativity*, 381–394.

55. A. M. Ludwig, *The Price of Greatness: Resolving the Creativity and Madness Controversy* (New York: Guilford Press, 1995); A. M. Ludwig, "Method and Madness in the Arts and Sciences," *Creativity Research Journal* 11 (1998): 93–101; D. K. Simonton, *Greatness: Who Makes History and Why* (New York: Guilford Press, 1994); Simonton, *Origins of Genius: Darwinian Perspectives on Creativity* (New York: Oxford University Press, 1999); Simonton, "Varieties of (Scientific) Creativity: A Hierarchical Model of Domain-Specific Disposition, Development, and Achievement," *Perspectives on Psychological Science* 4 (2009): 441–452.

56. C. R. Snyder and H. L. Fromkin, "Abnormality as a Positive Characteristic: The Development and Validation of a Scale Measuring Need for Uniqueness," *Journal of Abnormal Psychology* 86 (1977): 518–527; M. Lynn and C. R. Snyder, "Uniqueness Seeking," in *Handbook of Positive Psychology*, ed. C. R. Snyder and S. J. Lopez, 395–410 (New York: Oxford University Press, 2002).

57. R. F. Baumeister and M. R. Leary, "The Need to Belong: Desire for Interpersonal Attachment as a Fundamental Human Motivation," *Psychological Bulletin* 117 (1995): 497–529.

58. S. H. Kim, L. C. Vincent, and J. A. Goncalo, "Outside Advantage: Can Social Rejection Fuel Creative Thought?," *Journal of Experimental Psychology: General* (2012), doi:10.1037/a0029728.

59. S. M. Ritter, R. I. Damian, et al., "Diversifying Experiences Enhance Cognitive Flexibility," *Journal of Experimental Social Psychology* 48 (2012): 961–964.

60. D. K. Simonton, "Foreign Influence and National Achievement: The Impact of Open Milieus on Japanese Civilization," *Journal of Personality and Social Psychology* 72 (1997): 86–94.

61. C. S. Lee, D. J. Therriault, and T. Linderholm, "On the Cognitive Benefits of Cultural Experience: Exploring the Relationship Between Studying Abroad and Creative Thinking," *Applied Cognitive Psychology* 5 (2012): 768–778; C. S. Saad, R. I. Damian, V. Benet-Martinez,

W. G. Moons, and R. W. Robins, "Multiculturalism and Creativity: Effects of Cultural Context, Bicultural Identity, and Ideational Fluency," *Social Psychological and Personality Science* (2012), doi:10.1177/1948550612456560.

62. J. C. Kaufman and R. A. Beghetto, "Beyond Big and Little: The Four C Model of Creativity," *Review of General Psychology* 13 (2009): 1–12.

63. R. Richards, ed., *Everyday Creativity and New Views of Human Nature: Psychological, Social, and Spiritual Perspectives* (Washington, DC: American Psychological Association, 2007).

64. S. Kyaga, M. Landen, et al., "Mental Illness, Suicide and Creativity: 40-Year Prospective Total Population Study," *Journal of Psychiatric Research* 47 (2012): 83–90.

65. A. Furnham, M. Batey, K. Arnand, and J. Manfield, "Personality, Hypomania, Intelligence and Creativity," *Personality and Individual Differences* 44 (2008): 1060–1069.

66. Ibid.

67. K. R. Jamison, *Touched with Fire: Manic-Depressive Illness and the Artistic Temperament* (New York: Free Press, 1996); K. R. Jamison, *Exuberance: The Passion for Life* (New York: Vintage, 2005).

68. S. L. Johnson, G. Murray, et al., "Creativity and Bipolar Disorder: Touched by Fire or Burning with Questions?," *Clinical Psychology Review* 32 (2012): 1–12; R. Richards, D. K. Kinney, K. Dennis, I. Lunde, M. Benet, and A. P. C. Merzel, "Creativity in Manic-Depressives, Cyclothymes, Their Normal Relatives, and Control Subjects," *Journal of Abnormal Psychology* 97 (1988): 281–288.

69. S. B. Kaufman and J. C. Kaufman, *The Psychology of Creative Writing* (New York: Cambridge University Press, 2009); M. J. C. Forgeard, S. B. Kaufman, and J. C. Kaufman, "The Psychology of Creative Writing," in *Blackwell Companion to Creative Writing*, ed. G. Harper (Oxford: Wiley-Blackwell, in press); J. C. Kaufman and J. D. Sexton, "Why Doesn't the Writing Cure Help Poets?," *Review of General Psychology* 10 (2006): 268–282.

70. Kaufman and Sexton, "Why Doesn't the Writing Cure Help Poets?," 268–282.

71. D. K. Kinney, R. Richards, et al., "Creativity in Offspring of Schizophrenic and Control Parents: An Adoption Study," *Creativity Research Journal* 13 (2010): 17–25.

72. D. Nettle, "Schizotypy and Mental Health amongst Poets, Visual Artists, and Mathematicians," *Journal of Research in Personality* 40 (2006): 876–890.

73. M. Batey and A. Furnham, "The Relationship Between Measures of Creativity and Schizotypy," *Personality and Individual Differences* 45 (2008): 816–821.

74. S. B. Kaufman, "A Call for New Measures of Asperger's and Schizotypy," *Scientific American* (guest blog), August 17, 2011, http://blogs.scientificamerican.com/guest-blog/2011/08/17/a-call-for-new-measures-of-aspergers-and-schizotypy/; B. J. Crespi, "One Hundred Years of Insanity: Genomic, Psychological, and Evolutionary Models of Autism in Relation to Schizophrenia," in *Handbook of Schizophrenia Spectrum and Related Disorders: Conceptual Issues and Neurobiological Advances*, vol. 1, ed. M. Ritsner, 163–185 (New York: Springer, 2011); B. H. King and C. Lord, "Is Schizophrenia on the Autism Spectrum?," *Brain Research* 1380 (2011): 34–41.

75. S. N. Russell-Smith, M. T. Maybery, and D. M. Bayliss, "Relationships Between Autistic-Like and Schizotypy Traits: An Analysis Using the Autism Spectrum Quotient and Oxford Liverpool Inventory of Feelings and Experiences," *Personality and Individual Differences* 51 (2011): 128–132.

76. Buckner et al., "The Brain's Default Network"; C. Badcock, *The Imprinted Brain: How Genes Set the Balance of the Mind Between Autism and Psychosis* (New York: Jessica Kingsley Publishers, 2009).

77. Nettle, "Schizotypy and Mental Health"; D. Rawlings and A. Locarnini, "Dimensional Schizotypy, Autism, and Unusual Word Associations in Artists and Scientists," *Journal of Research in Personality* 42 (2008): 465–471.

78. B. Nelson and D. Rawlings, "Relating Schizotypy and Personality to the Phenomenology of Creativity," *Schizophrenia Bulletin* 36 (2010): 388–399.

79. R. Lubow and I. Weiner, *Latent Inhibition: Cognition, Neuroscience and Applications to Schizophrenia* (New York: Cambridge University Press, 2010).

80. R. E. Lubow, Y. Ingberg-Sachs, N. Zalstein-Orda, and J. C. Gewirtz, "Latent Inhibition in Low and High 'Psychotic-Prone' Normal Subjects," *Personality and Individual Differences* 15 (1992): 563–572; H. J. Eysenck, *Genius: The Natural History of Creativity* (New York: Cambridge University Press, 1995).

81. S. H. Carson, "Creativity and Psychopathology: A Shared Vulnerability Model," *Canadian Journal of Psychiatry* 56 (2011): 144–153.

82. S. H. Carson, J. B. Peterson, and D. M. Higgins, "Decreased Latent Inhibition Is Associated with Increased Creative Achievement in High-Functioning Individuals," *Journal of Personality and Social Psychology* 85 (2003): 499–506.

83. S. B. Kaufman, "Faith in Intuition Is Associated with Decreased Latent Inhibition in a Sample of High Achieving Adolescents," *Psychology of Aesthetics, Creativity, and the Arts* 3 (2009): 28–34.

84. S. B. Kaufman, "Beyond General Intelligence: The Dual-Process Theory of Human Intelligence" (PhD diss., Yale University, New Haven, CT, 2009).

85. Nelson and Rawlings, "Relating Schizotypy and Personality," at 396.

86. C. G. DeYoung, "Openness/Intellect: A Dimension of Personality Reflecting Cognitive Exploration," in *APA Handbook of Personality and Social Psychology*, vol. 3, *Personality Processes and Individual Differences*, ed. M. L. Cooper and R. J. Larsen (in press).

87. C. G. DeYoung, "Intelligence and Personality," in *The Cambridge Handbook of Intelligence*, ed. R. J. Sternberg and S. B. Kaufman, 711–737 (New York: Cambridge University Press, 2011); C. G. DeYoung, J. B. Peterson, and D. M. Higgins, "Sources of Openness/Intellect: Cognitive and Neuropsychological Correlates of the Five Factors of Personality," *Journal of Personality* 73 (2005): 825–858; C. G. DeYoung, L. C. Quilty, and J. B. Peterson, "Between Facets and Domains: 10 Aspects of the Big Five," *Journal of Personality and Social Psychology* 93 (2007): 880–896; C. G. DeYoung, N. A. Shamosh, A. E. Green, T. S. Braver, and J. R. Gray, "Intellect as Distinct from Openness: Differences Revealed by fMRI of Working Memory," *Journal of Personality and Social Psychology* 97 (2009): 883–892; K. L. Jang, W. J. Livesley, et al., "Genetic and Environmental Influences on the Covariance of Facets Defining the Domains of the Five-Factor Model of Personality," *Personality and Individual Differences* 33 (2002): 83–101; J. T. Cacioppo and R. E. Petty, "The Need for Cognition," *Journal of Personality and Social Psychology* 42 (1982): 116–131; J. A. Johnson, "Clarification of Factor Five with the Help of the AB5C Model," *European Journal of Personality* 8 (1994): 311–334; P. Mussel, W. Carolin, P. Gelleri, and H. Schuler, "Explicating the Openness to Experience Construct and Its Subdimensions and Facets in a Work Setting," *International Journal of Selection and Assessment* 19 (2011): 145–156; M. A. Wainwright, M. J. Wright, M. Luciano, G. M., Geffen, and N. G. Martin, "Genetic Covariation among Facets of and General Cognitive Ability," *Twin Research and Human Genetics* 11 (2008): 275–286.

88. Johnson, "Clarification of Factor Five."

89. C. G. DeYoung, R. Grazioplene, and J. B. Peterson, "From Madness to Genius: The Openness/Intellect Trait Domain as a Paradoxical Simplex," *Journal of Research in Personality* 46 (2012): 63–78.

90. K. E. Markon, R. F. Krueger, and D. Watson, "Delineating the Structure of Normal and Abnormal Personality: An Integrative Approach," *Journal of Personality and Social Psychology* 88 (2005): 139–157.

91. E. Klinger, V. R. Henning, and J. M. Janssen, "Fantasy-Proneness Dimensionalized: Dissociative Component Is Related to Psychopathology, Daydreaming as Such Is Not," *Journal of Research in Personality* 43 (2009): 506–510.

92. D. Watson, L. A. Clark, and M. Chmielewski, "Structures of Personality and Their Relevance to Psychopathology: II. Further Articulation of a Comprehensive Unified Trait Structure," *Journal of Personality* 76 (2008): 1545–1586.

93. J. L. Tackett, A. L. Silberschmidt, R. F. Krueger, and S. R. Sponheim, "A Dimensional Model of Personality Disorder: Incorporating DSM Cluster A Characteristics," *Journal of Abnormal Psychology* 117 (2008): 454–459.

94. R. L. Piedmont, M. F. Sherman, N. C. Sherman, G. S. Dyliacco, and J. E. G. Williams, "Using the Five-Factor Model to Identify a New Personality Disorder Domain: The Case for Experiential Permeability," *Journal of Personality and Social Psychology* 96 (2009): 1245–1258.

95. C. G. DeYoung, J. B. Peterson, and D. M. Higgins, "Sources of Openness/Intellect: Cognitive and Neuropsychological Correlates of the Fifth Factor of Personality," *Journal of Personality* 73 (2005): 825–858.

96. DeYoung, "Openness/Intellect"; J. B. Hirsh, C. G. DeYoung, and J. B. Peterson, "Metatraits of the Big Five Differentially Predict Engagement and Restraint of Behavior," *Journal of Personality* 77 (2009): 1085–1102.

97. C. G. DeYoung, D. Cicchetti, et al., "Sources of Cognitive Exploration: Genetic Variation in the Prefrontal Dopamine System Predicts Openness/Intellect," *Journal of Research in Personality* 45 (2011): 364–371.

98. DeYoung, "Openness/Intellect."

99. C. G. DeYoung, N. A. Shamosh, et al., "Intellect as Distinct from Openness: Differences Revealed by fMRI of Working Memory," *Journal of Personality and Social Psychology* 97 (2009): 883–892.

100. Note that DeYoung was a co-author with me on the earlier paper on implicit learning.

101. S. Blackmore and R. Moore, "Seeing Things: Visual Recognition and Belief in the Paranormal," *European Journal of Parapsychology* 10 (1994): 91–103.

102. A. F. Arnstein, T. W. Robbins, and D. T. Stuss, "Neurochemical Modulation of Prefrontal Cortical Function," in *Principles of Frontal Lobe Function*, ed. D. T. Stuss and R. T. Knight, 51–84 (New York: Oxford University Press, 2002).

103. L. Wilkinson and M. Jahanshahi, "The Striatum and Probabilistic Implicit Sequence Learning," *Brain Research* 1137 (2007): 117–130.

104. G. Winterer and D. R. Weinberger, "Genes, Dopamine and Cortical Signal-to-Noise Ratio in Schizophrenia," *Trends in Neuroscience* 27 (2004): 683–690.

105. O. D. Howes, A. J. Montgomery, et al., "Elevated Striatal Dopamine Function Linked to Prodromal Signs of Schizophrenia," *Archives of General Psychiatry* 66 (2009): 13–20.

106. J. B. Peterson, K. W. Smith, and S. Carson, "Openness and Extraversion Are Associated with Reduced Latent Inhibition: Replication and Commentary," *Personality and Individual Differences* 33 (2002): 1137–1147.

107. J. E. Sussmann et al., "White Matter Abnormalities in Bipolar Disorder and Schizophrenia Detected Using Diffusion Tensor Magnetic Resonance Imaging," *Bipolar Disorders* 11 (2009): 11–18; M. T. Nelson, M. L. Seal, et al., "An Investigation of the Relationship between Cortical Connectivity and Schizotypy in the General Population," *Journal of Nervous & Mental Disease* 199 (2011): 348–353.

108. R. E. Jung, R. Grazioplene, A. Caprihan, R. S. Chavez, and R. J. Haier, "White Matter Integrity, Creativity, and Psychopathology: Disentangling Constructs with Diffusion Tensor Imaging," *PLoS One* 5 (2010): e9818.

109. J. B. Taylor, *My Stroke of Insight: A Brain Scientist's Personal Journey* (New York: Plume, 2009); I. Gilchrist, *The Master and His Emissary: The Divided Brain and the Making of the Western World* (New Haven, CT: Yale University Press, 2009).

110. T. J. Crow, "Schizophrenia as the Price That *Homo sapiens* Pays for Language: A Resolution of the Central Paradox in the Origin of the Species," *Brain Research Reviews* 31

(2000): 118–129; S. Weinstein and R. E. Graves, "Are Creativity and Schizotypy Products of a Right Hemisphere Bias?," *Brain and Cognition* 49 (2002): 138–151.

111. C. Mohr, P. Krummenacher, et al., "Psychometric Schizotypy Modulates Levodopa Effects on Lateralized Lexical Decision Performance," *Journal of Psychiatric Research* 39 (2005): 241–250.

112. U. Wagner, S. Gals, et al., "Sleep Inspires Insight," *Nature* 427 (2004): 352–355; E. M. Bowden and M. Jung-Beeman, "Aha! Insight Experience Correlates with Solution Activation in the Right Hemisphere," *Psychonomic Bulletin & Review* 10 (2003): 730–737.

113. E. A. Poe, "Eleonara," in *The Complete Tales and Poems of Edgar Allan Poe* (1848; New York: Random House, 1975).

114. L. A. Sass and D. Schuldberg, "Introduction to the Special Issue: Creativity and the Schizophrenia Spectrum," *Creativity Research Journal* 13 (2000): 1–4; A. Kuszewski, "The Genetics of Creativity: A Serendipitous Assemblage of Madness," Metodo Working Papers no. 58 (2009).

115. A. Kozbelt, S. B. Kaufman, D. Walder, L. Ospina, and J. Kim, "Evolutionary Perspectives on the Creativity-Psychosis Association," in *Creativity and Mental Illness*, ed. J. C. Kaufman (New York: Cambridge University Press, forthcoming).

116. DeYoung, Grazioplene, and Peterson. "From Madness to Genius," at 76.

117. D. Nettle and H. Clegg, "Schizotypy, Creativity and Mating Success in Humans," *Proceedings of the Royal Society: B* 273 (2006): 611–615; also see H. Clegg, D. Nettle, and D. Miell, "Status and Mating Success Amongst Visual Artists," *Frontiers in Personality and Individual Differences* 2 (2011): 310.

118. M. L. Beaussart, S. B. Kaufman, and J. C. Kaufman, "Creative Activity, Personality, Mental Illness, and Short-Term Mating Success," *Journal of Creative Behavior* 46 (2012): 151–167.

119. G. A. Shaw and L. M. Giambra, "Task Unrelated Thoughts of College Students Diagnosed as Hyperactive in Childhood," *Developmental Neuropsychology* 9 (1993): 17–30; C. Fassbender et al., "A Lack of Default Network Suppression Is Linked to Increased Distractibility in ADHD," *Brain Research* 1273 (2009): 114–128.

120. H. A. White and P. Shah, "Uninhibited Imaginations: Creativity in Adults with Attention-Deficit/Hyperactivity Disorder," *Personality and Individual Differences* 40 (2006): 1121–1131; H. A. White and P. Shah, "Creative Style and Achievement in Adults with Attention-Deficit/Hyperactivity Disorder," *Personality and Individual Differences* 50 (2011): 673–677.

121. B. Cramond, "Attention-Deficit Hyperactivity Disorder and Creativity: What Is the Connection?," *Journal of Creative Behavior* 28 (2011): 193–210.

122. "The Essential Psychopathology of Creativity," Institute for Emerging Ethics and Technology, September 28, 2010, http://ieet.org/index.php/IEET/more/4236.

123. E. C. Nusbaum and P. J. Silvia, "Are Openness and Intellect Distinct Aspects of Openness to Experience? A Test of the O/I Model," *Personality and Individual Differences* 51 (2011): 571–574.

124. S. B. Kaufman, "Opening Up Openness to Experience: A Four-Factor Model and Relations to Creative Achievement in the Arts and Sciences," *Journal of Creative Behavior* (forthcoming).

125. S. von Stumm, B. Hell, and T. Chamorro-Premuzic, "The Hungry Mind: Intellectual Curiosity Is the Third Pillar of Academic Performance," *Perspectives on Psychological Science* 6 (2011): 574–588.

126. Kaufman, "Beyond General Intelligence"; S. B. Kaufman, "Intelligence and the Cognitive Unconscious," in *Cambridge Handbook of Intelligence*, 442–467 (New York: Cambridge University Press, 2011).

127. J. Bruner, *Actual Minds, Possible Worlds* (Cambridge, MA: Harvard University Press, 1985); J. St. B. T. Evans, "Dual-Processing Accounts of Reasoning, Judgment, and

Social Cognition," *Annual Review of Psychology* 59 (2008): 255–278; Evans, *Thinking Twice: Two Minds in One Brain* (Oxford: Oxford University Press, 2010); Evans and K. Frankish, *In Two Minds: Dual-Processes and Beyond* (New York: Oxford University Press, 2009); D. Kahneman and S. Frederick, "Representativeness Revisited: Attribute Substitution in Intuitive Judgment," in *Heuristics and Biases: The Psychology of Intuitive Judgment*, ed. T. Gilovich, D. Griffin, and D. Kahneman, 49–81 (New York: Cambridge University Press, 2002), 49–81; D. Kahneman, *Thinking, Fast and Slow* (New York: Farrar, Straus and Giroux, 2011); K. E. Stanovich, *The Robot's Rebellion: Finding Meaning in the Age of Darwin* (Chicago: University of Chicago Press, 2004); K. E. Stanovich and R. F. West, "Individual Differences in Reasoning: Implications for the Rationality Debate?," *Behavioral and Brain Sciences* 23 (2000): 645–726; Stanovich and M. E. Toplak, "Defining Features Versus Incidental Correlates of Type 1 and Type 2 Processing," *Mind and Society* 11 (2012): 3–13; Gabora, "Revenge of the 'Neurds'"; Wiley and Jarosz, "How Working Memory Capacity Affects Problem Solving"; Gilhooly and Fioratou, "Executive Functions in Insight; Lin and Lien, "The Different Role of Working Memory."

128. K. E. Stanovich, *What Intelligence Tests Miss: The Psychology of Rational Thought* (New Haven, CT: Yale University Press, 2010).

129. Stanovich and Toplak, "Defining Features," at 7.

130. Ibid., at 10.

131. S. Epstein, "Integration of the Cognitive and the Psychodynamic Unconscious," *American Psychologist* 49 (1994): 709–724; S. Epstein, "Cognitive-experiential Self-theory of Personality," in *Comprehensive Handbook of Psychology,* Vol. 5, *Personality and Social Psychology,* ed. T. Millon and M. J. Lerner, 159–184 (Hoboken, NJ: Wiley, 2003); S. Epstein, *Constructive Thinking: The Key to Emotional Intelligence* (Westport, CT: Praeger, 1998).

132. P. Norris and S. Epstein, "An Experiential Thinking Style: Its Facets and Relations with Objective and Subjective Criterion Measures," *Journal of Personality* 79 (2011): 1043–1080.

133. Ibid.

134. K. H. Kim, "Can Only Intelligent People Be Creative?," *Journal of Secondary Gifted Education* 2 (2005): 57–66. It should be noted that Paul Silvia and colleagues have found that the relationship between IQ and divergent thinking is a bit higher (moderately correlated) when researchers include multiple creativity tasks, use latent variables when assessing creativity, and look at higher-order factors of cognitive ability instead of lower-order cognitive abilities. See Nusbaum and Silvia, "Are Intelligence and Creativity Really So Different?"; P. J. Silvia, "Creativity and Intelligence Revisited: A Latent Variable Analysis of Wallach and Kogan (1965)," *Creativity Research Journal* 20 (2008): 34–39; P. J. Silvia, "Another Look at Creativity and Intelligence: Exploring Higher-Order Models and Probable Confounds," *Personality and Individual Differences* 44 (2008): 1012–1021.

135. S. Jaarsveld, T. Lachmann, R. Hamel, and C. van Leeuwen, "Solving and Creating Raven Progressive Matrices: Reasoning in Well- and Ill-Defined Problem Spaces," *Creativity Research Journal* 22 (2010): 304–319; S. Jaarsveld, T. Lachmann, and C. van Leeuwen, "Creative Reasoning across Developmental Levels: Convergence and Divergence in Problem Creation," *Intelligence* 40 (2012): 172–188.

136. K. H. Kim, "Can We Trust Creativity Tests? A Review of the Torrance Tests of Creative Thinking (TTCT)," *Creativity Research Journal* 18 (2006): 3–14.

137. J. C. Kaufman, S. B. Kaufman, and E. O. Lichtenberger, "Finding Creative Potential on Intelligence Tests via Divergent Production," *Canadian Journal of School Psychology* 26 (2011): 83–106.

138. K. H. Kim, "The Creativity Crisis: The Decrease in Creative Thinking Scores on the Torrance Tests of Creative Thinking," *Creativity Research Journal* 23 (2011): 285–295.

139. J. C. Kaufman, "Using Creativity to Reduce Ethnic Bias in College Admissions," *Review of General Psychology* 14 (2010): 189–203.

140. R. J. Sternberg & the Rainbow Project Collaborators, "The Rainbow Project: Enhancing the SAT Through Assessments of Analytical, Practical and Creative Skills," *Intelligence* 34 (2006): 321–350; R. J. Sternberg, C. R. Bonney, L. Gabora, L. Jarvin, L. Karelitz, M. Tzur, and L. Coffin, "Broadening the Spectrum of Undergraduate Admissions: The Kaleidoscope Project," *College and University* 86 (2010): 2–17; R. J. Sternberg, "The Assessment of Creativity: An Investment-Based Approach," *Creativity Research Journal* 24 (2012): 3–12; R. J. Sternberg, *College Admissions for the 21st Century* (Cambridge, MA: Harvard University Press, 2010).

141. J. A. Plucker and M. C. Makel, "Assessment of Creativity," in *The Cambridge Handbook of Creativity*, 48–73.

142. K. H. Kim, "Meta-Analyses of the Relationship of Creative Achievement to Both IQ and Divergent Thinking Test Scores," *Journal of Creative Behavior* 42 (2008): 106–130.

143. J. A. Plucker, "Is the Proof in the Pudding? Reanalyses of Torrance's (1958 to Present) Longitudinal Data," *Creativity Research Journal* 12 (1999): 103–114. For another 40+-year follow-up, see B. Cramond, J. Matthews-Morgan, D. Bandalos, and L. Zuo, "A Report on the 40-Year Follow-Up of the Torrance Tests of Creative Thinking: Alive and Well in the New Millennium," *Gifted Child Quarterly* 49 (2005): 283–291.

144. M. A. Runco, G. Millar, S. Acar, and B. Cramond, "Torrance Tests of Creative Thinking as Predictors of Personal and Public Achievement: A Fifty-Year Follow-Up," *Creativity Research Journal* 22 (2010): 361–368.

145. E. P. Torrance, "The Importance of Falling in Love with 'Something,'" *Creative Child & Adult Quarterly* 8 (1983): 72–78.

146. C. Cox, *The Early Mental Traits of Three Hundred Geniuses* (Palo Alto, CA: Stanford University Press, 1926).

147. Quoted in N. J. Mackintosh, *IQ and Human Intelligence*, 2nd ed. (New York: Cambridge University Press, 2011) at 238.

148. Cox, *The Early Mental Traits*, at 187.

149. L. M. Terman and M. H. Oden, *The Gifted Group at Mid-Life: 35 Years' Follow-Up of the Superior Child* (Palo Alto, CA: Stanford University Press, 1959), 147.

150. Simonton, *Greatness*; P. Sorokin, Fads & Foibles in Modern Sociology (Chicago: Regenery, 1956).

151. L. M. Terman and M. H. Oden, *The Gifted Child Grows Up*, vol. 5 of *Genetic Studies of Genius* (Palo Alto, CA: Stanford University Press, 1959).

152. D. Lubinski, R. M. Webb, M. J. Morelock, and C. P. Benbow, "Top 1 in 10,000: A 10-Year Follow-Up of the Profoundly Gifted," *Journal of Applied Psychology* 86 (2001): 718–729.

153. K. F. Robertson, S. Smeets, D. Lubinski, and C. P. Benbow, "Beyond the Threshold Hypothesis: Even among the Gifted and Top Math/Science Graduate Students, Cognitive Abilities, Vocational Interests, and Lifestyle Preferences Matter for Career Choice, Performance, and Persistence," *Current Directions in Psychological Science* 19 (2010): 346–351.

154. Lubinski et al., "Top 1 in 10,000."

155. D. Lubinski and C. P. Benbow, "Study of Mathematically Precocious Youth after 35 Years: Uncovering Antecedents for the Development of Math-Science Expertise," *Perspectives on Psychological Science* 4 (2006): 316–345.

156. Ibid., at 329.

157. Ibid., at 318.

158. http://www.possefoundation.org.

Chapter 13

1. Reprint: L. S. Gottfredson, "Mainstream Science on Intelligence: An Editorial with 52 Signatories, History, and Bibliography," *Intelligence* 24 (1997): 13–23, at 13.

2. R. J. Sternberg, "Culture and Intelligence," *American Psychologist* 59 (2004): 325–338; S.-Y. Yang and R. J. Sternberg, "Taiwanese Chinese People's Conceptions of Intelligence," *Intelligence* 25 (1997): 21–36.

3. Gottfredson, "Mainstream Science on Intelligence," at 14.

4. A. Jensen, *The g Factor* (New York: Praeger, 1998); R. J. Herrnstein and C. Murray, *Bell Curve: Intelligence and Class Structure in American Life* (New York: Free Press, 1994). L. S. Gottfredson, "Why *g* Matters: The Complexity of Everyday Life," *Intelligence* 24 (1997): 79–132; F. L. Schmidt, and J. E. Hunter, "The Validity and Utility of Selection Methods in Personnel Psychology: Practical and Theoretical Implications of 85 Years of Research Findings," *Psychological Bulletin* 124 (1998): 262–274; I. J. Deary and G. D. Batty, "Intelligence as a Predictor of Health, Illness, and Death," in *The Cambridge Handbook of Intelligence*, ed. R. J. Sternberg and S. B. Kaufman, 683–710 (New York: Cambridge University Press, 2011). For critiques, see S. Fraser, ed., *The Bell Curve Wars: Race, Intelligence, and the Future of America* (New York: Basic Books, 1995); S. Ceci, *On Intelligence . . . More or Less: A Biological Treatise on Intellectual Development*, 2nd ed. (Cambridge, MA: Harvard University Press, 1996); S. J. Gould, *The Mismeasure of Man*, 2nd ed. (London: Penguin Books, 1997); R. J. Sternberg and R. K. Wagner, "The *g*-ocentric View of Intelligence and Job Performance Is Wrong," *Current Directions in Psychological Science* 2 (1993): 1–5; P. L. Ackerman and M. E. Beier, "The Problem Is in the Definition: *g* and Intelligence in I-O Psychology," *Industrial and Organizational Psychology* 5 (2012): 149–188.

5. R. Colom and C. E. Flores-Mendoza, "Intelligence Predicts Scholastic Achievement Irrespective of SES Factors: Evidence from Brazil," *Intelligence* 35 (2007): 243–251; T. Strenze, "Intelligence and Socioeconomic Success: A Meta-Analytic Review of Longitudinal Research," *Intelligence* 35 (2007): 401–426; P. R. Sackett, M. J. Borneman, and B. S. Connelly, "High Stakes Testing in Higher Education and Employment: Appraising the Evidence for Validity and Fairness," *American Psychologist* 63 (2008): 215–227; Herrnstein and Murray, *Bell Curve*; D. Lubinski and L. G. Humphreys, "Some Bodily and Medical Correlates of Mathematical Giftedness and Commensurate Levels of Socioeconomic Status," *Intelligence* 16 (1992): 99–115; D. Lubinski, "Cognitive Epidemiology: With Emphasis on Untangling Cognitive Ability and Socioeconomic Status," *Intelligence* 37 (2009): 625–633; Deary and Batty, "Intelligence as a Predictor."

6. R. J. Sternberg, "The Theory of Successful Intelligence," *Review of General Psychology* 3 (1999): 292–316, at 298.

7. S. Ang, L. V. Dyne, and M. L. Tan, "Cultural Intelligence," in *Cambridge Handbook of Intelligence*, 582–602.

8. D. Goleman, *Ecological Intelligence: How Knowing the Hidden Impacts of What We Buy Can Change Everything* (New York: Broadway Books, 2009).

9. J. Menkes, *Executive Intelligence: What All Great Leaders Have* (New York: HarperBusiness, 2006).

10. G. Geher and S. B. Kaufman, *Mating Intelligence Unleashed: The Role of the Mind in Sex, Dating, and Love* (New York: Oxford University Press, 2013); G. Geher and S. B. Kaufman, "Mating Intelligence," in *Cambridge Handbook of Intelligence*, 603–622; D. T. O'Brien, G. Geher, A. C. Gallup, J. R. Garcia, and S. B. Kaufman, "Self-Perceived Mating Intelligence Predicts Sexual Behavior in College Students: Empirical Validation of a Theoretical Construct," *Imagination, Cognition, and Personality* 29 (2010): 341–362; G. Geher and G. Miller, eds., *Mating Intelligence: Sex, Relationships, and the Mind's Reproductive*

System (New York: Psychology Press, 2007); G. F. Miller, *The Mating Mind: How Sexual Choice Shaped the Evolution of Human Nature* (New York: Anchor, 2000).

11. D. T. Willingham, *Why Don't Students Like School: A Cognitive Scientist Answers Questions About How the Mind Works and What It Means for the Classroom* (New York: Wiley, 2009).

12. C. Riener and D. Willingham, "The Myth of Learning Styles," *Change: The Magazine of Higher Learning* 42 (2010): 32–35; J. Dunlosky, K. A. Rawson, E. J. Marsh, M. J. Nathan, and D. T. Willingham, "Improving Students' Learning with Effective Learning Techniques: Promising Directions from Cognitive and Educational Psychology," *Psychological Science in the Public Interest* 14:4–58.

13. A. Binet, T. Simon, and E. S. Kite, *The Development of Intelligence in Children (The Binet Simon Scale)* (Baltimore: Williams & Wilkins, 1916), at 122.

14. D. Wechsler, "Cognitive, Conative, and Non-intellective Intelligence," *American Psychologist* 5 (1950): 78–83, at 83.

15. D. Wechsler, *Wechsler Intelligence Scale for Children–Revised* (San Antonio: Psychological Corporation, 1974), at 37.

16. E. L. Thorndike, *An Introduction to the Theory of Mental and Social Measurements* (Oxford: Science Press, 1904); P. L. Ackerman, "Intelligence, Attention, and Learning: Maximal and Typical Performance," in *Current Topics in Human Intelligence*, Vol. 4, *Theories of Intelligence*, ed. D. K. Detterman, 1–27 (Norwood, NJ: Ablex, 1994).

17. L. Corno et al., eds., *Remaking the Concept of Aptitude: Extending the Legacy of Richard E. Snow* (New York: Routledge, 2001).

18. R. E. Snow, "Intelligence for the Year 2001," *Intelligence* 4 (1980): 185–199, at 194.

19. P. C. M. Molenaar and C. G. Campbell, "The New Person-Specific Paradigm in Psychology," *Current Directions in Psychological Science* 18 (2009): 112–117; L. T. Rose and K. W. Fischer, "Intelligence in Childhood," in *Cambridge Handbook of Intelligence*, 130–143.

20. Molenaar and Campbell, "The New Person-Specific Paradigm"; P. C. M. Molenaar, H. M. Huizenga, and J. R. Nesselroade, "The Relationship Between the Structure of Interindividual and Intraindividual Variability: A Theoretical and Empirical Vindication of Developmental Systems Theory," in *Understanding Human Development: Dialogues with Life-Span Psychology*, ed. U. M. Staudinger and U. Lindenberger, 339–360 (Dordrecht, the Netherlands: Kluwer, 2003); E. L. Hamaker, J. R. Nesselroade, and P. C. M. Molenaar, "The Integrated Trait-State Model," *Journal of Research in Personality* 41 (2007): 295–315.

21. S. Pinker, *How the Mind Works* (New York: W. W. Norton, 1999), at 34.

22. F. L. Coolidge and T. Wynn, *The Rise of Homo sapiens: The Evolution of Modern Thinking* (New York: Wiley-Blackwell, 2009); D. C. Geary, *Origin of Mind: Evolution of Brain, Cognition, and General Intelligence* (Washington, DC: American Psychological Association, 2004).

23. G. Marcus, *Kluge: The Haphazard Evolution of the Human Mind* (New York: Houghton-Mifflin, 2008); M. Changizi, *Harnessed: How Language and Music Mimicked Nature and Transformed Ape to Man* (Dallas: BenBella Books, 2011).

24. D. Dennett, *Kinds of Minds* (New York: Basic Books, 1996); A. S. Reber, *Implicit Learning and Tacit Knowledge: An Essay on the Cognitive Unconscious* (New York: Oxford University Press, 1993).

25. Pinker, *How the Mind Works*, at 62.

26. K. E. Stanovich, R. F. West, and M. E. Toplak, "Intelligence and Rationality," in *Cambridge Handbook of Intelligence*, 784–826.

27. M. Csikszentmihalyi, *The Evolving Self: A Psychology for the Third Millennium* (New York: Harper Perennial, 1994).

28. For some recent work on the dynamic development of engagement and ability, see M. J. Hogan, R. T. Staff, B. P. Binting, I. J. Deary, and L. J. Whalley, "Openness to Experience

and Activity Engagement Facilitate the Maintenance of Verbal Ability in Older Adults," *Psychology and Aging* 27 (2012): 849–854; M. R. Reynolds and J. J. Turek, "A Dynamic Developmental Link Between Verbal Comprehension-Knowledge (GC) and Reading Comprehension," *Journal of School Psychology* 50 (2012): 841–863.

29. K. E. Stanovich, *What Intelligence Tests Miss: The Psychology of Rational Thought* (New Haven, CT: Yale University Press, 2010).

30. Stanovich, West, and Toplak, "Intelligence and Rationality."

31. J. S. Renzulli, "Reexamining the Role of Gifted Education and Talent Development for the 21st Century: A Four-Part Theoretical Approach," *Gifted Child Quarterly* 56 (2012): 150–159.

32. S. B. Kaufman, E. M. Christopher, and J. C. Kaufman, "The Genius Portfolio: How Do Poets Earn Their Creative Reputations from Multiple Products?," *Empirical Studies of the Arts* 26 (2008): 181–196.

33. D. K. Simonton, "Creative Productivity: A Predictive and Explanatory Model of Career Trajectories and Landmarks," *Psychological Review* 104 (1997): 66–89.

34. D. K. Simonton, "Expertise, Competence, and Creative Ability: The Perplexing Complexities," in *The Psychology of Abilities, Competencies, and Expertise*, ed. R. J. Sternberg and E. L. Grigorenko, 213–239 (New York: Cambridge University Press, 2003).

35. D. K. Simonton, "Creative Thought as Blind-Variation and Selective-Retention: Combinatorial Models of Exceptional Creativity," *Physics of Life Reviews* 7 (2010): 156–179.

36. Cannon Design, VS Furniture, and Bruce Mau Design, *The Third Teacher: 79 Ways You Can Use Design to Transform Teaching & Learning* (New York: Abrams, 2010).

37. Beau Lotto, interview by author.

38. P. S. Blackawton et al., "Blackawton Bees," *Biology Letters* 7 (2010): 168–172.

39. Logan Smalley, interview by author.

40. B. S. Bloom, "The 2 Sigma Problem: The Search for Methods of Group Instruction as Effective as One-to-One Tutoring," *Educational Researcher* 13 (1984): 4–16.

INDEX